DISCARDED

THE RECONSTRUCTION OF WORLD TRADE

The Reconstruction of
WORLD TRADE

A SURVEY OF INTERNATIONAL ECONOMIC RELATIONS

By J. B. Condliffe

PROFESSOR OF ECONOMICS, UNIVERSITY OF CALIFORNIA

New York · W·W· NORTON & COMPANY · INC.

Copyright, 1940, by
W. W. NORTON & COMPANY, INC.
70 Fifth Avenue, New York, N. Y.

First Edition

PRINTED IN THE UNITED STATES OF AMERICA

Contents

FOREWORD	9
ACKNOWLEDGMENTS	11

I. The Background of Economic Policy — 15

Nationalism and Industrialism	15
The Making of Policy	26
National and International Regulation	37
Economic Policy and Peace	47

II. The Processes of Disintegration — 59

Closing Frontiers	59
The Breakdown of Monetary Equilibrium	71
Collapse of the Capital Market	79
A Liquidity Panic	90

III. The Causes of Breakdown — 99

Defects of Mechanism	99
The Victory of Political Realism	116
The Rejection of Economics	123
The Maintenance of Regulation	131

IV. Regulated and Unregulated Trading Systems — 144

The Spread of Regulation	144
The Criteria of Regulation	151
Varieties of Autarky	161
The Possibilities of Co-operation	167

CONTENTS

V. The Complication of Tariffs — 178

- The Importance of Tariff Barriers — 178
- Modern Tariff Methods — 189
- The Invisible Tariff — 196
- The Attack on Trade Barriers — 203

VI. Quota Politics — 210

- The Origins of Quotas — 210
- Government Through Producers — 217
- The Incidence of Quotas — 223
- The Value of Imports — 227

VII. The Monetary Weapon — 232

- The Advent of Monetary Nationalism — 232
- The Scaling Down of Debt — 242
- The Theory of an Autonomous Konjunktur Policy — 248
- Exchange Control as an Instrument of Commercial Policy — 256

VIII. Commercial Diplomacy — 263

- Treaty Degeneration — 263
- Compensation, Clearing and Payments Agreements — 272
- The Strategy of Bilateralism — 280
- The Tactics of Bilateral Bargaining — 288

IX. The Limits of Regionalism — 295

- The Teachings of Experience — 295
- Regional Initiatives in Europe — 300
- Imperial Consolidation — 308
- The Formation of Monetary Blocs — 316

X. New Aspects of International Organization — 328

- The Growth of International Business — 328
- International Commodity Controls — 334

CONTENTS

    The Financing of International Enterprise   341
    The Dilemma of Planning   347

XI. *The Conditions of Economic Co-operation*   355
    The Approach to Peace   355
    Autarky and Sovereignty   362
    The Economics of Insulation   371
    The Clearing of International Co-operation   382

APPENDIX   395
SUGGESTIONS FOR FURTHER READING   407
INDEX   413

Foreword

THIS volume falls naturally into three parts. The first analyzes the collapse of the international trading system that was restored, on the prewar model, after the last war. The second examines the challenge now presented by totalitarian methods of bilateral trade. The third surveys the problems that must be faced in any attempt to reconstruct world trade after the present war comes to an end.

Illustrations are drawn from the experience of many countries and emphasis is laid upon national economic policies as constituting the real substance of international economic relations. The clearing of economic co-operation through international institutions is discussed in the final chapter, but merely as one aspect of the interlocking conflicts of national policies in an interdependent world. Economic problems can no longer be discussed realistically as if they arose in self-contained national systems. On the other hand, there is no reality in discussing international problems except as the outgrowth of conflicting national policies. An attempt must be made to view such problems as arising in a series of interconnected and interdependent national economies.

The analysis that follows endeavors also to take due account of the political aspects of economic policy. It is a study in political economy rather than in economics or political science. It does not attempt, therefore, to analyze theoretical situations in logical detail. On the other hand, it does not present a cut and dried program of political and economic reconstruction. The aim of the author has been rather to present as clearly as possible the fundamental issues that must be faced in any such reconstruction.

J. B. C.

Acknowledgments

THIS book should have been a report of the International Studies Conference on "Economic Policies in Relation to World Peace." The materials on which it is based are drawn largely from research studies undertaken in preparation for a conference called to meet at Bergen on August 27, 1939.

In the circumstances it was not possible to hold detailed round-table discussion, but it was agreed that the prepared documents should be utilized as the basis of an individual and personal report. The scope and content of a possible report were discussed and the author has benefited greatly from this discussion. The analysis which follows, however, is not confined to the conference materials nor does it follow the conventional lines of a conference report. Liberal use has been made of the authority given to the author to write this book in his own way.

What follows is essentially a personal interpretation of the conclusions to be drawn from a great body of original research conducted in a co-operative spirit by scholars from many different countries. For its form and detailed expression the author alone bears responsibility; but his interpretation is based mainly upon the studies listed in the Appendix. To the authors of these studies, the National Committees through which their co-operation was enlisted, and the International Committees of the International Studies Conference is due the credit for the material here utilized. Particular credit is due to Mr. Malcolm W. Davis for his unfailing tact and organizing ability as Chairman of the Program Committee, and of the Conference itself. The International Institute of Intellectual Co-operation at Paris provided the secretariat without which the Conference could not have functioned. The author owes a special debt to his immediate assistants, Dr. H. O. Christophersen, M. André Piatier, Dr. Henry J. Tasca, and Miss D. E. Karmin, who not only carried through much of the detailed organization of the preliminary research studies, but in the period immediately prior to the conference co-operated in analyzing the documentation. The study-program prepared for the Bergen meeting was a result of this co-operative teamwork and the shape of this final report was largely determined by it. Finally, my thanks are due to the Director of the London School of Economics for permission to give so much time to the work of the conference, and to the University of California for the facilities necessary to complete the volume in its present form.

J. B. Condliffe

BERKELEY,
SEPTEMBER 1, 1940

THE RECONSTRUCTION OF WORLD TRADE

CHAPTER I

The Background of Economic Policy

Nationalism and Industrialism

THERE is a fundamental conflict in the modern world between political and economic forces or principles. This becomes particularly clear in any discussion of international economic relations. Why should it be necessary for State policy to aim at controlling and regulating economic activity? Surely because economic activity, left to itself, develops along lines that are not acceptable to those who exercise political power. Those aspects of economic activity that cross national boundaries tend to escape from the control of the State. Why else does the State intervene to regulate international trade and international economic relations in general? The degree of regulation at the present time seems to suggest that the integrity of the State is threatened by the evolution of economic activity unless such activity is controlled and regulated.

Preliminary questions such as these raise fundamental issues as to the purpose of social organization, the effectiveness of private economic enterprise, the function of such institutions as the State, the ultimate values they conserve and their validity in the modern world. Even in the armed peace before the present hostilities began, it was becoming necessary to ask whether unlimited national sovereignty was any longer compatible with the organization of economic prosperity, and whether private enterprise could function effectively in the modern world.

Since hostilities began these questions have become more insistent and urgent. It is already apparent that they will be actively canvassed and may be among the leading issues to be decided in any peace settlement. Is the nationally organized State to be accepted as the dominant unit of social organization and its interest allowed to take priority over considerations of economic welfare? Can private enterprise be relied upon to promote economic welfare? Or is the recent confusion of national economic policies to be regarded as a desperate struggle to escape from the necessity of limiting, if not destroying, State sovereignty, as local sovereignty was destroyed in an earlier period? Is it possible that the modern world has outgrown its traditional forms of political and economic organization and that the present anarchy results from the need for new forms of political and economic order in the world? [1]

These questions might not even have been asked, and would certainly have been answered more confidently, in the full tide of economic expansion that characterized the nineteenth century. There was a long period when Nationalism and Industrialism seemed to march together.[2] These twin forces that shaped the history of the nineteenth century were not inconsistent or in conflict as long as governments refrained from detailed interference with the private economic activities of their citizens.

In the modern world, however, Industrialism and Nation-

[1] Eugene Staley, *World Economy in Transition*, pp. 1–56, and Burky, de la Harpe, and Wackernagel, *La Suisse et l'autarcie*, pp. 1–29.

[2] Nationalism has been defined by a study group of the Royal Institute of International Affairs as "a consciousness on the part of individuals or groups of membership in a nation, or of a desire to forward the strength, liberty, or prosperity of a nation, whether one's own or another." See *Nationalism* (London, 1940), p. 18. Industrialism has been defined by Toynbee, *A Study of History* (London, 1935), Vol. I, p. 2, as follows: "The Industrial System has a human aspect in the Division of Labour and a non-human aspect in the application of modern Western scientific thought to the physical environment of human life. Its method of operation is to maintain, up to the maximum of its productive capacity, an incessant output of such articles as can be manufactured from raw materials by the mechanically coordinated work of a number of human beings."

alism are in sharp conflict. Economic activity more and more transcends national boundaries. State regulation penetrates more and more profoundly into every aspect of economic life. The conflict between these two opposing tendencies might well be dramatized as the resistance opposed by sovereign States to the creation of a world economic order based essentially on private enterprise. In recent years there has been a powerful resurgence of nationalism which, in Professor Toynbee's words, has "carried to victory every statesman who has managed to ride it."[3] In the guise of self-determination it was the leading principle of the peace settlement after the war of 1914–18. The League of Nations was built, and finally wrecked, upon acceptance of unfettered State sovereignty. A reawakened spirit of nationalism has transformed Italy and Turkey and stirred Spain into civil war. Transplanted to the ancient civilizations of Asia, it has launched not only Japan but China and India into the struggle for national self-expression. In Germany, the newest of the great States, it has been linked with a mystic revival of racial theories.

It would clearly be foolish to underestimate the power of such an idea, firmly rooted as it is in the deepest emotions of humanity—the love of home and family and country, a love "far-brought from out the storied past." Built on such primitive and powerful emotions, it is buttressed in every country by an elaborate system of formal education. Governments everywhere seek control of the educational processes by which the complex social heritage is transmitted to oncoming generations. In so doing they sweep aside conflicting loyalties to church, neighborhood, and even family, claiming the minds of the young for the service of the State. The love of country and undivided loyalty to the fatherland is the central theme of all systems of national education.

The forces that make for industrial expansion, however, are very powerful. They draw strength from motives that are at least as deeply rooted as those which reinforce the appeal of

[3] Arnold J. Toynbee, "A Turning Point in History," *Foreign Affairs* (January, 1939).

nationalism. Self-preservation is the first law of nature and the (so-called) acquisitive instinct is a recognizable and almost universal human attitude. The drive to build, to explore, to extend the boundaries of knowledge—what Veblen once called "the instinct of workmanship"—is very powerful also. Economic motives, however, have always been suspect by moralists. The "economic man" has never been able to compete successfully with man as a "political animal" in the writings and teachings of idealists. Economic motives have been represented as sordid and egotistical by contrast with the more romantic and less egocentric appeal of patriotism. Richard Cobden might link peace eloquently and truly with economic prosperity, but to Ruskin he was the "inspired bagman" of a "Calico Millennium." It has always been difficult to incorporate a rational explanation of economic activity in educational systems, but easy to stir youth with romantic history designed to encourage pride and love of country.

The real conflict between nationalism and industrialism is focused at this point—in the elementary school. The political organization of the modern world is built upon conceptions of nationality that do not, in fact, have a long history, but which are powerfully entrenched in all educational systems. They did not conflict with the developing forces of industrialism when the prime necessity of social life was to break down the powers of local government in order to make possible nation-wide economic activity. In the stagecoach and early railway eras national unification was a desirable goal at which to aim. Even when steam shipping began to link the continents in world-wide commerce, the abstention of governments from detailed interference in the economic activities of their nationals masked for a time the clash between political nationalism and economic internationalism. The progress of communications, however, is continuous and there is good reason now to question the adequacy of national citizenship in a world that flies.

Some of the reasons for this questioning are set forth clearly in the early chapters of Professor Staley's study entitled *World*

NATIONALISM AND INDUSTRIALISM 19

Economy in Transition. His book begins with a series of charts designed to show the shrinkage of time-distance in the last century. Measured in travel-time he is able to show that the most distant part of the world in 1938 was nearer to his center at Boston than the Southern or the Middle Western states of his own country had been in 1798. Europe was nearer than Philadelphia had been then, and Japan as near as Mt. Vernon.[4] As late as 1812 the distance from Berlin to Vienna was five days, and from Berlin to London ten; but ten days may now suffice to reach the most distant part of the world.

Apart from the increasing speed of communications, Professor Staley emphasizes certain broad technical reasons why modern industry tends to outgrow national boundaries. The first is the importance of a wide market for the new mechanical processes of mass-production which have come to dominate industry.[5] If mechanical inventions are to be economically utilized they must be produced on a large scale. Determined conservatives may be prepared to forego the use of automobiles and moralists may deplore their social consequences; but the average man wants them if he can afford them. A simple illustration suffices to indicate the importance, for the average man, of wide markets for such manufactures: "A $4,000,000 investment in new dies and tools might be quite impracticable for an output of 20,000 units (it would cost $200 a car), but not at all unreasonable for an output of 2,000,000 units (only $2.00 for each car)."[6]

If the finished product must be produced in quantity, its raw materials must be drawn from an even wider area. Economic geologists have in recent years emphasized this point, particularly in regard to the metals upon which modern mechanical production depends. In the older centers of industry, particularly in Europe, where metal ores have been worked

[4] Staley, *op. cit.*, pp. 8–11.
[5] For criticisms of this development, see below, Ch. III.
[6] Staley, *op. cit.*, pp. 20–21. Cf. also the trend towards wider markets as the stage of manufacture is raised, disclosed by Jean Jussiant, *L'Evolution du commerce extérieur de la Belgique*, pp. 56–112, and P. Lieftinck, *The External Economic Policy of the Netherlands*, p. 5.

for centuries, all but the commonest and cheapest ores are worked out. Raw materials must now be sought in areas far distant from industrial centers. The great demands of modern industry tend to concentrate production in a few such areas where large deposits make possible cheap methods of production. Professor Staley illustrates the world-wide search for raw materials rather neatly by listing 183 materials essential to the production of an automobile and printing them across a map of the world. The list is a varied one, ranging from acetic acid to arsenic, castor oil to chromium, diamonds to dyes, gasoline to gold, talc to tallow.[7]

The conclusion is well summarized:

To look back from this point in the twentieth century at the changes in the very foundations of economic (and cultural and political) life wrought by recent advances in the technology of distance leaves one gasping. The world has been shrinking at a rate unprecedented in history, and it continues to shrink. At the same time, new methods of production have been introduced. Large-scale industries and specialized products have put a premium on wide markets. More exact adaptation of materials to function, rising industrial outputs, new inventions creating new wants, have brought a mounting demand for an unimagined variety and volume of raw materials, to be satisfied adequately only by drawing on widely scattered sources. In all these ways our scientists, inventors and engineers have been pushing us in the direction of a unified, world-wide economic system. The profound consequences of this fact are as yet but dimly seen by citizen and statesman alike.[8]

Here then is a mighty trend—scientific, technical, economic —in direct conflict with the practice of nationalism, if not with the principle of nationality: a trend towards world markets. Given the deep emotional forces that lie behind patriotic feeling on the one hand and economic enterprise on the other, the conflict resolves itself into a clash between attempts to maintain national control of economic activity and the geographi-

[7] Staley, *op. cit.*, p. 28.
[8] *Ibid.*, p. 35.

NATIONALISM AND INDUSTRIALISM 21

cal necessity of organizing the means of a more abundant life for the average man by world-wide economic co-operation. The United States now displays industrial leadership even more markedly than nineteenth-century England. She has inherited leadership also in the struggle for freer trade, the organization of world markets, and the freedom of private trading enterprise. Other national governments do not accept this leadership and the battle is clearly joined between cosmopolitan trading and financial initiative on the one hand, and economic nationalism on the other.

It is too soon yet to say that nationalism, as represented by the all-powerful State, will succeed in dominating and controlling the forces tending to economic expansion on a world scale. It is possible that economic forces, at present throttled by State intervention, will in the long run destroy the State or, as in the past, enlarge its frontiers. Or that a return to more rational and less emotional conceptions of statecraft will facilitate the finding of ways in which legitimate national aspirations may be reconciled with the advantages of a worldwide organization of industry and trade. Such reconciliation demands that future generations be educated in a citizenship that extends from home to neighborhood and from nationality to humanity. On the other hand, they must be educated to be more concerned with real living and less concerned with "conspicuous expenditure."

One line of approach to such reconciliation is suggested by Professor Staley's conclusion at a later stage of his study that

> A policy that restrains modern man from using the knowledge he has acquired, that restrains him from using resources in ways that have become essential to his present modes of existence in some parts of the world, builds up pressures for an explosion. Economic walls at national boundaries, far from preventing conflicts, themselves create a grimly materialistic basis for future wars. One of the first principles for those interested in economic progress and political peace must be: *Lessen the economic significance of national boundaries.*[9]

[9] Staley, *op. cit.*, p. 123.

The realization of interdependence is perhaps greatest in small countries. In all of them the recent policies of trade regulation are in large part defensive, an attempt to save their national economies from the violent fluctuations and strains imposed by economic pressures originating in world markets. In some cases, as for example in Denmark [10] and Greece,[11] the pressures were focused by policy decisions in great markets. In all cases the catastrophic fall of prices for their export of agricultural products and raw materials was a considerable factor. The financial convulsions that placed them under the necessity of straining their balances of payments in order to meet a drain of capital was an effective cause of exchange restrictions and quantitative controls of imports. Though in certain cases a somewhat doctrinaire belief in the virtues of a planned economy led to such controls being welcomed,[12] and though practically every country has endeavored to achieve regulated stability and in doing so to build up a higher stage of manufacturing development, there is growing realization of the costs involved, and of the desirability of developing methods of regulation that need not sacrifice the advantages of international co-operation.[13]

In recent years, negative and restrictive types of regulation have necessitated a considerable transformation of domestic agriculture and industry in many countries. The smaller Eu-

[10] H. P. Gøtrik, *Danish Economic Policy, 1931–38.*
[11] S. D. Pintos, *Le Controle des changes en Grèce,* p. 7. "En Septembre 1931, la crise de la monnaie anglaise, provoqua une situation économique des plus graves pour la Grèce."
[12] Gøtrik, *op. cit.,* pp. 13 ff.
[13] V. Madgearu, *La Politique économique extérieure de la Roumanie, 1927–1938,* p. 45: "Nous avons rappelé, par ailleurs, qu'en dépit des difficultés inhérentes au methodes actuelles d'échanges économiques, la Roumanie avait réussi, par sa politique commerciale, à équilibrer les influences politiques extérieures. Mais ce resultat n'a été obtenu qu'au prix d'importants sacrifices matériels et il n'est que de nature precaire.

"La politique économique extérieure de la Roumanie, que s'est développée dans le cadre tracé par les difficultés provenant de l'instabilité économique internationale et les mesures d'isolement et de défense économique des autres pays, n'est pas sans presenter des éléments qui pourraient contribuer, a l'avenir, à certaines difficultés politiques."

NATIONALISM AND INDUSTRIALISM 23

ropean countries offer notable illustrations of this fact.[14] The specialized agricultural exporting countries of the world outside Europe suffered perhaps even more heavily by the contraction of their external markets.[15] Though cases may be cited where for economic or political reasons advantageous commercial arrangements were possible,[16] and industrial development was welcomed as a means of ultimately raising the standard of life,[17] the general effect of trade restrictions before the war began was quite clearly the achievement of a somewhat precarious balance of external payments at the expense of considerable economic dislocation, lower standards of living, and capital consumption.

While there was this growing sense of interdependence, there was little disposition to believe that the economic barriers at national boundaries were likely to be relaxed in the near future. Not only the smaller countries, but the great trading countries, were unwilling to relax their precautions while international conditions remained disturbed. German economists have argued that the "liberal" system of international co-operation which centered about the former gold standard not only had broken down in the abnormal circumstances after 1918, but contained fundamental defects that were impossible to remedy. Dr. Meyer, for example, in a closely argued paper on exchange restrictions, has analyzed the conditions necessary for the successful functioning of the gold standard as an international monetary mechanism and has shown that they were not realized in the interwar decades. One of the main lines of his argument is that creditor countries were unwilling to accept the adjustment of their economies in an international system and, by following a nationalistic pol-

[14] Cf., e. g., Wolfgang Heller (ed.), *Hungarian External Economic Policy*, and Erling Petersen, *The Repercussions of Modern Commercial Policies on Economic Conditions in Norway*.
[15] Cf. H. L. Harris, *Australia's Economic Policy*, and D. B. Copland, *Monetary Policy in Australia*; Angel Valle et Juan M. Ferrer, *La Politique économique de l'Argentine*.
[16] Cf. H. R. Hormi, *The Clearing and Compensation System of Finland*.
[17] Cf. Sir B. L. Mitter, *Indian Economic Policy*.

icy, drove the debtor countries into the necessity of still more developed nationalism.

"The creditor countries," he writes, "by their attitude have instituted a struggle of all against all. Driven by their obligation to transfer, for which the creditor countries were themselves responsible, the debtor countries had to put into action a mechanism which appeared dangerous to the creditor countries. To combat the actual or only imagined dangers, the creditors did not adopt the only correct measure, the elimination of the source of disturbance (consolidation or cancellation of the fluctuating international debt) or re-establishment of the conditions necessary for the functioning of the gold mechanism. Instead they permitted the actual causes of disturbance to remain and, in order to combat the dangers, made the functional conditions continuously worse." [18]

Without necessarily accepting this allocation of responsibility, it is important to notice the stress laid upon national economic policies as the cause of breakdown. Examination of the national economic policies of other great trading powers reinforces the impression that such policies have been concerned primarily, if not exclusively, with the safeguarding of particular national interests. M. Hoffherr, for example, after drawing attention to the breakdown of automatic international adjustments (*le crépuscule des automatismes*) argues for the development of the French colonial empire and a greater degree of national organization as the principal items in a reshaped economic policy.[19] The bilateral treaty policy followed by Great Britain in recent years was prompted mainly by concern for certain industries, particularly agriculture, coal, cotton, and shipping, that were hard hit by the depression.[20] In the United States, sectional influences are even more pronounced since

[18] Fritz Meyer (comp.), *Analysis of Exchange Restrictions at Present in Force* (Eng. Trans.), p. 43.
[19] René Hoffherr & others, *La Politique commerciale de la France*, pp. 1–90.
[20] Study Group of British Coordinating Committee for International Studies, *British External Policy in Recent Years*, pp. 23 et seq. Cf. also H. J. Tasca, *World Trading Systems: A Study of American and British Com-*

NATIONALISM AND INDUSTRIALISM 25

... the United States is at a lower level of national integration than England or France; at a higher level than Europe . . .[21]

While, therefore, it is perfectly true that

... the American system rests upon the premise that multilateral trade and payments, facilitated by the principle of equality of treatment and originating in private enterprise and initiative, provide the system most calculated to expand the world's real income and so improve the real standard of living of peoples of the world . . .[22]

it is equally true that

... the schedules of the Tariff Acts of 1922 and 1930 were incapable of rational defense, they were not, as a whole, popular, but there was little or no chance of a remedy as long as politics were sectional . . .[23]

for the simple reason that

... no bookkeeping which showed that the loss by the whole American people on a foreign debt default would be greater than the individual losses of protected private interests could move a prudent politician. A loss that was spread over the whole country would do him little harm while a loss that fell on any important interests in his district might be fatal.[23]

For a variety of reasons, therefore, differing from country to country, national economic policies were dictated by concern for national interests with scant regard for mutual interdependence and reliance on expanding world markets. The reasons were different in small and great trading countries, in

---

mercial Policies, p. 146: "The purposes of British bilateralism have been twofold—the immediate expansion of exports to certain markets, and debt collection from other countries."

[21] Arthur D. Gayer and Carl T. Schmidt, *American Economic Foreign Policy*, p. 10.

[22] H. J. Tasca, *op. cit.*, p. 141.

[23] Gayer and Schmidt, *op. cit.*, pp. 8–10. It might be added that "a loss that was spread over the whole country" might easily be attributed to foreign machinations and thus provide an effective political slogan for isolationist propaganda.

debtor and creditor countries, under totalitarian and democratic regimes; but, in all countries national interest, narrowly conceived, took undisputed precedence over the vaguer interests of all in a developing world system. Detailed analysis might place the responsibility for restrictive action on private vested interests, or on the desire to plan national economic activity so as to enhance social justice and afford more balanced vocational opportunities, or on the direction of trade to facilitate military preparations. The mechanism of restriction might be the simple use of a protective tariff (which in a great trading country need not be very high to be damaging in its restrictive effect) or a complex new apparatus of administrative controls. In every case the effective instrument of enforcement was the power of the Nation-State. When government policies result in such a general breakdown of economic activity and ultimately in political anarchy, it is time to ask whether the units of government, and the functions attributed to them, are the most effective that can be devised as instruments to promote general welfare.

The Making of Policy

Before any attempt is made to analyze the rather elusive forces responsible for the shaping of national economic policies, it is advisable to consider what is meant by "policy," who makes it, and how. It is only too easy, in analyzing the scattered and often incomplete record of actions taken by governments, or the reasons publicly advanced for such actions, to find somewhat facile explanations for what in reality were a series of improvised decisions taken under the stress of immediate necessity. A rather sharp distinction ought, therefore, to be drawn between the actual pressures responsible for decisions which in retrospect shape themselves into a more or less coherent policy, the arguments by which those decisions are publicly justified, and the rationalizations which at a somewhat later stage lend an appearance of theoretical consistency to them.

Something ought first to be said, however, concerning the actual phenomena of policy-making, as distinct from its justification. It is rarely the case that any government (or any individual) can lay down in advance, and adhere to, a line of policy which is the result of mature judgment and reflection. Wherever action must be adjusted to an ever-changing set of circumstances largely beyond the control of any individual, group, or government, policy must be in large degree improvised and pragmatic. Wherever a group process is involved, as in practical politics, compromises must be made. This is nowhere truer than in international politics where, in addition to the conflict of group interests within national boundaries, there is a continuous, if vague and confused, conflict of governmental attitudes and actions in defense of what are said to be "national interests."

It has been well said of economic planning within the confines of a national community that "the notion of complete understanding controlling action is an ideal in the clouds, completely at variance with practical life." [24] This is certainly truer of economic policy that must operate in the international field. No government, for example, can pursue a managed currency policy, or a tariff policy, without taking account of its reactions upon the policies of other governments. Management, in fact, must consist of a succession of adjustments and adaptations to continuously changing circumstances. The wider the range of contacts involved, and the more established routine becomes disorganized, the more improvised must be the decisions that in the aggregate form policy.[25]

It may be that, in certain rather exceptional cases, the foregoing observations apply rather to the tactics than to the

[24] A. N. Whitehead, "On Foresight"; Introduction to W. B. Donham, *Business Adrift* (New York, 1931).
[25]   "We sail a changeful sea, through halcyon days and storm,
     and when the ship laboureth, our stedfast purpose
     trembles as like the compass in a binnacle.
     Our stability is but balance and conduct lies
     in masterful administration of the unforeseen."
          Robert Bridges, "The Testament of Beauty."

strategy of policy-making. If political power falls into the hands of an individual or group committed to the pursuit of objectives that have been worked out, even vaguely, as the result of burning emotional conviction, those objectives may be steadily pursued by tactics that are adapted to shifting circumstances, even when adaptation gives an appearance of inconsistency. Many examples of such steadfastness of ultimate purpose might be cited from recent history. The clearest, quite naturally, are to be found where dictatorship not only retains power longer, but exercises it more effectively and over a wider range of social activity than is possible to any individual or group under the democratic process of government by persuasion and consent.

In the community of nations, deliberate policy, whether in the direction of economic aggrandizement or of co-operation, is largely confined to a few great powers. The smaller powers must, in the main, pursue policies conforming to the situation created by international pressures upon them. Their ability to initiate a greater degree of international economic co-operation is very circumscribed. Quite obviously also, no little powers in the modern world can do much effective saber-rattling. Their interest, and for the most part their desire, is to live at home at peace as far as their larger and more powerful neighbors will allow them. Collectively, the influence of the little powers might be very considerable—if exercised in a collective system. In a period of economic nationalism (which is equivalent in terms of government to international anarchy) the most co-operative intentions of the little powers cannot be much more than pious aspirations. On the other hand, their individual pursuit of nationalistic aims must in the aggregate greatly complicate the prevailing anarchy.

For the most part, therefore, and in most countries, policy consists of a mass of detailed actions in particular cases. The actions taken are nearly always of comparatively small importance, but they build up in the aggregate into important policy trends, and form commitments as well as precedents. From time to time a more important and spectacular decision has to be made, which has the appearance of a deliberate act of policy; but such decisions are nearly always predetermined by the accumulation of smaller decisions over a long period creating a situation in which freedom of action is very limited. Thus, in a sense, Great Britain may be said to have abandoned the gold standard, not in September, 1931, when a threatened exhaustion of the gold reserves forced a suspension of the Bank's legal obligation to sell gold at a fixed price in sterling, but in the preceding months, and even years, when successive decisions concerning the bank rate (to say nothing of a wide range of decisions concerning loans, wage-rates, etc., within Great Britain and in other countries) created a situation which strained the balances of payments and ultimately led to a run on the Bank's reserves. Dr. Tasca has drawn attention also to the way in which discrimination and modification of most-favored-nation treatment has crept into British commercial policy as the result of particular bilateral trade bargains.[26] The gradual attenuation of a still-accepted principle always leads to the likelihood that the time may come when the principle will have to be abandoned.

It will be noted that the illustrations given above are not confined to commercial policy. Commodity trade between the citizens of two or more countries is merely the most visible aspect of international economic relations. Much more is involved in the conduct of external economic policy than the regulation of external trade by tariffs, quotas, or treaty systems. Every aspect of policy which affects prices must be taken into account. In particular, the conduct of monetary policy is of primary importance as affecting the international balance of payments. It would, for instance, be a mistake to conclude that the active prosecution of a bilateral trade treaty program aimed at reducing tariffs and other barriers to international trade proves that any particular country is pursuing a consistent policy of international co-operation in the economic sphere. Account must be taken of the activities of other departments of government. If, in such a country, the agricul-

[26] H. J. Tasca, *World Trading Systems*, pp. 47 ff.

tural authorities subsidize both the production and the export of great staple commodities, so that agricultural exporters elsewhere find competition intensified, the results of such subsidization may go far to counteract the benefit of somewhat freer trade. If the monetary policy of government is such as to press harshly upon the exchange stability of other countries (as did the exchange depreciations of some of the great creditor countries, or the equivalent action by which the price of silver was raised), the consequences to international trade may be far greater than the raising of a tariff. Indeed, the persistence of depressed conditions in a great trading country, whether because of government policy or in spite of it, may outweigh the results of laborious efforts to free international trade from some of its more harassing restrictions.

It follows that any discussion of the forces that shape national economic policies in the international field cannot be narrowly confined to the field of commercial policy. It is, therefore, much more difficult to define and explain the springs of policy. This is particularly true in a democracy where government action is the resultant of a balancing of pressures. Unless policy is strictly co-ordinated under centralized direction pursuing clearly defined aims, it is apt to be confused and contradictory, one department of government acting inconsistently with the professed objectives of another.

Moreover, as long as private enterprise continues to play any considerable role in the organization of economic activity, government policy, even in the widest sense, must often conform to, and can seldom do more than moderate, tendencies which emerge from market processes.

This aspect of the problem may, perhaps, be put more clearly in another way, by asking who is responsible for making policy decisions. Before the international trading system broke down, while international monetary equilibrium was still maintained on the gold standard basis and even imperfect competition kept a rough working equilibrium between commodity prices, real wage rates, interest rates, and the profits of enterprise both within and between countries, the answer to such questions would have been at once clearer and more diffused. As the Gold Delegation of the League of Nations argued in its final report, the successful working of the gold standard depended upon the co-operative acceptance of, or acquiescence in, rather well-known and routine procedures of monetary policy. Those responsible for specific decisions, such as the raising or lowering of the discount rate, regarded themselves as neutral agents interpreting well-recognized signals. If there was a drain on the gold reserve the discount rate was raised and credit was made dearer. But the responsibility was on the trading community as a whole for the aggregate of transactions that had resulted in the drain which gave the signal for action.

In the same way, when trade was regulated mainly by tariffs that were normally the result of a long process of public discussion and legislative action, the ultimate responsibility for policy decisions rested upon the balance of economic pressures within the community as a whole.

One of the most significant developments of recent years, however, has been the passing of power in this respect from the legislative to the administrative side of government. This has been inevitable, not only because democracy has been replaced by a greater or less degree of dictatorship in so many countries, but also because the increasing opportunism of policy as established routine practices have broken down has rendered it necessary for decisions to be taken more quickly and in more complicated detail. A question may, of course, still be asked as to the pressures which are actually effective in the making of policy. Who has the ear of those who must act? Whose judgment and advice is mainly relied upon? How far are decisions based upon practical considerations concerning which responsible officials alone have, if not full, at least the best, information available? Do they tend to consult experts who must almost necessarily be individuals with a direct personal interest in the decision to be taken? Are they more or less open to the pressures of vested interests when their actions are further removed from public criticism?

Such questions as these are perhaps incapable of clear and decisive answers at present. It would be of the highest interest to know what influences make up the mind of a dictator—and this development clearly gives to a fairly considerable body of often unknown civil servants some of the minor attributes of dictatorship. With whom do they talk, what statistics and reports do they consult, what sort of experience and knowledge do they regard as worthy of consultation? The answers to all such questions are now more obscure, though more important, than they used to be, partly because the officials of whom they must be asked are less visible to public scrutiny, partly because there has been a noticeable shrinkage of information concerning the problems that confront them. The operations of a Stabilization Fund are necessarily secret and there is no means of knowing whether the powers entrusted to those who administer it are exercised in accordance with information known only to them, whether they are exercised upon information at all, or even whether they are exercised.

While more has now to be taken upon trust, certain broad generalizations appear to be justified. However high-minded and able may be the public officials upon whom devolves more and more of the responsibility for the conduct of day-to-day policy, there is a real danger in their progressive withdrawal from detailed public scrutiny and criticism. It is obvious that in the main they must be not only efficient but public-spirited. The increasing complexity of economic regulation would long before now have broken down in chaos if they had been self-seekers or muddlers. Complicated and more secret administrative procedures obviously offer greater opportunities for political corruption and graft, but the machinery of regulation would quickly have collapsed in confusion if such corruption had been general. The real danger is more subtle, and arises from the concentration of power exercised for long periods without the check of public criticism. Errors of policy tend to become cumulative. When power is diffused, as in a system of free enterprise, individual errors of judgment are not so serious and tend to eliminate those whose judgment is at fault. But this is not the case when power is exercised anonymously as a function of permanent employment not readily accessible to public criticism in detail.

A further fact seems clear in recent experience. Administrative control of policy-making puts a premium upon organized pressures from directly interested individuals, or groups of individuals, and lessens the consideration likely to be given to the general public interest and particularly the unorganized interest of the consumer.[27] It is true that in countries with a long and powerful democratic tradition, as for instance in Denmark, the machinery of regulation may be so constructed as to give representation to various group interests in the community, including consumer interests as represented, for example, in the consumers' co-operative movement. In most systems of economic regulation, however, there seems a clear tendency for organized interest groups (including in some cases a strong labor movement) to dominate the making of policy. Even though officials may strive to watch the interests of the general consuming public, it is difficult, in the absence of adequate publicity, to mobilize public opinion so as to withstand the pressures of organized producers who are al-

[27] This is not inconsistent with the view expressed by Professor P. W. Bidwell in arguing that the administrative procedure adopted by the United States in the Trade Agreements program has been successful. "For the first time in over a century," he writes, "lobbying, log-rolling and other obnoxious accompaniments of tariff revision have been relegated far to the background. The expert administrators who have the negotiations in charge are sufficiently insulated from contact with pressure groups to be able to consider primarily the public interest. Special interests are not neglected, but are placed in their properly subordinate position." Percy Bidwell, *The Invisible Tariff*, p. 13.

The essential point is that these administrators are not making, but executing, policy. They have been given power for a limited period to negotiate reciprocal tariff reductions. Every three years their power must be renewed after full debate and legislative decision. Moreover, their decisions are positive and constructive steps to implement a deliberate policy, not a series of improvised negative expedients out of which policy emerges. The same may be said of the public servants who implement the German policy of "autarky." In both cases there is positive direction; but in the former case policy is approved and power is granted to the executive by a free legislative assembly.

ways expert and have detailed and precise knowledge of the issues and of their own interests. There may be provision for consumer representation or for public discussion at certain stages; but the scattered and unorganized consumer interest can rarely make an effective case.

The result is that government regulation tends first to be influenced by, and in the long run to fall under the control of, organized producers. Many examples of this trend can be given. The machinery of corporative or totalitarian government frankly uses and promotes such functional organization —and is greatly influenced by it, at least up to the point where the interests of the Nation-State take precedence. Even in democratic countries the same trend is clear. The various international commodity control schemes regulating the production, trade, and prices of important raw materials are primarily designed to protect the financial structure of existing investments, even at the expense of new investment opportunities in areas of developing production. Agricultural marketing schemes in a great many countries are dominated by organized farming interests. The development in recent years of imperial marketing agreements in the British Commonwealth is avowedly aimed at "commodity councils, producer-controlled and financed." Since the war these somewhat rudimentary councils have been used as the foundation of war control schemes, and supplemented by parallel organization in a wide field of raw materials which have been handed over to the control of experts drawn almost wholly from the trade associations or even individual concerns in the industry.[28] A long step has been taken towards a "government of business men, for business men, by business men." [29] It is not laissez faire, but regulation, that leads most directly to this end.

Moreover, since regulation can be most effectively assured within the boundaries of a single national state by working

[28] "The Controllers," *Economist* (Dec. 9, 1939), pp. 363–364; "The Controllers," *ibid.* (Feb. 17, 1940), pp. 282–283.
[29] M. J. Bonn, *Wealth, Welfare or War*, p. 30.

with and through the machinery of national government, there is a constant tendency for the advocates of such regulation to adopt nationalistic attitudes and agree rather readily to restrictive measures of economic nationalism. Restrictions on international trade are almost indissolubly connected with the cartelization of industry. All such bodies as tariff commissions, in an era of national regulation and planning, tend to become instruments of protection assuring freedom from import competition to the reorganized national industries. In the same way, the advocates of autonomous monetary policies are inevitably led to deprecate the importance of international exchange equilibrium as placing the national economy at the mercy of international economic fluctuations. It is not an accident that the advocates of government regulation and planning have in recent years defended policies of economic nationalism.

The only escape from this conflict between national regulation and international equilibrium is, in fact, to be found in the creation of effective organs of international co-operation on a regulated basis; but in the present state of political and economic anarchy this task appears extremely difficult. Indeed, such an enlargement of the scope of planning makes more obvious the impossibility of effective economic regulation by such day-to-day decisions of detail as have now become the rule. The best practical prospect of restoring international equilibrium lies in the re-establishment of known and accepted routine rules of policy, based upon a relatively moderate degree of national planning in the sense of assuring to each national community reasonable minima of security and livelihood.

The most important and alarming trend revealed by the recent shift of power from legislative to administrative authorities is, however, the facility it affords to governments which desire, or are forced, to direct and mobilize economic activity for other than economic purposes.[30] The most dangerous

[30] For illustrations of the use of indirect protection for political reasons see Bidwell, *op. cit.*, p. 19.

vested interest in a system of State-regulated industry and trade is the interest of the State itself. There are innumerable illustrations of this tendency, ranging from the interest of a bureaucracy in its own perpetuation to the totalitarian mobilization of economic activity for political aggression. Governments represent and act for the national community, and it is fatally easy for the distinction between the public interest and the government interest to become blurred. Thus, monetary policy may be conducted largely, if not primarily, so as to facilitate the financing of government expenditures, the gold standard being replaced by a "gilt-edged standard."[31] Trade may be regulated not according to the possibilities of profitable exchange, depending ultimately upon meeting individual demands of consumers, but according to the needs of the government which is embarked upon a program of economic preparedness for war. The transition from "welfare economics" to "power economics" is more readily made when the conduct of policy is concentrated in the hands of administrators rather than of legislators responsible to public opinion.

Discussion of the motives for economic policy cannot, therefore, be simple or clear-cut. There is, at the present time, a wide variety in the political organization of States—ranging from developed democratic institutions responsive to public opinion, through many forms of administrative oligarchy, to totalitarian dictatorship. National economic policies vary as widely—from intervention calculated to interpret and give effect to the common will as expressed in the aggregate result of individual actions working within an accepted framework of economic and social organization, through intermediate forms of regulation designed to achieve disciplined reorganization of the national economy, to single-minded and often ruthless mobilization of all economic activity in the real or supposed interest of the State. At one extreme the analysis of motives involves an attempt to appraise the dispersed and conflicting individual decisions that in the aggregate produce an equilibrium of social forces. At the other extreme all that

[31] N. F. Hall, *Treasury Control and Cheap Money* (Manchester, 1937).

matters is the aims and ambitions of a small ruling group and the means by which they are able to secure for their policies the continued acquiescence, or support, of the mass of the people.

As the world has moved in recent years from the former towards the latter, the established routine of international economic relations has broken down. Policy has, in consequence, become less stable and less measurable, indeed less known. It is inevitable that such a development should call for improvisation and innovations in policy, and that national policies should become more erratic and confused. This is very clear in the rapid growth of new restrictions on international trade. In the early stages of its development the new mercantilism bore all the marks of hasty and often inconsistent expedients devised to combat the destructive forces unloosed by disintegration of the world trading system.

National and International Regulation

Even those economists who criticize and reject the nineteenth-century system of international economic cooperation by reliance on competitive market processes, recognize the necessity and desirability of building a new system not only of international trade, but of foreign investment and exchange stability between national currencies.[32] There is a sharp divergence of opinion, however, between those who believe that the restoration of world markets can be successfully achieved only by a substantial restoration of economic freedom to private enterprise, and those who argue, on the contrary, for "an expanding system of regulated trade."

There is a good deal of confusion in the current usage of the terms "nationalism" and "internationalism." "Economic internationalism," in Dr. Heilperin's words, "can be defined simply as a policy intended to prevent political boundaries from exercising any disturbing effect on economic relations be-

[32] Cf. von Mickwitz, *The Economic Structure of Capital Exports to Southeastern Europe,* and Kurt Kroyman, *Problems of German Trade Policy.*

tween areas on the two sides of the frontier. The full realization of economic internationalism is found in free trade, combined with the freedom of international migration and of financial transactions. In a protectionist world, economic internationalism means a development towards reducing obstacles to trade, migration and financial transactions between countries." [33]

An essential part of such economic internationalism would seem to be the conduct of national economic policies so as to reconcile freedom of trade and financial transactions with stable exchange-rates between the currencies. "Ultimately," Dr. Heilperin remarks, "this amounts to an international co-ordination of national economic policies," but such co-ordination, in the view of laissez-faire liberals, can be achieved only as the result of competitive forces working in a free market.

If the political aspects of the question are left on one side for the moment, the chief reasons advanced in support of economic nationalism derive from the increased importance attached in recent years to national as opposed to foreign markets and the belief that national markets can be brought to, and maintained in, a state of full employment by judicious policies of credit expansion. A distinction must, of course, be drawn between the *practice* of economic and monetary nationalism, which in most countries has been the fortuitous result of an accumulation of expedients designed to protect segments of the national economy in successive emergencies, and the *theoretical* justification of regulating measures designed to expand national economic activity and ultimately to develop an expanding system of regulated trade.

It is important, however, not to confuse the issues by identifying internationalism with a return to laissez faire. There is, it is true, some historical justification for such an identification. In the nineteenth century, international trade, world-wide investment, and exchange stability pivoted on the gold standard were associated with freedom of economic enterprise. Economic nationalism has developed rapidly since governments

[33] Heilperin, *International Monetary Organization*, p. 16.

have imposed increasing limitations on such freedom and it is easy to demonstrate that increased State intervention in domestic economic activity has been intimately connected with the recent increase of trade barriers and the breakdown of exchange stability.

Nevertheless, the two problems are logically distinct. It is possible to conceive, at least theoretically, a system of economic planning directed towards expanding international trade. And, in a world where international cartels and private trading agreements flourish, it does not necessarily follow that complete liberty of private enterprise would lead to expanding trade. It is certainly true that the intervention of governments in economic activity requires, if international trade is to increase, not only more skillful planning of the national market, but international planning, or at least international co-ordination of national plans. But the converse is equally true. The restoration of world trade along laissez-faire lines would involve in some degree the reversal not only of government action in regard to such matters as wages and hours of work and labor conditions, but also revocation of the legal privileges that have enabled great financial corporations to build up rigidities in the price systems of different countries. When trade was expanding on a laissez-faire basis in the nineteenth century, not only were systems of factory legislation rudimentary, but trade-unions were weak and industry was still largely in the hands of small masters who were closely in touch with the processes of manufacture. Short of a reversion to these conditions (from which some thoroughgoing modern liberals would not shrink, but which seems practically impossible), the advocacy of international economic co-operation by laissez-faire arguments beats vainly against the inescapable fact that government regulation is firmly rooted in national markets. This being so, national economic policies independently pursued are in practice bound to issue in strained international economic relations that cause recourse to measures of economic nationalism.

The real roots of economic nationalism are to be found,

therefore, in the domestic economic policies of governments. This is plainly stated in Dr. Meyer's argument referred to in the preceding section of this chapter. One aspect of his argument may be quoted to illustrate this point further:

> The thesis that a revival of international trade can only take place on the foundation of sound national economic systems is no empty phrase which, without any factual basis, attempts to give a belated scientific sanction to the specific development of Germany's currency and economic system or even to make a virtue of necessity. On the contrary, sober facts and reasoning in our report prove that the dependency of the individual national economic system's "Konjunktur" on the world market must of necessity lead to a unilateral struggle for markets—to a struggle in which the necessary counterpart is missing, as any corresponding increase of imports is held to be detrimental to the economic situation. From this again spring those innumerable forms of protectionist trade and currency policies. Any attempt to clear the way by doing away with these is doomed to failure from the very outset upon the causes and not upon the symptoms. In other words the urge to import must have its origin in the demands of a fully occupied economic system.[34]

No one would quarrel with the thesis that a durable recovery of world trade and a restoration of international economic equilibrium depend very largely upon a prior, or parallel, restoration of national prosperity in at least the great trading countries. It is inconceivable that any government could plunge its citizens into economic distress merely to show its good will by participating in international measures to restore international trade. It is difficult even to envisage any government inflicting economic loss on important groups of its citizens in order that the national community as a whole might participate in the expanding prosperity of a restored international system. The essential fact is that effective government at the present time is organized on a national basis and that the national units claim complete independence of action. It is all but impossible, therefore, to

[34] Meyer, *op. cit.*, pp. 69–70.

find any government willing to take the risks of initiating a program of expanding trade, if only for fear no other government will follow its lead.

The fact is too often overlooked also that there is usually a very close connection between the domestic and external economic policies of governments. Not only are they governed by the same philosophy at any given time, but action in one sphere conditions and governs action in the other. Measures taken to regulate wages, interest, and other costs and prices in the national market affect the demand for imports and the possibilities of competitive export. While it may well be argued that, given readiness to accept the international repercussions of domestic policies, a substantial degree of domestic regulation is not inconsistent with a relatively liberal external policy, it is important to realize that the repercussions of such a policy may involve heavy sectional losses to the national economy concerned. For example, if a country with a relatively high standard of living imposes minimum standards of wages and working conditions that raise real labor costs in certain industries, a choice may need to be made between protecting those industries against the competition of cheap imports or allowing them to go out of production. The case for domestic regulation in combination with free trade, therefore, rests essentially upon the extent to which efficiency of production is stimulated, rather than hampered, by the imposition of minimum standards of wages and labor conditions.

Even more clearly, monetary policies designed to cheapen credit so as to encourage economic expansion in the national market directly affect the balances of international payments. Imports are encouraged and exports made more difficult while at the same time short-term funds are drained from the country. If these developments continue for any length of time, the strain on the balance of payments will force either exchange depreciation or exchange control. "New Deal" policies in Belgium, France, Italy, New Zealand, and other countries in recent years may be cited in illustration of this sequence. In these circumstances, the only possibility of maintaining stable exchange rates is, as Dr. Meyer correctly argues, to separate the national market from the world market by instituting exchange control and with it increasingly severe control of all external and ultimately all domestic economic transactions. This leads inevitably to a situation in which the world market breaks up by centrifugal action into a series of national markets, each with its own price structure. Not only are prices of particular commodities divergent, but the relations between different sorts of prices differ from country to country so that there is no exchange parity at which currencies can be stabilized so as to allow greater freedom of transactions without creating the necessity for serious national adjustments of wages, interest, and other costs.[35]

As long as the gold standard mechanism worked effectively, national price structures were kept in equilibrium within and between national economies. If wages rose in one country out of proportion to other costs of production, exports—particularly of goods in which labor was a high proportion of the total cost—fell off and imports increased. The result, accelerated by the monetary consequences of strain on the balance of payments, was that real wages were adjusted or that the country lost ground in the production of such goods. There was never complete equilibrium, but an incessant series of adjustments tending to equilibrate not only commodity prices but labor costs, interest rates, and all other elements of the price structure.

For such a mechanism to function, however imperfectly, two main conditions were necessary. In the first place, the countries that formed part of this international system had to accept the necessity of adjusting their national economies to the continuous but relatively small fluctuations of the world market. Dr. Meyer, following Lutz, points out that this involved the repudiation of independent monetary policies aimed exclusively at regulating the national market. It also postulated the necessity of keeping restrictions on imports

[35] Cf. J. B. Condliffe, "Exchange Rates and Prices," *Index* (January, 1935), pp. 1–17.

within bounds and the necessity of maintaining elasticity in the price system. To these three aspects of adaptation to international equilibrium must be added the imponderable factor of confidence in the national currency. Under the gold standard, this was maintained by enforcing on the national economy such adjustments as kept the monetary reserves intact and the exchange rates stable.

But a positive factor of regulation was equally necessary. The gold standard mechanism functioned as successfully and as long as it did not only because of the degree to which trading countries conformed to the requirements of international equilibrium, but also because there was a clearinghouse in which adjustments could be made and absorbed. As long as the London Money Market functioned effectively in this respect, positive leadership was available. London's powerful creditor position, especially on short-term, enabled it to act as a regulating center for credit. An increase in bank rate drew short-term credit from every important trading center. Great Britain's free trade policy developed a market also for temporary world surpluses of commodities. In its dual capacity as wholesaler and banker, London acted as the clearinghouse for world trade, investment, and finance as long as sterling was managed primarily as an international rather than a national currency.

Both these aspects of the world trading system as it developed in the nineteenth century were essential—the negative aspect of national readiness to adjust to the changing equilibrium of world markets, and the positive aspect of co-ordinating and regulating leadership. Both are now lacking. Every nation, including Great Britain, is following a policy, more or less consciously thought out, of economic and monetary nationalism. It is almost certainly impossible to envisage a return to the nineteenth-century system. The disequilibria and discrepancies between national price systems are now too great, and the growth of national controls is too deeply rooted, to expect that governments can submit their peoples to the violent upheavals and dislocations that would suddenly be brought about by restoring freedom of international trade and financial transactions. Nor is it likely that any one country can again act as a regulating and co-ordinating center for an international monetary, financial, and trading system. Some of the problems that arise are treated in later chapters, but before accepting the conclusion that international economic relations must in future be based upon nationally regulated markets sheltering behind exchange control and linked together by an elaborate system of bilateral clearing agreements, certain questions must be asked.

The first concerns the suitability of modern States as units within which full and balanced employment is first to be sought. The world at present consists of a curious conglomeration of large States and small, which differ in economic development in almost every respect but which are alike in claiming to exercise unfettered sovereignty. Whatever considerations were effective in drawing their boundaries, their suitability as units within which autonomous economic policies might be conducted was certainly not dominant. Political self-determination in the settlement of Versailles, for example, created a great number of small States and carved up others without much regard for their economic structure.

It is often argued that an acceptable solution of this problem might be found by grouping numbers of small States within the economic orbit of a great trading power which regards itself as competent not only to follow an independent national economic policy, but to dominate the economic arrangements of its smaller neighbors so that they become satellites and feeders of a metropolitan area. Regionalism of this type, however, might well result in the creation of great rival economic empires between which the difficulty of harmonizing imperial economic policies would remain acute. In any case, it is unlikely that the smaller States would willingly sacrifice either their autonomy or the advantages of participation in a world trading system offering them the possibilities of alternative markets. Indeed, other great trading nations, dependent as they are upon access to world markets, could hardly acquiesce in a system which confined their trading and investment within a certain sphere of influence. World economic activity, like world peace, is in fact indivisible.

Apart, however, from the geographical suitability of States to act as units of economic organization, there arises the question whether the modern State, large or small, can safely be entrusted with such tasks. The machinery of States is based upon military force. National security is their first, and often their overwhelming, preoccupation. If they are to be strong, they must subordinate the economic welfare of their citizens to strategic considerations. Limitation of their economic sovereignty under modern conditions of warfare is tantamount to limitation of their military capacity. If anything approximating world economic co-operation is to be achieved, such limitation of sovereignty is essential; but it is not likely to be achieved except in a federation, or at least a confederation, of States which succeeds in removing the overwhelming necessity for self-defense.

Questions may well be asked also concerning the effectiveness of the mechanisms now advocated for the prosecution of autonomous credit policies, or policies of social planning, within national boundaries. The monetary policies which are commonly advocated in this connection are, at best, non-proven. Full employment in a closed national economy is certainly capable of achievement, as recent experience has shown. Whether this is in fact a desirable goal at which to aim as far as national economic welfare is concerned has yet to be demonstrated. It would take the argument too far afield to launch into a detailed discussion of monetary theories at this point; but two problems may be raised.

The first concerns the nature of the violent fluctuations of economic prosperity which have been suffered in recent years. It may be questioned whether the concentration of economic analysis on the problems of the so-called business cycle does not ignore one of the basic elements in the situation. That there is a more or less rhythmical oscillation of business activity seems clear, though the shifting manifestations of that oscillation seem to indicate that its causes may be very complex and compounded of varying elements from cycle to cycle. The intensity of the phenomenon in recent years is, however, largely due to underlying structural disequilibria that would in any case have caused serious economic difficulties. Unemployment due to structural dislocations of industry caused by maladaptation to changing international equilibrium, or to misdirection of economic activity dating from the war of 1914–18, has proved intractable to monetary manipulation. It is difficult to see how any autonomous business cycle policy can overcome the difficulties of the shrinking markets for British coal and cotton or sweeten the angry vintage of the dust bowl in the United States. Or how the essential impoverishment of Europe by war and war preparations can be remedied by easier monetary conditions.

Moreover, regulated economic activity based upon present national groupings encounters fundamental difficulties in facilitating change and economic development. Not the least of the merits of the nineteenth-century system of world trade was the way in which it functioned as an instrument of economic change and growth. It called a new economic world into existence to redress the balance of the old. The present distribution of world population and the present organization of world production were determined by, and postulated upon, the facilities for world trade provided by British leadership in the nineteenth century. The situation indeed is even more precarious, since cycles of population increase were started that have not yet reached their culminating peak, great investments were made and specialisms developed which are uneconomic except on the assumption that world trade will continue to expand. It is not easy to see how this necessity for continued growth of developing national economies can be accommodated in a system of closed national planning.

One fact, at least, is clear. As long as independent Nation-States claim unfettered and unlimited sovereignty, what matters in international economic relations will continue to be the conduct of national economic policies. The real front is the home front. The aims sought and the methods followed, particularly by the powerful creditor nations, in their domestic economic policies will largely determine the possibilities of reconstructing some workable system of voluntary international economic co-operation. If such a voluntary system cannot be restored, the only alternatives are some system of federation which will give power to central authority in a world-state to discipline and regulate economic activity in the national units, or the building up of great economic empires.

Economic Policy and Peace

The persistent effort to restore international economic co-operation in the troubled years following the war of 1914-18 is perhaps the best indication that such restoration was regarded by governments as essential to peaceful international relations and expanding prosperity. When M. van Zeeland, at the invitation of the British and French governments, visited the capitals of the great trading nations during 1937 and 1938, he reported universal agreement with this view—but equally universal reluctance on the part of any government to take any decisive initiative in the matter.

After the cessation of hostilities in 1918, and the conclusion of a treaty settlement in the following year, the urgent necessity of restoring monetary stability and international trade between the belligerent and neutral countries was hampered by the first postwar financial crisis in 1920 and then by a series of runaway inflations in several European countries. It did not prove an easy task to re-establish confidence in national currencies, control public expenditure, and get trade moving again. Nevertheless, a series of international conferences, beginning as early as 1920, endeavored to lay down the principles of international reconstruction. The Brussels Conference (1920), the World Economic Conference (Geneva, 1927), and the Monetary and Economic Conference (London, 1933) are merely the outstanding examples of such meetings. Committees of the League of Nations, intergovernmental conferences on a regional basis, and private gatherings such as those of the International Chamber of Commerce met at frequent intervals. Whatever their constitution and their immediate objects, they invariably emphasized the overwhelming importance of restoring international trade and international economic co-operation in general. The experts who participated in the financial and economic reorganization of Austria and Hungary gave the same advice: that no emergency measures could be of lasting benefit unless international trade could be restored.

After the immediate chaos of the interwar inflations had been cleared up, there was a short period from about 1925 to 1929 when trade did begin to flow again and, indeed, to increase faster than national production. During this period an effort was made to re-establish an international monetary system. One after another, the leading countries returned to the gold standard by unilateral action. The exchange stability thus restored was, however, always precarious and even before 1929 a heavy fall of agricultural prices had endangered the stability of certain great agricultural-exporting countries such as the Argentine and Australia. It is now generally realized that the period of apparent recovery from 1925–29 rested largely upon the extension of liberal credit to the stricken European countries. When the flow of loans began to slacken, the instability of the recovery was rapidly revealed. Despite the moratorium on reparation payments and war debts, the debtor countries became unable to meet their external obligations without severe financial and economic strain. In May, 1931 the difficulties of the Austrian Credit-Anstalt revealed the essential bankruptcy not only of Austria, but of the whole of central and southeastern Europe. At once a wave of financial panic spread westward. The German banking system was affected in July, and by September the drain of funds from London forced Great Britain off the gold standard. With the central pillar of the international mechanism broken, it was only a short time before the whole interwar economic system collapsed. The United States left the gold standard in April, 1933 and, while a group of western European countries clung to the gold parities of their currencies for another three years, their national economies were contracted by deflation and their balances of payments were strained by recurrent flights of capital. One by one they dropped away from the gold parity until, in September, 1936, the last of them—France, the Netherlands, and Switzerland—were forced into devaluation. By this time, a network of exchange control systems, quotas, and bilateral clearing agreements was spread widely not only over the greater part of continental Europe, but in Asia and Latin America.

Meantime, the political relations of the leading powers in Europe and elsewhere steadily grew worse. It is certainly not a mere coincidence that the years of deepening economic depression were also years in which the interwar political settlement broke down in a series of diplomatic and military coups. The Sino-Japanese conflict in Manchuria in 1931 came even before the breakdown of the Disarmament Conference, which met in 1932 and was disrupted by the German withdrawal of the following year. The occupation of Ethiopia by Italian troops, despite economic obstacles interposed by the member-states of the League, undoubtedly increased the drive for economic self-sufficiency, not only because it was a heavy blow to any remaining hopes of collective security, but also because the countries which were seeking political expansion drew the obvious moral of the attempted economic blockade. Civil war in Spain, undeclared war in China, the occupation of Austria, the reduction of Czechoslovakia, the disappearance of Albania as an independent state, and the invasion of Poland followed in quick succession.

The bearing of these political events upon economic policy does not need emphasis. It is clear that the ever-growing danger of actual hostilities, and indeed the mere pressure of economic mobilization for national defense, was fatal to any hopes of freer trade leading to a greater degree of international interdependence. Apart from these direct influences, the general trend to protectionism and self-sufficiency was greatly strengthened, especially after the complete failure of the Monetary and Economic Conference in 1933 to provide even the bases for an alternative system of international economic co-operation.

On the other hand, the influence of economic policies upon political events, though often vaguely referred to, is not so clear. It is apparent, however, that economic mobilization has become a more and more vital part of war preparation, as economic factors have become more and more important in the actual conduct of military operations. Professor Moritz J. Bonn has analyzed the reasons for this development which is, of course, merely the continuation of a long historical process.[36] It is natural that soldiers should utilize the improved weapons that industrial progress puts in their hands. It is equally natural that governments at war, or preparing against the possibility of war, should draw upon the economic resources of their citizens for the provision of such equipment. Governments have never hesitated also to supplement diplomacy and military operations by such economic and financial weapons as they were able to mobilize. In a mechanical age warfare has become mechanized. For the provision of modern weapons of offense and defense it is necessary to draw heavily upon the varied economic capacities of modern industry. The lines of military concentration go back deeper into the economic structure not only for the provision of armaments, but for supplies and means of communication. Moreover, as government intervention and control penetrate new strata of economic activity, such control itself offers a potent weapon for use in diplomatic negotiation and ultimately in the conduct of hostilities. As long as international relations are overshadowed by the fear of war, it is inevitable that the possibilities of totalitarian war must be accompanied by totalitarian organization of economic activity in preparation for war.

It may perhaps be argued that the breakdown of international co-operation based upon private enterprise, by creating the necessity for State intervention and regulation, greatly

[36] M. J. Bonn, *op. cit.*

facilitated the concentration of economic as well as political power in the hands of government officials. Since the operation of competitive forces could not be relied upon to promote individual welfare, the State took over the responsibility for regulating and controlling economic activity. In theory it is conceivable that such responsibility might be exercised not to strengthen the power of the State, but solely to promote the individual welfare of its citizens. In practice it is difficult to avoid decisions of policy being influenced by State necessities. From this point of view the growth of economic nationalism has obviously facilitated the subordination of economic to political considerations in the conduct of policy even in the economic sphere.

It does not follow, however, that restoration of private enterprise and economic freedom from detailed government regulation would be sufficient, in itself, to improve international political relations. As a foregoing quotation from Dr. Meyer shows, there is a school of thought which indicts the system of free trading enterprise as a cutthroat scramble for inadequate export markets, leading to international friction in which governments have not hesitated to use all the economic and financial weapons at their disposal to bring pressure upon reluctant buyers or debtors. Attempts at large-scale political bribery in the shape of loans or trading concessions to strategically placed small powers were not unknown in prewar Europe and elsewhere.[37] Large capital investments, particularly those destined to produce raw materials or oil, were facilitated by diplomatic pressure exercised by powerful governments on behalf of their nationals. Railways and mines have frequently been the precursors of annexation in colonial territories. The struggle for markets, and even more the struggle for free access to raw materials and investment opportunities, have often enough tempted governments to supplement and reinforce the activities of their citizens, especially in dealing with weaker powers. It is, indeed, obvious that the situation at the end of the nineteenth century could not last

[37] Cf. L. Baudin, *Free Trade and Peace*, p. 38.

in face of the developing industrial power of latecomers in the international arena. Further scope for colonial expansion was limited and the great bulk of undeveloped resources had passed into the possession of a few colonial powers, some of which like Belgium, Portugal, and the Netherlands were small states, while Great Britain maintained the sea supremacy won a century earlier.

It is very easy to push this argument to extreme lengths as an attack upon capitalist-imperialism, or as a justification for nationalist expansion upon the model, and at the expense of, those countries which in the past have built up, but failed fully to utilize, great colonial empires. While instances may, no doubt, be found of vested interests creating diplomatic situations that involved the risk of war, there is no necessary and inevitable connection between the extension of trading enterprise across national boundaries and territorial imperialism. The strongest argument, indeed, by which the liberal free traders of the nineteenth century defended their advocacy of a world-wide trading system was that it was the surest basis for international peace.

The connection between free trade and peace, however, can be demonstrated only by assuming that political attitudes and economic policy are both dominated by a rational desire to promote the economic welfare of the individual.[38] This point is made very clearly by Professor Baudin in his monograph on "Free Trade and Peace." He comes quickly to the conclusion that such an assumption lies at the very foundation of liberal thought, but is equivalent to assuming away the whole problem with which we are concerned.

It assumes that economic considerations are not only separable from all others, but also that they end by entirely dominating

[38] It also assumes that unfettered private enterprise will promote economic welfare both in the world as a whole and for each national unit. Cf. G. Haberler, *The Theory of International Trade* (London, 1936), p. 221. "It can be proved that, at any rate under the usual assumptions of economic theory (free competition, absence of friction and so on), the unrestricted international exchange of goods increases the real income of *all* the participating countries."

social life. The day when all men are moved solely by strictly economic motives, it is evident that nationality will cease to count in economic activity. The factors of production will then be able to combine with one another without any question as to origin. The entrepreneur can place the centre of his operations wherever he likes without considering whether or not he has crossed the boundary of his own country. The merchant will set up as easy relations with foreigners as with his own countrymen. Economic activity will not think of seeking the support of political power.

But this does not demonstrate that liberalism is capable of settling conflicts between nations. It rather assumes that such conflicts have been solved. One of the statements of Dr. L. von Mises shows this very plainly. "The man who recognises that the economic interests of all nations are interdependent, who is indifferent to the problem of the extent and the boundaries of a State, who has so far cast off all collectivist ideas that expressions like 'the honour of the State' have become unintelligible to him, that man will never be able to find a plausible motive for an offensive war." [39]

The liberal assumption, therefore, takes as solved the whole vast problem of the conflict between nationalism and industrialism; but since that problem is far from being solved in the actual world, Professor Baudin has no difficulty in citing many cases where political intervention has created pretexts and occasions for war even under a relatively free trading system. It is very clear that foreign investment, whether rather closely supervised by the State as in prewar France, or free as in Britain and the United States, or actively supported by diplomacy as in Germany, has followed the line of political understanding and preferences.[40] It is equally clear that territorial conquest or domination, by the mere fact of government purchases, language teaching, and commercial connections, gives a preferential position to merchants from the dominant metropolitan state, even where the Open Door is pursued. Private foreign investment also, often of the participating type of

[39] Baudin, *op. cit.*, p. 26.
[40] Baudin, *op. cit.*, p. 36.

direct as distinct from public investment, creates extranational vested interests which in times of difficulty seek diplomatic support.[41]

While, therefore, it is perfectly true that the nonregulated system of international trade based upon private enterprise is not in itself a cause of war, it can occasion pretexts for war. The motives for war are irrational and mystical; but this does not prevent their proponents from seizing upon economic arguments in support of their aims. The thesis of "The Great Illusion" that in modern times war is an unprofitable enterprise may be irrefutable; but this does not mean either that particular interests may not gain from an aggressive policy and even from war, or that a State will not go to war in spite of rational economic considerations.

"The system of non-regulated international trade," concludes Professor Baudin, "cannot ensure peace. It can help to create a peaceful atmosphere, on one condition: that men have a peaceful mental attitude." [42]

The great leaders of the liberal and free-trade movement that was centered in mid-nineteenth-century England sought to create such a peaceful atmosphere by the negotiation of a network of commercial treaties, the basic objects of which were first to establish the principle of "national treatment" for foreign traders and secondly, by friendly negotiation, to break down tariff and other barriers to the expansion of international trade. The principle underlying "national treatment" was that traders should have the same security under the law as local residents in any country—the same right to reside, own property, trade, pay equal taxes, have access to courts of law, and protection from discrimination or injustice by the State as did private citizens. It was believed that if private enterprise was thus enabled to take the whole world for its province while friendly negotiation gradually removed the barriers to commodity trade, there was no incompatibility between political self-government and world-wide

[41] *Ibid.*, p. 40.
[42] *Ibid.*, p. 77.

economic co-operation. Thus, Cobden and Bright welcomed and supported such movements for national independence and unity as Garibaldi's campaign in Italy, at the same time as they advocated the leveling of barriers to international trade. They miscalculated the emotional forces of nationalism, largely because of their overoptimistic belief in the power of human reason. It did not follow that governments, having achieved national unity and independence, would become convinced of the value of an expanding system of world trade. Instead, they sought to buttress and support particular forms of national economic development primarily for political and strategic rather than for economic reasons. The conclusion is inescapable that, in Professor Baudin's words:

> The origin of wars is mystical, not rational. It does not involve a utilitarian calculation, as Ferrera said; for we grant to Sir Norman Angell that any calculation of this sort, accurately made, would, on the contrary, prevent war from occurring. In our own day a war, even if victorious, does not pay. As Dr. Le Bon puts it, "Rational logic builds science, but does not create history." The field we must enter is that of convictions created by hypnotic suggestion or by mental contagion . . .
> In the last analysis we do not know whether war is really a "dynamic current obeying natural laws," or at least—for this determinism seems hard to accept—a "dynamism derived from psychism, from the passion inherent in man, a concrete aspect of life," as certain philosophers affirm; but we do know that it "transcends our reason," as Spinoza long since declared, and that a society "has need of fictions and of irrational sources of energy." In 1914, clear-sighted men were not deceived. At the origin of the war there was a "mental attitude." [43]

If there is no proof that freer international economic cooperation, however much it may contribute to the welfare of the common people in every country, can solve the essentially political problem of creating a "mental attitude" which will effectively abolish war as an instrument of national policy, there is certainly less proof that national regulation of

---

[43] Baudin, *op. cit.*, p. 29.

international economic relations will do so. It is sometimes argued that "by reducing economic complications between the nations we diminish the chances of conflict," but as Professor Baudin points out, to accept this argument "we must sacrifice, for the sake of security, all the undeniable advantages of the international division of labor." This, in face of the powerful trend towards world economic interdependence outlined above, is hard doctrine indeed.

But the case against regulated international relations from the viewpoint of peace is much stronger than this. State regulation involves what has been called the "politization" of economy. What, in a system based upon private enterprise and free trade, are essentially private conflicts of interests, even though those concerned may on occasion seek the support of their governments, inevitably become conflicts of governments when trade is regulated and controlled. Every sharp clash of competition, every attempt at price-cutting or dumping, every loan or arrangement of credit accommodation, every debt default or attempt to collect an overdue account, is elevated to a diplomatic dispute. The increasing sharpness of diplomatic exchanges on commercial matters in recent years is sufficient proof of the danger of such developments.

Moreover, regulation of trade, conducted almost inevitably by bilateral bargaining, leads, as will be shown, to a concentrated search for essential raw materials on the one hand and for markets on the other, while every country tries to become as self-sufficient in foodstuffs as possible. There was a period in the middle of the nineteenth century when international trade consisted mainly of an exchange of manufactured goods, especially capital goods, for the staple foodstuffs grown cheaply in the newly settled temperate grasslands. But this rather simple and early stage of modern trading was rapidly passing even before 1914, and the greatest opportunities for trade expansion were between highly industrialized areas. The way in which recent trade restrictions have broken up the specialized interchange between the whole industrial region of northern France, Belgium, Luxembourg, Germany, and Great Britain offers a highly instructive illustration of the costs of economic nationalism. Much of the heavy, basic production, as in the first processes of steel-making, was carried on in Belgium which drew ores and fuel from surrounding countries and supplied its neighbors with the semi-finished manufactures that were the raw materials of their highly developed industries.[44]

The barriers put in the way of such specialized interchange of manufactured products have not only struck a heavy blow at the quantum of international trade, entailing very extensive reorganization of national industries; they have also concentrated trade more and more upon the exchange of finished manufactures for raw materials. The increased importance of raw materials in the total quantum of world trade is readily seen in the statistics regularly published by the Economic Intelligence Service of the League of Nations.[45] The distribution, particularly of mineral resources, in the world is such that it is less possible to develop national self-sufficiency in this respect than in respect of foodstuffs. It is true that substitutes may be developed in some degree: petrol from coal, nitrates from the air, bakelite and other plastics, and even glass, to replace metals in many uses. But the increasing demand for the bulkier minerals—iron, copper, tin, petroleum, lead, zinc, aluminum, nickel—cannot be met in any country without a considerable volume of imports, while the important "poundage" minerals needed for alloys—antimony, chromium, manganese, molybdenum, titanium, tungsten, vanadium—are widely distributed over the earth and incapable of substitution. The search for raw materials becomes ever more intense as their consumption increases and new sources of supply must be sought in more distant countries.[46]

The difficulty is not only that these and other raw materials must be bought in increasing quantities and paid for by man-

---

[44] J. Jussiant, *op. cit.*
[45] See League of Nations, *Review of World Trade*, annually.
[46] League of Nations, *Report of the Committee for the Study of the Problem of Raw Materials*, II Econ. and Fin. 1937. IIB.7 (Geneva, 1937).

ufactured exports. The increasing canalization of bilateral trade limits the supply of free exchange that can be obtained by exporting to third markets. The sources of raw materials are controlled by a comparatively few States. Their production is now regulated by international agreements in which these States have a predominant influence. There arises, therefore, a problem of access to raw materials and, even if access is reasonably free, prices are held at levels governed primarily by the financial interests concerned in raw material production. Moreover, exports become more and more difficult except as a counterpart to imports from the country of their destination. There thus arises a scarcity of free exchange, available for purchases of raw materials. A new kind of mercantilism develops in which there is a necessity to secure a surplus of exports, not to acquire treasure but to acquire the exchange needed for raw material imports. In this mercantilism, under regulated trade, the whole diplomatic power of great States is mobilized. They must "export or die." This is obviously a dangerous political development. Trade becomes an instrument of national policy. Commercial treaties are governed by strategic interests as much as are treaties of mutual assistance. Every effort is made to integrate the national economies of weaker States with the political and economic requirements of their stronger neighbors. In this sense, regulation leads to "power" as contrasted with "welfare" economics, and the conduct of State-regulated trade in the interests of national power politics becomes a fruitful source of international conflicts leading ultimately to war.

CHAPTER II

The Processes of Disintegration

Closing Frontiers

SOMETHING has already been said of the changes that have taken place, and are still taking place, in the nature of international trade; but it is necessary to push the analysis a stage further in order to reveal the true nature of the problem and dispel certain misconceptions that are very prevalent at the moment. There is a disposition in many quarters to argue, first, that the importance of international trade has been exaggerated and, secondly, that the continuous and rapid expansion of international trade in the past hundred years or so was a fleeting historical episode due to peculiar circumstances that have now come to an end. It is sometimes added that, in any case, these circumstances led to unstable and economically unfortunate international specialization resulting in unbalanced national economies and precarious international equilibria.

The first argument can be dealt with briefly, since it is based upon a popular misconception of the relative importance and true value of international as compared with domestic trade. In its simplest form, the argument is that the trade across national frontiers has always been small compared with the trade within national boundaries. It is sometimes put in the form that economists, striving always for quantitative measurements, have found it easiest to work in the field of international trade where statistics have long been compiled as a by-product of revenue collection. The much more complex exchanges within a national community, it is argued, are in fact more important in the aggregate, but more difficult to measure. Not having statistics at hand in this field, economists have preferred to investigate the more measurable, but less important, problems of international trade.

It may be conceded, at once, that domestic trade is quantitatively far greater than international trade has ever been. Trade across the frontiers is, in fact, merely an outgrowth of domestic production and interchange. Though lead, tin, grain, and salt were important staples in Roman times, trade was mainly confined in later centuries to the exchange of luxury goods which, combining great value with small bulk, yielded profits adequate to compensate for the risks, delays, and heavy costs of transport before the age of steam. The growing trade in bulky staple products is a modern development, the result of regular, cheap, and certain means of modern transportation. Even with this development, the great bulk of production in most countries finds a local market. The larger the country, the smaller the proportion that international trade bears to local trade. Indeed, this argument can be carried much further. The commodities which in the aggregate are produced in the greatest value are not those such as wheat, sugar, and wool which bulk large in the statistics of international trade, but are such familiar products as milk, vegetables, and eggs which are usually consumed at home.

But this acknowledged fact does not detract from the qualitative importance of international trade. It is equally clear that the trade carried on in any locality, such as a great town, is quantitatively greater than the trade between that locality and others within the same national boundaries. This fact has been seized upon recently in the United States as one justification for the barriers that have begun to hamper interstate commerce. There can be few, however, who would argue that the crippling of interregional trade would conduce to the economic welfare of the national community as a whole. Local patriotism does at times reach this extravagance;[1] but the argument is more usually applied to trade beyond national frontiers.

The value of international trade cannot be measured, any more than the value of territorial division of labor within a national community, by the aggregate value of the goods which cross local boundaries. It brings within the purchasing power of consumers in every country the specialized products of every region. The whole world is given access to the fruits of tropical agriculture and northern sea fisheries, of large-scale agricultural and pastoral production in the thinly populated countries of the New World and the elaborated manufactures of highly industrialized regions in the Old. By its efficient organization the luxuries of the rich have become the conventional necessities of the poor and there are still great possibilities of raising standards of living by its improvement. This is particularly true in regard to the new "protective" foodstuffs and the new mechanical inventions towards which demand turns as living standards rise. In the process of organized interchange, also, price-competition keeps down the consumer's costs and prevents the application of labor and capital to relatively wasteful and unprofitable uses, while spurring on the production of those commodities in which

---

[1] "Nothing's wrong with Texas, except entirely too many of us get up in the morning at the alarm of a Connecticut clock, button a pair of Ohio suspenders to a pair of Chicago pants. Put on a pair of Massachusetts shoes, wash in a Pittsburgh tin basin, using Cincinnati soap and a cotton towel made in New Hampshire, sit down to a Grand Rapids table, eat pancakes made from Minneapolis flour spread with Vermont maple syrup, and Kansas bacon fried on a St. Louis stove. Buy fruit put up in California, seasoned with Rhode Island spices, sweetened with Colorado sugar, and pay our bills with a check made in New York. Put on a hat made in Philadelphia, hitch a Detroit mule fed on Oklahoma gasoline to an Ohio plow, and work all day on a Texas farm covered with a New England mortgage, send our money to Ohio for tires, wondering why Texas taxes are $2.75 per acre while Ohio farmers pay $1 tax and drive on paved roads, and at night we crawl under a New Jersey blanket to be kept awake by a bulldog, the only home product on the place, wondering all the time where all the money went in this wonderful State of ours." Business Circular quoted by James Harvey Rogers, *Capitalism in Crisis* (New Haven, 1938), p. 135.

each region has economic advantages from its location and climate, the efficiency of its labor, or merely the ability of its organizers.[2] There is, therefore, good ground for the conclusion to which M. van Zeeland came in the course of his investigations, that, although the quantitative importance of the international market may have been exaggerated in certain cases, "its relative importance appears today to be as great as ever, and its marginal influence is real and powerful."[3]

While this is as true today as it was when international trade was expanding rapidly and continuously in the nineteenth century, it is often argued that this expansion was a historical and geographical accident, the result of the new methods of steam transport both on land and at sea, opening up the last frontiers of permanent settlement, the open grasslands of the Temperate Zone. This swarming of the European peoples, it is argued, could not be more than a temporary historical episode, and has already come to an end. As a result largely of British initiative, enterprise, and capital, these new lands have all been brought into effective occupation, if not full use. Just as the frontier age in the United States has come to an end and given place in many areas to a reverse movement of population, so, it is argued, there are no longer available any international frontier regions of settlement. The American experience is, in fact, only one aspect of the larger development, and the Immigration Restriction Act of 1924 merely the leading illustration of a general tendency towards the closing of migration outlets.

The statistical material is lacking for a thorough investigation of the effect of migration restrictions upon the still increasing populations of many European countries, and what is available is not in a form suitable for precise analysis.[4] The extent to which the stoppage of migration outlets has con-

[2] For the cultural importance of international trade see L. Hogben, *Mathematics for the Million* (London, 1936), pp. 32–34.

[3] Great Britain, Cmd. 5648, msc. No. 1, 1938.

[4] W. W. Fitzhugh, *Memorandum on the Economic Effects caused by Diminished Emigration from Europe*.

tributed to the banking up of populations in already congested areas, and so to a complication of the occupational opportunities available, particularly to rural populations, is extremely difficult to measure. Emigration was never great enough to take away more than a small proportion of the annual increase of population. The effects of its cessation are merged with a host of other demographic and economic developments. Field surveys of typical communities from which migrants were formerly recruited in considerable numbers might yield valuable information; but in default of such surveys, only general a priori statements are possible.

It seems clear, however, that the possibility of even limited emigration contributed to population increase both by relieving occupational pressures and by raising living standards through substantial emigrants' remittances increasing the survival rate at home. The emigrants were, for the most part, adults in the reproductive ages, and this for a time slowed up the absolute increase in numbers and also tended to decrease the birth rate. The retention of these young adults at a time when a cycle of population increase had begun (though counteracted by a tendency of the birth rate to fall as a result of rising living standards and the gradual introduction of conscious control) must tend to intensify not so much the absolute pressure of numbers as the consciousness of such pressure at a time when higher living standards are being demanded. Coming at a time when agriculture in countries of emigration was meeting intense competition from the war-stimulated production of extra-European countries, it may have been a factor in stimulating the agricultural protectionism of interwar Europe. Since the surplus population of the countryside, and particularly the more enterprising young people who might formerly have emigrated, naturally sought occupation in the towns, there was added pressure to build up local industries to relieve urban unemployment.[5]

[5] The related problems of Population, Colonies, and Raw Materials were the subject of the International Studies Conference at Paris, July, 1937. See the documents prepared for that conference and the final reports.

The effect of reduced immigration into the receiving countries (which at the depth of the depression became an actual emigration in many cases) [6] was to accelerate the slowing up of population increase which was already in evidence as a result of a rapidly falling birth rate. Although the absolute figures of births and deaths continue to record a substantial natural increase in the newer countries of European settlement, this is largely the result of an abnormal age-grouping of the population which, partly because of the previous immigration, is heavily weighted in the reproductive age-groups. Recently it has been demonstrated that the net reproduction rates in these countries are below the figure necessary, if allowance is made for normal wastage of the population, to replace the mothers of this generation. Thus, unless a rise occurs in the birth rate, the time is approaching when the populations of the newly settled countries will cease to increase and may even decline.[7]

On the basis of these statistical facts (which, however, are indicative of a probable future development rather than a present condition), it is argued that it would be unwise to count upon a continuance of the expansion of international trade. That expansion, it is argued, depended largely upon the exchange of manufactured goods, both for the consumption of the rapidly expanding populations in the new countries and for the capital investment necessary to bring these countries into profitable production, against the export of foodstuffs and raw materials to the increasing populations of the Old World. Since there is in most of the countries of western Europe, and in the United States, the same strong tendency for population increase to slow up, and for an increasing proportion of the population to pass into the older age-groups, there is, it is argued, less need for an ever-increasing production of cheap staple foodstuffs.

[6] Imre Ferenczi, *L'Optimum synthethique du peuplement* (Paris, 1938).
[7] There has in many countries appeared to be a slight rise in the birth rate in the last year or two and some population experts look for a stabilizing rather than a declining tendency in the future.

The probability that the exchange of manufactures against foodstuffs and agricultural raw materials will tend to decrease in importance, even apart from the imposition of trade barriers, is enhanced by the fact that recent advances in the biological sciences in such fields as plant and animal selection and breeding have increased the possibilities of national self-sufficiency in respect of foodstuffs. In some countries of western Europe there appears recently to have been a temporary increase in production per acre as well as an extension of acreage devoted to the production of staple foodstuffs.

At the same time, reckless exploitation of the virgin fertility of the newer countries, in the form of long-continued, specialized production of particular crops and overstocking as well as overcropping, without much care for the replenishment of the soil, has created a widening area in which the soil has been chemically impoverished and physically deteriorated. It is now known that there is in the soil a nutritive balance as delicate as that upon which human nutrition depends. The earth needs organic matter as well as a wide variety of chemical constituents and must, moreover, be kept in a physical condition suitable for cultivation if it is to continue producing plants for human consumption directly or indirectly. The exhaustion of essential, though often minute, chemical elements in the soil has been found to be the cause of widespread plant and animal deficiencies and diseases.

The widespread and destructive appearance of various types of erosion is in large part a consequence of the deterioration of the physical condition of soils that have been overcropped or overstocked, or merely used for the production of unsuitable crops. In extreme cases water erosion has carried away vast areas of soil and in so doing has choked great river systems and produced serious flood damage, or wind erosion has blown away great tracts of formerly cultivable land. It is now known that these extreme cases are merely symptomatic of a very widespread condition which exists in various forms in many continents. There is scientific ground, therefore, for attempts to preserve balanced cultivation and soil conservation where it is still practiced, as over a large part of northern Europe, and to develop it in regions hitherto devoted to unduly specialized and predatory methods of farming.[8]

It is difficult, in a world where so much poverty and undernourishment persists in many countries, to believe that there is surplus production of food. The accumulation of stocks and waste of perishable commodities, even their organized destruction, is due either to reckless expansion of certain types of specialized production, to low purchasing power in potential markets, or to failure to solve the problems of marketing. Even in the extreme case of coffee, where large quantities have been deliberately destroyed, there are now shortages in many European countries. Overproduction of cotton or wheat, while masses of people are underclothed and ill-fed in such countries as China, seems a contradiction in terms.

It may be conceded, however, that the trade built mainly upon an exchange of finished manufactures for cheap staple foodstuffs will probably tend to decline. This does not necessarily involve either the impoverishment of agricultural countries or the abandonment of balanced agricultural production in industrial countries. It has recently been made very clear that a greater degree of trading freedom and price competition might well result in solving both aspects of this problem by directing consumption into channels which accord with the newer knowledge of nutrition.[9]

The fact is that, if consumers, who are now becoming aware of the value of protective foods, were able to draw freely upon the varied production of agricultural industry the world over, and to take advantage of the cheaper prices resulting from specialized production in low-cost areas, there would be room both for local agriculture specializing upon the production of perishable products such as milk, vegetables, fruit, and eggs (with a certain proportion of the older forms of production to obtain proper rotation) and also for a greater

[8] G. V. Jacks and R. O. Whyte, *The Rape of the Earth* (London, 1939).
[9] F. L. McDougall, *Food and Welfare* (Geneva, 1938).

trade in agricultural commodities—the bread grains produced on a large scale in the temperate, and oilseeds and fruits from the tropical, zones.

Trade in agricultural products, both foods and raw materials, has greatly decreased in recent years not because of economic or scientific developments, but because government policy has restricted it. In part such policy has a pseudo-economic base, the protection of existing methods of production and vested interests that could not survive the competition resulting from freer trade. The competition was admittedly severe, particularly at the depth of the great depression; but the tragedy has been that government intervention, as in so many other fields, has been mainly negative. Little constructive effort has been made in most countries to shift production in the directions necessary if standards of living are to rise and agriculture is gradually to be switched from the less to the more efficient and profitable avenues of production. One of the most depressing aspects of government intervention, negatively practiced as it has recently been almost everywhere, is the premium it has placed upon stagnation, inefficiency, and economic timidity. Moreover, it is now very clear that one of the basic reasons for increasing restrictions upon trade in agricultural products has been the fear of war and the desire to promote a high degree of national self-sufficiency and independence of foreign food supplies.

In any case, it is a mistake to argue that the exchange of manufactured goods for staple foodstuffs was the most important form of developing trade in the nineteenth century. There is ample statistical evidence to prove that trade was greatest, and developed fastest, between already highly industrialized countries. There is obviously a tendency for certain forms of rather simple trade to diminish as newly developing regions come to a certain stage of economic maturity. Local manufactures spring up and after a time such a new region of settlement does not need to rely upon the outside world for practically everything but the bare necessities of existence. It is, indeed, natural that the older manufacturing countries should find their export markets for the simpler manufactures disappear as local industries develop in one country after another. A clear case of such development is to be found in the spread of textile production in recent years. But this does not mean that trade diminishes. In more normal circumstances than those of recent years, it increases faster as one country industrializes after another, if only because greater production gives greater purchasing power. The largest and most rapidly developing trade in the nineteenth century was between Great Britain and Germany and the United States, and later the industrial progress of Japan led to exactly the same development of both imports and exports. The example has already been cited of the high degree of specialization and the vast trade that grew up in the industrial regions of western Europe. The subdivision of processes was carried to great lengths and very keen price-competition often led to cross-traffic that, on a superficial view, might seem wasteful. One effect of such competition, however, was not only to promote technical progress, but to spur efficiency of organization and to keep costs low. Since economic nationalism has broken up such areas of international specialization, there has been an incentive to vertical integration of processes within great industrial combinations serving national markets. Not only have the advantages of price-competition disappeared, but with them part at least of the incentive to technical progress.

From whichever angle the economic history of recent years is reviewed, therefore, there is little solid support to be found for the argument that international trade must in any case have tended to decline for economic or technical reasons. It must, of course, have changed its character; but such changes were a striking feature of the period of expansion in the nineteenth century. Indeed, it is one of the greatest merits of a freer trading system that it is an efficient instrument of peaceful change and growth.[10]

[10] Cf. D. H. Robertson, "The Future of International Trade," *Economic Journal* (March, 1938), pp. 1–14.

In such a disturbed period as that which followed the war of 1914–18, the changes necessary to restore economic equilibrium between the nations, after it had been dislocated in a long and bitter struggle in which great use was made of the economic weapon, proved so great as to be socially intolerable to many governments. To this extent there were economic and social reasons for the policies of restriction that finally caused the international trading system to collapse; but these economic disequilibria were themselves the products of the war and of the inflamed nationalism which it provoked, and which was continued into the peace settlement and interwar national economic policies.

It was in this period of disturbed equilibrium that there developed the difficulties of payments between debtor and creditor countries with which German economists have made such play in an attempt to prove that the unregulated system of international trade based on private enterprise had broken down and must be replaced by regulated systems centering upon exchange control.[11] There was no insuperable difficulty in preserving exchange equilibrium and facilitating payments for many decades before 1914. The London Money Market functioned smoothly and efficiently in gathering up surpluses of short-term credit and using them to finance the world's trade and make productive long-term investments all over the world. Debtor countries found their surpluses of exports readily absorbed in an expanding world market. Even in periodic financial crises (which at that period were less severe than in the troubled interwar years) the organized wholesale markets of free-trade England acted as a reservoir to absorb temporary surpluses of production. In these years also the natural expansive tendency of the credit mechanism was reflected in a steady but gradual rise in average price-levels which not only eased the position of debtors, but gave an additional incentive to enterprise. Accumulating disequilibria, the result of ill-judged negative and restrictive government

[11] Fritz Meyer (comp.), *An Analysis of Exchange Restrictions at Present in Force*, pp. 50 ff.

policies, together with a growing lack of confidence in investment opportunities, and above all the political tensions that have finally culminated once again in economic war preparations and war itself, were responsible for the failure to reconstruct freer trade and monetary stability in the postwar period.

The primary responsibility for the breakdown, therefore, lies not with economic facts but with economic policy. The problem is a political one, even in the sphere of economic developments. Governments, fearful of their strategic and political security, have interposed barriers to the progressive interdependence which is inevitable if economic tendencies are allowed to work freely in the modern world. The first intensification of restrictions came in the field of migration. More effective barriers to commodity trade quickly followed. Limitation of capital movements and, finally, extensive controls of other items in the national balances of payments, leading to more stringent quantitative restrictions upon commodity trade and finally to more and more complete regulation of both domestic and external economic activities, were a natural consequence.

At every stage in this process, restrictions of economic movements across national boundaries led to, or aggravated, economic difficulties within every national economic community. These difficulties were used not only as an argument for further restrictions, but also to whip up emotional attitudes hostile to international co-operation.[12] This is certainly true of the use of ill-founded statements about population pressures.[13] It is also true of low price-levels and agricultural surpluses, as well as of unemployment. Entangled throughout

[12] "A rational study of the alternatives in any population situation of the modern interdependent world, from a purely economic point of view, seldom suggests a military or colonial policy—a fact which confirms the conclusion that the objectives of foreign policy, among leaders who understand and who make the policy, are generally in only small degree economic. The rank and file who do not understand, may frequently be influenced by bad economic arguments." Quincy Wright in *Annals of the Academy of Political and Social Science* (November, 1936), quoted by Fitzhugh, *op. cit.*, p. 88.

[13] Fergus Chalmers Wright, *Population and Peace* (Paris, 1939).

all recent discussions of the economic policies to be followed in clearing away the debris resulting from the breakdown of international economic co-operation is the "attitude of mind" which, by placing the interest of particular groups before that of the community as a whole, and, in particular, seeking to preserve and buttress the unfettered sovereignty of the Nation-State, not only brought about the war which was the original cause of the breakdown but has now led to a ghastly repetition of the tragedy.

The Breakdown of Monetary Equilibrium

The multiplication of trade restrictions after 1931 was due primarily to the disappearance of exchange stability after the depreciation of sterling and the consequent disorganization of international price comparisons. The improvised, and at times confused, new measures of trade restriction that were hastily adopted when the exchange rates were fluctuating and commodity prices were falling rapidly, were later consolidated and integrated into more systematic and often simpler administrative controls; but it is clear that at the beginning they were expedients rather than policies, the result of uncertainty and disequilibrium rather than of improvements in administrative procedure.

If any single event can be said to mark the collapse of the international trading system that was reconstructed after the war of 1914–18, on the prewar model, it was the departure of Great Britain from the gold standard in September, 1931, which has been described by Sir Arthur Salter as "the victory of economic forces over monetary action." [14] This dramatic event, in other words, was merely the culmination of a long period of economic strain.

In part, the strain upon the London Money Market in the interwar period is traceable directly or indirectly to the war of 1914–18. The dislocation of peacetime activities in order to stimulate production for war purposes has many of the

[14] Sir Arthur Salter, *Recovery* (London, 1932), p. 69.

characteristic features of an exaggerated investment boom. The industrial structure of both belligerent and neutral countries is distorted, so that when the abnormal war demands cease there are heavy capital losses and widespread unemployment. The problem of demobilization after a great war is not simply one of fitting the fighting forces again into peacetime occupations; it also involves the reconstruction of industry and commerce in general. Strained public finances and inflated currencies add to the difficulties of national economic reorganization.

International economic relations are affected adversely also. Part of the disorganization of productive activity takes the form of a distortion of international specialization. In the war of 1914–18, for example, the production and export of wheat from the United States grew rapidly after a long period of gradual shrinkage. There were accumulated great surpluses, both of stocks and of productive capacity, in agriculture and in industry. It was not easy to make a connection between these surpluses and the needs of impoverished countries intent upon restoring their own production. There were dramatic changes also in the international balances of payments of many countries and particularly in their debtor-creditor relationships. The United States, which had been a substantial debtor on balance before the war, emerged as a great creditor country but with stimulated export industries and no change in its high tariff policy except a stiffening of protection when the first interwar depression revealed the vulnerability of many of the war-stimulated industries.

It should be recalled also that the former Russian Empire was transformed after a prolonged period of inflation, revolution, and slow reconstruction into a great autarkic region, cut off in large measure from the main body of world production and trade. The loss of an important market, of raw material supplies, and of great investments in that region was later followed by new forms of trading which were, at times, disturbing to international equilibrium. In the depth of the depression, for example, in 1931, the U. S. S. R. sold wheat, oil, and timber at low prices. Later, large quantities of gold were exported, at a time when there was a "gold scare." The transformation of the Russian economy, however, was merely the outstanding example of social revolution in the inflationary period. Not only were many new States created and new frontiers erected; there were also considerable alterations in the economic organization within the new frontiers.

Great changes of economic structure were called for in almost every country before there could be any restoration of international equilibrium; but these changes were difficult to make and were, in fact, avoided for a time by an expansion of credit and large international loans that seemed to achieve miracles that economists had declared impossible. The United States continued for a time to have large export balances of both agricultural and manufactured goods, while increasing its creditor position on international account. Agricultural production was restored in central and eastern Europe without any contraction, but a continued increase, of competitive production in the great agricultural countries outside Europe. There seemed room for both the reconstruction of industrial manufactures in Europe and for their rivals in the newly industrializing countries. Production increased rapidly, and international trade even more rapidly, in the years 1925–29, and in those years one country after another rejoined the gold standard system so that international monetary equilibrium seemed to be restored.

The whole of this interwar reconstruction, however, was in fact built upon the flow of credit in large amounts from the United States to Europe. There were crosscurrents and the whole world was involved in the credit expansion, but the net movement was from America to Europe. Great Britain, which had been the financial center of the prewar world, took part in the international investment, but was severely handicapped not only by the disorganization of her formerly strong export industries, but by high costs of production. Return to the gold standard at the prewar ratio of sterling to the dollar (and to gold) further increased the high-cost difficulty so that the British balance of payments was laboring in difficulties all through this period of expansion.

It is not sufficient, however, to trace back the collapse of the interwar reconstruction simply to the dislocations of the last war. It is undoubtedly true, as an American business economist argued at the depth of the depression, that "the true lesson of this depression is that the world cannot afford any more great wars." [15] But it is also true that at many turning points in the interwar period different decisions of policy might have mitigated, if not overcome, the difficulties of international co-operation. It is, indeed, very easy to compile a long list of "ifs." If the United States had not raised but lowered its tariff in 1922 and again in 1930; if Great Britain had returned to the gold standard at a lower parity; if Germany had been less burdened by reparation obligations; if the new (and old) European States had pursued less nationalistic economic policies, the worst of the breakdown might have been avoided. The economic dislocations were serious, but not irremediable. What was fatal throughout the interwar period was the growing influence of political factors in economic decisions.

It must be remembered, on the other hand, that one of the inevitable results of a long and bitter war is the unloosing of extreme nationalistic propaganda and the building up of strong nationalist emotions. The argument is often heard, again now as it was in 1914–18, that war releases new social forces which, properly used, may result in the creation of a better world after the war. There is truth in this argument; but hard experience proves that war acts as a social solvent in many directions and the chances of rational idealism gaining the upper hand over revengeful and destructive attitudes are not as great as idealists might wish. At the close of a great and bitter war, when the whole machinery of economic activity is disorganized and deep currents of national emotion are reinforced by fears of impoverishment and insecurity, it is asking a great deal of human nature to suffer the immedi-

[15] Leonard P. Ayres, *The Economics of Recovery* (New York, 1933).

ate costs and risks of what must in any case be a prolonged and laborious effort to reconstruct international economic cooperation.

After the war of 1914–18, Great Britain was not able for long to resume the role of international shock absorber. The United States, which had come to be an even greater creditor nation, not only showed no sign of sharing this regulating function, but at the first onset of postwar difficulties increased its tariffs. Throughout the interwar years both agricultural and industrial tariffs were steadily increased in all but two or three countries. An increasing stream of agricultural surpluses, particularly after Germany recovered her tariff autonomy in 1925, was directed to an ever-narrowing world market. At the same time markets for manufactured goods were closing because of the economic difficulties of the newly developing agricultural countries and also because of heightened industrial tariffs everywhere.

The dangers of this situation were clearly recognized, as the repeated efforts to reverse the tide of economic nationalism show. There was no lack of warnings as to the economic and political consequences to be expected from the threatened breakdown of the international trading system. The forces of nationalism were, however, too strong. In 1929 the credit expansion which had for some years staved off the collapse, and even given the illusion of a rapidly expanding prosperity, came to a sudden end. For a time, as Sir Arthur Salter suggests, monetary policy endeavored to avert the impending international financial crisis, but a weak link in the chain of international payments broke when the Austrian Credit-Anstalt difficulties were revealed and it was only a matter of months before these difficulties spread to London.

The final explanation of the fall of sterling, therefore, is to be sought not in an analysis of monetary technique, nor even in a probing of economic, as distinct from monetary, disequilibria. Sterling, and with it the concept of a world-wide trading system, was wrecked on the unwillingness of national governments to accept policies of adjustment to economic interdependence organized by private enterprise. The motives for such unwillingness are discussed later. At this point all that is necessary is to recognize that the driving forces of the present tragedy are mental concepts of national interest and national security. The breakdown is not a result of technical defects in the economic mechanism, or of natural economic and geographical limitations, but of human decisions. It is essentially a political, rather than an economic and technical, problem that must be solved.[16]

Just as technical mistakes were made in the developing crisis which may perhaps have hastened, though not caused, the breakdown, so it is clear that the disruption of monetary equilibrium was very influential in spreading the need for new and more effective means of national insulation from the shocks which spread rapidly from one country to another after 1931.

Exchange control was introduced in one country after another after the fall of sterling. The reasons given for its introduction vary in detail and in emphasis from country to country, but they form differing combinations of the same basic difficulties. The drying up of capital imports upon which the developing countries had come to depend, the withdrawal of foreign short-term credits, and the liquidation of longer-term investments were reinforced by flights of domestic capital in anticipation of the cumulative strains on national balances of payments resulting in currency depreciation. The visible signs of strain were usually a weak tendency of the national currencies on the exchange markets and a drain on monetary reserves. Movements of capital were in most cases the immediate cause, but behind these distress signals were more fundamental economic disequilibria, notably the contraction of export outlets and falling prices for agricultural export surpluses. Karin Kock has shown how intimate was the connection between abnormal capital movements and the rapid spread of restrictive commercial poli-

[16] Moulton, Edwards, McGee & Lewis, *Capital Expansion and Economic Stability* (Washington, 1940).

cies.[17] The connection runs both ways. The gradual and, after 1929, rapid fall of agricultural export prices caused a heavy strain on the balances of payments of agricultural debtor countries. These countries had made strenuous efforts to discharge their international obligations by increasing their production and enlarging their exports, while suffering some currency depreciation and cutting down their imports of manufactured goods. Their efforts were largely nullified by the continuing fall in agricultural prices and strain on their balances led inevitably to nervous withdrawals of capital which accentuated the strain and caused an intensification of tariff and other barriers to international trade.

On the other hand, the reduction of imports into the debtor countries and their strenuous export efforts led to increased passive import balances in the trade of great creditor countries. Thus arose the "chronic deficits" in commodity trade to which M. Hoffherr points as one of the major causes of quantitative import restrictions in the case of France.[18] The great bulk of these surplus agricultural exports was directed towards the few remaining free-trade countries, Great Britain, Belgium, and the Netherlands, all of which in turn took steps to protect their domestic agriculture from the mounting flood of cheap imports. The flood even lapped over the tariff barriers of those European industrial countries which had always protected their peasant agriculture. Many of them were bound by commercial treaties which had stabilized their tariff duties at moderate levels that were rendered universally applicable by the operation of most-favored-nation treatment.

When the depreciation of sterling carried with it the currencies of many of the great agricultural exporting countries, some of which were depreciated relatively to sterling, the already low prices of agricultural commodities were further reduced in terms of those currencies that had not depreciated. A Swiss or French peasant, already faced with Australian wool and wheat prices that were severely competitive, sud-

[17] Karin Kock, *International Capital Movements and Economic Policy*.
[18] See René Hoffherr & others, *La Politique commerciale de la France*.

denly found those prices halved in terms of francs. Sterling drifted in a few months 40 per cent below its former parity and the Australian currency remained 20 per cent below sterling, while commodity prices expressed in sterling did not rise but continued to fall. The costs of peasant agriculture are relatively rigid and exchange dumping could not be met by a parallel currency depreciation since there was a lively memory of recent inflations in the peasant communities. In many cases, tariff rates could not be raised because of the conventions by which they were bound. It is hardly surprising, therefore, that new and more effective trade restrictions were rapidly improvised. Import licensing systems were introduced and soon developed into the use of quantitative import quotas as measures of trade restriction. Customs formalities were multiplied. Sumptuary laws, such as milling regulations requiring the admixture of a fixed proportion of home-grown wheat in the making of flour, safeguarded the market for local production. Veterinary and quarantine regulations were strictly enforced and a whole new and complicated apparatus of quantitative, monetary, and indirect protectionism was rapidly developed.

The mere fact that there was such a confusion of procedures in these early years of the new mercantilism is sufficient to indicate that these events must be classed as phenomena of disintegration. Once the collapse of international monetary equilibrium had gathered a certain momentum, there was an entanglement of causes, one currency depreciation leading to another, and one set of trade restrictions provoking retaliation almost universally. Vagabond capital shifting nervously from one financial center to another, in search of security, did not receive its name of "hot money" until most of it came to rest in the United States after the dollar was devalued. As this process of cumulative collapse proceeded, it was obvious that each successive stage of restriction in every country could be justified by urgent economic and political considerations; but however urgent these considerations might be, they were not the real causes, but themselves the consequences, of the breakdown of international equilibrium. The true causes must be sought further back, in the gradual hardening of national economic policies until flexible adjustment to a constantly shifting international equilibrium became impossible.

Collapse of the Capital Market

Passing allusion was made in the preceding section to the intimate connection between international capital movements and international commodity trade. The breakdown of the international capital market, which culminated in the disastrous liquidity panic of 1931, was clearly connected with the growing restrictions imposed on international trade in the interwar period. Equally clearly it was the major cause of new and more effective trade restrictions. The liquidity panic was in fact a paroxysm caused by accumulating strain over a long period, and marks a definite stage in the disintegration of the world trading system.

It is significant that the whole problem of international investment is clouded by facile generalizations arising largely from emotional bias. Within a national community conflicts of distributive interest are acute enough. Modern industrial methods inevitably place the initiative in economic organization upon those who can gather command over capital resources. Such command is obtained by mobilizing credit, and in a system of private enterprise the initiative therefore rests with financial specialists. There is, no doubt, much to be said in criticism of the way in which financial initiative has been exercised and of the extent to which it has resulted in continuing and profitable control of economic activity by powerful financial interests. The fact remains that, until it is replaced by some alternative method of organizing productive activity, the seeking of profit is the mainspring of economic enterprise.

As soon as such enterprise crosses national boundaries, the emotional reactions of nationalism reinforce the objections, valid or invalid, to financial leadership and the control of everyday life that goes with it. Capitalism is in any case a target of attack. Capitalist-imperialism encounters the criticism not only of those who resent the domination of economic activity by financial leadership, but of those who resent foreign domination.

The combination of these emotional forces has crippled international capitalist enterprise. Such a statement is perhaps as close as economic analysis can come to the ultimate causes of breakdown discussed in the following chapter. The system of world-wide economic specialization and cooperation built up in the nineteenth century was essentially capitalist and cosmopolitan. Free movement of capital across national frontiers, even more than free commodity trade, was its essential characteristic. This fact has been stated by Professor Iversen when he writes that "capital sets out in search of the other immobile factors (of production), in order to get combined with them in the most advantageous proportions. Its movements tend to neutralize the disadvantage of the uneven productive equipment of different countries." [19]

In the heyday of nineteenth-century development, Bagehot drew an almost lyrical picture of the "cosmopolitan speculative fund" which was the main instrument of international investment. "The truth is," he wrote in 1880, "that the three great instruments for transferring capital within a nation, whose operations we have analyzed, have begun to operate on the largest scale between nations. The 'loan fund,' the first and most powerful of these, does so most strikingly. Whenever the English money market is bare of cash it can at once obtain it by raising the rate of interest. That is to say, it can borrow money to the extent of millions at any moment to meet its occasions: or what is the same thing, can call in loans of its own. Other nations can do so too, each in proportion to its credit and its wealth—though none so quickly as England, on account of our superiority in these things. A cosmopolitan loan fund exists which runs everywhere as it is wanted, and

[19] Carl Iversen, *Aspects of the Theory of International Capital Movements* (London, 1936), p. 156.

as the rate of interest tempts it. . . . The 'speculative fund' is also becoming common to all countries, and it is the English who have taken the lead, because they have more money, more practical adaptation to circumstances, and more industrial courage than other nations. Some nations, no doubt, have as much or more of one of these singly, but none have as much of the efficiency which is the combined result of all three. The way in which continental railways—the early ones especially, when the idea was novel—were made by English contractors is an example of this. When Mr. Brassey, the greatest of them, was making the line from Turin to Novara, for the Italian Government, Count Cavour sent one morning for his agent, and said, 'We are in a difficulty: the public have subscribed for very few shares, but I am determined to carry out the line, and I want to know if Mr. Brassey will take half the deficiency if the Italian Government will take the other half.' Mr. Brassey did so, and thus the railway was made. This is the international speculative fund in action, and the world is filled with its triumphs." [20]

For such operations to take place two sets of conditions were necessary. The first may be summarized as confidence that capitalist enterprise motivated by the search for profit would lead to the general enrichment of the community. The second was willingness of national communities to accept and utilize such enterprise originating in other countries. There has been a progressive undermining of both in recent years.

In order to show clearly how essential was such freedom of capital movements to the functioning of international economic co-operation, and to bring out the magnitude of the recent breakdown, it is necessary to summarize the way in which capital transactions were integrated with the expansion of international trade that characterized the nineteenth century. Much more is involved in the breakdown, however, than a diminution of international trade and a rearrangement of productive enterprise in the world. The whole concept of peaceful co-operative trading relations based on private enter-

[20] Walter Bagehot, *Economic Studies* (London, 1880), pp. 67–70.

prise is challenged, if it is not already destroyed. In its place is set up a concept of nationally regulated and controlled economic systems which inevitably impairs the international specialization so far achieved. The relations between such nationally regulated economies seriously complicate international politics, not only because every economic transaction that crosses national boundaries becomes a measure of government policy, but also because governments can now utilize the whole range of economic activity as instruments for the execution of their policies.

One elementary but very common misunderstanding may be disposed of briefly.[21] As the Industrial Revolution extended its range there was a steady evolution in the character of international trade. In its early stages the mechanization of industry in the manufacturing countries of western Europe and notably in England enabled them to become the "workshop of the world." They drew from other countries increasing supplies of foodstuffs and raw materials and sent in return finished manufactures, largely consumers' goods. It was in this way that the textile industries of Lancashire and Yorkshire grew rapidly. In order to develop the resources of their markets so as to obtain access to raw materials and also to increase purchasing power, capital goods were exported in the next stage of evolution, but these were mainly such goods as transport equipment which enlarged the export markets. Inevitably, however, a third stage of development was reached in which capital equipment was exported as a means of erecting competitive industries in other countries. In the minds of nineteenth-century economists this was a natural development entailing the necessity of the older industrial countries keeping ahead of their newer rivals by improved technical methods and by moving readily from the simpler to the more complex manufacturing processes.

The essence of the international economic system that has now broken down was to be found, however, not in the free

[21] For more detailed exposition of this point cf. Iversen, *op. cit.*, pp. 27 *et seq.*

export of capital goods but in the existence of an international capital market in which the direction and disposal of free credit available for new capital investment was determined on a cosmopolitan basis. Not the gradually changing character of international trade, but the financial leadership that lay behind it, was the crucial matter. Though in fact the development of new areas did increase international trade, there was never any guaranty that any particular financial decision, implemented later by export of capital goods, from the country supplying credit or from elsewhere, would increase international trade directly. Still less did it guarantee that production and employment would be increased or would develop along socially desirable lines in the country supplying the original credit. There was a general presupposition that world production would increase, and with it world trade, since the factors of production would be combined in more advantageous proportions. The modern world has less confidence that the forces of competition will result in such increased production raising the standard of life of the ordinary man. Still less are national communities willing to face the risk of immediate sectional losses in the confident expectation that the enrichment of world production will in the long run bring more than corresponding gains to other sections of the national community.

The most developed international capital market was that of London. Indeed in the difficult financial circumstances of the years after 1918, a famous Royal Commission reported that the London Money Market was organized in such a way as to facilitate the raising of international loans much more readily than loans for domestic industry.[22] The mechanism of this market and its international ramifications have often been described. On the whole, its operations proceeded smoothly, though there is some tendency in the anarchy of recent monetary and financial convulsions to exaggerate the regularity and efficiency of its workings. Perhaps the most

[22] Great Britain, Cmd. 3897, 1931, *Report of the Committee on Finance and Industry* (June, 1931).

impressive feature of its operation was the flexibility with which short- and long-term capital movements were co-ordinated on a world-wide scale. Credit was always available for a great variety of demands at prices determined by competitive market conditions. The movement of goods was facilitated by the acceptance and discounting of bills, short-term accommodation was available to bankers and traders, and longer-term investments could be readily placed.[23] Almost incidentally a mechanism was provided whereby national credit systems could clear their balances and maintain equilibrium, at the same time as credit surpluses could be gathered up and directed into productive long-term investment.

In so far as the distribution of capital was concerned, the money market might have been compared with a great reservoir through which the currents of trade flowed. Trickles of credit from private savers and great corporations holding unused balances were stored in the reservoir, the level of which could be controlled within rather wide limits. From the reservoir, streams of capital were directed to irrigate productive fields of investment. The flow of these streams was regulated not only by the level of the reservoir, but by the controls at the sluice gates, controls operated by financiers interested in the immediate profits to be gained by opening the gates even more than by the ultimate increases of production to be expected from the irrigation process.

London's primacy did not prevent the development of other great money markets, and it has often been remarked that there was increasing evidence of cross-traffic between national markets clearing through London. There was such a variety of investment demands and so many different types of investors that individuals in one country might be subscribing to long-term loans or buying shares in another country at the same time as their compatriots were borrowing on short-term from financial institutions in that country. The same processes

[23] For the way in which the replacement of trade bills by short-term deposits as the means of financing international commodity trade aggravated the instability of the money markets, see Karin Kock, *op. cit.*, p. 50.

of specialization mentioned earlier in connection with industrial manufacture in northwestern Europe were developed to a very high degree in the closely connected money markets of the great financial centers.

Such progress towards cosmopolitan finance, however, depended essentially upon relatively free movement of commodities. The only way in which the balance of financial transactions between countries could ultimately be adjusted was by movements of goods. Such a statement indeed unduly simplifies, and tends to give a misleading impression of, the elaborate and intricate working of the money markets. The whole organization of international trade took place in a medium of credit so that commodity prices, as well as the volume of goods traded, were essential aspects of the continuous balancing of international accounts. Without entering here into an analysis of these complicated processes, the historical fact may be recorded that the practical results of an immensely intricate series of financial and trading operations included both the direction of large amounts of capital to the newer developing countries and a practically continuous expansion of international trade and enrichment of living standards all over the world.

It is a tribute to the efficiency of this intricate mechanism that the regular flow of international trade came to be taken for granted. In the classical exposition of international trade theory, capital movements, especially on short-term, came to be regarded as equilibrating factors needed to balance payments on account of commodity trade. It was argued that changes in productive efficiency in one country or another brought movements of commodity trade that affected the balances of international payments in such a way as to call forth corrective movements of short-term credit that bridged the gap in payments until adjustments could be made in the national productive organization. It came to be believed that the volume of foreign investment adjusted itself to changes in the terms of international trade, rather than that the quantities and prices of goods traded were governed largely by financial decisions which distributed capital resources advantageously around the world.[24]

Moreover, the system functioned so smoothly that, at a price, liquid capital was always available for transference between countries. The only form of capital that can be transferred is free or floating capital; but only rarely was there a crisis of liquidity involving the wholesale realization of assets to provide the credit needed for international transfers.

As the organization of the market improved, the forms in which investment was made across national boundaries grew more varied and complex. Concrete examples of this variety of investment may be cited from a modern Polish investigation.[25] Dr. Wellisz, after pointing out the various evidences of Poland's need for capital, lists schematically a great number of ways in which foreign capital was put at Poland's disposal in the reconstruction of the country after 1918. Beginning with various obligations to the governments which helped the independence movement and with Poland's share in the liabilities of the Austro-Hungarian monarchy, the categories of foreign obligations which are listed in detail comprise much more than the government loans publicly issued in the leading money markets. Issues of the National Bank and of various local government bodies, often with a government guaranty, are fairly well known; but in addition there are outstanding credits given to various government departments in cash or goods by foreign contracting firms; loans advanced as payments for monopolies and concessions, private banking loans and contractors' advances to local bodies, the obligations of Mortgage Loan Associations, bond issues of private companies, credits extended to commercial banks, cash credits to industrial and commercial companies, deferred payments for goods supplied to such companies, foreign participation in Polish companies, and the capital and credits allocated to Polish branches of foreign companies. Dr. Wellisz points out that different roles were played in this complex financing of

[24] Cf. Iversen, *op. cit.*, p. 69.
[25] Leopold Wellisz, *Foreign Capital in Poland* (London, 1938).

Polish enterprise by British, French, German, Italian, and American capitalists. Because of historical or political connections, the economic needs of the lending country, the temper of its investors, or their trading connections, variant forms of investment were worked out that met Poland's needs and the desires of the lenders.

One other feature of the international capital market as it developed in the nineteenth century and was restored, at least imperfectly, after 1918, deserves to be stressed. Just as commodity trade was multilateral rather than bilateral, with balances cleared ultimately through London, little attempt was made either to link foreign investment with exports or interest payments with imports. The lack of such provision has sometimes been criticized; but that criticism overlooks the essentially multilateral character of trade and capital movements as long as a world market functioned with reasonable freedom.[26] A loan publicly issued in London, for example, might be used by the borrowing country to buy capital goods either in England or elsewhere, payment being made by bills on London. Or the borrower might proceed to employ domestic labor and materials, the disbursements for which in the borrowing country increased purchasing power and led to greater imports, largely of consumers' goods, payment for which was ultimately made by drawing on London funds. So far from attempting to link loans and exports, reliance was placed upon the effective working of the world market to keep international balances in equilibrium. Both commodity trade and financial payments were conducted in long chains of multilateral exchanges, equilibrium being maintained by the complicated market processes that were mainly cleared through the London Money Market. That market, in the prewar period, was essentially competitive and speculative. Individualistic traders in the various specialized sections of the money and commodity markets incessantly sought opportunities of profit by bridging any gaps that appeared in interest rates, exchange rates, commodity prices, or other compo-

[26] Cf. Karin Kock, *op. cit.*, p. 73.

nent elements of the price structure. They operated in anything that could be bought and sold, and the result of their operations was a balancing of the very diverse market forces.

This highly developed and cosmopolitan competitive equilibrium was an object of admiration and satisfaction to nineteenth-century economists and business leaders who saw in it the working out of natural laws. Its efficiency was impaired by the growth of monopolistic elements; but its deathblow was dealt when popular distrust of the power it placed in the hands of those able to control the financial mechanism without which economic enterprise was unable to function, was reinforced by the growing desire of national governments to control economic activity within their own borders.

The combination of these two powerful forces of antagonism to cosmopolitan financial leadership in world economic activity may perhaps be illustrated by the argument recently propounded by a Mexican economist.[27] "The system of industrial economy established by England," writes Professor Quintana, "did not envisage machinery as an instrument designed to enhance the welfare of humanity, by enabling men to enjoy a greater supply of goods at reduced labor-cost while production increased, which is the end of true economic organization. England was obliged to capitalize itself in order to build its great factories, means of communications, ports, merchant shipping, and navy, all of which have given it industrial supremacy. The extraordinary capitalization of this nation is due largely to mechanization and to the ability of its people in making industrial use of their coal and iron; but it should not be forgotten that this mechanization and resulting large-scale industry was the work of wage-earners earning low wages for long hours. The English industrialist has always had, and still has, a very marked slave-owning mentality. He is a great exploiter of human labor, not only the labor of the four hundred millions that he holds under his colonial sway, but that of his own nationals and the nationals of other countries. English imperialism is of the Roman type. It believes

[27] Miguel Quintana, *Memoire sur les problemes économiques et la paix.*

firmly that industrial production must use slaves toiling for the profits of a group of industrial, commercial and banking barons, who hold in their hands all the wealth of England.[28]

It is not surprising that this reading of history leads Professor Quintana not only to the conclusion that the war of 1914–18 was a struggle of rival imperialisms, but to a similar interpretation of the "industrial and commercial war" which preceded the present hostilities. The final conclusion of the Mexican author follows logically:

> To achieve economic peace, which will also be spiritual peace, there is no alternative to socialism which levels wealth and makes impossible a system of potentates confronting unfortunates. But capitalism will continue to defend itself and in the coming war, which is very near, the proletariat will fight again for the dominance of some capitalist group and not for its own interests. Until the working masses, tired of enduring an unduly prolonged insecurity, take political power by a revolution like the Russian revolution in 1917 and finish off the capitalist era.[29]

These Marxian presentations of "capitalist-imperialism" illustrate the extreme form in which social and national criticisms of the system of private enterprise are combined. Without necessarily going to these lengths, there has in recent years been widespread and growing distrust of the operations of great international productive, trading, and financial enterprises. The petroleum companies have met this opposition in many fields, mineral enterprises such as those exploiting tin deposits in Bolivia, though providing a large proportion of tax revenues, are suspect; still more, banking groups endeavoring to secure payment of past loan obligations, and even the scat-

---

[28] Miguel Quintana, *op. cit.*, p. 5 (translation by this author). Cf. also the following curious passage: "There is a certain parallelism in the development of England and that of Japan. One is forced to conclude, indeed, that one of the most powerful reasons for the progress of these two countries is the fact that the upper classes, the landowning nobility of England, and the Samurai, the landowners of Japan, placed themselves at the head of industrial and commercial enterprises and organized them rapidly, thanks to their wealth and their training."

[29] *Ibid.*, p. 13.

tered foreign owners of shares in industrial and commercial enterprises, have encountered growing resentment and experienced discriminatory pressure or default on an increasing scale.

The "national conservation" policies of undeveloped countries, however, have been less responsible for the breakdown of world-wide investment than the policies pursued by the governments of the great industrial and trading nations. In order to understand the development of those policies and the manner in which they contributed to the breakdown of international economic co-operation, it is necessary to analyze the liquidity panic that spread from country to country at the depth of the great depression.

A Liquidity Panic

There is no doubt that the proximate cause, not only of the Austrian Credit-Anstalt difficulties in May, 1931, but of the German banking failure in July and the fall of sterling in September, as well as of the disequilibria that led to exchange control measures in so many countries after the depreciation of sterling, was a liquidity panic marked in each case by sudden withdrawals of short-term credits.[30] The liquidity panic that spread from country to country was certainly the most severe and the most disastrous in its consequences of any financial crisis since the modern international capital market was developed.[31] Before the war there were serious crises, for example in 1893, which were complicated by unwise international capital commitments. Severe credit stringency affecting many money markets, and entailing not only industrial, but banking, losses on a great scale, were the result; but exchange stability was preserved and after a brief period of depression, financial reconstruction, and bankruptcies, credit

[30] Up to a few weeks before the actual breakdown, expert international banking committees believed in the possibility of funding operations to relieve the strain. Cf. Karin Kock, *op. cit.*, p. 35.

[31] No comparison is possible with 1920, since so many European countries were at that time pursuing independent monetary policies.

expanded once more. There was at that time a resilience and recuperative power in the capital market that was notably lacking in the years after 1918.

In part, this lack of resilience is to be explained by a widespread fear of political and economic insecurity, aggravated by monetary instability during, and after, the serious currency inflations that occurred in the interwar years. There was a notable lack of confidence in long-term investment possibilities. For a time, indeed, the credit expansion that was centered in the United States brought an unrealistic and uncritical readiness to invest in foreign enterprises, but before 1925, and after 1929, long-term investment was hampered by a marked sense of insecurity. Even between 1925 and 1929 there was less private investment than banking loans. In part also, the difficulties of capital movement in this whole interwar period were caused by the impoverishment and wastage of capital resulting from the war of 1914–18. The flow of new capital was diverted to reconstruction of European enterprises and public services. In the years of rapid credit expansion such reconstruction did not prevent heavy borrowing by the newer developing countries; but it is significant that the first signs of distress came from these countries. Australia was in difficulties with its balance of payments as early as 1928.

Moreover, the sources of capital for new investment were changed as a result of the war. Great Britain had drawn heavily upon her accumulated assets and emerged from the war less able to provide the new capital that was called for in the reconstruction period. Germany became the greatest borrowing country. France went through long years of currency instability until the franc was stabilized in 1928. The United States became, for the first time, a great source of foreign investment, but lacked the experience and equipment of a lending country, as was clearly revealed later in the very heavy losses sustained on its European investments.[32] The London Money Market, moreover, suffered subtle changes that crippled its efficiency as an international lending and regulating

[32] Cf. Karin Kock, *op. cit.*, pp. 1–13.

center. The great joint-stock banks and the national industrial and commercial enterprises dependent upon them came to overshadow the private international banking houses and the individualistic financial specialists who had formerly dominated monetary policy.

It must be remembered also that the capital market was greatly complicated by the abnormal strain of political payments, such as those necessitated by reparations and war debts. These were one-way transfers not offset by equivalent payments in the opposite directions, and were in fact made only as long as American loans provided a counterpart on the exchange markets. Such transfers would have been difficult to arrange even if an expanding volume of international trade had been available to carry them; but international trade had been reduced by the war of 1917–18 and after the war its restoration was hampered by economic nationalism.[33]

It is not surprising to find, therefore, that the capital market functioned erratically even in the years of apparent recovery. Such long-term investment as was made was in large part directed towards the rebuilding of industrial Europe and helped to accentuate its competition with the productive capacity that had expanded during the war period in the countries outside Europe. Its effect, therefore, was fundamentally a misdirection of production along lines that were already overequipped.

Perhaps the most significant development, however, was the emergence of a great mass of short-term credit that moved rapidly from one financial center to another in search of security, or in payment of political debts, without being absorbed into productive long-term channels of investment.

[33] Karin Kock, *op. cit.*, p. 21 comes to the conclusion, however, that, "looking at the matter merely as a transfer problem, the conclusion might be drawn from these figures that German capital exports (apart from credits intimately connected with exports) would have sufficed to pay for reparations actually paid in cash and that transfer could have been made without recourse to borrowing. The capital imported can thus be said to have been used for increasing the productivity of German industry, for raising the national income and the standard of living of the German people. To this must be added that the use made of the capital in many instances was open to criticism."

This problem was aggravated after the breakdown of exchange equilibrium in 1931; but it was a serious menace before then. A recent listing of the causes of abnormal short-term capital investments is sufficient to indicate that they were operative throughout the interwar years. These causes were the payment of reparations and war debts, flight from high taxation or the fear of such taxation, flight from political or social motives such as the avoidance of high production costs resulting from economic regulation or social welfare legislation, distrust of national credit policies, and fear of depreciation or devaluation.[34]

In this connection, the great currency depreciations that finally got out of control in many European countries had consequences even more serious than the impoverishment of the propertied classes and the undermining of confidence in the national currencies. There was also a serious loss of faith in the wisdom of saving for the future. Even the wisest investments vanished when the currencies in which they were held lost their value. There developed not only a reluctance to forego present satisfactions in order to save, but an even greater unwillingness to sink resources in long-term investments. Such margins of credit as became available were held in the form of free credits, readily realizable, and readily transferable into other currencies that for the time being appeared safer.

There arose also a burning resentment against those who by speculative enterprise, often international in scope, were able not only to avoid losses, but to grow rich and flaunt their riches in ostentatious expenditure at a time when the hardworking, frugal, and disciplined sections of the community were being impoverished. The already marked distrust of financial speculative enterprise received a great reinforcement from such experiences, and was readily joined with national resentment against those cosmopolitan individuals who

[34] Cf. Marco Fanno, "Normal and Abnormal International Capital Transfers," *University of Minnesota Studies in Economic Dynamics* (November, 1939), No. 1.

could escape the common misfortune by transferring their capital abroad at opportune moments. It was not difficult to fan this double resentment by the invocation of racial feeling in countries where Jewish financiers and speculators were prominent in the trading community, even though the mass of Jews suffered from inflation with the rest of the population.

The investment of capital in the reconstruction of European enterprise largely took the form of bank loans based upon credits or deposits, both national and foreign, that were subject to withdrawal at short notice. This was not an unusual method of floating continental enterprises, but the subsequent transference of ownership to private individuals proved more difficult than it had been in the prewar period. It is true that large amounts of government and industrial securities were sold to private individuals in the United States, and smaller amounts to individuals in Great Britain and other countries. Such private investment, however, lasted a relatively short time, and was less in the aggregate than the financing of European industry by bank loans. When the flow of private credit from the United States first tapered off and then abruptly ceased after the stock market crash in October, 1929, short-term loans continued to bolster up the European markets for more than a year. London was borrowing short and lending long; the German banks were also borrowing short in London and elsewhere and lending long; Vienna, mainly through the Credit-Anstalt, was also borrowing short and had spread its investments over central and southeastern Europe. When its balance sheet was challenged, a precarious situation was revealed and despite government and international banking aid the Credit-Anstalt was not able to stall off the massive withdrawal of foreign and national deposits.

The crisis that ensued was a liquidity panic, a run of nervous depositors on a greater scale and over a wider area than in any previous financial crisis. The German banking system as well as the Austrian was completely prostrated and the banks lost all their capital. Their reconstruction was possible only with government aid, so that direct control of the whole credit system passed to the State, a fact that greatly facilitated the subsequent evolution of totalitarian economic policy. In the absence of confidence in either national or foreign investment, industry was more than ever dependent upon banking assistance and banking was dependent upon government control.

The overstrained London market also suffered heavy withdrawals of short-term credits and was not able to withstand the storm. While there were no banking failures, sterling was forced off the gold standard, and there has since been a notable increase of Treasury influence in banking policy.

One further aspect of the demoralized capital market must be noted in the interwar period. Large and erratic, sudden movements of capital dominated the exchange markets and greatly disturbed international balances of payments and therefore exchange rates, international price relationships, and credit policies. The greater ease with which monetary claims could be transferred, even by telephone, as contrasted with the painful and costly implementing of such transfers by changes in commodity trade provoking serious disturbances of national economic activity, was very marked. It was clear that the financial market was more sensitive and more highly organized, even more nervous, than the great commodity markets. Three important results followed.

The first was a realization of what came to be called the "transfer problem." [35] A great part of the economic writing on international problems in the nineteen twenties was devoted to the mechanism by which transferences of monetary claims could be implemented by changes in the commodity trade between debtor and creditor countries. If commodity trade is not large enough to carry the financial transfers, no mechanism can avoid the obvious fact that such transfers become merely an exchange of titles to wealth that cannot be realized and in the end must be defaulted. As long as investors in the United States were willing, by their purchases of European securities, to provide the dollars against which checks

[35] Cf. Karin Kock, *op. cit.*, p. 71.

could be drawn in payment of reparations and war debts, these unilateral financial transfers continued. When the flow of credit from the United States ceased, it was not long before not only the political debts but a large proportion of the newly contracted loans were in default.

The second effect was quite clearly to stiffen the reluctance of most countries to lower their tariff barriers. The devastating effects on national production and trade of erratic capital movements justified those economists who, like Mr. Keynes, stressed the undesirability of placing national employment and productive activity at the mercy of such unpredictable international influences. An economist well placed to watch the interaction of international trade and capital movements in these years did not hesitate to ascribe the breakdown of international equilibrium to the latter.[36]

Finally, it must be recognized that the ever-present danger of strain on the international balances of payments inhibited the initiation of expansionist credit policies such as normally brought recovery after previous depressions. This was particularly important in the case of Great Britain which had been struggling against the depressing influence of an overvalued currency throughout the years of apparent recovery. Great Britain was not only a great international commodity market, but the effective center of a great international monetary system, so that deflationary influences were widely spread. The prolonged and heavy fall of commodity prices aroused serious concern everywhere. No escape from it seemed possible as long as national currencies were interconnected by their common link with gold. National credit expansion ran the risk of leading to a drain on monetary reserves, a risk that was realized by one country after another that attempted to combat deflationary influences. Attempts to initiate concerted policies of credit expansion were balked by the unwillingness to participate of a group of countries that adhered resolutely to the gold parities restored after a pre-

[36] Folke Hilgerdt, "Foreign Trade and the Short Business Cycle," *Economic Essays in Honor of Gustav Cassel* (London, 1933), pp. 273–293.

vious period of inflation and exchange depreciation. In the end, the burden of continuous deflation proved intolerable and the international gold standard system was broken. Though the gold bloc countries continued for some years to maintain their currencies on the old basis, they were plunged into severe deflation and their balances became strained so that one by one they dropped away.

Since the depreciation of sterling in 1931, long-term international investment has virtually ceased, except for certain forms of direct investment by large-scale business enterprises. There has, in fact, been a great liquidation of previous investment. That liquidation has been due in part to the depreciation of currencies in which loans had been contracted, in so far as those currencies have depreciated below the levels of the borrowing countries. In large part also it has been the result of widespread default. Even where the default has been technically merely a stoppage of transfer with debtors continuing to pay interest and amortization service into blocked accounts in their national currency, the resultant fall of security prices on foreign markets has enabled many individuals and governments to repatriate their debts at bargain prices. There developed, indeed, a circular process by which the announcement of default caused lower prices enabling debtor governments to buy in their foreign obligations. The use of free exchange for this purpose instead of for debt service induced the necessity for further default.[37]

The seriousness of the present situation, therefore, arises from the fact that the mainspring of the nineteenth-century international economic system has been broken. That system rested essentially on the organizing initiative of private capitalists in search of profit. The opportunities of substantial profit are now severely limited, not so much by the disappearance of territorial frontier regions as by the increased regulation and discriminatory taxation imposed by national governments, particularly upon foreign capital. On the other hand, the risk of heavy losses has been greatly enhanced. Confisca-

[37] Karin Kock, *op. cit.*, pp. 41–45, 91–98.

tory policies pursued in some countries that formerly tolerated, if they did not welcome, foreign capital, are merely one, and by no means the most important, of the risks that must now be run. The most serious of these risks arise from the restrictions on international trade that make it difficult to envisage the export of new products at satisfactory prices, and from the prevailing chaos of monetary policies with its prospect of fresh exchange depreciations and transfer difficulties.

Long-term investment across national boundaries now requires government approval in most capital-exporting countries and in many receiving countries. If Signor Mussolini were to approach a modern British businessman with a proposition similar to that which Count Cavour made to Mr. Brassey, it could not be accepted without the permission of a Treasury Committee. If permission were given, which is rather rare for countries outside the sterling area, it would be conditional upon the loan being spent for the purchase of British exports. The most likely way for the loan to be supplied would be by utilizing the machinery of the Export Credits Guarantee Department. It is not so long a step from such supervision and assistance to complete government operation of the machinery for foreign lending. In some countries that step towards complete government regulation of international capital movements has already been taken, but the countries where private enterprise has been so completely eliminated are debtors on balance. The great creditor countries, at least till the outbreak of war in September, 1939, retained the principle of private enterprise. The international capital market, however, had broken down completely.

CHAPTER III

The Causes of Breakdown

Defects of Mechanism

IN THE preceding chapter attention was drawn to the manner in which, as long as an effective trading system operated with reasonable freedom, economic equilibrium between national communities was determined by the interaction of a great mass of individual decisions in a series of interconnected markets. These individual decisions were taken within a framework of accepted rules and procedures. National governments, it is true, had the power to change tariffs as well as other legislation governing economic activity. In particular, they had the power to alter the legislative bases and the operative principles of national monetary systems. But in practice tariffs were relatively moderate, stable, and nondiscriminatory, a wide network of commercial treaties established the principle of "national treatment" by which foreign traders received the same legal status as national citizens, and the pivot of most monetary systems was exchange stability, such stability being ensured by defining the national unit of account in terms of gold or some currency readily convertible into gold.

Such a system kept the volume, turnover, and price of credit, as well as commodity prices, profits and wages, and therefore the whole organization of economic activity in every country, moving in parallel with the corresponding phenomena in other countries. Mutual interdependence was created, subject only to mild limitations resulting mainly from tariff restrictions.[1] In such conditions continuous price comparisons were possible, leading to profitable trade and to a continuous extension of the international division of labor. It was upon this basis that the great growth of international investment and the continuous expansion of international trade in the nineteenth century brought such an enrichment of living standards to rapidly growing populations.

The mutual interdependence of national economic activities in such an international system clearly involved limitations, voluntarily accepted, of national economic sovereignty. If exchange stability was to be preserved, governments were forced to refrain from monetary and financial policies likely to disturb the international balance of payments. Individual traders and trading groups, including bankers, had to accept the discipline imposed upon them by central bank action designed to safeguard monetary reserves and ensure the value of the national currency in the exchange market. This meant that, from time to time, national economic activity was temporarily arrested and depressed to prevent it from getting out of line with economic activity elsewhere. Bankruptcies and unemployment were produced in periods of cyclical depression by influences outside national control. The structure of industrial production and employment within a country was subject to the same influences over longer periods of time. Any industry which could not compete with cheaper imported products was left to shrink, as British agriculture did in the latter half of the nineteenth century. In most countries, however, tariffs were invoked to counteract such tendencies to world-wide specialization as threatened important national industries.

Change was incessant, but not abrupt. Cyclical fluctuations of economic activity spread over a world-wide market were less severe than they have been in recent years. Moreover, accommodation was readily found in an expanding system of

[1] There were similar limitations, e. g., in the imperfect internationalism of the monetary systems. Cf. F. A. von Hayek, *Monetary Nationalism and International Stability* (London, 1937).

world trade for the longer-term processes of economic growth and industrial development that altered the pattern of international relationships in the nineteenth century. Though the necessity of adaptation was largely thrust upon a small group of free-trade countries, and notably upon Great Britain, it did not prove an intolerable burden, but was a net advantage to those free-trade countries, as was proved by their increasing wealth and rising standards of living.

Attempts in the interwar period to reconstruct international economic equilibrium on the prewar model ended in failure. The central events in that failure were the adoption of a protectionist policy by Great Britain in 1931–32 and the depreciation of sterling. There is now no central regulating market in which surpluses of goods may be absorbed and from which they can be distributed. Nor is there any free money market operating as a regulating reservoir for credit. The result has been not only a multiplication of barriers to international economic co-operation, but a centrifugal segregation of what were formerly interconnected markets.

The causes of this breakdown of the international trading system are not easy to disentangle with any certainty. It is easy enough to point to various symptoms of disintegration and demonstrate how they acted and reacted upon each other —falling price-levels causing trade restrictions and these in turn accentuating the fall in prices, unemployment causing a demand for credit policies which strained the balances of payments and led to exchange control in many countries, and so on, in many tangled sequences. The intricate connections between these various developments are of great interest to economists. Their analysis throws much light upon the various stages of disintegration; but such analysis does not reveal the operative underlying causes of breakdown.

There is a school of thought which argues that fundamental defects in the gold standard mechanism rendered it incapable of coping with the strains that were thrust upon it in the difficult circumstances of the first postwar period. There are really three strands in this argument. The first is that the restoration of exchange stability and freer trade in this period would have demanded such severe adaptations of price-levels and productive activity in many countries that the social consequences of such restoration would have been intolerable for any government. The second is that the essential conditions were not present for the effective working of the gold standard mechanism and are not likely again to be present within any foreseeable time. The third strand of the argument is that the mechanism was, in fact, designed not to promote social welfare but to maximize profits and to concentrate the control of economic activity in every country in the hands of small but powerful groups of international financiers. A corollary of this latter argument is that free international trade concentrated power in the hands of great creditor nations.

The first of these arguments may be discussed briefly since it amounts to a statement that the real cause of disequilibrium in the interwar period was not any defect in the monetary or trading mechanism, but the disorganization of international relationships that was a legacy of the war and was aggravated by the continuance of war policies into the peace. For at least forty years before 1914—after the adoption of the gold standard by Germany in 1873—there was no insuperable difficulty in accommodating the processes of industrial growth and peaceful change, as well as cyclical fluctuations, within the framework of a trading system based upon exchange stability. All of the national economic policies discussed later in this section as causes of the breakdown were widely practiced before the war of 1914–18. Tariff protection, financial amalgamation, and social legislation were well advanced in the nineteenth century, but did not unduly strain the balances of international payments or cause the mechanism of equilibrium to break down.

The second argument has already been referred to briefly in the first chapter. It is that the absence of relative freedom of international commodity trade, migration, and capital payments, the increasing inflexibility of price systems, and the growth of independent monetary policies designed to combat cyclical fluctuations of industry made the restoration of the gold standard system in the interwar period a futile gesture since the necessary conditions were not present for its successful operation. Like the first, this second argument is to some extent inconsistent with the third, since no mechanism could be expected to work in unsuitable conditions and therefore failure can hardly be imputed to defects in the mechanism itself. The whole interest of the present discussion lies not in the absence of free trade, price-flexibility, and national readiness to adjust to international equilibrium, but in the reasons for the absence of these conditions.

As in every aspect of this complex problem there is obviously an interconnection of causes, so that the discovery of primary causes, as distinct from consequential complications of causation, is difficult. It is this complication which accounts for the differing emphasis laid by economists upon various elements and stages in the causation. There is, for example, no doubt of the strain thrown on the balances of payments by the progressive restrictions imposed on international commodity trade after 1913. No method of measuring the effective height of tariff barriers is fully satisfactory, but all attempts at measurement agree that tariffs were raised abruptly and greatly even before 1931.[2] Threefold, and even greater, in-

[2] Cf. H. Liepmann, *Tariff Levels and the Economic Unity of Europe* (London, 1938). The following table (p. 414) summarizes the tariff increases of certain countries:

Changes in Prewar and Postwar Tariff Levels
(Base: 1913=100)

COUNTRY	FOODSTUFFS		SEMI-MANUFACTURED GOODS		MANUFACTURED INDUSTRIAL GOODS	
	1927	1931	1927	1931	1927	1931
Germany	125	380	95	153	190	183
France	65.5	180	96	125	153	178
Italy	75	188	114	198	193	286
Belgium	46	93	138	204	122	137
Switzerland	146	288	157	208	189	236
Austria *	56.6	204	76	103	109	143
Czechoslovakia *	125	288	108	148	185	188
Sweden	65	117	71	71	85	96

(*Table continued on next page*)

creases are indicated in many countries and it is obvious that such heightened barriers to commodity trade greatly increased the difficulty of balancing international payments. It was a sound instinct that led economic experts to concentrate their attack upon this point, since in fact a freeing of commodity trade would have relieved any population pressures that might have been aggravated by migration restrictions and would also have greatly facilitated both new long-term productive investment and the service of past debt. It was not sufficient, however, simply to plead for freer trade, since the trade restrictions were themselves the result of deeper underlying causes.

It is perhaps necessary to make these points somewhat clearer. The closing of migration outlets has been pointed to as one of the basic causes of the breakdown of international equilibrium.[3] From an economic viewpoint, however, it seems clear that freedom to expand international trade might have provided a vicarious substitute for migration, the products of labor being exported instead of the labor itself. This, indeed, was the policy pursued for many years by Japan and other countries of rapid population increase. It is true that the stoppage of migration outlets produced an acute feeling of frustration in some countries, particularly when the restrictions conveyed a stigma of racial or national inferiority. The political resentment thus produced fed the rising tide of national feeling. The process of industrialization in most of these countries was not an easy one since they were poor in raw ma-

Finland	117	208	107	106	47.5	60.5
Poland †	103	158	52.5	63	65.5	61.0
Roumania	131	252	108	153	190	215
Hungary *	108	206	132	162	165	220
Yugoslavia ‡	138	238	135	180	175	205
Bulgaria	320	540	204	270	385	465
Spain	109	193	150	190	148	177

*—compared with Austria-Hungary, 1913
†—compared with Russia, 1913
‡—compared with Serbia, 1913

[3] I. Ferenczi, *L'Optimum synthetique du peuplement.*

terials and had little accumulated capital relatively to their population, which indeed was the reason why they were countries of emigration. The spread of migration restrictions was a factor in economic nationalism as expressed in a readiness to promote industrial development by imposing higher tariffs on imports. While, therefore, a policy of industrialization may be regarded as a substitute for emigration, it is an effective substitute only when the products of industrialization can find ready markets so that needed raw materials may be imported and capital equipment built up. A certain aggravation of trade restrictions by the countries of former emigration is to be expected when their migration outlets close and if this coincides with a stiffening of protection elsewhere, as it did in the interwar years, there is a cumulation of restrictions.

In much the same way the stiffening of tariff protection, and particularly the narrowing of European markets for agricultural commodities and the consequential fall of agricultural prices, gravely aggravated the difficulties of debtor countries. There was a double absurdity in the interwar years when every country seemed anxious to sell but not to buy, while the great creditor countries were willing, and indeed eager, to lend, but reluctant to receive interest payments in the shape of increased imports. The strenuous efforts made by debtor countries to discharge the service of their international obligations were largely nullified as expanded exports to a narrowing market constantly depressed prices. Now it is perfectly true, as expert advice constantly urged, that freer commodity trade might have averted some of these difficulties, but it is also true that the swamping of world markets by exports from debtor countries anxious to pay their debts increased the reluctance of the creditor countries to lower their tariff barriers. Their reluctance was further increased by the shrinkage of their exports of manufactured goods as purchasing power contracted in the debtor countries, while increased restrictions were imposed on imports to those countries and, finally, the exchange value of many debtor currencies fell and they were forced to such methods as exchange control to protect their balances of payments.

There was no great problem of interest payments in the prewar period, when international trade was less restricted and great free-trade markets were capable of absorbing temporary export surpluses in periods of financial strain. From time to time one or more debtor countries found the strain of international payments intolerable and suffered exchange depreciation; but these were, on the whole, isolated and relatively unimportant incidents. The explanation of the interwar problem must be sought, therefore, in the reasons responsible for the imperfect functioning of the international marketing systems after 1918.

A closer approach to the fundamental causes of breakdown is evident when an attempt is made to analyze the growing inflexibility of various elements in the national price structures. International equilibrium pivoted on fixed exchange ratios between the trading countries demands, for its successful maintenance, sufficient flexibility of commodity and other prices to make possible rapid adaptation of national economic activity to the changing competition of imported commodities and external investment opportunities. Such flexibility is necessary not only in commodity prices, but in profits, interest rates, and the remuneration of labor, since economic activity is likely to be disorganized if commodity prices change violently while costs of production are sluggish. The growing inflexibility of prices in recent years derives partly from the increasing scale of manufacturing production based on heavy capital investment which gives added importance to overhead costs that cannot readily be reduced. In larger part, however, it derives from developments in the financing of industry. The control of production tends to pass from the hands of masters familiar both with the workers and with the processes they employ into the hands of organizers whose interests are primarily financial. The invention of limited liability and the subsequent rapid development of absentee ownership led to processes of flotation, combination, and amalgamation which have produced giant businesses.[4] Financial rigidities developed in this way have led to greater inflexibility of prices and have been buttressed by trade understandings, monopolies, cartel agreements, and other devices, sometimes depending solely upon the economic power of the industries concerned but at times receiving legislative sanction as in laws prohibiting price cutting on proprietary articles. In every country in recent years a greater range of commodity prices has been "fixed" rather than "free."

It should be noted, however, that these processes began long ago and until within the last few years did not prove incompatible with the maintenance of international economic equilibrium pivoted on exchange stability. This was partly because, in certain great industries of international scope, business organization itself regulated international price competition by such methods as the delimitation of selling areas, the allocation of market quotas, or price agreements. More important, however, was the fact that as long as a reasonable degree of freedom was maintained in international trade, import competition provided an effective check upon cartelization and monopoly, at least in commodities capable of being produced in many areas. Moreover, legislative and, even more, administrative, support, including tariff protection, for vested interests was less easy to secure before the inflated financial structures that were a legacy of the war boom were faced with the violent fluctuations of prices in the interwar period.

In the same way labor costs of production have become more rigid in recent years. This fact is often regarded as an inevitable consequence of social legislation and trade-union activity, which is either condemned as one of the root causes of the rigidities that have strained the balances of payments, or regarded as a desirable development, the corollary of which is the extension of government regulation to other aspects of

[4] Cf. J. H. Clapham, *An Economic History of Modern Britain* (Cambridge, 1937), Vol. III, Ch. V.

economic activity. Wage rigidities were emphasized particularly after the return of sterling in 1925 to its prewar parity with the dollar. This involved a price deflation in Great Britain estimated at 10–12 per cent. Such a deflation was difficult to achieve, especially in industries where labor-costs were a high proportion of the price and labor was strongly organized. Union resistance, for example in the coal-mining industry, to a reduction of nominal wage rates led to a bitter strike and to the loss of export markets with a consequential increase of unemployment. State relief of the unemployed was a factor enabling the unions to put up a stiff resistance to wage reductions, and it was repeatedly argued that this combination of union organization and social legislation was a major cause of inflexibility in the price system. As Mr. Keynes was quick to point out, however, "deflation does not reduce wages 'automatically.' It reduces them by causing unemployment." [5] And the argument against unemployment relief and wage maintenance was, in fact, an argument for throwing the major cost of an ill-considered policy decision upon the workers.

The fact that union organization to secure adequate wages and working conditions, and legislation designed to check social abuses and relieve distress, are not necessarily incompatible with international equilibrium has been amply demonstrated by the experience of many countries, and notably of free-trade England, during the nineteenth century. This historical evidence has recently been confirmed by investigations made by Professor Tinbergen, who concludes that wage rigidities have been much less influential than financial rigidities and monetary uncertainties in disturbing economic equilibrium.[6] Whatever may be said of trade-union practices, in regard not only to wage negotiation but also to the demarcation of occupations and the obstruction of rationalized production, these practices are not a major factor in our prob-

[5] J. M. Keynes, *The Economic Consequences of Mr. Churchill* (London, 1925), p. 19.
[6] J. Tinbergen, *Business Cycles in the United States of America, 1919–32* (League of Nations, Geneva, 1939), Ch. VII.

lem. Moreover, labor pressure for protection to industries threatened with wage reductions and unemployment by reason of import competition—a real and powerful reinforcement of economic nationalism in recent years—has been immensely increased by the disastrous dislocations of industry in the interwar period.

It must, however, be admitted that in the particularly difficult circumstances of the years immediately following 1918 ambitious social legislation was responsible, in countries such as Austria, Italy, and Germany, for serious economic difficulties and exacerbation of class conflict. These countries were impoverished and loaded with heavy obligations of war debt. Even when inflation lightened this burden, there were heavy political payments to meet and a new burden of debt was rapidly accumulated. Strict economists might argue that these conditions should have been met by a general and severe lowering of living standards and long years of intensive work and hard saving. But there was a great deal of unemployment and social unrest. The example of Russia and of the Béla Kun regime in Hungary was always present in the minds of workers and employers. It was inevitable that, in a city such as Vienna where the socialist vote was predominant, or indeed in Germany under a socialist government, an effort should be made to ameliorate the conditions of the distressed workers. Many of the experiments undertaken in Vienna, especially the housing program, were admirable, but probably beyond what the country could afford in the circumstances. They led to taxation that was in many respects confiscatory, to inequity of income distribution between workers in town and country, and later to excessive expenditure of loan moneys. Class conflict became acute. Political factors thus reinforced the economic conflict over social legislation and its costs. Ultimately, this struggle took the form of an offensive against socialist democracy as represented in the city government of Vienna.

The class conflict between the urban socialism of Vienna, and the rising discontent of the surrounding countryside and the owners of urban property, was perhaps the clearest example of the social struggle in an impoverished Europe; but there can be little doubt that such a struggle was played out in Italy, Germany, and Hungary also. Indeed, the case is more general. Wherever social legislation was pushed too fast and too far beyond the economic possibilities of production and the political possibilities of income redistribution, it was a cause of economic dislocation and of political bitterness.

The financial necessities of governments have also played an important role in the interwar period. In this respect, indeed, the spread of government intervention has given national governments a direct financial interest in protecting certain industries, and national industry in general, from undue losses by reason of import competition. The drain of unemployment payments, and still more of various kinds of subsidies, is heavier in a time of depression. Moreover, the increasing tendency of governments to operate certain public services and, in doing so, to limit contracts as far as possible to local materials is a factor making for trade restrictions. The rapid increase of tariffs in many European countries, and particularly in the newly created States, is partly explainable also by the urgent need for revenue.

But the most important element of economic policy in recent years has been the development of monetary nationalism involving reluctance to follow credit policies of adaptation to shifting international equilibria. In some degree this monetary nationalism is due to the fact that government debt is now much greater, primarily as a result of war expenditures, and later of rearmament expenditures, but also because of expenditure on social services which, since the breakdown of international equilibrium in the great depression, have mounted rapidly. Governments now have not only a greater direct interest in the perpetuation of cheap-money policies, but also more abundant means of influencing money markets by manipulating the funds under their control. It is not an accident that there has been steady encroachment everywhere upon the functions of independent central banks which formerly used to register and implement the changes of credit policy necessary to adapt national economic activity to changes in international equilibrium.

Since cyclical fluctuations have been so much more severe and the combination of national and international economic disequilibria has brought unemployment and financial losses of much greater magnitude than in the prewar period, there has been irresistible pressure to use the power of the State to counteract depression, avert bankruptcies, and prevent unemployment. National adaptation to international competition based on fixed exchange rates and relatively free trade involved the acceptance of disciplinary monetary policies designed to check economic activity resulting from credit expansion in one country out of line with the rest of the world. Such policies brought temporary depression and resulted in a crop of bankruptcies and an increase of unemployment. As long as the departures from equilibrium were not great, monetary discipline as expressed, for instance, by a rise in the discount rate, was not severe and its consequences were temporary, not unduly harsh, and often salutary. They were, in any case, the price to be paid for participation in the benefits of an expanding system of world trade.

In the interwar world there has been not only reluctance to accept such discipline, and difficulty in applying it, but more radical departures from equilibrium calling for much more severe and destructive monetary policies if equilibrium was to be restored or maintained. It is not difficult to make out a strong case for avoiding such policies, if only on the grounds of the social injustice that is caused by widespread unemployment. Indeed, most of the abnormal restrictions placed upon international trade in recent years can be brought within the scope of Adam Smith's famous exception to the case for free trade on the ground of humanity, when a sudden irruption of competitive imports would inflict heavy financial losses and throw large sections of the population into distress. As soon as one gets past the technical and proximate reasons given for the new protectionism, this is the argument upon which real reliance is placed and which is the most stubborn obstacle to any removal of trade restrictions. In the tangled circumstances of recent years it is indeed an unanswerable argument, so that even those who are convinced that freer trade and exchange stability are desirable objectives at which to aim, and the only alternative in the long run to a contracting spiral of economic disorganization and political conflict, are forced to admit the necessity of working at the same time for both national and international equilibrium. In doing so, the necessity of caution in removing the barriers to international economic co-operation is freely admitted.[7]

This does not mean, however, that independent or autonomous monetary policies pursued behind exchange control systems are desirable in themselves or economically more advantageous than flexible credit policies adapted in happier circumstances to a shifting international equilibrium. The impossibility of immediately restoring fixed and free exchanges in a freer trading system and so exposing national economies to the full blast of unregulated competition is generally admitted. The necessity, within those national economies, of restoring production and employment, and of using appropriate credit policies for that purpose, follows naturally. But there is a vast cleavage of principle between those who would accept the necessity for such national policies as an inevitable consequence of the present international anarchy and those, on the other hand, who regard the independent national direction of monetary policy as permanent and desirable. The former would endeavor so to restore national production and employment as to work towards an organization of industry that could in due course become once again an integral part of an international trading system. They look, therefore, to a gradual and progressive lifting of the barriers to international trade and, as national reorganization proceeds along lines compatible with international co-operation, to renewed readiness to accept limitations of national economic

[7] Cf. Adam Smith, *Wealth of Nations,* Book IV: "Humanity may in this case require that the freedom of trade should be restored only by slow gradations, and with a good deal of reserve and circumspection."

sovereignty in an international trading system. The latter repudiate such a conception not only as unrealistic daydreaming, but as undesirable, since unfettered national sovereignty is an end in itself transcending any real or supposed economic advantages that may come from participating in a system of international specialization.

At this point the purely political argument for nationalism is reinforced in some countries, and paralleled in others, by criticism of the international trading system as it was practiced under the gold standard. It is criticized as leading to the control of economic activity by international financiers whose primary interest is profit rather than the livelihood and creative satisfactions of the working population. A curious similarity of invective is to be found in the writings of those who denounce the workings of international finance either because they regard it as thwarting national aspirations or because they conceive it as withholding the material resources of better and more secure livelihood from an awakening laboring class.

It would require a long and unprofitable discussion to examine such criticism in detail, since the literature is extensive and the argument somewhat vague, being based upon emotional conviction rather than on observed fact or reasoned conclusions. Some aspects of the question are examined later. The vehemence of the literature, however, is sufficient evidence that a world-wide system of international economic co-operation does enable the owners of capital to escape in great measure from controls imposed by a national State. As long as credit, and even the means of long-term investment, remain more mobile than labor, they will be transferred wherever their owners can find security and profit opportunities. To mobilize economic resources in the service of the State, therefore, requires the imposition of restrictions on international capital movements and such restrictions are incompatible with the working of a free international economic equilibrium. In the same way, those who advocate the regulation of national economic activity, as by a sort of extended town planning, soon become aware that there are narrow limits to such national planning as long as international investment and trade remain free. The logical solution of their dilemma is the institution of international planning, or at least the international co-ordination of national plans; but such a solution is not only vastly more difficult to conceive, but lacks the necessary organs of international government for its enforcement.

It is necessary, however, to distinguish sharply between the developments that caused the collapse of international economic equilibrium in the interwar period and the reasons now advanced for the maintenance, consolidation, and extension of the government regulations introduced in that emergency. The present argument is concerned with the causes of breakdown, and it is clear that in the last analysis these resolve themselves into the growing interference of national governments with the organization of economic activity. While at every stage of the breakdown there can be found reasons for further interference in the economic interest of important groups of producers, threatened by heavy loss as a result of prior intervention, the ultimate causes of the breakdown are dominantly political and social in character. It may, with justice, be argued that there never was any period, even in the so-called free-trade era, when economic forces were left to operate unchecked by government controls. The peasant agriculture of Europe successfully invoked government intervention to check the competition of cheap imported grain, and in doing so invoked political and social, as well as economic, arguments. Few States have ever been content to rely largely upon imported food supplies, or to expose the manufacturing industries necessary for war to the full blast of international trading competition. But before the war of 1914–18 such considerable qualifications of international trading freedom did not overstrain the mechanism by which equilibrium was maintained between the trading nations.

Since 1918 there has been not only a great dislocation of economic specialization and a reluctance to face the costs and sacrifices involved in a gradual reduction of that dislocation.

More important have been the continuation of war policies in peacetime and the gradual subordination of economic welfare to the totalitarian mobilization of economic activity in systems of power economics. Political insecurity has brooded over the whole interwar period and no government can follow policies leading to mutual interdependence as long as such insecurity dominates all political decisions. International economic co-operation is incompatible with war preparedness and is, indeed, the only practical alternative to it; but the settlement of political disputes, or at least the establishment of effective machinery for their negotiation, is a prior condition of co-operation. Neither such a settlement nor the establishment of such machinery could be achieved in the world between the wars.

It is significant in this respect that the greatest economic progress was made after the Locarno treaties seemed to presage a better understanding between the leading European States. Recovery from the great depression coincided also with the hopes of settlement arising from the Lausanne Conference. Whenever political tension has lessened, the prospects for effective restoration of economic equilibrium have improved. Despite the complexity of the issues involved, there seems no insuperable technical difficulty in such restoration, provided only that economic considerations are paramount and are not thwarted by overriding political objectives. Undoubtedly, both the economic insecurity which has increased in recent years, and the awakened social conscience which is no longer content to allow the costs of economic change to be borne by those least able to protect themselves, have buttressed the demand for government regulation of economic activity. It will be argued later, however, that there is no inherent conflict between such regulation and the restoration of international economic co-operation.

The question at issue, therefore, cannot be answered in economic terms. The causes of economic nationalism are political in character. They must be sought by an investigation of mental attitudes and loyalties. Men will not fight for gain, nor suffer hardship and privation to make profits for interested groups. The appeal must be made in moral terms, in terms of loyalty and adherence to principles. The use of State power in the economic sphere has been defended as a means of advancing national interests, safeguarding national security, remedying national injustice. No doubt, arguments for social justice have been used and vested interests have worked behind the smoke screen of national sentiment. In these respects the setting has not changed in essentials since Adam Smith wrote in 1776.[8] But the primary cause of the exaggerated economic nationalism of recent years is education conceived exclusively in terms of national citizenship, so that, as soon as disaster is threatened, there is an almost instinctive rally to the support of the Nation-State. This has long been true, but such national cohesion has gained new importance since the last war because disaster has seemed to be more imminent in the chaos of interwar circumstances.[9]

The Victory of Political Realism

The reasons for, and consequences of, the breakdown of world-wide economic organization have recently been analyzed from the angle of political realism. The breakdown is ascribed to the collapse of an illusory and Utopian concept of natural harmony in international relations. "The characteristic feature of the present crisis," writes Professor Carr, "seen in the light of the twenty years between 1919 and 1939, has been the abrupt descent from the visionary hopes of the first post-War decade to the grim despair of the second, from a

[8] "To expect that the freedom of international trade should ever be entirely restored in Great Britain is as absurd as to expect that an Oceana or Utopia should ever be established in it. Not only the prejudices of the public, but, what is more unconquerable, the private interests of many individuals, irresistibly oppose it . . . like an overgrown standing army, they have become formidable to the government, and, upon many occasions, intimidate the legislature."

[9] "As protectionism naturally arises in a period of warfare, so it is likely to be continued when that period has passed." C. F. Bastable, *The Commerce of Nations* (London, 1892).

VICTORY OF POLITICAL REALISM 117

utopia which took little account of reality to a reality from which every element of utopia seems rigorously excluded. The mirage of the post-War years was, as we now know, the belated reflexion of a century past beyond recall—the golden age of continuously expanding territories and markets, of a world policed by the self-assured and not too onerous British hegemony, of a coherent 'Western' civilisation whose conflicts could be harmonised by a progressive extension of the area of common development and exploitation, of the easy assumptions that what was good for all and what was economically right could not be morally wrong. The reality which had once given content to this utopia was already in decay before the nineteenth century had reached its end. The utopia of 1919 was hollow and without substance. It was without influence on the future because it no longer had any roots in the present." [10]

There seems little reason to dissent from the argument that the international political and economic system erected on the prewar model after the war of 1915–18 was unrealistic. The preceding chapters of the present volume contain many detailed illustrations of the manner in which both economic and political obstacles inhibited the effective organization of international economic co-operation in the interwar period. The explanation, however, has run in terms somewhat different from those set forth by Professor Carr. It has run mainly in terms of the growing importance of political factors in the determination of national economic policies.

The thesis that economic progress in the nineteenth century was largely based upon the possibilities of territorial expansion, while not essential to the realist argument, is so often advanced that there is every possibility that it may come to be generally accepted. If it comes to be believed that natural limitations have put an end to what was admittedly an era of economic prosperity and peace, that belief will undoubtedly produce its own justification. The thesis is that there are no more new lands into which economic activity can expand and,

[10] E. H. Carr, *The Twenty Years Crisis* (London, 1939), p. 287.

therefore, that the clashes of economic interest, between social groups and between nations, inherent in free enterprise directed by cosmopolitan capitalism, can no longer be postponed or avoided. It is obvious enough, as has already been argued, that such clashes of interest have come to the surface and have rung the death knell of the nineteenth-century system—political and economic. It is also clear that the necessity, if expansion was to continue, of capital investment being lodged in areas already politically organized and conscious of their nationalism made the conflict of cosmopolitan economic enterprise and political nationalism more obvious and acute. The disappearance of frontier regions open to settlement and economic exploitation is a fact. But the problem is not essentially territorial. Throughout the nineteenth century the opportunities for capital investment and economic expansion were greater on the intensive than on the extensive margins of settlement. Capitalism is thwarted not by geography but by politics.[11] The pseudo-internationalism of the nineteenth century was clearly an outgrowth of British financial leadership and trading enterprise, backed ultimately by the economic supremacy of London and by the British Navy. That hegemony has come to an end and nothing has been put in its place, so that international relations have lapsed into anarchy.

Professor Carr's analysis of the decline of laissez faire, as far as it affects international economic organization, runs along two connected lines. There is, first, a demonstration of the wishful thinking involved in the assumption that conflicting interests can be reconciled by competition so that a natural harmony of interests, or at least a survival of those best fitted to serve the community, is achieved. "Laissez-faire in international relations as in those between labour and capital," writes Professor Carr, "is the paradise of the economically strong. State control, whether in the form of pro-

---

[11] This conclusion is consistent with the wealth of historical evidence adduced by Professor Toynbee in his analysis of the causes of breakdown in earlier civilizations. Cf. *A Study of History*, Vol. IV.

tective legislation or of protective tariffs, is the weapon of self-defence, invoked by the economically weak."

The second line of reasoning rejects the laissez faire assumption of the separability of economic and political organization. This assumption, so strongly defended in the nineteenth century, especially in its applications to international relations, is quite clearly rejected now by the practice of governments.

The concept of a world in which governments did not interfere unduly with economic activity, but left it to be organized by private enterprise on a world-wide basis, was defended by the classical economists as the system best calculated to enhance the economic prosperity of the masses of the people in every country. Professor Carr does less than justice to the economists' position at this point. His explanation of the extraordinary divergence between the theories of economic experts and the practice of those responsible for the economic policies of their countries is vitiated by his misrepresentation of the economists' viewpoint as naïvely cosmopolitan.[12] It may be that the economic argument for freer trade secured political acceptance in Victorian England because of the rationalization by which British politicians believed that what was in Britain's interest at the time must be in the general interest of every national community. The economic argument for free trade, based on the assumption of laissez faire, however, is neither cosmopolitan nor a rationalization of the economic interests of a dominant nation. It has been stated very clearly by a modern economist.

"It can be proved that, at any rate under the usual assumptions of general economic theory (free competition, absence of friction, and so on), the unrestricted international exchange

[12] "The economic expert, dominated in the main by laissez-faire doctrine, considers the hypothetical economic interest of the world as a whole, and is content to assume that this is identical with the interest of each individual country. The politician pursues the concrete interest of his country, and assumes (if he makes any assumption at all) that the interest of the world is identical with it." Carr, *op. cit.*, p. 71.

of goods increases the real incomes of *all* the participating countries." [13]

This theoretical demonstration, it may be added, takes account not only of the aggregate real income of each country participating in international trade, but of the distribution of that income between regions, among classes and occupations, among individuals, and over periods of time, as well as its stability and security. Granted the premise of free competition, economists are prepared to demonstrate that free trade between national communities brings more effective production and increases the economic welfare not only of the world as a whole and of the dominant trading nation, but of *all* the nations participating in the freer trading system. Indeed, the classical theory goes further and demonstrates (upon the assumption mentioned) that the division of the gain from international trade is likely to favor the smaller rather than the larger trading countries—as long as a free world market is maintained.

Criticism of the economists' thesis should be directed, therefore, not against a vague and unrealistic cosmopolitanism which they never professed, but against the validity of the assumptions upon which their analysis rests. If the conclusions from theoretical analysis are to be any guide to practical policy, the assumptions upon which it rests should bear some relation to reality. Few economists would now contend that the assumptions of classical theory are valid as an approximation to modern economic conditions. It is precisely for this reason that theoretical analysis of national economic problems is now concerned with problems of imperfect competition and with those that arise from the organization of economic activity in a socialist state. There is need for similar analysis in respect of international economic problems.

The doctrine of free trade as a maxim of practical policy must be clearly distinguished, however, from the assumption of laissez faire as a basis for theoretical reasoning. The doctrine of free trade has always been recognized by economists

[13] Haberler, *The Theory of International Trade*, p. 221.

as a Utopia, a daydream, an ideal towards which practical policy should be directed. Adam Smith specifically declared that complete free trade was as unlikely to be adopted as an "Oceana or Utopia." The historical episode in which that Utopia came closer to practical realization than Adam Smith had believed possible may have given rise to illusions and false reasoning. It was brought into being by the economic power and authority of a great trading country, with naval power not far in the background. The political realist has no great difficulty in demonstrating this fact and the equally clear fact that the acceptance of free trade was in the economic interest of the manufacturing and banking groups who displaced the landowners as the dominant political power in nineteenth-century England. Nor is there any difficulty in demonstrating that the episode is ended. While it lasted, the common people in every country gained more in economic prosperity and political power than in any previous period of history.

The decisive factor in its ending was the rejection by governments of the economists' Utopian dream of international economic co-operation free from political interference. That rejection, it has been argued, was decisive when the forces of nationalism were joined to those of social discontent. Both worked through the institutions of the Nation-State to impose limitations upon private enterprise that finally crippled its operations so effectively as to bring about a complete breakdown.

Professor Carr has stated the results vividly:

> The breakdown of the post-War utopia is too overwhelming to be explained merely in terms of individual action or inaction. Its downfall involves the bankruptcy of the postulates on which it is based. The foundations of nineteenth-century belief are themselves under suspicion. It may be not that men have stupidly or wickedly failed to apply right principles, but that the principles themselves were false or inapplicable. It may turn out to be untrue that if men reason rightly about international politics they will also act rightly, or that right reasoning about one's own or

one's nation's interests is the road to an international paradise. If the assumptions of nineteenth-century liberalism are in fact untenable, it need not surprise us that the utopia of post-War international theorists has made so little impression on reality. But if they are untenable today, we shall also have to explain why they found such widespread acceptance, and inspired such splendid achievements, in the nineteenth century.[14]

One obvious reason why the assumptions of nineteenth-century liberalism are untenable today is to be found in the unstated assumption that underlies the whole of Professor Carr's analysis, the dominance of the Nation-State as the supreme social grouping in which men organize themselves. This assumption is realistic. The modern State has absorbed economic as well as political functions. The Utopia to which nineteenth-century liberals clung—that economic activity was best organized by private enterprise operating on a world-wide scale, with the barest minimum of government regulation and intervention—has been rejected. Intervention, primarily to build up the military power of the State, has finally resulted in such complete anarchy of international economic relations, and such disorganization of national economic activity, that the State has been forced itself to take over the direction and operation of economic life. Inevitably, the purposes of the State have come more and more to take precedence over those of the community it exists to serve. The logical result of such a development is a condition of almost continuous economic war, breaking out sporadically into actual armed conflict.

This ultimate result of political realism, however, must lead, if civilization is not to be sacrificed on the altar of the State, to renewed attempts at formulating a Utopian ideal towards which policy can be shaped. It is perhaps significant that the Utopia which is projected by a political realist does not differ in essentials from the ideal of national economic policies pursued in a spirit of consideration for their effects beyond, as well as within, national frontiers to which

[14] Carr, *op. cit.*, p. 53.

economic Utopists have always clung.[15] Moreover, the clash of economic and political motives may not finally end in the victory of the unitary and completely sovereign Nation-State over a pluralistic conception of society in which economic organization transcends national boundaries. It is clear that the territorial organization of Nation-States is in process of evolution and that "the concept of sovereignty is likely to become in the future even more blurred and indistinct than it is at present." [16]

Whatever the future may hold in these respects, it is clear that the nineteenth-century system, based essentially on the competitive organization of private enterprise by the initiative of cosmopolitan financiers, is wrecked. As far as can be judged now, it is very unlikely to be restored on a worldwide scale or, without considerable modification, even on a more restricted scale. In many countries it has been superseded almost completely by State enterprise, or at least by detailed State regulation of all important economic activities. But it is too soon yet to believe that the State has gained permanent and final control of economic life, or that, henceforth, economic activity across national frontiers must be confined to what serves the purposes of the all-powerful State.

The Rejection of Economics

The reasons so far advanced to account for the breakdown of international economic co-operation have been concerned mainly with the choking of economic enterprise by political

[15] "The more we subsidise unproductive industries for political reasons, the more the provision of a rational employment supplants maximum profits as an aim of economic policy, the more we recognise the need of sacrificing economic advantage for social ends, the less difficult will it seem to realise that these social ends cannot be limited by a national frontier, and that British policy may have to take into account the welfare of Lille or Düsseldorf or Lodz as well as the welfare of Oldham or Jarrow. The broadening of our view of national policy should help to broaden our view of international policy; and, as has been said in an earlier chapter, it is by no means certain that a direct appeal to the motive of sacrifice would always fail." Carr, *op. cit.*, pp. 306–307.

[16] *Ibid.*, p. 296.

intervention. The argument may, for clarity, be summarized briefly. It is that the nineteenth-century system of economic activity organized on a world-wide basis of specialized production and trade depended essentially upon freedom of private enterprise. The active organizing initiative devolved upon capitalist financiers in their search for profits. Long before the war of 1914–18 brought extensive dislocation of international economic relationships and heightened economic nationalism, the cosmopolitan activities of these financial organizers met with increasing distrust and opposition on both social and national grounds. The attempt after 1918 to reconstruct a world trading system on the nineteenth-century model was doomed to failure because the essential conditions for its effective operation were lacking. The most essential of all these conditions was popular belief that free capitalist enterprise could be trusted to bring about economic progress and prosperity.

It can be demonstrated that free enterprise has in the past brought solid economic benefits to the masses. Theoretically it can be argued that, given a reasonable basis for operation, similar results might be achieved once again. If there were even a moderate degree of freedom for private enterprise, combined with certainty and stability in the restrictions imposed upon it, economists are prepared to demonstrate that production could be increased and made more efficient than it is at present. The real income of all the national communities participating in a freer trading system could be increased, standards of living could be raised and rendered both more stable and more secure. The ordinary man could have access to greater quantity, a wider range, and an improved quality of consumers' goods. Such a theoretical demonstration, supported by the experience of the nineteenth century, need not shirk a frank recognition of the chicanery, wastes, and inefficiencies that have in the past accompanied private enterprise. It would be, in the main, an argument that these abuses were outweighed by abundant production and economic growth.[17]

[17] Cf. Carl Snyder, *Capitalism the Creator* (New York, 1940).

One reply has already been given to such theoretical reasoning—the reply that it is sheer Utopian, wishful thinking since in fact the conditions essential for the restoration of private enterprise are not likely to be achieved in the foreseeable future. The fusion of economics and politics has gone too far. It is mere daydreaming at the present time to analyze economic forces in abstraction from the political realities of the modern world. In recognition of these rather obvious facts, many economists are now concerned to explore practicable systems of socialist organization, or various compromises between State regulation and free enterprise.[18] It is possible to argue that, given a common will to use State machinery for economic ends, systems of socialist enterprise could be effectively organized so as to increase production, promote technical efficiency, and at the same time remedy certain injustices of income distribution. Alternatively a "mixed system," retaining some of the driving force of private enterprise while substituting public for private enterprise in large sectors of economic activity, might be worked out in theoretical detail.[19]

All such theoretical analyses, however, whether postulated upon freedom of economic enterprise, upon socialist organization, or upon some compromise between them, use economic tests and criteria. They attempt to measure the efficiency of various forms of organization and types of policy by their probable results in promoting efficient production, raising standards of living, securing a more equitable distribution of income, and increasing the real economic satisfactions of consumers.

It is necessary to record the fact that the revolt against such theories and the policies that may be built upon them goes far beyond criticism of their practicality in the modern world. The merits of free, as opposed to socialist, enterprise are not the main issue. A good economic case can be made for either, if it is contrasted with the twilight state that in most coun-

[18] Cf. Staley, *World Economy in Transition*, pp. 173 ff.
[19] Staley, *op. cit.*, Ch. 5.

tries at present is characterized by nominal adherence to the principle of private enterprise while government policies dominated by noneconomic motives effectively hamper its working. The mixed systems which are criticized by economists at the present time seem to destroy what is best, and promote what is worst, in both public and private enterprise. Since in fact such mixed systems are dominated by political, or even by war, considerations, it is not surprising that they fail to meet economic tests.

The real explanation for their immunity to economic criticism is that public opinion, or at least that section of it that has power, rejects economic reasoning and economic criteria of judgment. It is no longer sufficient to argue, as it was for a time in the nineteenth century, that a given policy is economically justified or unjustified. The mere fact that a certain course of action is likely to diminish productive efficiency, and reduce the aggregate of goods available for distribution among individual consumers, is not regarded as sufficient reason for condemning it.

It is not only that moralists and social reformers are willing, as they have always been, to accept a diminution of production and a limitation of abundance if, in so doing, more wholesome ways of living can be promoted. The simple life has always had its advocates and there is so much social injustice, artificiality, and unwholesomeness in modern industrial and urban ways of living that direct attacks upon bad housing, insecurity of employment, and subordination of human skill to machine processes can be justified even where they entail immediate economic costs. Economists have increasingly fought this battle for human, as distinct from monetary, values, if only on the ground that in the long run a virile, independent, and energetic working population is the most important economic asset a nation can have, as well as the true end and aim of all economic activity.

It must be remembered, however, that a high level of productivity is an essential basis for communal well-being. Artistic and cultural achievement in the past has not been correlated with poverty, but with wealth. The "good life" is possible only when the rudimentary necessities of food and shelter are assured. In the past this assurance has been the prerogative of a privileged few. It still remains more important to increase production than to equalize its distribution—desirable as a greater measure of economic equality is, for economic as well as social reasons. This is so, if only because production is still inadequate, however it is distributed, to afford facilities for leisure and cultural development to all sections of the population.

Much nonsense is talked and written about the use of mechanical methods in modern industry. The whole development of production in the past has depended upon the use of scientific knowledge and invention to lighten manual labor. Inevitably, craft skills have been displaced; but new skills have been developed. The true case against mass methods of production is not that they subordinate labor to the machine and throw skilled craftsmen out of occupation, but that they have not been developed far enough to liberate human beings from heavy labor and set them free to have greater leisure and opportunity for cultivating new and more personal skills. If leisure is misused and mechanical production develops ostentatious standards of expenditure and bad taste alongside of proletarian insecurity of employment, the fault lies not with the machine, but with ineffective economic organization and educational methods.

The really destructive criticism of economic reasoning and economic values comes, not from social reformers whose ranks are recruited in large part from students of political economy, but from those who reject entirely both the economic calculus of the "nicely calculated less or more" and the concern for individual welfare upon which it is based. Edmund Burke deplored the increasing influence of "sophists, economists and calculators" in his lament for the disappearance in the French Revolution of the class privilege and romanticism that constituted for him "the age of chivalry." The replacement of that age by the much derided "rule of reason" in the nineteenth century not only enriched the real living standards of the masses of the people, but placed them in a position to demand a greater measure first of political, and later of economic, equality. Universal suffrage, popular education, limitation of the hours of labor, relief of old age and unemployment, and lengthening of the average expectation of life were fruits of rational economic organization, not of romantic chivalry.[20] However great the abuses of urban industrial civilization may have been, and however glaring the inequalities of wealth and ostentatious exhibitions of bad taste that often resulted from the accumulation of wealth in hands that had not been trained to use it, it must be admitted that increasing productivity gave the organized workers greater real income and a consciousness of even greater possibilities for the future. The very discontent that was engendered was a wholesome result of living standards that were rising, but not as fast as seemed desirable. There was despair but little constructive discontent in the stratified medieval society to which so many modern reformers look back, as to a golden age.

In many countries at the present time there is a new age of chivalry. It is the unrealistic and romanticized outgrowth of a decaying nationalism, as medieval chivalry was the outgrowth of a decaying feudalism. It scorns the fustian virtues and painstaking calculations of rational economics. Its appeal to youth is directed along noneconomic channels. Security rather than abundance, honor rather than profit, State power rather than individual welfare, position and prestige rather than comfort, identification with the mass rather than expression of individual personality are its slogans.[21]

Against such appeals to emotion rational economic calculations at the moment are discredited and powerless. It is, indeed, the most disquieting symptom of a disintegrating civilization that there should be such widespread abandonment and discrediting of the somewhat naïve but fruitful

[20] Cf. Graham Wallas, *Men and Ideas* (London, 1940), Ch. I.
[21] Cf. Peter F. Drucker, *The End of Economic Man* (New York, 1939).

nineteenth-century faith in reason and rational compromise. The anti-intellectualist teachings of the late nineteenth century, based upon realization of the complex and obscure emotional elements that enter into all human thought, have been used to justify an acceptance of primitive emotional attitudes instead of reinforcing the necessity of disciplining such attitudes and dispositions. The "glowing heart" is exalted and glorified instead of being recognized as a treacherous organ in great need of constant watchful control by a cool head. We now know that more people think with their glands (or their blood) than with their brains; but such glandular (or bloody) thinking is encouraged and glorified by the new chivalry.

No country has been immune from such irrational and emotional thinking. The errors of policy that caused the breakdown of co-operative international relations preceded the advent to power of the more extreme political philosophies. The collapse cannot be credited to totalitarian aggression, but was the product of selfish interests and muddled nationalism before such aggression took shape. Indeed, it is only in a period of frustration that extremists are able to seize and retain power. They represent the incarnation of ideas and philosophies that have been prevalent in every country, but were not revealed in their naked ugliness until a period of social disintegration gave an opportunity for their assertion.

The rejection of economic thought, therefore, is only partly due to the inadequacy of the traditional forms of organization in which such thought has been applied to practical, everyday life. The forms of organization are inadequate because the thought behind them has been inadequate and in many respects unrealistic. But no economic theory, and no application of it in economic organization, is acceptable in an age where the appeal to reason is discredited. The very notion of scientific economic reasoning, however fumbling and inadequate its expression may be, is a rational concept, an attempt to use intellectual processes of analysis and argument to understand the complicated relationships of cooperation in the everyday business of producing and distributing goods and services.

It is possible to question the success of such analysis as has been attempted in the past. It is also reasonable to set aside the conclusions from such analysis on the ground that there are other and more important criteria for public policy than the accumulation of material wealth. These are matters for rational consideration in which the final word must lie with social philosophy. But when appeal is made to emotional considerations such as national prestige, national honor, or the soul of a people, there is no possibility of rational discussion. These are the stuff of which wars are made, and against the emotions they arouse economic argument is futile.

Graham Wallas has pointed out that when Shakespeare wished to describe the ills that drive men to suicide, he defined them as:

> The oppressor's wrong, the proud man's contumely,
> The pangs of despised love, the law's delay,
> The insolence of office, and the spurns
> That patient merit of the unworthy takes.

The applicability of these lines to international, as to individual, situations does not need emphasis. In a period when such psychological states are widespread, and capitalized by skillful playing upon mass emotions, rational discussion of economic or political remedies is thrust on one side. The passions that lead to war do not arise from hunger, privation, and fatigue, but from "wounded self-respect, helpless hatred and thwarted affections."[22] Economic remedies are powerless to heal such states of mind and economic costs are disregarded in expressing them.

A distinction should, perhaps, be drawn in this respect between the ultimate purposes of social organization, the methods by which it is carried out, and the myths that are

[22] Graham Wallas, *Our Social Heritage* (London, 1921), p. 157.

created in order to secure acceptance of those methods. At the present time there is an open conflict of social purposes which has led to war between great nations—the nations that have revived military virtues against the "plutocratic democracies." It may be that, if the military virtues prove victorious, the end which is sought may be held to be rational, as giving more living-space and opportunity for economic expansion. The costs of modern war and the demoralization that follows it may, on the other hand, turn such a victory into disaster.

Even if the ultimate ends of totalitarian organization are uncertain of success, there is little doubt that the methods of such organization are highly rational, in the sense of being logically calculated to achieve the desired end. As will be shown in later chapters, State intervention in such fields as exchange control and clearing arrangements has been logically and methodically calculated to enhance the military strength of the totalitarian States. It is in respect of the arguments by which the individual sacrifices such policies entail are justified that irrationality is most evident. Every national community has its myths and historical fictions, its social creeds and ideologies. Social purposes must always be represented by symbols; but there has been a notable change in the overtones of emotion to which such symbols make appeal. Peace and prosperity may have been illusions, but they unloosed less dangerous emotional forces than are unloosed by appeals to race prejudice, to primitive combativeness, and to revenge.

The Maintenance of Regulation

The preceding sections of this chapter have been devoted to a preliminary consideration of the more fundamental and longer-term social and political forces that prevented the effective restoration of a freely working international economic equilibrium in the interwar period. A distinction has been drawn between those forces and the immediate pressures that were responsible in particular instances for the decisions taken by various governments to intervene in specific ways intended to protect or buttress threatened segments of their national economies. Behind the immediate pressures were mental attitudes that are not easy to define and still less easy to exemplify. They might even be summed up as a loss of faith in formerly accepted principles, modes of behavior, and institutions. There was, at any rate, a distinct loss of faith in the system of free trading enterprise.

It is necessary, however, to stress the fact that the government regulation which was introduced was not in any country a complete and symmetrical substitution of government planning for the unorganized competition of private enterprise. It was, at least in the first years of confusion after the breakdown of international equilibrium, a series of *ad hoc*, improvised, and partial expedients designed to cope with specific situations as they arose. Necessarily, such intervention was not always well considered. Something had to be done quickly in an emergency. The first attempts were not uniformly successful in their immediate objectives. Secondary consequences, such as reactions in other segments of the national economy and reprisals abroad, were seldom foreseen. The history of the imposition of quantitative, monetary, and indirect restrictions imposed upon imports after 1931 is one of confusion, of the hasty improvisation of new mechanisms of administration, of almost continuous amendment and reinforcement as weaknesses and gaps became apparent, and of search for principles of application. Systems of regulated trade did not spring complete from the brains of their creators, but were evolved by a rather long and costly process of trial and error.

Necessarily, they were not only restrictive but cumulatively so, one set of restrictions calling forth others in different fields and in different areas. Necessarily also, they protected existing interests and so acted as an obstacle to the restoration of equilibrium and to changes of national economic structures in the directions required by economic progress.

There is little need to prove, or even to illustrate, the first of these statements. The Smoot-Hawley tariff of 1930 called forth a crop of retaliatory and consequential tariff increases. The depreciation of the Japanese yen in 1931 was the immediate cause of quantitative import restrictions in the British and Dutch colonial empires and later in several South American countries. The depreciation of the New Zealand currency was followed by that of Denmark within a few days, and it was not long before the international butter market was complicated by export subsidies almost as much as the market for sugar. The adoption of a protectionist tariff by Great Britain greatly disturbed the trade and production of many European countries and led to an intensification of their protective measures. Though justified largely as a bargaining weapon which would enable Britain to use its trading position as a lever to free trade, both the preferential treaties entered into at Ottawa in 1932 and the subsequent negotiation of bilateral treaties with Scandinavian and South American countries have, in fact, further restricted trade and at times placed the other contracting countries in embarrassing situations. The depreciation of sterling is cited in more than one country as the chief cause of exchange depreciation and exchange control. The closing of the German market at first accentuated the agricultural crisis and later led to the wholesale negotiation of bilateral trade treaties as the attempt of creditor countries to retain the proceeds of German exports for the payment of debt service led to widespread use of clearings. Once begun, restriction was countered by restrictions elsewhere.

The spread of disequilibria as restrictions increased can be illustrated with equal facility. Indeed, the cumulative process of restriction is itself evidence of accumulating disequilibria. In order to maintain a precarious balance of payments in and out of the weaker financial countries, more and more extensive and rigid controls had to be established over all items of the balance of payments, including tourist traffic, shipping receipts, financial commissions, and above all security transactions and other capital transfers. The continued extension of such controls was evidence that restrictive regulations were not curing, but aggravating, the disequilibria responsible for their imposition.

It has been argued that these new systems of trade regulation are capable of transformation into more effective means of regulated international co-operation than the system of free trading enterprise could ever have yielded.[23] It is obvious enough that the arrangements which, until war recurred, allowed a certain quantum of international trade to be carried on were preferable, and in many cases the only alternative, to upheavals and dislocations of the price system that might have brought economic chaos in many countries. It is also true, and has been repeatedly demonstrated, that the initiative and ingenuity of traders will accommodate itself to, and find ways of carrying on with, a surprising degree of government interference and regulation. Given a certain amount of stability in the regulating system and some freedom of private enterprise, traders will find ways over and around tariffs and other trade restrictions.

Before concluding, however, that government restrictions have little or no influence on economic prosperity, it is desirable to examine the statistical facts. The total quantum [24] of world trade, after falling steadily from the onset of depression in the last quarter of 1929, increased slowly from the

[23] Cf. Fritz Meyer, *An Analysis of Exchange Restrictions at Present in Force.*

[24] The "quantum" of trade is a more precise expression for volume as distinct from value. It is defined (cf. League of Nations: *Review of World Trade,* 1939, p. 8) as follows: "The value of world trade is measured by adding together the figures of the recorded external trade of the numerous statistical areas of the world, after converting them to a common monetary unit. If the average movement of prices of goods entering into trade is known, it is possible to estimate roughly the movement of the quantum of world trade, which may be defined as the change in value after elimination of the effect of price changes since the base year chosen."

middle of 1932 onwards. This increase, however, was far slower than the recovery of national production in most countries and in the world as a whole. In the preceding period of recovery after the disorganization of the first postwar depression, international trade, supported by large foreign loans, had outstripped national production. The gradual expansion of international trade from the middle of 1932 till another recession of business activity set in at the close of 1937 was, moreover, far from uniform. In part, it was a function of recovery in that part of the trading world where restrictions remained relatively moderate. In part, especially in the closing stages of the upward swing, it reflected a persistent search for raw materials as the rearmament boom got under way. Examination of the detailed statistics for particular countries makes it very clear that trade with and between countries where restrictions were most elaborated lagged far behind the increase in the rest of the world.

There was a noticeable deterioration also in the character of world trade. It became more concentrated upon the search for raw materials. The chains of trading transactions were broken as bilateralism increased and the world market was replaced by a series of disconnected national markets. Trade become more erratic and more dependent upon political arrangements between particular countries, while a larger proportion of it was carried on by discriminatory methods involving the use of subsidies, differential exchange rates, preferential quotas, and similar arrangements. As trade was forced by political considerations into noneconomic channels there was opened a wide series of price discrepancies between national markets, the prices of important staple commodities such as wheat, sugar, butter, and meat differing between neighboring areas by multiples of the world market price. Production was fostered in high-cost areas and discouraged where costs were low. French peasants, for instance, were subsidized to grow wheat unprofitably at three times the price ruling in the United States, where farmers were being subsidized to take wheat land out of cultivation.

The political aspects of such policies were even more important than the economic consequences. Standards of living were lowered, but, in addition, economic trading considerations were subordinated to political objectives. Trade treaties were influenced not only by the economic necessities of rearmament programs, but by the desirability of securing allies and collaborators. The allocation of exchange for imports was determined more, in some cases, by national plans for totalitarian warfare than by the needs of consumers. Trade, like every other aspect of economic activity, tended more and more to be used as an instrument of national policy. War having been officially abandoned as such an instrument, totalitarian mobilization of economic resources and totalitarian trade tended to replace it.

These economic and political facts must be taken into account before the persistence of international trade in a period of increasing restrictions can be regarded as justifying government regulation as a sound basis for an expanding system of international co-operation. The historical facts are: that the recent multiplication of trade barriers was the result of a breakdown of trading equilibrium; that these barriers were at first improvised and only later consolidated into regulated systems; that trade began to increase slowly as soon as recovery set in at the bottom of the depression, but the increase was confined largely to the countries which had not indulged in the new quantitative restrictions to any great degree; [25] and that the expansion of trade was first distorted and then halted by the consolidation of trade restrictions into systematic policies dominated by political rather than economic considerations. The ultimate result, not so much of this use of trade as an instrument of national policy, as of the mental attitude which lay behind that development, was the present war.

[25] The trade of Germany valued in marks and converted into gold dollars, at the official parity—which, in fact, is used only for a fraction of the trade—rose after 1935 but at its peak in 1937 was only equal to the predepression share of world trade. Measured at any real parity, or in quantum, the proportion of world trade was less than in other countries.

MAINTENANCE OF REGULATION 137

Theoretically it is possible to conceive the imposition of regulations designed to encourage production of the kinds of commodities for which there might be anticipated an expanding demand which the national economy concerned was advantageously placed to meet. But, since the regulations were imposed primarily to protect those industries most threatened by external competition, precisely the opposite result has been inevitable. Production was maintained and even extended in high-cost areas, so that, for example, France accumulated a surplus of wheat that had to be disposed of to Great Britain at prices much lower than those supported by heavy subsidies in France itself and those guaranteed to English wheat growers. The burden of adaptation was, in consequence, thrown upon the areas of efficient low-cost production elsewhere. In the same way, expensive substitute products were developed, notably in Germany, while the natural raw materials fell heavily in price and their production was restricted.

It is true that there emerged cases where the reorganization of national economic activity broke through certain rigidities and established more efficient means of production. This seems to have happened in some German industries, together with a galvanizing of scientific research in many directions. Industrial progress of this character has by no means been confined, however, to countries where reorganization took place behind the shelter of exchange control and other trade restrictions. Some notable illustrations might be drawn from the success of the Swedish cooperatives in breaking through to wider strata of demand by efficient large-scale and low-cost production. In so far as industrial progress was an incidental by-product of restriction, it was no more than a minor exception to the broad general rule that such restriction retarded and hampered the efficient utilization of the world's natural resources.

It must be remembered also that, in the first years of the new protectionism, restrictions were imposed unilaterally with little regard to their effects outside the national economy concerned. The negotiation of bilateral agreements, in which attempts were made at least to stabilize, and if possible to expand, trade between complementary areas, was a later development. They did not take any great amplitude till Germany initiated extensive purchases, particularly of raw materials, in central and southeastern Europe in 1935–36. Indeed, their efficient operation was hardly possible until a measure of rationalization had been introduced into the various systems of national regulation so that machinery became available to conduct negotiations in which not only prices but exchange rates, import premia, and export subsidies could be combined in the bargaining process.

Discussion of the manner in which different countries struggled to solve the technical administrative problems with which the new apparatus of protectionism confronted them, is now largely a matter of historical academic interest. The lack of administrative machinery with which they were at first confronted has now been remedied. The necessary co-ordination has been effected between the private industrial and other interests affected and the appropriate departments of government. In many cases the national industries had to be more effectively organized, so that a considerable impetus was given to cartelization. These new industrial groupings, as well as previously existing voluntary organizations such as Chambers of Commerce, have been given some of the minor responsibilities of government and at the same time have been more definitely subordinated to government direction and control. Gaps in the controls have been closed as they were revealed by experience. Procedures have, to some extent, been improved and even simplified, though trading is a much more complicated and cumbersome business than it used to be under the system of free enterprise. A greater degree of co-ordination has been effected between the various organs of control and notably between the departments of government responsible for price control, the allocation of raw materials, the organization of industry, the stimulation of exports by subsidies, and the allocation of import quotas. All have been brought in greater degree under the governing influence of exchange control administrations, while the negotiation of commercial treaties has come to provide a framework within which administrative bargaining may proceed with the officials of other regulated countries and even private banks and traders in countries where trade remains relatively free.

It has become possible, therefore, to envisage a system of regulated trade, proceeding for the most part on the basis of bilateral bargaining, but with the possibility in certain cases of triangular clearing of balances. A great part of the trade of central and eastern European countries has been conducted for some years now on this basis, and there has been a strong tendency for complementary methods to be adopted by many other countries in their trade with these closely regulated European countries. Indeed, this is in most cases the only basis on which such trade can be conducted since the more closely regulated countries usually lack sufficient free exchange to buy except against equivalent exports. For some years there was a strong tendency for bilateral trade to extend between the closely regulated European countries and many Latin-American countries, but, even before the present European war began, this transatlantic trade tended to become more difficult and to diminish.

The reasons for which restrictions on international economic co-operation were originally introduced are not necessarily the same as those for which it is now maintained and justified. Both must be distinguished from the theoretical rationalizations which are now being advanced in advocacy of such regulation as a permanent policy. The real reasons responsible for the maintenance of regulated trading systems in their present form are indeed similar to those which prompted the adoption of such regulations, being a combination of immediate detailed necessities and vaguer attitudes of mind which shape the trend of policy that emerges from detailed decisions in particular cases. But there are important differences of emphasis, particularly in the latter respect, which call for some examination.

It is clear, in the first place, that the most important practical reason for the continuation of trade restrictions is the persistence of the disequilibria originally responsible for their introduction. While the simplification of procedures, and in many countries the co-ordination of import premia and export subsidies so as to approximate to a uniform depreciation of the currency, has at times appeared to offer a possibility of relaxing exchange control and quota systems, in fact such relaxation has invariably led to renewed strain upon the balances of payments. A good example is provided by the experience of Rumania in 1936.[26]

This persistence of disequilibrium is only partly due to imperfect measures of adaptation in particular countries. Each country has proceeded unilaterally with little regard to the fact that similar action in other countries causes shifts in the basis to which adjustments must be made. It has been a common experience for long and arduous efforts at adaptation, either by deflation or by currency depreciation, to be nullified by further restrictions or depreciation in other countries, rendering it necessary to undertake a fresh program of adaptation to new price relationships.

Moreover, international economic equilibrium is not a static, but a dynamic concept. It can be maintained only while commodity trade and capital movements continue to operate on a basis of business confidence. If, at the first relaxation of restrictions, national capital seeks an opportunity of fleeing the country in search of greater security elsewhere, or even if needed capital imports cannot be brought to enter the country on a business basis, still more if exports are blocked by lack of buying power or trade restrictions elsewhere while imports are deflected from advantageous markets by lack of free exchange, painfully acquired equilibrium will be strained again and restrictions must be reimposed. The essence of international economic equilibrium is a continuous process of

[26] Cf. V. Madgearu, *La Politique économique extérieure de la Roumanie* (1927–38).

balancing the international accounts. It is only in an active system of trading that equilibrium can be preserved.

Moreover, new vested interests have been created not only in the sense that bureaucratic institutions have been built up to handle the new regulated systems of trade, but also in the sense that these systems have been interwoven into the economic and political structure of many countries. It is inevitable that there has been a shift of industry behind the shelter of quota restrictions and exchange control reinforcing heightened tariffs. But, in addition to these sheltered economic groups, the fact has now to be reckoned with that the new systems of regulation have placed in the hands of many governments instruments of supervision and control, even of intimidation, that are peculiarly effective in disciplining what might otherwise become recalcitrant business groups. Exchange control is especially effective in this respect since it must rest upon detailed knowledge of international trading transactions that can be thwarted, curbed, or directed as government policy demands, simply by the withholding of exchange allocations.

The chief differences between the reasons which now operate to maintain trade restrictions and those originally responsible for their imposition are to be found at this point. They may be summed up in the statement that whereas at the depth of the depression government intervention was largely negative in character, in many countries it has now developed a positive momentum. The first efforts at regulation endeavored to preserve existing industries from the effects of destructive external competition. They did not normally seek to reorganize those industries or subordinate them to the purposes of the government itself. Essentially they were in the nature of protective barrages against the threatened flood of foreign competition.

The development of these essentially conservative and temporary measures into an instrument of national policy has put more effective power into the hands of governments than was ever known before in times of peace. It may even be doubted whether in previous war periods there had ever been fashioned such complete and smoothly functioning instruments for the detailed regulation of economic activity and external economic relations. Much more than discouragement of trading with the enemy or inducements to serve State purposes was now achieved even before war broke out. The possibilities of economic regulation and mobilization were recognized earliest and most clearly by the German military economists who developed the theory of *Wehrwirtschaft* as a basis for *Kriegwirtschaft*. As early as April, 1936, the chief of the department of war economy in the German War Ministry stated the new conception of economic regulation very clearly.

Strategic economy (*Wehrwirtschaft*) merges entirely with the economy renewed and transformed by national-socialism. Strategic economy covers all human life and therefore transforms the social structure. It rests on the absolute will to be prepared from the military point of view. It is the economic principle of the totalitarian state and constitutes the economic preparation for future war which will also be, in the highest degree, totalitarian.

Such frank statement of the purposes for which the new weapon of economic regulation was being forged out of what had at first been regarded as abnormal and temporary measures of limited intervention leaves no doubt as to the main motive for the maintenance of such regulated systems of national economy. Even where regulation was less effective and less systematic, the shadow of war preparations fell across all discussions of international co-operation. Where political insecurity had been a potent cause of restrictions on international trade, those restrictions were now fashioned into a powerful instrument that accentuated insecurity.

Such enslavement of the economic forces that, given freedom to operate, might have led the nations out of the impasse into which they were drifting, was an effective preparation for the final apotheosis of the State as the supreme end for the preservation of which men are prepared to die. It marked the final subordination of a rival philosophy and the breaking down of a major obstacle to State-worship and obedience. Thereafter, only the voice of religion remained, and governments at war can always identify and confuse their cause with that of God.

CHAPTER IV

Regulated and Unregulated Trading Systems

The Spread of Regulation

THE PRECEDING chapters of this volume have argued in some detail that the new protectionism of the years immediately preceding the present war sprang from a collapse of the nineteenth-century trading system. That system was based largely upon the economic leadership and naval strength of Great Britain which used its economic and political power to establish and maintain what has been called an "empire of trade." The British Empire was essentially based upon freedom of private enterprise. Organizing initiative was provided by financial capitalism operating on a world-wide, cosmopolitan scale. Even before the war of 1914–18, however, there was growing opposition to British supremacy in world finance and world trade. Anticapitalist criticism was gathering strength in most countries and was reinforced by economic nationalism. The war dealt a heavy blow at international co-operation, and particularly at British leadership. It left legacies of disorganization and disequilibria within and between trading nations, of political and economic insecurity, and of inflamed nationalism.

The international economic system reconstructed on the old model after the immediate interwar monetary and financial crises had passed lacked real stability. Trade never flowed freely enough to cope with the tremendous readjustments of national economic systems that were necessary if workable equilibrium was to be restored. Foreign investment was directed into dubious channels. In practically every country economic insecurity provoked national policies designed to cope with unemployment and safeguard local industry. Political insecurity inhibited the acceptance of mutual interdependence. Britain lacked the power, and lost the will, to enforce international co-operation as she had done throughout the nineteenth century. After a very brief period of apparent stability, the newly restored international monetary standard broke down again. It had been based largely upon a great credit expansion and its collapse wrecked the international capital market.

Between the collapse registered by the depreciation of sterling in September, 1931, and the outbreak of major hostilities almost exactly eight years later, there developed a great complication of regulating and protectionist mechanisms designed to direct and control the flow of commodity trade and capital movements. In the beginning these mechanisms were stopgap expedients; but the time had passed when they could be regarded as abnormal restrictions on international co-operation, likely to disappear when economic recovery and political agreement should make it possible to re-create another trading system based on private enterprise. Even before the present hostilities began they were being consolidated into systematic policies of State-regulated production and trade. This consolidation has been hastened by the outbreak of war. Totalitarian mobilization of human and material resources on either side must be matched by corresponding measures on the other, so that the belligerent nations must regiment and mobilize their whole force for the struggle to survive.

Nor have the neutral nations escaped this pressure. Those most closely involved in the conflict, whether by their proximity to the battlefield or by their economic and political connections with the belligerents, are themselves on a war footing. Many of them are mobilized, and all of them have had to take further steps to protect their currencies, safeguard their industries, and control their external trade. Almost alone, the greatest neutral, situated far from the conflict, adheres to its initiative in favor of freer trade and peaceful international economic co-operation based on private enterprise. In a world at war, and fearful that the war may be prolonged and rage more bitterly over a wider area, that initiative is necessarily halted. The tenacity with which it is maintained, however, raises an issue of first-rate political importance. Is the organization of a world-wide trading system a practical ideal at which to aim? Can it give the opportunity again of adjusting the real economic pressures and aspirations of the warring nations in an expanding system of world production and trade? If there is any such hope, on what basis can international trade be reorganized? Must there be a reversion to laissez-faire principles, entailing the abandonment of present regulated policies and probably the overthrow of authoritarian governments? Or is it conceivable that trade may be restored between countries whose economic systems range from closely regulated to relatively free enterprise? If such a mixed system can be worked, what are the devices by which trade may be carried on?

It is obvious that, in the brief historical period covered by this study, the economic policies actually followed have failed to maintain world peace. It cannot be assumed, however, either that they were the primary or contributing causes of war rather than the instrument of preparations for war, or that their complete reversal is an essential condition of a peaceful world in the future. Indeed, if the preceding analysis has any validity, it is clear that present trade restrictions rest, at least partly, upon forces that provoked the collapse of the laissez-faire system. Those forces persist and must be reckoned with in any future reorganization of the economic relations between independent trading nations. It is probable, therefore, that their techniques will survive in some modified form, so that an examination of their evolution is by no means an academic exercise.

The first point to be noted is the wide scope of the new mechanisms of regulated trade. Essentially the international trading system of the nineteenth century was based upon freedom of capital investment, productive activity, and trading enterprise, limited mainly by tariff duties imposed at national frontiers. It is now clear, as was argued in the preceding chapters, that economic developments within national boundaries, stiffening resistance to the constant adaptations of national economic activity necessary for conformity to a shifting international economic equilibrium, were mainly responsible for the breakdown of the trading system as it was restored after the war of 1914–18. To some extent these national developments were reflected in rising tariff schedules, but for the most part they were regarded as of purely national concern. The fact is that an international trading system postulated upon freedom of private trading enterprise became unworkable when in most countries trading enterprise was limited by monopolies, financial controls, State regulation, and dependence upon managed monetary policies.

Since the breakdown in 1931, such internal regulation has been greatly stimulated in almost every country. This is clearest, and most important, in the rapid spread of monetary policies designed to stimulate national production and employment. Currencies are no longer regulated mainly by reference to some indication of external equilibrium, such as the gold reserve or exchange parity with other great trading countries. It has been necessary to devise policies based upon national considerations. These policies have not always been successful, nor have they been entirely able to neglect external factors. Nevertheless, the attempt by monetary means to regulate national economic problems, such as disparities of costs and prices, unemployment and investment, has both stimulated the more rigid organization of national economic activity and built up resistance to international adaptation.

There has, however, been action and reaction between the more definite organization of national economic activity and the regulation of international economic relations. The attempt by independent national action to solve local problems has entailed a considerable increase of government regulation and this, in turn, has led to the promotion of trade and industrial associations. Quite often the reorganization of industrial (or agricultural) activity has entailed a combination of protection from foreign competition, financial assistance both directly and indirectly by cheap money policies, cartelization and control of production, together with regulation of prices and of wages. Examples may be cited from the British marketing schemes for agricultural produce; the co-operation of the Import Duties Advisory Board in measures to reorganize the British iron and steel industry; the close connection between wage regulation, modification of the antitrust legislation, tariff protection, and monetary policy in the National Industrial Recovery movement in the United States; and, above all, the much more definite and far-reaching organization of industrial activity, and the incorporation of such organization in the machinery of government, that has been an essential development in the dictatorship countries.

More than ever before, therefore, the decline of laissez faire and its replacement by regulated trade organizations closely linked with government policy has made the revival of world-wide trade on laissez-faire lines impractical. Apart from the fact that the new mechanisms of external regulation are intimately linked with trade organizations that would be difficult to modify, and if modified would necessitate drastic readjustments of economic activity within national boundaries, the mere abolition of external controls would not suffice to restore international trade.

Such restoration must depend upon a simultaneous loosening of both external and internal regulations. It is true that somewhat freer international trade would tend to weaken the national controls that are most vulnerable to competition, but, unless there is a determined will to direct national regulation into channels compatible with international co-operation, such weakening would certainly bring a demand for reimposition of the trade barriers.

Closer integration of internal and external regulation of national economic activities makes the attack on trade restric-

THE SPREAD OF REGULATION 149

tions a much more complicated problem than it used to be. In many countries not only the whole machinery of organized economic activity, but government policies and indeed the very forms of government, depend upon rigid control of all external economic and financial transactions. Some attempt is made below to examine the various possibilities of expanding trade between such closely regulated countries and those countries which would prefer to retain a greater or less degree of private enterprise in their economic activity. Here it is sufficient to note that, short of a complete reversal of present policies and probably a change of government in the closely regulated countries, there is no possibility of restoring a world-wide system of expanding trade based upon free enterprise.

Apart from this closer connection of internal and external regulation, however, there is a great and significant complication of the mechanisms of external regulation in the sense that they now go far beyond the time-honored use of protective tariffs. Tariffs have by no means been abandoned. Instead they have been greatly expanded and refined. They are now much higher than they were even in 1931, more detailed and minute, less uniform in their application to different exporting countries, more arbitrary and flexible, less bound by conventional agreements, and less stable. They are also supplemented in far greater measure by tariff legislation conferring upon the administration power to impose differential duties, arbitrary valuations, or more minute classifications. Like most other economic legislation in recent years, they have tended to become less a fixed and definite code of law than a framework of legislative authority within which administrative discretion may be exercised in applying the law.

There is an essential difference, however, between the economic effects of a tariff and the newer administrative methods of discriminatory rationing of imports by quotas, exchange allocations, and the use of indirect controls such as quarantine or milling regulations. Tariffs impose an extra cost on the price of a particular import. This charge is imposed at the most sensitive point of the whole price mechanism, the wholesale price. Its effects are diffused backward to the exporter and forward to the importer and through them ultimately to the producers and consumers. There is a whole range of price bargaining, including the related supply and demand for by-products, joint-products, materials and substitutes, in which the trader can work, so that even very high tariffs on particular commodities often permit a considerable volume of trade to pass.

The rationing of imports by quantitative, administrative, or monetary measures, on the other hand, is directed against that portion of the supply which must be imported, and is absolute. The effect on prices and on demand is apt to be very different from the effect of a tariff, more erratic and more arbitrary; but, whatever the effect, no increase in the quantity imported is possible. The destructive consequences to international trade are much greater in this case.

Moreover, rationing regulation of this character almost necessarily involves discrimination between sources of supply, irrespective of price competition. This, indeed, is a major reason why these new methods of trade control have been used to supplement tariffs. Inevitably the multilateral character of trade is seriously impaired so that it becomes necessary to build up a network of detailed, and frequently revised, bilateral treaties to regulate commodity trade and the means of payments. In the negotiation of such treaties administrators are able to use not only quotas and exchange allocations, but tariffs and exchange rates. Indeed, the bargaining becomes so much a matter of administrative detail that there is a strong tendency for the bilateral treaties to develop, like the tariffs, into a legislative framework within which particular bargains may be struck.

Detailed examples of these various developments are cited in the chapters that follow. The general problem has been raised at this point to illustrate the degree to which current practice in many great trading countries has departed from the principle of free trading enterprise and equality of trading opportunity. The growing concentration of power in the hands of government officials to determine not only what trade shall pass national frontiers, but the conditions under which it shall pass, is in striking conflict with nineteenth-century conceptions of international trade. Before discussing how far these types of international trade are compatible, it is necessary, however, to examine the extent to which the new methods of trade regulation have been employed in various countries. This raises the question whether it is possible to divide countries into those practicing a close regulation of external trade and those retaining relatively free trading systems.

The Criteria of Regulation

It used to be an axiom of foreign policy that the domestic affairs of a country were matters of purely national concern. The international game of power politics was played without much regard to conflicting conceptions of government. Democratic nations sought and maintained friendly relations with absolutist countries; republics allied themselves with monarchies. While private individuals, particularly in Anglo-Saxon countries, at times expressed decided criticism of government policies in other countries, the occasions were rather rare when such political or humanitarian movements influenced the practical policies of foreign offices. Though examples, such as Gladstone's denunciation of Turkish policies or missionary influence upon American policy in China, might be cited in disproof of this statement, and political sympathies were always apt to influence the recognition or nonrecognition of revolutionary governments, these were exceptions to the general rule that international friendships and enmities were formed mainly on realistic considerations of strategic and commercial interest.

Trade was freely conducted also between free-trade and protectionist countries, quite irrespective of their forms of government. It is only in recent years that public opinion, moved by noneconomic considerations, has brought pressure to bear on governments to restrict trade with, and use "economic pressure" against, countries whose domestic or external policies were disliked. On the other hand, the increasing degree to which trade has come to be regulated for political rather than economic reasons has fostered discriminatory methods of trading regulation. Moreover, both national regulation and external economic controls have become so closely identified with the form of government in many countries that it has become difficult to separate trading transactions from diplomatic relationships with those governments.

The question rises, therefore, whether a division has grown up between two types of political and economic organization, which may be broadly designated as regulated and nonregulated, with the implication that, in the latter, international economic relations are separable, and, in the former, inseparable, from international political relations. In the present confusion of national economic policies this question is not easily answered. Difficulties become apparent as soon as an attempt is made to classify the varieties of regulation now practiced in the leading countries into one or other of these groups. It is obvious, in a world where regulation is so widely practiced, that the distinction must be drawn, if it is drawn at all, in terms of the purposes for which regulation has been introduced, or is now maintained, rather than in terms of the degree of regulation practiced. If such a criterion of division can be established, the further question arises whether or not ways can be found to preserve and extend peaceful trading relationships between countries in the two groups, or whether the economic and political aspects of their differences are so interwoven that trading contacts between them are bound to lead to conflict.

A first approximation to a classification of trading policies may perhaps be found in an examination of the degree to which various countries have supplemented customs tariffs by the new protectionist methods. It has already been pointed out that there is an essential difference between the old and the new protectionism in the fact that the former relies primarily upon methods of regulation which affect the price

THE CRITERIA OF REGULATION 153

mechanism, while the latter is based essentially upon procedures of rationing that involve direct interference with the supply of commodities or services. Not only customs duties, but monetary policies designed to regulate exchange rates, whether by currency depreciation or by the operation of an exchange equalization fund, fall in the former category. On the contrary, quota and clearing systems and exchange control fall in the latter category.

The most important difference between these two sorts of government control lies in the fact that the former is more, and the latter less, compatible with the nineteenth-century principle of "equality of trading opportunity." It is true that careful classification and minute subdivision of tariff items may result in tariff manipulation which in fact discriminates between imports from different countries, even while maintaining the literal application of unconditional most-favored-nation treatment. Such discriminatory manipulation of tariff schedules, however, is more difficult to work out, and less effective, than direct discrimination in the allocation of quotas and foreign exchange. In recent years there has been tacit acquiescence in the literal interpretation of most-favored-nation obligations, as being confined to the application of uniform rates of import duties. Quotas and exchange control systems have escaped these obligations.

Rationing methods also lend themselves more readily than tariffs to discriminatory management in two other respects. It is possible, and indeed it is the primary reason for lengthening tariff schedules, to impose differential duties upon various classes of goods so as to discriminate between imports by commodities; but such tariff discrimination is not easy to change rapidly and traders are adept in finding ways around and over tariffs. Quotas were first developed because they provided an easier method of shutting out the particular import commodities it was desired to control. The second aspect of discrimination that is facilitated by the new protectionism is even more important. The control of quota permits and exchange allocations places in the hands of governments very effective means of discriminating between traders and industrialists within the regulating country. Industry can be directed along the lines conforming to government policy, industrial organization can be fostered and controlled and, in extreme cases, individual producers can be disciplined. This development can, in fact, lead to an identification of government and business organization, one essential element of which is the rationing of external trade.

The facilities for discriminatory policies offered by the devices of the new protectionism have been greatly increased also by the manner in which the centralized trade controls in many countries have been endowed with discretionary powers in their administration. As this development has proceeded, not only tariff schedules, quota, exchange, and subsidy regulations, but commercial treaties also, have become little more than a framework of legislative authority within which trade is conducted, transaction by transaction, by administrative decision in accordance with government policy at the moment.

It is perhaps necessary to stress the fact that the introduction of these new quantitative controls with necessarily large elements of administrative discretion and improvisation has given wide opportunities for the evasion of most-favored-nation obligations. The principle of equality of trading opportunity has a long history. Under the tariff system it was worked out in detail until the specific definition of its application in particular circumstances became conventional. There is a large body of precedents and accepted rules of application as far as customs duties are concerned. But these precedents and rules are not readily applicable to the granting of quota permits and it was not to be expected that satisfactory principles of most-favored-nation treatment in respect of quotas could be rapidly improvised. Some of the problems encountered in this respect are discussed later.[1]

Moreover, the new discretionary powers which quota systems placed in the hands of officials have been used in many

[1] See below, Ch. VI.

countries to control and silence the protests of trading interests, both national and foreign. Such interests have in the past been vigilant in defense of equal trading opportunities; but their very existence now depends upon the possibility of securing quota allocations. There are many cases where allocations have been granted on conditions that approximate to the establishment of partial monopolies. The profits made possible in this way have been a powerful inducement to silence. In this way potential opposition was bought off until the new systems of quantitative control were established firmly enough to defy such opposition. Few business enterprises will refuse immediate short-term gains in order to insist upon the maintenance of fundamental principles, even though the abandonment of those principles means, as in this case, destroying the possibility of profitable trading in the long run.

It is obvious, however, that the mere adoption of direct quantitative and monetary rationing in supplement of tariff restrictions on international trade cannot be regarded as final evidence that a country is unwilling to participate in the restoration of an international trading system based on freer reliance upon market mechanisms as opposed to economies directed and controlled in detail. It is possible to draw a distinction in principle between countries which, even before the present war, were using the whole apparatus of quantitative and monetary rationing in a highly integrated policy of trade regulation and those which, while making use particularly of quantitative import controls, endeavored to retain free exchange systems; but it is not possible to make this distinction very clear-cut.

The *World Economic Survey, 1938–39*, written by Mr. J. E. Meade for the Economic Intelligence Service of the League of Nations, includes a very interesting discussion of this problem.

"Although the tendency since 1929 for the formation of 'economic *blocs*' and for the development of bilateral trade has been widespread," writes Mr. Meade, "yet there is at present a sharp contrast between two distinct commercial policies. On the one hand, there are countries, such as Germany, whose trade is organised bilaterally through clearings and quantitative control of imports, whose foreign exchanges are closely regulated, and whose exports are frequently directly subsidised. On the other hand, there are countries—typified by the United States of America—whose foreign exchanges remain uncontrolled and whose imports are restricted by tariffs rather than by quantitative quotas. . . . While the distinction between the two types of commercial policy is in some cases very marked, it is not always clear-cut. For example, as the following figures show, even in the case of countries which have maintained freedom of exchange dealings, a considerable percentage of imports is subjected to quantitative, as opposed to tariff, restrictions." [2]

If the use of quantitative restrictions, and also of barter transactions, is not a conclusive test of nonregulated as opposed to regulated trade policies, the adoption of exchange control is not a conclusive test either. Even before war broke out, the number of countries which had adopted some measure of exchange rationing was very considerable. In a great number of cases, however, and particularly in the smaller and financially weak agricultural countries, the adoption of exchange control was quite clearly involuntary.

There is, in fact, no clear line of division to be drawn by attempting to classify national policies according to the methods employed. Even if the employment of both exchange control and quotas, and the integration of both these rationing methods in a highly centralized and detailed control of international economic transactions, be regarded as the test, and

[2] The figures are contained in the following table:
Approximate Percentage of Total Value of Imports in 1937
Subject to License or Quota Restrictions

France	58	Ireland	17
Switzerland	52	Norway	12
The Netherlands	26	United Kingdom	8
Belgium	24	Sweden	3

World Economic Survey, 1938–39, pp. 188–189.

countries employing such controls be contrasted with those where trade and other external economic relationships are maintained on as free a basis as is compatible with watchful regard to the balance of international payments, it is still difficult to get a clear-cut and satisfactory division. Denmark, for example, has one of the best organized systems of trade regulation, pivoted on exchange control. New Zealand has also adopted a trading policy in which the conservation of exchange assets is a prime consideration. Yet both of these countries, together with numerous others that in recent years have gone some distance along the path of trade regulation by rationing methods, are commonly placed within the group that might be expected to form part of a freer trading system in the future.

The United Kingdom, which in the nineteenth century was the citadel of free trade, has made many compromises with the new forms of protectionism. Her system of agricultural protection is based upon licensing and quotas. The program of bilateral trade treaties negotiated with Scandinavian, Latin-American, and other countries in the sterling area, while adhering in principle to the unconditional form of the most-favored-nation clause, has included quantitative provisions, both for the limiting of agricultural imports and for the assurance of exports or the means of their payment.[3] In certain cases, these quantitative provisions have made it difficult for the other contracting countries to fulfill their most-favored-nation obligations to other powers. They have also rendered more difficult the extension of the United States bilateral trade treaty program.

In the last analysis, however, the criterion of distinction between regulated and free trading systems must be subjective rather than objective. The test must lie not in the methods adopted, but in the purposes for which they are adopted. Such a qualitative test, involving interpretation of motives, is obviously more difficult to apply objectively and is more dependent upon individual judgment. It is possible, and in-

[3] *World Economic Survey 1938–39*, pp. 189–190.

deed probable, that elements of economic or political aggression enter in some degree into the trading policies of most governments. No nation has a monopoly of righteousness, or its opposite, in this or any other aspect of foreign policy.

The adoption of discriminatory tactics, however, provides an objective test that throws a good deal of light upon the subjective aspects of national policy. Whether such policy uses frankly direct methods of rationing, as do Germany and many other countries, or indirect methods such as the industrial purchasing agreements, which paralleled many of the British bilateral trade treaties, and the voluntary quotas accepted by Japanese textile exporters after negotiations with American textile interests, the extent to which it makes use of discriminatory practices in its rationing is a fair indication of noneconomic motives.

Abandonment of the principle of "equality of trading opportunity," therefore, while not a conclusive indication of the conscious subordination of economic to political considerations in the conduct of trading policy, is ground for suspecting such subordination. A later section of this chapter examines the extent to which devices have been found in the trade between regulated and unregulated countries by which equality of trading opportunity can be assured even under the new quantitative and monetary regulation of trade. It is obvious that the problem is a difficult one; but in certain cases attempts have been made to find at least an approximately satisfactory solution for it. Wherever discrimination is practiced, voluntarily, or involuntarily because of pressure from the other party to a trading bargain, price comparisons are discarded as the criterion of trading possibilities. This means abandonment in some degree of reliance on the mechanism of the market and price competition, and the substitution, instead, of bargains that achieve political objectives.

As the quotation cited above points out, the protagonists of the two opposed systems before the outbreak of the present European war were the United States of America, whose trad-

THE CRITERIA OF REGULATION 159

ing policy, though highly protectionist, was avowedly based upon "equality of trading opportunity," and Germany, which was frankly pursuing a totalitarian trading policy in which economic were subordinate to political objectives. It is perhaps significant that the clearest case in which American policy had discriminatory aspects was in its toleration of the unofficial textile quotas aimed at Japan. Germany remains in 1940 the only country from which the United States has withdrawn most-favored-nation treatment and Japan the only country with which the United States has abrogated its commercial treaty.[4] The countervailing duties which can be imposed under various sections of the United States tariff legislation [5] have in practice been invoked mainly against imports from these two countries. At one extreme, therefore, may be placed the American practice of trading equality modified only by the isolated and unofficial use of discriminatory quotas by direct industrial agreement between Japanese and American traders, and the American use of countervailing duties and refusal of most-favored-nation treatment as reprisals for discriminatory treatment of American exports. At the other extreme is the totalitarian control of trade as an instrument of national policy, which is practiced not only by Germany, but also by Italy, Japan, and the U. S. S. R. Between these extremes there is a gradation of discriminatory practices which is largely determined by the degree to which various countries are linked by trade and political rivalries with the totalitarian countries. Turkey and Iran have practiced trading monopolies on the Russian model. A great many of the central and southeastern European countries and, at times, some of the Latin-American countries, have been drawn within the orbit of the German trading system and have necessarily

[4] Most-favored-nation treatment was withdrawn from Australia in August, 1936, as a reprisal against the Australian trade diversion policy described by N. F. Hall in "Trade Diversion: An Australian Interlude," *Economica* (February, 1938). Germany denounced its commercial treaty with the United States on Oct. 13, 1934, taking effect as from Oct. 13, 1935.

[5] Cf. P. W. Bidwell, *The Invisible Tariff*, pp. 86 ff.

adopted complementary trading policies. The discrimination that was creeping progressively into the British trading system before the present war was largely in its relations with countries where rivalry with German trade was acute.

It is significant also that all of the totalitarian countries have been involved in war since 1931 and, with the exception of Germany, whose occupation of Czechoslovakia and invasion of Poland, Denmark, Norway, Belgium, and the Netherlands were not brought before the League of Nations, all have been formally designated by neutral opinion as aggressors in those hostilities. If the connection between war preparations and discriminatory trade policies was not clear enough before, it has been abundantly demonstrated by events since September, 1939. All the belligerent powers have been forced towards complete mobilization of economic resources within their home territories, colonial empires, and allied or dependent countries. Germany intensified its bilateral trading relations with neutral European countries and reopened active trade connections with the U. S. S. R. The Anglo-French alliance was quickly developed into a joint economic organization working with exchange control and co-ordinated purchasing policies based upon maximum use of the resources of the two empires. In their effort to conserve foreign assets for essential military purchases in foreign countries, as much as possible of the trade in nonmilitary commodities was arbitrarily switched to sources within the areas they controlled. After the defeat of France, Great Britain pursued this policy within its own empire.

As a practical matter, therefore, it may be reasonably concluded that the essential difference between the trading systems which are so generally recognized as opposites lies in the fact that, whatever may be the superficial resemblances in their methods and practices, one has used external trade as an instrument of national policy in the preparation for, or conduct of, war, while the other clings to the ideal of trade conducted with the minimum of government interference and upon the basis of equality of trading opportunity.

Varieties of Autarky

The experience of Switzerland is illuminating in regard to the pressure of autarkic systems upon a small country with a traditionally liberal trading policy.[6] Switzerland is an economic island. Its four million people inhabit a small inland territory, much of which is mountainous. Few of the raw materials of modern industry are found within its borders. For centuries, therefore, the Swiss have striven to build friendly and profitable trading connections with the outside world. At one time their young men sought service as mercenaries; but the development of international trade in the nineteenth century opened up expanding markets for the products of Swiss craftsmanship. Population and wealth grew as trade was extended, and Switzerland became a center of banking and financial organization. It is not surprising that practically every Swiss economist who has written on the subject has declared autarky to be "a policy of suffocation."

There are also strong political and social reasons to explain why Switzerland should have embarked in recent years with considerable reluctance and misgivings upon a policy of regulated and reciprocal trade. Composed of linguistic and confessional groups whose only common link is their citizenship and participation in a strong democratic tradition, organized in a federation built upon strong cantonal patriotism, and surrounded by powerful neighbors, the Swiss have always endeavored to derive strength from their weakness. Democratic toleration inhibits disunity, neutrality preserves their inde-

[6] Cf. Burky, de la Harpe, et Wackernagel, *La Suisse et l'autarcie*. "The word autarky derives from the Greek autarkeia and ought to be written with a k; it means 'the art of being self-sufficient,' the tendency to withdraw oneself from dependence on the external ties which link one human group to others. It should not be confused with the idea of autarchy, from the Greek autarcheia which means something else, the government of a group by its own representatives to the exclusion of foreign powers. Between these ideas there is some connection since both are based on an ethno-centric principle, but to be politically independent and to be economically self-sufficient, far from being synonymous, can in certain circumstances be the opposite."

pendence, and local patriotism checks undue centralization of power in the hands of the federal government.

Yet, in 1931, suffering from the effects of the Hawley-Smoot and other tariffs, and more immediately from the depreciation of sterling, this little country was forced into taking bold measures of trade regulation, including the abandonment of most-favored-nation treatment, the adoption of quantitative import controls, and the frank prosecution of a reciprocal bargaining policy, "cashing in" on the high purchasing power of the country.[7] In doing so it took what the experience of other countries has since shown to be a pioneer step towards preserving as great a degree of trading freedom as was practical in the circumstances. Quotas were chosen in preference to exchange control and as a means of bargaining for reciprocal concessions. Clearing agreements were made at a later stage in order to collect some payment on defaulted debts. But there is much evidence to prove that Switzerland endeavored to conduct a restrictionist policy, when it was forced upon her by necessity, in a liberal spirit. The most-favored-nation principle was renounced, but reciprocal bargaining was conducted in an effort to preserve and extend trade outlets. Switzerland is one of the few countries employing the new protectionist methods with which the United States has found it possible to negotiate a bilateral trade treaty based upon equality of trading opportunity. Efforts were made, in 1937, after the negotiation of the Tripartite Agreement and the devaluation of the Swiss franc, to liberalize the quota system and even to revive the capital market.[8] There is little reason to doubt repeated statements that the new measures of trade restriction were for Switzerland a necessary evil, that every opportunity of relaxing them has been seized upon, and that public opinion is

[7] Burky, etc., *op. cit.*, pp. 56–72, especially the characteristic passage (p. 67): "Bien que différents milieux le lui aient demandé, la Suisse n'a jamais exigé une compensation intégrale de l'étranger, ne n'a voulu imposer a celui-ci les organisations d'importation et d'exportation compliquées qui eussent été nécessaires. Elle s'est contentée de monnayer son pouvoir d'achat."

[8] Burky, etc., *op. cit.*, p. 76.

categorically in favor of their abolition whenever international pressures may permit.[9]

While it would perhaps be difficult to find parallels in other countries to the quasi-unanimity and vehemence with which the leaders of public opinion in Switzerland adhere to the principle of freer trade, even while they are forced to adopt practical policies of restriction, it is clear that many of the smaller European countries have embarked upon the new protectionism reluctantly and hesitantly. Those in the north and west which are creditors on balance have refrained from the introduction of exchange control. Nearly all have utilized import quotas to protect their agriculture and to control their balances of payments. The financially weaker countries of central, southern, and eastern Europe have been forced to utilize exchange-control systems as well as quotas in order to forestall capital flights and to safeguard their monetary stability. It is abundantly evident, however, that such measures are in the main defensive rather than aggressive, negative rather than positive, involuntary rather than voluntary.

Care needs to be exercised, therefore, in discussions of autarkic policies, to differentiate the circumstances under which such policies have been adopted, and still more the purposes for which they are now maintained. The definition of autarky, when traced back to its origins in Greek political thought, clearly indicates that certain forms of autarky are not incompatible either with international trade or with peaceful international relations.[10] In Greek thought, continued into medieval doctrine, a certain degree of economic self-sufficiency was one of the essential requirements of independent statehood. No community which did not contain within itself the minimum degree of economic self-sufficiency could develop the culture and political life that was deemed an essential attribute of independent nationality. This idea has survived, particularly in the small countries with vivid national

[9] *Ibid.*, p. 71.
[10] Burky, etc., *op. cit.*, p. 94.

traditions. To them, political independence and the preservation of their characteristic ways of living are more important than great wealth. They are prepared to justify measures which, even at some economic cost, check the tendency towards extreme specialization; but they are more than willing to participate in a world market which is complementary to their own resources.[11] Their quarrel is not with internationalism, but with a cosmopolitanism that would submerge and destroy their individuality. Their attitude is that many moral values and cultural ideals are interwoven with political independence, which must be regarded as worth preserving for its own sake, even at some economic cost.

The difficulty of this attitude in the modern world is that it "encounters a national and international system of rapid transport, based on petrol and electricity, a highly developed technical organisation of industry, a formidable urban concentration of human masses that have now become colossal, and a concentration also of economic and financial power. Introduced into a world so internationalised and concentrated, a world all the component parts of which form the threads of a closely woven net, it cannot help but take on at first a destructive and violent character, and be pushed by the very obstacles it encounters to a state of extreme tension." [12]

In other words, the defense of economic autarky as a means of preserving the individuality and independence of national cultures again raises the question whether the technical progress of modern industry has not outgrown national boundaries, as in an earlier age it outgrew the boundaries of City-

---

[11] Burky, etc., *op. cit.*, p. 108. "La politique autarcique de principe ne veut nullement renoncer au commerce sur le marché mondial ou, en tout cas, ce trait n'est pas une de ses caractéristiques éminentes. La politique autarcique de principe se borne à avoir une attitude différente à l'égard du commerce mondial de celle qu'adoptent les méthodes libérales, pour lesquelles les économies nationales ne sont en un certain sens que des parties de l'économie mondiale. Au contraire, pour les Etats autarciques, l'économie mondiale apparaît comme un complément parfois nécessaire et parfois simplement désirable de l'économie nationale, auquel on devrait, si c'est nécessaire, pouvoir renoncer, mais aussi auquel il ne faut pas renoncer sans nécessité."

[12] Burky, etc., *op. cit.*, p. 20.

VARIETIES OF AUTARKY 165

States. In these circumstances, attempts to cling to traditional forms of political organization, by putting back the clock of scientific knowledge and industrial technique, run the risk of inducing social regression.[13]

Such a risk may perhaps be discounted when autarkic tendencies, particularly in small countries, consist primarily of defensive measures of protection from unduly sweeping economic and social changes imperiling national independence. The real danger comes when autarky becomes aggressive, rather than defensive, and extends far beyond the economic sphere. Not small, but great, countries, practicing not nationalism, but imperialism, and utilizing the whole armory of economic, political, and cultural weapons, are the centers of "regressive autarky" which, "in its extreme form, consists of monopolising and organising the whole national market by more and more systematic planning and by bureaucratic regimentation sustained by pitiless police power, while at the same time squeezing out a surplus of exports sufficient to enable its directors to procure essential raw materials from abroad, by barter or by clearing." [14]

The transition from defensive to aggressive autarky, which is possible only to a great power, has come, and could only come, as part of the preparation for renewed warfare. That preparation has, as ever, taken the traditional Shakesperian form.[15] It has been necessary not only "to stiffen the sinews" and "summon up the blood," but also to "disguise fair nature with hard-favoured rage." In modern terms this means propaganda, what a Swiss writer has called "cultural autarky," and particularly "autarky of the press," as well as economic mobilization.

[13] *Ibid.*, p. 18. "C'est de cette catastrophe historique que va renaître l'autarcie féodale que dura environ deux siècles, du IXe au XIe siècle: la navigation est morte, sauf dans la région de l'adriatique. Les marchands disparaissent et avec eux la vie urbaine; le mot de 'mercatores' lui-même a disparu, on ne trouve plus que l'expression de 'judaei.' L'Europe du VIIIe siècle est retombée dans un régime exclusivement agricole."
[14] Burky, etc., *op. cit.*, p. 21.
[15] *Henry V*, Act III, Scene I.

In the final analysis, therefore, the test of differentiation between autarkic systems that represent the passive defense of a cherished national culture, and the aggressive mobilization of economic power for national assertion and expansion, lies not in the economic, but in the political and psychological sphere. Discrimination is necessarily more marked in the latter than in the former. The most deadly of all imports to an authoritarian country are "dangerous thoughts." Autarky that strives to preserve national modes of existence without placing constraint upon the free expression of opinion, or free access to foreign ideas, is not likely to threaten the peace. But "if all free opinion is throttled, if all opposition has been suppressed, the masters of power no longer have resistance against which to buttress themselves; on the contrary they have every reason to mistrust the unknown and the inconstancy of popular prejudices with their moments of exaltation and brusque reversals. They know only the collective feeling that they themselves feel or that which is in sympathy with them: every test of collective psychology has ceased to exist. They have only one resource, to base themselves on the most general and primitive herd instincts, to nourish, cultivate and, if need be, lash them into excitement, and constantly to make theatrical appeal to them in an impressive setting of pomp. Demagoguery, from being a revolutionary instrument, becomes the ordinary procedure of government. Their action finds itself amplified by the immense loud-speaker they have themselves built and may equally well produce results that are akin to genius or absurd, useful or dangerous. The brakes being off, all that is left is a dynamism to which is forbidden any repose, any mature reflection or any halt. In the long run only two alternatives remain, triumph or catastrophe, at the sacrifice of everything that is normal and constructive in a truly enduring sense." [16]

The difficulty that arises for international relations when any country is possessed by such a driving psychology is that it cannot be arrested at the national frontiers. Like the great

[16] Burky, etc., *op. cit.*, p. 30.

POSSIBILITIES OF CO-OPERATION 167

landowner who always had the urge to acquire adjoining properties, the positive achievement of autarky demands the extension of complementary organization in neighboring territories. Full employment is succeeded by labor shortages that must be filled by adding to the population. Economic mobilization develops shortages of raw materials and the necessity for export markets that must be met by the conversion of economic activity in other lands into tributary streams that feed the insatiable needs of an accelerating nationalism. The national economy that is whipped into such acceleration must spin ever faster and faster since any loss of speed threatens loss of equilibrium.

The characteristic features of such economic systems are the characteristics of war economy. Indeed, the very definition of national economy, in the writings of those who advocate autarky as a principle, is identical with war economy.[17] It is, therefore, difficult to dissent from the conclusions of Professor de la Harpe that, in the modern sense, autarky comprises four essential attributes—an economic territory large enough to have a sufficiency of raw materials and food supplies; a State police organization powerful enough to impose planned direction upon the whole of economic life; an extremely powerful communal mysticism and a specific creed, albeit variable from one national group to another, assuring internal cohesion that is extremely strong and steady; and, finally, a "systematic preparation for war justifying the fundamental interest of an autarkic policy and economy and keeping the mind in a state of constant tension against a permanent enemy, an enemy who can be anonymous and not designated until a favourable moment and may even, at the right time, change his true incarnation." [18]

The Possibilities of Co-operation

In principle there is direct conflict between the two types of trading systems discussed in this chapter. They differ dia-

[17] Cf. citation in Burky, etc., *op. cit.*, p. 28.
[18] Burky, etc., *op. cit.*, p. 29.

metrically at every important point. The type that may, for convenience, be called "unregulated" endeavors to revive and extend private trading enterprise by assuring equality of trading opportunity. It tolerates, but endeavors to reduce, tariff barriers and seeks to discourage the use of quantitative and still more of monetary trade restrictions. Above all, it insists upon the elimination of discriminatory practices so that trade may be conducted by price bargaining, and noneconomic considerations may be reduced to a minimum. The clearest and most consistent policy of this type followed by any country in recent years has been that of the United States.

American policy, however, labors under the obvious handicap of working from a high and wide tariff. Although, in the twenty-one agreements so far concluded under the Reciprocal Trade Treaty program, there have been extensive concessions, those concessions have been made from the schedules of the extremely high Hawley-Smoot tariff. It is difficult as yet to judge whether, in the process of reciprocal bargaining, the concessions made by the United States have, on balance, been greater than those made by other governments. The trend of trade in recent years appears to indicate that this has been the case; but, even before the present war offered new opportunities to United States exports and crippled the export trade of the belligerents, the United States continued to have an active balance of commodity trade. This fact, in itself, made it difficult to extend the trade treaty program, since the United States was not able to use its buying power to force other countries to make concessions, and was not willing to accept greatly increased quantities of the only kind of imports that many countries were able to offer.

Moreover, the already complicated and extensive tariff schedules have been further complicated by the subdivision, reclassification, and redefinition of items so as to preserve the literal application of most-favored-nation treatment while limiting its effective scope. There can be cited numerous instances where concessions to a particular country have been generalized by most-favored-nation treatment to the advan-

POSSIBILITIES OF CO-OPERATION 169

tage of third parties; but such generalization has not been as important a factor in promoting imports to the United States as it might have been if there had not been such an amount of tariff elaboration.

At various times also, the action of other departments has not appeared to be thoroughly consistent with the principles upon which the trade agreement policy was based. There was a period, for example, when Treasury rulings permitted trade with Germany by practices difficult to distinguish from those to which the United States objected in Germany's trade with other countries.[19] Export subsidies, for example, on cotton, and the negotiation of barter transactions with the United Kingdom, whereby cotton was exchanged against rubber, would also seem to be similar in character to the subsidies and compensatory trade which the United States has found objectionable in other countries. Reference has already been made to the negotiation by private textile interests of voluntary quotas upon Japanese textile exports. Neutrality legislation, and official suggestions for "moral embargoes" upon the export of war materials in particular cases, have introduced political elements into the conduct of international trade which are not strictly consistent with reliance on market mechanisms and equality of trading opportunity.

When all these qualifications have been given their full weight, it still remains true that there is a clear conflict of principle between the American type of trading policy and that which is best typified in German trading practice. In the latter, private enterprise is supervised by detailed government regulation, tariffs are less important than quantitative and monetary restrictions, and equality of trading opportunity has given place to frankly discriminatory bargaining so that direction of trade has passed into the hands of government officials who negotiate specific transactions by manipulating prices, subsidies, tariffs, quota allocations, exchange allocations, and exchange rates. The contrast between the two systems is indeed so great that it becomes doubtful

[19] Cf. Tasca, *World Trading Systems*, pp. 36–41.

whether ways and means can be found to facilitate trade between them.

The experience of the two protagonists in this conflict of principles is not very encouraging. Almost as soon as Germany embarked upon its new policy it gave notice (on October 13, 1934) to abrogate its trade treaty with the United States. When the abrogation took effect, the United States found that German exports were being subsidized and imports strictly controlled. Germany was, therefore, denied most-favored-nation treatment and has not participated in the tariff reductions generalized by most-favored-nation treatment as the reciprocal trade treaty program developed. In addition, German imports were penalized by heavy countervailing duties, over and above the general tariff, in order to neutralize the effects of subsidies. Though for a brief period Treasury rulings permitted the use of blocked accounts in such a way as to be equivalent to export subsidies, countervailing duties were reimposed on March 23, 1939. The stringent application of legal provisions regarding the marking of imports also rendered more effective a growing disposition on the part of American consumers to boycott German goods.[20] On the other side, Germany has increasingly diverted purchases from the United States to countries where advantage could be taken of clearing arrangements. It is not surprising therefore that, even before the war shut Germany off from the American market, trade between the two countries fell heavily.

Finally, it may be remarked, no basis has been found for the negotiation of a reciprocal trade treaty with Germany. Though in August, 1938 a responsible German official made a public suggestion that such negotiations would be welcome, the reply of the Secretary of State, when asked at his press conference to comment on the suggestion, was uncompromising. Mr. Hull was reported to have said that "he would naturally be glad to find a basis for increasing our trade with Germany, and that a great deal of study had been given to that matter during the past few years. The system under which

[20] Cf. Bidwell, *op. cit.*, pp. 70 ff.

POSSIBILITIES OF CO-OPERATION 171

Germany operates, however, is bilateralism and barter. Not only is this contrary to the principles upon which the United States is making its agreements, but, upon the basis of past experience, bilateralism results in a balance of trade at a lower and not at a higher figure, and hence does not increase world trade. Therefore, the Secretary continued, as sympathetic as this country is to increasing its trade with Germany, it has been, up to now, difficult to find a basis for a trade agreement." [21]

Agreements have been negotiated, however, with other countries that in fact have utilized, and still utilize, quantitative and even monetary restrictions. This fact, and the reported wording of Mr. Hull's reply, laying emphasis on "the system which Germany operates," support the argument of the preceding sections of this chapter which distinguished between the actual use of the new protective devices and the spirit and purpose in which those devices are used. It has not proved impossible, though the actual arrangements made have not always been very satisfactory or fruitful of results, to find ways and means of facilitating trade between regulated and unregulated countries.

The actual expedients adopted have been examined in detail by Dr. Henry J. Tasca. It is not necessary here to recapitulate his summary of American experience in this respect. Attention may be drawn, however, to the emphasis he lays upon the many ways in which formulas drawn up to ensure fair treatment for American exports in return for tariff concessions by the United States may be evaded by a government which is prepared to utilize a flexible system of trading control for that purpose. Where the arrangements agreed upon have worked satisfactorily, they have done so by the good faith and good will of the government concerned. The conclusion to be drawn would appear to be that it is not impossible, given the will, to expand trade and to administer quantitative restrictions fairly between competing countries. Transitional methods can be found to expand trade between nonregulated

[21] Tasca, *op. cit.*, p. 42.

countries and those which have adopted quantitative import controls reluctantly. It is more difficult to discover such devices when the effective instrument of trade regulation is exchange control, and at this point the United States has had to accept less success, greater compromises of principle, and even emphasis on quantitative regulation as a lesser evil.

Moreover, while the experience so far gained goes to show that such transitional devices are not wholly ineffective at a rather early stage in the evolution of the new protectionism, they rapidly lose touch with any real basis of competitive trade and degenerate into stereotyped bilateral arrangements of an arbitrary character. Dr. Tasca's final conclusion, therefore, is that "the principle of equality of treatment as the cornerstone of commercial policy cannot be satisfactorily applied to trade with regulated countries. As time passes, any devices which have so far been conceived become more and more arbitrary, until completely devoid of meaning in terms of equality of treatment. There appears to be no method by which exports of the unregulated country can be accorded treatment on the part of the regulated economy which bears even an approximate relation to the basic competitive positions of the different supplying countries. Nor is this surprising, for under close regulation through State interventionism the forces determining the origin of imports are subordinated to the various aims of the national economy, which may be completely divorced from market considerations. The principle of equality of treatment by its very nature cannot function where market forces and private initiative are suppressed." [22]

What does remain is the possibility of *ad hoc* trading bargains between private traders in unregulated countries and State trading monopolies or the officials controlling regulated trading systems. The United States has had a somewhat disappointing experience with attempts to develop such trade with the U. S. S. R. The agreements under which trade was attempted were frankly reciprocal bargains in the nature of

[22] Tasca, *op. cit.*, p. 159.

POSSIBILITIES OF CO-OPERATION 173

barter transactions. Some increase in bilateral trade resulted, but whether this increased the aggregate of world trade cannot be determined. Nor does it point to any likelihood of regular trade based upon agreements which will offer the opportunity of rebuilding a system of equal opportunity and drawing the U. S. S. R. into closer multilateral trading connections with an expanding system of world trade. In negotiations with trading monopolies in respect of particular commodities in other countries, the United States has been able to procure the assurance of fair treatment by the allocation of percentual or absolute quotas of imports. The effect of all such arrangements, however, is to secure fair treatment for United States exporters in a restrictive system rather than to achieve the larger objects of the American program—an expansion of world trade and the restoration of free trading enterprise.

The experience of the United States has been cited because its policy at the moment is the most outstanding example of a policy based essentially upon equality of trading opportunity. Other countries which, until war came in September, 1939, maintained adherence to that principle as expressed in the unconditional form of the most-favored-nation clause in commercial treaties, have made various compromises in their relations with countries of regulated trade. For many of the smaller countries, whose economic activity was dependent in large measure upon a continuance of trade with powerful neighbors whose trade was conducted upon a bilateral barter basis, there was no option but to adopt complementary methods. Thus, Switzerland denounced the most-favored-nation principle at an early stage and proceeded to make the best bargains she could by reciprocal treaties and later by clearing arrangements. Czechoslovakia was forced into exchange control largely because so many of the countries with which her trade was conducted had already adopted it, so that the only possibility of collecting arrears of commercial debts and payment for current exports was by clearing arrangements. The freer trading initiative launched by Belgium and Holland at

Ouchy in July, 1932, and the negotiations of the Oslo group of Scandinavian countries, depended for any prospect of success upon the assent of the larger trading countries to modification of the most-favored-nation principle—assent that was not forthcoming. Practically all of the smaller European countries, however, and many in Latin America, were forced to enter into bilateral arrangements and to adopt quantitative or monetary restrictions, or both, that were contrary to the principle of trading equality.

Great Britain also has made many compromises in its trading arrangements with the regulated countries, and particularly with Germany. It continues to adhere strictly to the unconditional application of most-favored-nation treatment in its own policy, and, at least till war broke out, conducted its limited quantitative restrictions on agricultural imports by the same principle. This fact, together with the recognition by the United States of imperial preference as a special arrangement compatible with most-favored-nation treatment, made it possible to negotiate the Anglo-American trade treaty of 1938. The British bilateral treaty policy that followed the conclusion of the Ottawa treaties in 1932 entailed, however, concessions, particularly from the Scandinavian and Baltic countries, and also from the Argentine, that placed those countries in the position of infringing the principle of equality of trading opportunity. In the negotiation of these agreements, and also of the clearing agreements made with exchange-control countries, Britain made effective use of the bargaining power of her great market. Unlike the United States, she had large passive import balances with these countries, a fact which enabled her to obtain considerable concessions at the cost of guaranteeing continued access to her markets.

The intricate detail of these British bilateral negotiations, together with the criticisms leveled against British policy particularly by American experts, have been analyzed by Dr. Tasca in the work already cited. His conclusion may perhaps be quoted, though it would be tedious and misleading to summarize the careful detail in which he has discussed the problem.

"The British Government has, then, used to the hilt its enormous bargaining power to secure preferential and trade canalizing agreements. The meaning of the most-favoured-nation principle in British commercial policy has undergone a peculiar transformation in recent years. Time and again in recent years, the British authorities have officially approved the most-favoured-nation clause, yet, as this study has demonstrated, Great Britain has done violence to the principle of which that clause is an embodiment. If the British concept of most-favoured-nation relations can be compressed into a single statement, it would be that they are willing to grant equality of treatment in the British market for something more, in some cases a great deal more, in return as regards their exports.

"A real conflict exists between the commercial policy systems of the United States and Great Britain. British bilateralism must seriously impede the efforts of the United States to promote multilateral trade upon the basis of non-discrimination. This obstruction results from the destruction of the multilateral system which the British agreements aggravate, and the difficulties which they offer to the American trade agreements programme itself. The United States, by the very nature of its trade policy, cannot negotiate a trade agreement with a country already bound to accord wide preferential treatment to the United Kingdom. Such countries as Argentina, Denmark and the three Baltic countries, for example, can hardly undertake to grant American products equality of treatment when they are under heavy pressure from the United Kingdom to accord products of the latter country preferential treatment in line with the principle of bilateral trade balancing." [23]

The emphasis thus laid upon the British trend to bilateralism since the adoption in 1931 of protective tariff policies is

[23] Tasca, *op. cit.*, pp. 151–152.

borne out by statistical analysis and measurement of bilateral tendencies.[24]

The conclusion to be drawn from mature consideration of this whole problem of the relations between regulated and unregulated trading systems, therefore, can hardly differ from the view expressed by Dr. Tasca,[25] that "it is becoming ever clearer that the world is dividing up into sharply defined commercial policy blocs under the influence of the great commercial Powers. In the absence of political upheaval, the question of reconciliation between these blocs must develop an increasing importance and concern for the nations of the world. The American, British and German systems of commercial policy differ greatly in their aims and methods. But the sharpest distinction appears between the policies of the United States and Germany. Britain's policy appears to be midway between these two with the German system exerting a strong pull in its direction. It is believed that the success or failure of American policy will exercise a profound influence upon the future of the British system. This will in turn be conditioned, in part, by the presence or absence of British collaboration."

Since these lines were written, war has driven British policy into exchange control and retrenchment within the economic resources of the empire and the countries within the sterling area. Long strides have been taken in the direction of regulated trade; but there is still the possibility expressed by Professor Charles Rist before France was defeated and Anglo-French collaboration came to an end that "the end of the war will mean the end of autarky, if we win. For the moment our Franco-British collaboration is only a pooling of resources for the war, but it can, of course, be used as a nucleus for after the war, tending towards a lowering of tariff barriers which would automatically extend to all countries through the working of the most-favored-nation clause. Diminishing

---

[24] Albert Hirschmann, *Etude statistique sur la tendance du commerce extérieur vers l'equilibre et le bilateralisme.*
[25] Tasca, *op. cit.*, p. 165.

POSSIBILITIES OF CO-OPERATION 177

of trade barriers, after the war, will be the only way for the world to recover from its wounds." [26]

Before such a possibility can be envisaged, even as a distant and none too certain hope, some consideration must be given both to the strategy of bilateralism and to the problem of regionalism. The following chapters are devoted to an examination in somewhat more detail of the practices of the new mercantilism and their regional aspects.

[26] The New York *Times Magazine,* March 31, 1940, p. 23.

CHAPTER V

The Complication of Tariffs

The Importance of Tariff Barriers

IT IS not proposed, in this and the following chapters, to attempt an exhaustive summary of tariff developments and the administrative elaboration of the new protectionism. Such a summary would be laborious and confusing rather than illuminating. What is attempted here is rather an analysis of the political implications of these developments. Illustrations are drawn from the experience of particular countries as they seem pertinent. For fuller detail reference should be made to the documents cited in the appendix or to official publications.[1]

The first point to be made is that the time-honored method of trade regulation by customs tariffs still remains an important factor in commercial relations. In many countries, particularly on the continent of Europe, its importance, even before war broke out, had come to be overshadowed by the newer and more directly effective methods of trade regulation such as quotas and exchange control. These newer methods had also penetrated rather deeply into the trading systems of countries outside Europe. Nevertheless, until the European war began again in September, 1939, the greater part of the trading world was regulated by tariffs rather than quotas. The United States, the British Commonwealth and Empire, and

---

[1] Cf., e. g., the excellent annual statements prepared by Dr. Henry Chalmers for the U. S. Department of Commerce, under the title "Foreign Tariffs and Commercial Policies"; or successive numbers of the League of Nations *World Economic Survey*.

most of Latin America were still working mainly under a tariff system. The evolution of their tariff policies was not a negligible factor in international economic relations.

Even where, after 1931, quantitative and monetary trade restrictions were paramount, tariffs were intimately linked with the new controls and stood at inordinately high levels. In the years before 1931, chief reliance was in fact placed upon tariff protection as a means of regulating imports. Though no longer the chief instruments of trade restriction in the exchange-control countries, tariffs remain formidable barriers to any resumption of normal trade. While any attempt at trade revival must, by common consent, begin with a relaxation of the new discriminatory trade controls, such an attempt would quickly encounter the fact that tariffs at their present levels, and in their present complexity, are formidable obstacles. It is not sufficient, therefore, to concentrate attention upon exchange-control and quota systems. Still less is it practical to contemplate the replacement of such controls by consolidated and heightened tariff barriers. If ever trade is to flow more freely, tariffs must come down too.

The experience of the years that followed the war of 1914–18 is, unfortunately, again relevant in any discussion of the immediate future. When that war ended, there was a complication of trade controls, but in the first months and years of acute shortages and rapidly deteriorating currencies, import barriers were not of primary concern. The immediate and urgent need was to conserve and replenish such national stocks of food and raw materials as remained. Prohibitions and licensing arrangements were directed at imports of luxury articles—and the definition of "luxury" proved very elastic—but they were directed also at exports of necessities. The receipts from export duties in Bulgaria in the fiscal year 1920–21 were greater than those from import duties.[2] Export controls

[2] C. Bobtcheff, *Memorandum sur la politique commerciale extérieure de la Bulgarie après la guerre*, p. 19. "Il est à remarquer que durant l'année financière 1920–21 le fisc a touché plus des droits d'exportation que des droits d'importation (219 millions contre 171 millions)."

remained important until the brief period of monetary stabilization began about 1925, and vestiges of them remained until the imposition of exchange controls in 1931 initiated an intensified struggle for export markets.[3] The interest of this phenomenon lies in the fact that it may be repeated. Even before the present war began, German trade negotiators had discovered that exchange-rates could be manipulated so as to conserve exports and increase imports, a technique now urged upon other belligerents.[4] It is at least possible that, when hostilities end, the imperative need of imported goods in most European countries will lead to slackened tariff barriers and relatively high exchange-rates despite a weak currency position and high domestic prices. Imports encouraged in this way cannot be paid for by exports, and the only result must be an aggravation of international disequilibrium since it is the neutral countries, and particularly the United States, that should lower their tariffs and appreciate their exchange-rates even while their domestic price-levels should be rising. These are contradictory phenomena made possible only by credit expansion; but if the contradiction appears in the form of rising prices, high exchanges, and heavy imports into the borrowing countries, it will be fatal to any hopes of restoring equilibrium.

A second lesson to be drawn from the experience of the last postwar period is that, apart altogether from the follies of exaggerated nationalism in newly created States, there is inevitably a period during which the regrouping of economic factors within new boundaries leads to confusion and uncertainty of tariff policy. This is very well illustrated by the immediate postwar reorganization of such countries as Hungary,

[3] *Ibid.*, p. 18. Cf. also Wolfgang Heller, *Hungarian Economic Policy*, p. 10; E. Taylor, *La Répercussion des difficultés monétaires sur la politique extérieure de la Pologne*, pp. 8–9; M. Tuveng, *External Economic Policy of Norway in Recent Years*, p. 13; S. D. Obradovic, *La Politique commerciale de la Yougoslavie*, pp. 11–13.

[4] Cf. T. Balogh, "Foreign Exchange and Export Control Policy," *Economic Journal* (March, 1940), p. 18.

Turkey, and Yugoslavia.[5] In the latter country, for example, the first definite postwar tariff could not be formulated till 1925. Up till then the whole situation was fluid and handled by *ad hoc* administrative methods. In all the smaller European countries, as soon as the period of inflation, uncertainty, and reorganization was passed, an effort was made to establish definite tariff arrangements, to adopt most-favored-nation treatment, to abandon emergency exchange controls, prohibitions and licensing systems, and as far as possible to follow liberal tariff policies. Only the more stable of these countries, however, mainly the neutrals of the last war—a melancholy list in the light of recent events—Denmark, Norway, Sweden, Belgium, Holland, and Switzerland, were able to follow moderate tariff policies. Finland should perhaps be added to this list.[6] In the other small countries of Europe a desperate need for revenue and the desire for rapid national consolidation resulted inevitably in high tariff levels. The attempts at measuring these levels are well known and need not be summarized here.[7] It is of some interest, however, to note that the revenue problem was an important factor in the formation of these high tariffs.[8] Protection of local industries, or the promotion

[5] Cf. Heller, *op. cit.*, Ch. I; H. A. Kuyucak, *Exchange Control in Turkey*, Chs. I–II; and S. D. Obradovic, *op. cit.*, p. 10. "L'adaptation nécessaire des différentes régions yougoslaves aux besoins de la nouvelle communauté économique fut compliquée par la nécessité de faire face aux troubles monétaires, économiques et sociaux dûs à la guerre et de réparer les dégats materiels énormes dans ce pays, qui, pour autant qu'il ne servait pas de champs de bataille, se trouvait dans la zone de guerre."

[6] Cf. H. P. Gøtrik, *Danish Economic Policy;* M. Tuveng, *op. cit.;* G. Boos, *Survey of Sweden's External Economic Policy;* J. Jussiant, *L'Evolution du commerce extérieure de la Belgique;* Ch. Burky, etc., *La Suisse et l'autarcie;* T. Voionmaa, *Finnish Commercial Policy;* P. Lieftinck, *External Economic Policy of the Kingdom of the Netherlands.*

[7] Cf. League of Nations, *Tariff Level Indices* (Geneva, 1927); and H. Liepmann, *Tariff Levels and the Economic Unity of Europe.*

[8] Cf., e. g., Bobtcheff, *op. cit.*, pp. 25–26. "Ainsi nous pouvons dire que le facteur fiscal dominait la politique extérieure du pays jusqu'en 1931. . . . A partir de 1931 le facteur fiscal cède la primauté au facteur des devises, mais malgré cela il joue encore un grand rôle et reussit a faire découvrir des sources de revenus aussi dans les mesures de devises prises par l'Etat."

of new industrial development, was a factor also, and the necessity of safeguarding exchange stability was always present; but a detached observer cannot escape the feeling that the tariff policies of these little countries were forced upon them by the hopelessly uneconomic circumstances of their constitution or reconstitution after 1918.

In the smaller countries outside Europe there had been a considerable expansion both of agricultural production and of industrial development. India, Canada, Australia, and the Argentine are good examples, but the outstanding industrial development was that of Japan.[9] Even after the interwar boom gave way to sharp depression and a period of uncontrolled inflation in many European countries, there seemed to be an insatiable market for the expanded agricultural production of the world. There was need also for much capital equipment and, as long as credit expansion lasted, for manufactured consumer's goods. In 1919, and again from 1925 to 1929, the world market seemed big enough, despite tariffs and monetary strain, for the wheat growers of Australia, Canada, and the Argentine, as well as for those in the Danubian countries, and for the manufacturers of Japan as well as Germany. But an essential link was missing in the chain of transactions, the means of payment by the countries whose need for imports and for loans was most desperate. At the first onset of depression, the greatest creditor country in the world had sharply raised its already high tariff. The Fordney-McCumber tariff of 1922 was the first heavy blow directed against any hope of effectively restoring a world trading system. It was followed in 1924 by a drastic Immigration Restriction Act, which cooped up the surplus population of southeastern Europe and led immediately to an intensification of both agricultural and industrial protection in those countries. The restoration of tariff autonomy to the defeated countries was completed when

[9] Cf. Sir B. L. Mitter, *Indian Economic Policy;* H. L. Harris, *Australia's Economic Policy;* J. F. Parkinson, *The Bases of Canadian Commercial Policy;* Angel Valle et Juan M. Ferrer, *La Politique économique de l'Argentine;* Tetsuji Kada, *Social and Economic Factors determining Japan's External Economic Policy.*

IMPORTANCE OF TARIFF BARRIERS

Germany regained control of its tariff in 1925 and immediately proceeded to raise duties on agricultural imports.[10]

During the next few years, despite the apparent progress made in the stabilization of currencies and the mitigation or abolition of many postwar obstacles to trade, such as import and export prohibitions and licensing systems, exchange-controls, emergency customs duties, excises, primage, exchange-taxes, and statistical dues, there was a consolidation of tariffs. In many instances the consolidated rates appeared to be, and were, less restrictive of trade than the confusion of protective and revenue devices which they replaced; but they were consolidated at high levels. Even though trade increased very fast—faster even than national production—under the impulse of expanding credit and a great volume of international lending, there was increasing realization after 1925 of the fundamentally precarious nature of the monetary and trading equilibrium that had been restored. The credit expansion upon which the increase of trade was based made it possible for the borrowing countries to receive large imports, both of consumer's goods and of capital equipment, payment for which was made in the meantime by using the foreign exchange accruing from loans. When the credit expansion, and with it international investment, ceased abruptly towards the end of 1929, banking accommodation filled the breach for a few months. Little progress had been made meantime in the efforts to break down tariff barriers so that an increasing flow of trade could provide the foreign exchange with which to pay for current imports and interest on the loans that had been contracted.[11] In default of such means of payment there ensued a violent contraction of imports to the debtor countries. Prices fell heavily and international trade was greatly reduced. Interest payments were suspended and eventually a large proportion of the debts contracted during the interwar period fell into default.

[10] Cf. also Bobtcheff, *op. cit.*, p. 1; Heller, *op. cit.*, pp. 6 and 17 ff.
[11] W. Rappard, *Post-War Efforts for Freer Trade*, Geneva Studies (March, 1938), Vol. IX, No. 2.

184 THE COMPLICATION OF TARIFFS

It was in an effort to avert just such catastrophes that strenuous attempts were made in the period of prosperity to break down the barriers to international trade. The remarkable assemblage of businessmen, bankers, economists, and statesmen who were assembled at Geneva for the World Economic Conference of 1927 laid down the strategy, but lacked the power, of effective attack upon these trade barriers. Expert opinion might agree on the measures to be taken, but governments did not take them. The British Government, still clinging to free-trade principles, led a vain struggle for a tariff truce and the Oslo group was formed largely to support its initiative. There was, however, little abatement of economic nationalism elsewhere. Germany, still weak and pursuing an uphill task of reconstruction, stiffened its tariffs. France, having finally stabilized its currency, began to rebuild its gold reserves. The newer manufacturing countries outside Europe fought to preserve their home markets. Most important of all, the United States tariff wall remained impregnable. When the second interwar depression broke precipitously in October, 1929, the United States again raised its tariff, this time to levels that proved disastrous. The Hawley-Smoot tariff of 1930 was a fatal blow to any remaining hope of international economic equilibrium. It was followed almost immediately by a crop of tariff increases in other countries.[12] In some cases the reprisal motive was very strong. In others there was a strong defensive reaction against the loss of export markets and the fear of enhanced import competition.

It is perhaps significant that the most overt reprisals against the Hawley-Smoot tariff were taken by Canada, which felt its impact most directly.[13] So seriously were its effects viewed, that the leader of the Conservative Opposition suggested keeping Parliament in session while Congress was considering the bill, in order to enact measures of retaliation.[14] There was

---

[12] Cf. League of Nations, *World Economic Survey, 1931–32* (Geneva, 1932), p. 281.
[13] J. F. Parkinson, *op. cit.*, Ch. V.
[14] *Ibid.*, p. 104.

a general election in Canada in 1930 and the tariff situation was a major issue. The leader of the Conservative Opposition became Prime Minister and Canada embarked on a high protective policy. One curious illustration of the way in which trade barriers cause unexpected repercussions and reprisals is worth citing in this connection.

"In 1925," writes Mr. Parkinson, "the special concessions given (by Canada) to Australia in the trade agreement of that year were extended also to New Zealand. Under the agreement, New Zealand butter was therefore charged only a nominal duty of one cent per pound, and in subsequent years a large export trade to Canada in butter was built up. Canada, herself an exporter of dairy products, exported butter, milk and cream across the boundary to the United States. With the erection of prohibitive barriers against such imports by the United States in 1930, the dairymen of Canada lost an important market. At the same time New Zealand butter, also excluded from the United States, was imported into Canada in larger quantities and the price fell rapidly. The dairy farmers of the Prairie Provinces, Ontario and Quebec therefore protested the importation of New Zealand butter. Indeed this complaint was one of the principal issues in the general election of that year."

This illustration is typical of a whole series of trade diversions and protective reactions caused by the imposition of an important tariff. It is not suggested that the Hawley-Smoot tariff was the source of all evil in the commercial policies of the years after 1930. The same kind of illustration could be drawn from the tariff history of almost any country. But the United States was not only a big market; it was also the chief creditor country of the whole world. The Hawley-Smoot tariff is, therefore, a landmark in the disintegration of world trade.

The great reversal of British commercial policy in 1931–32 was another landmark, the historic importance of which has yet to be fully appreciated. No one would contend that it was a reprisal against the United States; but the Hawley-Smoot tariff facilitated both the adoption of protective tariffs in Great Britain and the negotiation at Ottawa of preferential agreements within the British Empire. It did so partly because it gave Canadian imperialists an opportunity they did not fail to accept, of launching a successful campaign for Canadian protection and Imperial reciprocity. Perhaps more important in the long run, it precipitated a series of tariff reprisals in many countries, the ultimate result of which was a canalizing of world export surpluses upon the few remaining free-trade markets. What happened in the case of New Zealand butter exported in larger quantities at lower prices to Canada was repeated in almost infinite variety with other products elsewhere. The New Zealand butter, shut out of Canada, went to Britain, and so did the growing surpluses of many other commodities from many countries. These were the years in which all creditor countries, except the United States, found themselves with mounting import balances, the result of desperate efforts by the exporting debtor countries to discharge their obligations. Such massive import balances alarmed public opinion nearly everywhere as prices fell precipitately and unemployment spread.[15] Tariffs were raised and new means of import restrictions devised, but the flood mounted and was increasingly canalized towards the few free-trade countries. All of them—the Scandinavian group, Holland, Belgium, Switzerland, and Great Britain—were driven to protectionist measures.

The process by which Great Britain imposed emergency tariffs in 1931 and 1932, created an Import Duties Advisory Committee, and rather quickly evolved a tariff of substantial proportions supplemented by agricultural import quotas, is

[15] Cf. René Hoffherr, *La Politique commerciale de la France,* pp. 16–17. "C'est précisément le déficit de la balance générale du commerce français qui constitue le signe le plus apparent des perturbations actuelles de notre politique commerciale. Aux yeux du public, ce deficit, qui atteint près de 16 milliards de francs in 1937, prend figure de symbole menaçant. Il surgit avec une obsession de fantôme de toutes les études, de toutes les conversations. C'est lui le pelé, le galeux d'où vient tout le mal."

IMPORTANCE OF TARIFF BARRIERS 187

well known and rather quickly summarized.[16] The economic effects and historical importance of these measures, together with the abandonment of the gold standard, the restrictions imposed on international lending, bilateral treaty negotiations and private compensation agreements, clearing and payments agreements, and a long list of State interventions in various fields of international economic relations,[17] are as yet difficult to grasp in their entirety. It is evident that in a very short space of time Great Britain changed from a free-trade organ-

[16] Cf. *Memorandum on British External Economic Policy in Recent Years* and *Supplement*, prepared by a Study-Group of the British Coordinating Committee for International Studies, 1939.

[17] British Coordinating Committee, *op. cit.*, Part II. The title page listing various administrative organs for the regulation of external economic policy contains the following:
  A. Financial Policy
  B. Commercial Policy
    (i) General Tariff Administration
      a) Protective Duties and the Import Duties Advisory Committee
      b) Retaliatory Duties
      c) Revenue Duties
      d) Merchandise Marks Acts
    (ii) Statutory Quotas
      a) In connection with Marketing Schemes
      b) Under Ottawa Agreements Act
      c) Under Sea Fishing Industry Act
      d) Dyestuffs
      e) Importation of Cinematograph Films
      f) Admission of Aliens
    (iii) Processing Duties
      a) Wheat Act
      b) Empire Cotton Growing Corporation
    (iv) "Voluntary" Administrative Machinery
      a) "Voluntary" Quantitative Restriction of Imports
      b) "Voluntary" Action by Cartels
      c) "Voluntary" co-operation in Statutory Import Quotas
    (v) Administration of Government Subsidies
      a) North Atlantic Shipping
      b) British Shipping (Assistance) Act, 1935
    (vi) Developing Trade Relations
      a) Credits for Export
      b) Department of Overseas Trade
      c) Marketing Schemes
    (vii) Administrative Protection

ization, the center of a world trading system, to a highly developed protectionist and bilateral bargaining policy. Even before the present war began, very large compromises had been made with the new systems of totalitarian trade restriction, many of the expedients of which had been adopted.

The immediate effects of this abrupt reversal of British policy were far-reaching. It was a decisive factor in the widespread adoption of exchange control, the raising of tariffs, and the adoption of quantitative trade restrictions and regulated national economic systems. It threw the smaller manufacturing countries of Europe, as well as agricultural-exporting countries the world over, into something approaching consternation. The longer-run effects deriving from the collapse of the world trading system that had rested upon sterling for over a century cannot yet be assessed. The decisions of 1931–32, it is becoming clear, marked the end of an era not only for Great Britain itself, but for the rest of the world. Nineteenth-century concepts of monetary stability, of international specialization and co-operation, and of the relations between politics and economics, were revealed as no longer operative or adequate. The end of the story cannot yet be foreseen, but the significance of these historic events does not diminish as the passing years reveal the amplitude of their repercussions.

The remainder of the narrative of the years between the wars is not concerned primarily with tariff developments. The British tariff and its immediate consequences ushered in a period when more direct and drastic forms of economic regulation became widespread. After the collapse of the Monetary and Economic Conference of 1933, preceded as it was by the breakdown of disarmament negotiations and by the accession to power of the National Socialist party in Germany, the whole of Europe began to look to its defenses. Trade restrictions were multiplied and quickly took the form of positive policies dominated by war preparations. The unsuccessful attempt of member-states of the League of Nations to restrain Italy from reaping the fruits of its invasion of Ethiopia brought swift reinforcement of autarkic policies. Only in the United States, where Mr. Hull painstakingly pursued his policy of bargaining tariffs down, was there real conviction that multilateral trade regulated only by moderate tariffs could, and should, be restored. After long and discouraging negotiations the American policy scored its most spectacular, if not greatest, success in the treaty signed with Great Britain on November 17, 1938. That treaty did something to reduce duties on both sides and to modify the imperialist bargains struck at Ottawa. It took Great Britain back a step towards the traditions of free trade that had been the foundation of its former prosperity. But it was too late. Within little more than a year the catastrophe fell and plans for international economic co-operation became a mockery in a world at war.

Modern Tariff Methods

Before giving some illustrations of the way in which recent tariff policy in most countries has been directed towards the elaboration of flexible tariff schedules, it is well to reflect that a high degree of administrative complexity is not necessarily proof of efficiency. The new systems of trade regulation are new only in the sense that they have adapted old devices to modern monetary and administrative conditions in what is essentially a reversion to trade practices more primitive than the multilateral trade characteristic of the prewar period. The ideas that lie behind the most recent trade policies are very old. Over most of them might well be written the seventeenth-century precept: "We must ever observe this rule: to sell more to strangers yearly than we buy of theirs in value." [18] The persistence of certain broad general notions, such as the desire for "a favorable balance of trade," is well recognized.[19] The

[18] Thomas Mun, *England's Treasure by Forraign Trade* (London, 1664).
[19] Cf., e. g., the long discussion of "Mercantilism as a Monetary System" in Eli F. Hecksher, *Mercantilism* (London, 1935), Vol. II, Part IV, with J. M. Keynes's "Notes on Mercantilism" in *The General Theory of Employment, Interest and Money* (London, 1936). Cf. also Hecksher's discussion of "The Policy of Provision," Vol. I (Part III, Ch. III), with export policies after the war of 1914–18.

setting is new, but the ideas are old. Modern governments regulate the balance of trade by credit controls where their Mercantilist predecessors were concerned with the precious metals. Highly elaborated bargaining tariffs are a more formal means of achieving essentially the same results as the variable, discriminatory, and opportunist use of import duties achieved centuries ago.

The specific devices now used to regulate trade are often streamlined versions of old practices. Prohibitions, quotas, export monopolies and duties, and bilateral bargaining are notions that occurred to administrators long ago. Indeed, the degree to which modern practice has enhanced the discretionary power of officials is in itself a striking illustration of the reversion to medieval ideas. The very expression "customs duties" denoting, as Adam Smith observed, "customary payments that have been in use from time immemorial," [20] recalls the struggle of merchants to pin their rulers to traditional and stable rates of taxation. The complication of tariffs in recent years and the increasing use of supplementary administrative devices to regulate trade represent a check to the steady progress made during the nineteenth century towards simple, known, and relatively stable trade regulations. The ingenuity of modern tariffs and the complications of tariff bargaining ought not to blind anyone to the fact that they represent a change from the agreed to the arbitrary, from the known to the uncertain, from the economic to the political regulation of trade. It is not the only field in which there has been a reversion to tyrannical methods of government, but it is not the least important.

The first important change to be noted is the almost universal adoption of "three-decker," or multiple tariffs. The actual title of the schedules varies from country to country; but in general they represent a penal list of duties, an intermediate list, and a preferential schedule or schedules, varying from

[20] Cf. Palgrave, *Dictionary of Political Economy*, Vol. I, article: "Custom —customs duties" for early instances of import duties superimposed on the customary rates.

time to time with the commercial treaties in force. Not only does the possession of such a multiple tariff give scope for bargaining, which has often been enlarged by the temporary enactment of higher rates on particular goods before the opening of trade negotiations. It also increases the administrative obstacles to trade by making it necessary to secure evidence of the origin of goods eligible for preferential rates. Moreover, it offers a rather obvious temptation to combine preferential advantages with protection of home industries by increasing the intermediate, rather than by lowering the preferential, rates. The United States may be cited as an example of the abandonment of "its traditional single column autonomous tariff system." [21] By the Trade Agreements Act of 1934 "a multiple schedule tariff was to be expected. The non-generalization of tariff reductions accorded in the reciprocal trade agreements . . . meant the maintenance of the general, or Hawley-Smoot, rates against certain countries. Further, the placing of Cuba within a special category creates, in a sense, a limited third column of tariff duties." [22]

Another illustration may be cited from British experience.[23] The long nineteenth-century process of simplification and reduction by which Great Britain finally achieved a single tariff of very few items, primarily designed for revenue purposes, was reversed in the interwar period. The adoption of protection and the subsequent negotiation of bilateral treaties brought into being an elaborate tariff with different schedules of rates according to the origin of imports in British countries, in countries with which bilateral concessions had been negotiated, or elsewhere. Many other illustrations could be cited, since the whole trend of tariff policy has been towards the elaboration of the tariff structure in order to give scope for trade bargaining. These cases have been cited because they illustrate the opposite possibilities of such tariff elaboration.

[21] H. J. Tasca, *The Reciprocal Trade Policy of the United States* (Philadelphia, 1938), p. 7.
[22] *Ibid.*, p. 42.
[23] *British External Economic Policy in Recent Years*, Part I, Chs. I and III.

The United States trading agreements have been used to make concessions from an already high tariff, and in so far as these concessions have been matched by concessions elsewhere and generalized by most-favored-nation treatment, the adoption of a "three-decker" has led to the lowering of tariff barriers. Before Great Britain could begin to follow this procedure a tariff had to be created from which concessions could be made, so that the complication of the British tariff has increased trade barriers. There is much evidence that the British rather than the American case is typical of general experience.

A second development to be noted is the strong tendency almost universally for tariff schedules to become longer and more minute in their definitions. Protection is particularized. This creates a very real administrative problem since the classification of imports becomes a highly technical and complicated procedure leading to much delay and increased cost. Simple broad categories of goods are divided into specific commodity groups, many of which are defined in terms that need expert interpretation and even laboratory tests. Apart, however, from such administrative effects, the minute classification of tariff items, and their reclassification in the course of bilateral bargaining, severely limits the scope of most-favored-nation treatment. Concessions are given on commodities that come chiefly from the other party to a reciprocal bargain and, if necessary, the tariff item is subdivided so as to make the concession specific. Thus, the United States can safely promise most-favored-nation treatment to "Cornwall building stone" originating in any country.

There has been, as will be pointed out in a later chapter, a subtle evolution in the character of commercial treaties and agreements by which tariff duties on certain items were formerly "bound" or "conventionalized" or "frozen." In prewar, and even predepression, practice, these agreements were normally the subjects of long negotiation and were entered into for a term of years. Normally they continued in force beyond their original term, subject always to a substantial period of notice before they could be denounced. Such semipermanent arrangements, generalized by most-favored-nation treatment, were a stabilizing factor in international economic relations. The American and British treaties follow this tradition; but the commercial agreements of most countries practicing the new devices of trade regulation are for periods as short as three months. The availability of preferential rates in continuous bargaining of this type makes possible what is virtually a discretionary tariff.

Another common development has been the creation of tariff commissions or equivalent bodies with power to recommend, or even to make, changes in tariff rates. Where, as in most of the continental European countries, tariffs have become linked with exchange control and quota systems, the degree of responsibility delegated to administrative bodies is necessarily considerable. This type of administrative action is best considered later.[24]

In countries where parliamentary institutions are still effective and tariffs are still the chief means of regulating trade, the functions of such bodies as the Import Duties Advisory Committee in Great Britain and the Tariff Commission and Trade Agreements Division of the State Department in the United States are less extensive. It is significant, however, that under the system of ministerial responsibility in Great Britain, the Import Duties Advisory Committee has less formal power, but appears in practice to have more real power, of tariff making than the comparable bodies in the United States. It can only recommend to the Treasury, which must issue orders that are laid on the table of the House.[25] Members may, if they wish, protest privately or challenge the Chancellor of the Exchequer in debate. In fact, it is improbable that a British government could be overturned on any particular tariff decision and while the House retains the right of criticism, the Chancellor, guided by his administrative officers, has effective power. As the variation of tariff duties on iron and steel bears witness, this power has been used to enforce cartelization and to assist

[24] See below, Ch. VIII.
[25] *British External Economic Policy in Recent Years*, Part II.

British participants in international cartel negotiations. It has also been used to build up a tariff of far more effective proportions than the modest 10 per cent basic duty imposed in the governing legislation.

The Tariff Commission of the United States is primarily a fact-finding and advisory body.[26] In the actual alteration of tariff rates its limited powers of recommendation are now far less important than the powers of actual negotiation delegated for a three-year period (renewed in 1937 and 1940) to the President by the Trade Agreements Act of 1934. This Act gives power to the Executive, after stipulated procedures, to negotiate reciprocal treaties involving concessions up to 50 per cent of existing duty rates on particular commodities. This is a specific delegation of power for a limited period. The procedures of public hearings stipulated under the Act give an opportunity for public ventilation of objections to proposed tariff reductions.[27] The differences between British and American practice arise from the fact that in the former an administrative body with little publicity is guided largely by evidence coming from business interests seeking additional protection, whereas in the latter an administrative body is empowered to carry out tariff reductions to which certain business interests object.

[26] Gayer and Schmidt, *American Economic Foreign Policy*, p. 45. "The Commission has described itself as 'an arm of Congress and the President for obtaining special types of information and for performing certain special work.' Specifically, it has the following legally defined activities, which are subject to change with each new tariff act or amendment, or under other laws dealing with foreign trade:
1. To investigate and report on tariff matters in general;
2. To co-operate with other governmental establishments;
3. To investigate and report to the President the difference in the cost of production of domestic commodities and like or similar foreign articles, and any necessary tariff changes to equalize these differences;
4. To investigate and report upon unfair trade practices in importation and sale of foreign merchandise;
5. To keep informed of discriminations against the foreign trade of the United States;
6. In conjunction with other government departments to inform and advise the President before the conclusion of foreign trade agreements."

[27] *Ibid.*, pp. 57–58.

From time to time in recent years, the exploded fallacy of a scientific tariff administered by a nonpolitical administrative body has been resurrected. The usual form of its resurrection is that tariffs should be adjusted to price differentials. If this could be done it would obviously kill all trade. An attempt was made at the Ottawa Conference to devise Tariff Commissions to regulate British and Dominion Tariffs and provision was made whereby representations from interested exporters could be made to the Commission in the importing country.[28] It should, however, be recognized that such commissions are, and ought to be, administrative devices for executing government policy. They cannot be, and ought not to be, bodies of independent authority, except where limited powers, strictly defined, are granted for a definite term and are subject to review. There is no cost, price, or other criterion on which they can build a "scientific tariff."

The Ottawa proposal, however, contains the germ of an idea that may come to have international importance. Essentially it is that the producers and merchants of many countries beyond the one in which tariff changes are proposed have a direct interest in such changes and ought to be heard in the matter. Even the Imperial Conference of the British Commonwealth, however, did not take the logical step of constituting an Imperial Tariff Commission to which proposed changes of national tariffs should be submitted for comment, if not for approval. Since the present war broke out, a suggestion has been made with increasing urgency that an International Tariff Commission should be created as an important part of any postwar settlement.[29] This suggestion is often correlated with proposals to extend the system of international cartels and establish some sort of international supervision over them.[30] Some of the aspects of such proposals are canvased in the final chapter of this volume. Here it is sufficient to point

[28] J. F. Parkinson, *op. cit.;* also W. S. Kelly, *The Australian Tariff*, pp. 11 ff.
[29] Cf. E. Staley, *World Economy in Transition*, pp. 225–334; Alfred M. Bingham, *The United States of Europe* (New York, 1940), Ch. IX; Raymond L. Buell, *Isolated America* (New York, 1940), Ch. XV.
[30] Cf. P. E. P., *Report on International Trade* (London, 1937).

out that recent developments in tariff mechanisms, whether correlated with quantitative and monetary trade controls or maintained as the chief instrument of trade regulation, have all been in the direction of greater complexity, flexibility, arbitrary application, and administrative discrimination. Inevitably, they have placed more power in the hands of government officials. The manner in which such power has been, or may be, used depends primarily upon the purposes of national governments, and the ability of public opinion to influence those purposes has, in most countries, been drastically curtailed. Since trade has become an instrument of national policy, it is inevitable that tariffs and other trade controls have been transformed into flexible means of manipulating such a powerful instrument.

The Invisible Tariff

Indirect, or administrative, protectionism has necessarily come more into use as governments have taken power to deal with emergency situations in a period of disturbed international relations. The devices used range from penal duties imposed in certain circumstances at the discretion of government officials to the use as measures of trade restriction of veterinary, health, quarantine, or similar restrictions imposed for specific purposes, or merely the literal application of the wide powers usually taken by governments to ensure adequate inspection, classification, statistical recording, or valuation of imports.

A preliminary caution is perhaps necessary in regard to this subject. In general, legislative draftsmen endeavor to foresee and provide against every conceivable contingency. Governments habitually take wider powers than it is necessary to use in practice. There is a well-recognized legal procedure by which, in most countries, such extensive powers are subsequently limited by judicial interpretations of the legislation. Any estimate of the effectiveness of such laws or regulations ought, therefore, to be made by investigation of the actual administrative practice followed in each country rather than by analysis of the powers granted by legislation.

The experience of recent years, however, is sufficient to show that wide powers, even if seldom used, can in an emergency become a potent instrument of trade regulation. If, for example, under the authority to impose antidumping duties contained in the United States customs legislation, an appraiser should notify the Customs Department that a particular shipment may be liable to such duties, his notification will be circulated as a matter of routine throughout the service. The result may well be that in every port shipments of similar goods may be held up or cleared only after bonds have been lodged or the extra duty deposited. The mere possibility that delays and extra charges may be incurred is often sufficient to cause cancellations of orders. The administrative discretion entrusted in this way to officials is very considerable. In normal times, a routine tends to be set up, regulations are interpreted liberally rather than literally, and there is a good deal of sampling or acceptance of verbal or written statements. Most customs (or other) systems would in fact be unworkable if all official instructions and regulations were literally executed. The more complicated tariff formalities become, however, and the wider becomes the range of tariff legislation as distinct from the tariff schedules themselves, the more likelihood there is that in a national emergency these formalities of procedure may be used to harass and restrict trade. There is also more likelihood that, for political, or even at times for personal, reasons, officials may be able, within the law, to hamper the movement of particular kinds of trade, or trade from a particular country.

It was for these reasons that the Economic Committee of the League of Nations devoted so much attention to the problem of simplifying customs formalities.[31] Their efforts have

---

[31] League of Nations, *International Convention Relating to the Simplification of Customs Formalities* (Geneva, 1924) (1924. II. 36); also *International Conferences on Customs and Other Similar Formalities* (Geneva, 1924) (1924. II. 23).

been nullified, however, since 1931 by the unwillingness of most countries to relax trade controls, and above all by the introduction of new forms of trade regulation such as quotas and exchange control requiring still more forms to be filled in and more official channels to be passed through. Required to buy the necessary forms of application, to fill them in with much detail of past transactions, to negotiate their progress through a series of official bodies, to pay quota or license fees that are often substantial, and to await decisions that may or may not be prompt and favorable, the individual trader is apt to be discouraged. Inevitably, such regulated trade tends to fall into the hands of trade associations or big businesses able to work out co-operative relations with the officials concerned. The odd trades conducted by individual enterprise become too difficult to handle and interchange is restricted more and more to the barter in bulk of rather simple commodities negotiated by government agencies.

Apart from the multiplication of formalities, with their direct and indirect costs, there has been a growing tendency for governments to equip themselves with extraordinary powers to cope with various types of imports whose competition is deemed dangerous or unfair. There is a whole range of regulations designed in the public interest—the prohibition of obscene or politically dangerous publications; of narcotics and dangerous drugs; of foods unfit for consumption; of articles dangerous to the health of human beings, animals, or plant life; of articles that infringe patents, copyrights, and trade marks. There are also provisions, necessary when tariffs discriminate between goods originating in different countries, for the marking of goods to show their national origins.[32] For

[32] Cf. League of Nations, *Marks of Origin* (Geneva, 1927) (1927. II. 11); *Veterinary Questions* (Geneva, 1930) (1930. II. 49); *Draft Conventions on Veterinary Questions* (Geneva, 1934) (1934. II. B.2); *International Convention for the Campaign against Contagious Diseases* (Geneva, 1935) (1935. II. B.1). See also Ruben Ricalde, *Les Mesures sanitaires appliquées au commerce d'importation et d'exportation dans les ports mexicains;* Bidwell, *The Invisible Tariff;* Australian Institute of International Affairs, *The Department of Commerce* (*Commonwealth of Australia*), pp. 12–14; Jussiant, *op.*

practically all of this legislation a good case may be made in principle; but its application in practice may provide a whole armory of weapons with which to restrict trade. Veterinary, health, and quarantine regulations may be strictly enforced even when the danger of infection has passed, or extended more widely than is absolutely necessary. For example, under a provision of the United States Tariff Act of 1930, intended to check the spread of rinderpest or foot-and-mouth disease, imports of live animals and meats are prohibited from a long list of countries. The only countries from which meat can be imported are "North America, countries in the Caribbean area, a few countries in northern Europe, Japan and Australasia." [33] There seems little doubt that this prohibition is largely protective in intention. It is one of the major issues of dispute between the United States and the Argentine.[34]

It is, of course, very difficult to form a sound judgment concerning the degree to which a country makes unfair use of precautions which are legitimate in certain circumstances. The introduction of parasites may be so very dangerous to a great industry that the utmost care may be needed to avoid their importation. Those interested in the industry may be trusted to make the strongest representations against any relaxing of precautions. Officials aware of the probable consequences of laxity are inclined to play safe by taking no risks whatever. It is, therefore, not a simple matter to determine when precautionary measures are unjustified and are, in fact, simply a method of indirect protectionism. This is perhaps truer in regard to quarantine and veterinary regulations than in regard to health regulations and, still more, to controls over imported publications.

The most complete national study of this general problem of indirect protectionism is Professor Bidwell's study of United States practice in this regard.[35] The range of government

---

cit., pp. 99–104; Parkinson, *op. cit.*, pp. 109–133; S. Kawashima, *The Trend of Japan's Foreign Trade Policy and Her Indirect Protective Measures;* etc.

[33] Bidwell, *op. cit.*, pp. 211–212.

[34] See the New York *Times,* Jan. 6, 1940, and ff.

[35] Bidwell, *op. cit.*

controls, in addition to tariff duties, revealed by this study is impressive and various instances of arbitrary action by officials are cited. In practically every instance, however, a reasonable defense can be made of the principle embodied in a particular regulation, and machinery is provided for judicial review of the application of such regulations in detail. Mr. Bidwell claims that "American customs procedure is not nearly so burdensome from the point of view of importers as the corresponding procedure in many foreign countries," [36] and the same claim may fairly be made in regard to other aspects of indirect protectionism in the United States. It is always well to be vigilant in criticizing the arbitrary use of delegated powers; but, in fact, there is a case for the precautions that have been taken and appeal from administrative decisions is provided by a relatively simple and effective procedure.

Few persons would now be prepared to advocate the abandonment of government powers to inspect imports for health, quarantine, veterinary, and social reasons. Private enterprise cannot always be trusted to safeguard the public interest in these matters and consumers are not expert enough to protect themselves from fraud or positive risks. It is possible, however, to use these necessary precautions, particularly in an emergency, as an extra form of protection and the line is always difficult to draw.

Moreover, the growth of State intervention in many countries has been so extensive that new forms of indirect protection have developed. A Polish document gives interesting cases of indirect protection affecting Polish exports.[37] It begins with various forms of subsidies to national production, or marketing regulations, in countries which are markets for Polish exports or compete with Polish exports in other markets. In Switzerland, import permits for Polish poultry or eggs

[36] *Ibid.*, p. 6.
[37] Wojciech Zaleski, *Le Protectionnisme indirect dans les divers pays et ses répercussions sur les exportations de la Pologne;* cf. also Bronislaw Oyrzanowski, *Le Protectionnisme indirect en Pologne;* both memoirs directed by Adam Heydel.

are conditional upon the purchase of stated proportions of the local product; in most European countries milling regulations stipulate the admixture of stated proportions of local flour. Contracts for government supplies, a matter of increasing importance with the growth of state intervention, are reserved by law or administrative decision for national producers. In India, or the French colonies, for example, Polish cement or coal has no opportunity of competing successfully for public tenders. Even the powers of local government may be effective in this respect as in the administration of health regulations.[38] The marketing of imported products becomes very complicated when they must conform to differing state legislation in a federation such as the United States.

Differential transport charges, either on state-owned railways or by the arbitrary fixation of port dues (or private discrimination by carrying companies linked with competing national production), offer another important means of indirect protection. Discrimination in the administration of quota and exchange-control systems, the administration of national monopolies such as those controlling the sale of tobacco, matches, wheat, etc., discrimination in local taxation, and delays in the transport of perishable produce are other examples of indirect protection facilitated by the growth of economic nationalism in recent years. The fact is that a government anxious to support and protect its local industries can find more ways in which to do so when a greater degree of government intervention is practiced.

An even more important field of administrative protection has been opened up by the elaboration in practically every

[38] Cf. the following curious illustration—Zaleski, *op. cit.*, "Tous les transports de chevaux de boucherie venant de l'étranger doivent être dirigés sur le marché de Paris. Les taxes municipales qui y sont en vigueur sont bien plus élevées que sur les autres débouchés locaux, qui sont souvent plus rapprochés du pays éxportateur que Paris.

"En outre, on assigne à la vente des chevaux 2–3 jours seulement par semaine et, pendant ces 2 ou 3 jours, ou ne peut vendre les chevaux que durant la dernière heure ou les deux dernières heures du marché. De cette façon, quand la demande est couverte par la marchandise nationale, il devient impossible d'ecouler la marchandise étrangère."

country of tariff legislation designed to give power at the discretion of government officials to impose penal duties in certain circumstances. In minor degree, these powers are related to the forms of indirect protection already cited.[39] For the most part, however, such administrative powers have grown from the provisions directed at dumping and unfair competition which now form part of practically all tariff legislation. The strict definition of "dumping" is sale below the fair market price in the country of origin; [40] but in popular usage the term tends to mean sale at a price below that of the national product. "Unfair competition" is an equally elastic term.[41] It covers such practices as unfair or misleading branding, violation of copyrights or patent rights, and simulation of other products. In order to establish infringements of fair practice, an elaborate machinery of investigation is necessary. It is probable, however, that the deterrent effect of a threatened investigation is the most powerful weapon at a government's disposal, at least as long as judicial rather than arbitrary procedures of government are followed. In the United States, for example, "during the progress of the Tariff Commission's investigation, all entries of the goods in question may be suspended, except under bond." [42]

Antidumping legislation has acquired new importance in recent years since the breakdown of monetary equilibrium has rendered international price comparisons peculiarly difficult. A new category of unfair competition, known as "ex-

[39] Cf. Bidwell, *op. cit.*, p. 75. "One importer, for example, found that 20,000 bags of cocoa from British possessions in Africa were illegally marked because the French language was used. In order to avoid a penalty of $15,000, the cocoa was returned to Liverpool. Another importer was assessed $350 in penalty duties because the dustcovers on imported books (held by the courts to be 'containers') were not marked 'France.' Rubber marked 'Burma' was held not legally marked. The correct marking should have been 'British India.' But this decision was later reversed. A manufacturer of chocolate almond bars who imported shelled almonds in bags marked 'Portucues' had to pay $2,000 in penalty duties although all the almonds were to be used in his own business."

[40] J. Viner, *Dumping* (Chicago, 1923).
[41] Cf. Bidwell, *op. cit.*, Chs. III–IV.
[42] Bidwell, *op. cit.*, p. 61.

change-dumping," has made its appearance. Moreover, the development of extensive systems of export subsidies in many countries, particularly in those where regulated autarky is practiced, has provoked the invocation of additional protective measures. In the United States, most-favored-nation treatment has been withdrawn from, and countervailing duties applied to, German imports as reprisals for export subsidies.[43]

To follow all the ramifications of administrative or indirect protectionism in detail would be not only a hopeless, but a futile task. Sufficient illustrations have been cited to indicate the range and importance of the problem. From the viewpoint of international relations it is obvious that this development of arbitrary administrative powers, however justifiable in particular cases, is a definite regression to primitive and combative forms of government intervention. It clearly reinforces the tendency for trade to become subject to government direction and control. Officials must be constantly vigilant and their discretionary powers are greatly increased. Traders are faced with baffling uncertainties and with complicated formalities. The inevitable trend, therefore, is towards an even greater degree of government regulation and planning.

The Attack on Trade Barriers

Throughout the years between the wars a vigorous, but almost wholly unsuccessful, attack was maintained upon tariffs and other barriers to international trade. There is no need to recapitulate the history of the numerous conferences and discussions that fill the interwar years. Professor Rappard's Cobden Lectures at the University of London cover the ground adequately.[44] Many methods of attack were tried in succession. "The difficulties encountered in abolishing import and export prohibitions in general led to an endeavor to concentrate on certain specific products. The unsatisfactory results of strictly limited negotiations led back to the idea of a gen-

[43] *Ibid.*, Ch. IV.
[44] W. Rappard, "Post-War Efforts for Freer Trade," *loc. cit.*

eral concerted action, to be initiated by a tariff truce. Repeated failures on the world plane suggested the idea of the apparently less ambitious scheme of a union purely European. More recently and more generally, the discouragement engendered by the impossibility of securing any measure of significant agreement by means of multilateral conventions has caused most Governments to fall back on the time-honoured, but far more modest form of bilateral treaties." [45]

As will be argued in a later chapter, the great majority of the bilateral treaties negotiated in recent years have been restrictive of multilateral trade. Under the powerful impetus of German trading drives they have been used on the continent of Europe to build up a new trading system radiating from Berlin; but this system is destructive of multilateral trade. The antithesis and negation of nineteenth-century principles and ideals, it is designed not to promote individual welfare in a world at peace, but to develop a powerful military State.

The British bilateral treaty system, as Dr. Tasca has pointed out, has been essentially opportunist in character. "Instead of any attempt to build a general framework of commercial relations based upon a multilateral system, there is what might be described as an improvised policy designed to fit easily, according to the consideration of the British interests involved, into the trade regulation and commercial policy structures found in different countries. If the term 'policy' can be used, then it may be said that British policy has been purely opportunist in character in contrast to the uniform policy which the American Government has devoutly pursued. The outstanding fact about British external trade policy since the

[45] *Ibid.*, p. 31. For a more recent approach along a new line, cf. F. L. McDougall, "Food and Welfare," *loc. cit.* The explanation given by Professor Rappard for the consistent failure to make headway against trade restrictions is essentially similar to that advanced in this volume. "But all recent experience," he writes, "shows both that international trade cannot be free in a world of hostile or potentially hostile and therefore suspicious sovereign States and that trade alone cannot ban international hostility and suspicions. The problem is thus more complex, because less exclusively economic, than it appeared to Cobden."

adoption of full-blown tariff protectionism is its strong bilateral flavour. . . . The purposes of British bilateralism have been twofold—the immediate expansion of exports to certain markets, and debt collection from other countries." [46]

By contrast with both the British and the German systems, American policy since 1934 has been directed towards a restoration of multilateral trade. To quote Dr. Tasca once more: "The cornerstone and basis of America's foreign trade policy is the principle of equality of treatment. The American system rests upon the premise that multilateral trade and payments, facilitated by the principle of equality of treatment and originating in private enterprise and initiative, provide the system most calculated to expand the world's real income and so improve the real standard of living of the peoples of the world. . . . It is essentially the classical economic conception of the benefits flowing from international specialisation of the world's resources and its obverse, the mutual economic interdependence of nation-states." [47]

Tribute must be paid to the single-minded and effective persistence with which the Secretary of State, Mr. Cordell Hull, has pursued these ideals since the passing of the Trade Agreements Act in 1934.[48] In many respects his policy has been a sharp break with cherished tradition. In a country where the tariff has for a century and a half been almost an article of faith and where there is always deep-rooted suspicion and mistrust of powers delegated to the Executive, he has twice obtained from Congress renewal of authority to negotiate reciprocal agreements avowedly designed to reduce the tariff. The twenty-one agreements negotiated in five years have made a definite breach in the high protective wall erected by the Hawley-Smoot tariff. It is a notable and courageous achievement, perhaps the outstanding piece of sane and constructive economic statesmanship in recent years. Yet, ham-

[46] Tasca, *World Trading Systems,* pp. 145–146.
[47] Tasca, *op. cit.,* p. 141.
[48] Raymond Leslie Buell, "The Hull Trade Program and the American System," *World Affairs Pamphlets* (March, 1939), No. 2 (Revised).

pered by nationalist sentiment and political obstacles at home and by reluctance to co-operate abroad, this "good deed in a naughty world" has not, in fact, been able to do a great deal to break down the obstacles to a restoration of world trade. Unless it can be used in the distress of the coming postwar period to bring about greater sanity of trade relations, the verdict of history upon this latest turn of American foreign policy is likely to be that so often applicable in the confusion of recent years—"too late and too little."

The reciprocal trade treaty program began with the initial handicap of negotiating from the preposterous levels of the Hawley-Smoot tariff. It got under way rather slowly and in the face of much suspicion and opposition from vested interest. Before the first agreement could be negotiated, further barriers had been added to the already high tariff structure by the depreciation of the dollar and the imposition of extra duties as a safeguard against import competition with industries to which higher wage-rates had been granted under the National Industrial Recovery Act. Designed primarily to reduce tariffs, it was launched in a world where new and discriminatory trade restrictions were rapidly being consolidated into an effective apparatus for mobilizing economic activity in preparation for war. Every step in negotiation was taken in the face of mistrustful opposition by powerful national interests likely to be affected even slightly. Political pressure forced a procedure of public hearings that was necessarily slow and calculated to give full opportunity for opponents of tariff reduction to ventilate their opposition.[49] Perhaps the most serious handicap of all was presented by the delays and difficulties that ensued in negotiating the agreement with Great Britain, the country that had most to gain in the long run from a restoration of multilateral trade. Hindered by the

[49] Carl Kreider, "Democratic Processes in the Trade Agreements Program," *American Political Science Review* (April, 1940), pp. 317–332. See also John Day Larkin, *Trade Agreements; A Study in Democratic Methods* (New York, 1940).

protectionist psychology that had come to dominate the former center of world trade, as well as by preferential commitments at the Ottawa Conference and the bilateral obligations incurred in succeeding years, the negotiation of the Anglo-American treaty dragged on till 1938 and, when finally concluded, the agreement was of limited scope. Nevertheless, the objectives of multilateral trade and equality of treatment were patiently and steadfastly pursued, even with countries committed to discriminatory regimes of trade regulation, and in the aggregate substantial results have been achieved.

After the negotiation of the Anglo-American agreement, further progress was barred not only by the growing tension of international relations, but by a series of adverse political developments at home and abroad. Many of the countries to which an extension of the program would seem a natural development have already contracted bilateral treaties with Germany or Great Britain, or both, that seriously restrict their ability to offer reciprocal concessions to the United States. In some of them, notably the Argentine, Chile, and other Latin-American countries, worth-while concessions by the United States would inevitably encounter powerful political opposition within that country. This is particularly the case since concessions would be generalized by most-favored-nation treatment and it would be difficult to define such commodities as wool, wheat, meat, corn, and copper in such a way as to restrict concessions to specific countries. A lower duty on copper granted to Chile would be extended automatically to Northern Rhodesia and the Belgian Congo, and induce competition that would be ruinous to Arizona interests. It so happens that the pastoral products and minerals likely to be affected are produced in states that are thinly populated but politically influential, since each state sends two Senators to Washington whatever its population. In the case of the Argentine, the long-standing application of veterinary restrictions already referred to constitutes an additional obstacle to agreement that is not easily removed. Moreover, the continued depression of American agricultural exports, notably cotton, corn, and wheat, has led to policies of intervention, and even subsidies, that are difficult to reconcile with the principles underlying the Trade Agreements Program.

It is difficult, therefore, to resist the conclusion that the conflict of tariff policies in the world just before the present war mirrored the international political situation only too accurately. The British trading system based on the unchallenged stability of sterling and a great free-trade market had broken down and been replaced by an opportunist policy conservatory of vested interests. Totalitarian policies were making vigorous and determined attempts to create new centers of world trade designed to strengthen the economic bases of military power. The United States was moving in the direction necessary to restore world trade, but slowly and with reservations deriving essentially from a profound reluctance to accept the consequences of effective and responsible participation in an interdependent world.

How far reciprocal trade negotiations in an impoverished and distraught world can be effective in maintaining some degree of economic equilibrium, and gradually restoring prosperity after the present conflict ends, is a question that no one can answer. A victorious and unbroken Germany would obviously seek to strengthen and extend the economic mobilization upon which her military success had been built, and would be joined in the scramble for plunder by other totalitarian States. Even impoverishment, provided morale was unbroken, would not deter such an attempt, since the first costs of reconstruction could probably be thrown on to other countries by massive imports purchased under clearing agreements to be liquidated by German exports at a later date. Any other issue of the war, however, whether a British victory, a compromise peace, stalemate, or economic breakdown, would clearly offer an opportunity for effective American intervention in the reconstruction period. In such circumstances, the powers embodied in the Trade Agreements Act might prove to be effective instruments of negotiation; but their effectiveness will depend in large part upon the readiness of the United States to make tariff concessions that will result in import surpluses consistent with the balance of payments of a great creditor nation.

CHAPTER VI

Quota Politics

The Origins of Quotas

THE DEVICE of rationing imports (and exports) is not a new one. It is, indeed, a rather obvious necessity when trade can no longer be conducted smoothly by the price bargaining of an effectively organized market. It represents a reversion to barter methods, blocks of goods being sold against other goods. In this respect it resembles the primitive bargaining of African tribes rather than civilized market processes conducted on a credit basis. It was known and used by the Mercantilists and recurred in modern times under the stress of war or preparation for war. During the war of 1914–18 rationing at home and quantitative control of trade abroad were adopted by all the belligerent countries and a great many neutrals. Import quotas disappeared, but export quotas were reinforced, in the scarcity of the immediate postwar years. Not until national currencies had been reconstituted after the inflation period, and exchange stability restored, was it possible to go back to trading methods based on international price comparisons. Even then tariff quotas were preserved in many countries, and where the penal duties imposed on imports beyond a certain maximum were sufficiently high, they had the effect of absolute quota restrictions.

The reintroduction of import quotas in recent years was occasioned by the drastic fall of agricultural prices in the first stage of the depression that began in 1928–29, and by the collapse of international monetary equilibrium in the summer and autumn of 1931. International trade was thoroughly disorganized since shifting exchange rates, without compensating price movements, threw into chaos the comparative prices of staple commodities in different national markets. Drastic measures were necessary to safeguard the producers, particularly of agricultural foodstuffs and raw materials, in countries threatened by exchange dumping. The peasant countries of Europe were placed in an exceedingly awkward situation when the depreciation of sterling carried with it most of the currencies of the agricultural exporting countries of the world outside Europe, many of them to levels below depreciated sterling. Some of their competitors in Europe promptly depreciated to the same levels; but there were many European countries that could not take this drastic step. Such countries were threatened by a flood of agricultural imports, at prices much below competitive levels, into their main export markets and even into their own domestic markets. Unlike manufacturing enterprises which are apt to meet reduced demand by maintaining prices and diminishing production, the scattered, unorganized, and small-scale agricultural producers in most countries usually meet depression by increasing their production, even though such an increase aggravates the fall in prices.

The peasant countries of continental Europe had never freely admitted the products of cheap mechanized and specialized agriculture. Much more was involved in the preservation of national agriculture, for a country like France, than the loss of agricultural capital that would have been involved in a free-trade policy.[1] The land was owned in small parcels, inheritance of which was the cement of the social structure. The peasant lived his own life, relatively independent and hardly troubled by international fluctuations—a life hard but rewarding, limited but safe. To have allowed cheap imported grains and other foodstuffs to have disorganized the national market would have been to destroy this security and the way of life upon which it was based. It would have struck at the

[1] Cf. René Hoffherr, *La Politique commerciale de la France*, p. 121.

most stable and conservative, as well as the most powerful, segment of society, throwing the hard-earned and frugal patrimony of generations into a bottomless pit of economic and social disorder. What was true of France was equally true of Switzerland and, in large measure, even of countries such as Belgium, Germany and Italy, where industrial development had gone relatively further. Even in the Netherlands, where international trade was of paramount importance, the plight of the agriculturist led to the abandonment of free trade and the introduction of a whole battery of interventionist measures.[2] Production subsidies, milling regulations, excise and processing taxes, import monopoly fees, marketing regulation, price fixing, and control of production as well as import quotas, were among the measures taken by the liberty-loving Dutch in this great emergency.

One reason why extraordinary measures of import restriction and national regulation were necessary to protect European agriculture from the flood of imports cheapened by exchange depreciation was the intense opposition manifested by most peasant communities to a renewal of currency depreciation. In many countries they had only recently emerged from uncontrollable inflations that had wiped out the accumulated savings of generations. There was widespread fear that devaluation might lead again to inflation. Flights of capital and withdrawal of foreign funds caused the necessity for exchange control to be imposed in the financially weaker countries. In those where strong commercial and financial interests fought against exchange control, quota systems were introduced.[3] The list of countries where such systems have been adopted is now a very long one, and most of them date from 1931 or 1932.[4] It is clearly impossible to trace the application

[2] Cf. P. Lieftinck, *The External Economic Policy of the Netherlands*, pp. 20–31.
[3] For the proportion of imports subject to quota in some free exchange countries see League of Nations, *World Economic Survey, 1938–39*, p. 189.
[4] An incomplete list is as follows:
   Before 1931: Austria, Czechoslovakia, Hungary, and Lithuania
   1931: Belgium, France, Iran, Spain, Turkey

THE ORIGINS OF QUOTAS

of these systems in detail.[5] In some countries the use of quotas is very small, as for example in the United States which has made only a limited use of tariff quotas in its trade with Canada and the Philippines, of sugar quotas, and of voluntary quotas in the case of Japanese textiles.[6] In other countries the use made of quotas is largely voluntary or contractual, as a result of treaty arrangements with countries following policies of trade regulation. In the United Kingdom it is confined mainly to a limited number of agricultural imports.[7] The discussion which follows is concerned mainly with issues of policy arising in countries where extensive use has been made of quantitative restrictions as a means of trade regulation.

Quotas were introduced into these countries as a more effective and immediate means of protection to national production than tariffs. Apart from the difficulty of raising duties abruptly and to the heights necessary to be effective, most European countries were in the position of France, which, in the period of apparent prosperity preceding the debacle of 1931, had negotiated commercial treaties that were generalized by most-favored-nation treatment. It was estimated that no fewer than 72 per cent of French imports were subject to duties that had been "bound" or "conventionalized" in this way. Since the treaty obligations could not be denounced

1932: Chile, Eire, Germany, Greece, Netherlands, Poland, Rumania, Switzerland
1933: Bulgaria, Greece, Netherlands Indies
1934: British Colonies, India, Latvia, Uruguay
1935: Italy
1936: Yugoslavia
1937: Japan, Manchukuo
1938: Afghanistan, New Zealand

Partial use has been made of quotas also in Albania, Australia, Brazil, Cuba, Estonia, Norway, Peru, Portugal, Sweden, and the United States.

[5] Cf. Margaret S. Gordon, *Barriers to World Trade: A Study of Recent Commercial Policy* (shortly to be published) for a thorough discussion of the mechanisms of trade regulation, including quotas. I am indebted to Mrs. Gordon for some of the points made in the present chapter.

[6] P. W. Bidwell, *The Invisible Tariff*, Ch. V.

[7] *British External Policy in Recent Years*, Part I, pp. 35–39; Part II, pp. 37–45.

without a long period of notice, some other method of import restriction had to be found. For many European countries the enforced introduction of exchange control solved the problem, and the necessity for securing import licenses and exchange permits soon resulted in an integration of control. In some of the free-exchange countries, and notably in Poland until 1936, a rigid administration of import quotas served the same purpose as exchange control in safeguarding the balance of payments.

In some countries, notably Switzerland and Poland, quota restrictions were introduced frankly as a bargaining instrument. Reference has already been made to the Swiss policy of "cashing-in" on the purchasing power of their market.[8] A Polish statement may be quoted in the same sense. "As a result of the progressive regulation of world trade," writes Professor Strzeszewski, "export possibilities are no longer conditioned by the competitive power of commodities, but depend above all on the conclusion of bilateral commercial agreements based on reciprocal concessions. Import prohibitions have been introduced in view of future commercial agreements, the system being clearly conceived as a negotiating instrument."[9] Another way in which to put this argument is that used by Professor Madgearu when he states that Rumanian import quotas were introduced in order to stimulate exports.[10] Something further is said of the correlation of import controls and export policies later in this chapter.

Meantime, in order to round out the story of government assistance to harassed agricultural producers, it is necessary to mention briefly some of the many other devices adopted in various countries to regulate the national markets. It is not surprising to find that governments display great concern over their food policies. Even in an industrial age food supplies remain the first necessities of national existence, and no gov-

---

[8] See above, p. 198.
[9] Czeslaw Strzeszewski, *La Politique du commerce extérieur de la Pologne.*
[10] Virgile Madgearu, *La Politique extérieure de la Roumanie,* p. 10.

ernment can afford to risk scarcities or shortages. Most of the direct interventions of European governments—whether by way of subsidies, production controls, price fixing, import monopolies, or grain battles—have revolved around wheat. This is, in itself, a symptom of international disorder, since the declining importance of bread in modern diets is counterbalanced by the fact that a greater degree of self-sufficiency for a given population can be achieved by utilizing the soil for bread grains rather than for the production of a more varied and balanced diet. The various devices used are, of course, capable of application to other important commodities. Thus, milling regulations, requiring the admixture of stated proportions of domestic wheat, find their parallels in the admixture of alcohol with gasoline, national film quotas, the blending of butter with margarine, and the mixture of wool or silk with staple fiber. In the same way the system of linked-purchasing, illustrated in the preceding chapter, can be applied to other goods, as when the New Zealand Government required purchasers of woolpacks to buy a given proportion of packs made of native flax (*Phormium tenax*) as a condition of receiving permits to import packs made of Indian jute. Import monopolies can be used to conserve supplies of important products other than wheat. Indeed, import monopolies can become complete, as in the U. S. S. R. and Iran. Nevertheless, it is in regard to food supplies, and particularly to wheat, that governments have been most solicitous in recent years.[11] So solicitous have they become, in fact, that the whole balance of agricultural production has been changed—former net wheat-importing countries, such as France and Sweden, appearing as net exporters and adding further to the confusion of world markets. Sugar has long been subject to a complication of production and export subsidies, import controls, and international agreements. Wheat

[11] Milling regulations were introduced in Norway (1927); France (1929); Sweden, Czechoslovakia, Latvia, Persia, Greece (1930); Tunis, Belgium, Luxembourg, Italy, and the Netherlands (1931).

is almost as badly affected. Other important staple products such as butter have also been thrown into the same marketing confusion in recent years.[12]

Quotas had their origin in this concern for agricultural interests; but the application of quota restrictions has by no means been confined to agricultural imports. Indeed, it is one of the characteristics of such restrictions that they tend to extend the scale of their operation. The history of quotas in practically every country where they were introduced repeats, with variations, the experience of Rumania which began on November 29, 1932 by submitting 120 articles to quota restrictions; "but, the introduction of quotas for a limited number of articles could not yield results, and that is why on July 1, 1933, the number of articles subject to quota was increased to 500, being about 80 per cent of the total imports."[13] Such an extension of quotas, to industrial as well as agricultural products, was a common experience. French quotas, introduced in May, 1931, covered one seventh of the tariff items by July of the following year, and by 1934 over 3,000 items, about half the total, were covered. In some cases, as in Belgium, industrial quotas on certain products had preceded agricultural quotas, but these were mainly the products of small-scale industries.[14] Small-scale manufacturers faced much the same problem as peasant agriculturists. It was not long, therefore, before the smaller-scale industrialists, and even the large-scale enterprises of many countries, were being sheltered by import quotas. In the latter case cartel negotiations were often the real basis of quota arrangements. This was the case, for example, with the first industrial quotas in Belgium.[15] It was also the case for the licens-

[12] Carl Major Wright, "Butter as a World Staple," *Index* (November, 1935), pp. 254–269.

[13] Madgearu, *op. cit.*, p. 11.

[14] Cf. J. Jussiant, *L'Evolution du commerce extérieur de la Belgique*, p. 88.

[15] Cf. Jussiant, *op. cit.*, p. 88: "En ce qui concerne les products chimiques azotés, l'établissement d'un régime de licences, qui est le premier en date, était justifié par une surproduction générale; il fut adopté du reste à la suite de négociations entre producteurs faisant partie du cartel international de l'azote."

ing of iron and steel imports into Great Britain in 1936.

As the disintegration of international trade proceeded, however, other and more fundamental reasons became responsible for the extension and integration of quantitative and monetary restrictions. Considerations of the balance of payments and of monetary stability became more and more important. Control at the frontier was linked with regulation of domestic production. Not particular commodities, but the whole organization of economic activity came under government control. But when this stage was reached, exchange control rather than import prohibitions, licensing, or quotas became the effective instrument of regulation.

Government Through Producers

The corporative State is essentially an attempt to organize society along occupational lines. It governs through organizations of producers. Associations of general welfare are relegated to a subordinate role. Individual citizenship and the interest of the ordinary consumer are disregarded. The State emerges as the supreme reality without which individual activities and interests are meaningless. Productive organization is dominated by State necessities, and these necessities are inevitably conceived in terms of military power. This is the logical end of organization that disregards individual satisfactions. The end may be rationalized in mysticisms offering to frustrated peoples the symbols of national greatness in substitution for the satisfactions of ordinary life. In a desperate crisis, individual liberties may be surrendered in order to gain cohesion of unified effort. Such conscious adoption—voluntarily or involuntarily—of national discipline for definite ends is at least logical and prescient. But much of the drift towards government through producers has been the result of less conscious attempts to save at least something of existing property interests from the maelstrom of disorganization created by the breakdown of world trade. It may well be true that those responsible for such negative policies of State intervention would repudiate any belief that their actions were leading towards a corporative State. The representatives of Farmers' Unions from Great Britain and the Dominions, for example, who met at Sydney in July, 1937 and drew up plans for the quantitative regulation of agricultural production and trade by "commodity councils, producer controlled and financed," may well have been innocent of the political implications of their proposals. But agricultural quotas under the Livestock Marketing Act, and the whole apparatus of quantitative restrictions, necessarily entailed more effective organization of producing interests. Governments administering quota systems were bound to consult the interests affected, if not to hand over to them the actual administration of the regulations. In this way long strides were taken towards the corporative form of State.

The administrative problems of quota policies are now largely a matter of academic interest. They revolve around such questions as the form of quota to be used, the base upon which it should be calculated, its distribution over time among importers and among exporters, the replacement of customs revenue by quota fees, the control of monopolies created by the exclusive right to import, and the correlation between import restrictions and export outlets. There was much confusion while staffs were being organized; systems of recording established; relationships worked out with manufacturers, Chambers of Commerce, trade associations, and individual importers; negotiations undertaken with exporting countries and international cartels; and co-ordination arranged between different departments of government in the restricting country. The solution of all these problems, while differing in detail from country to country, has inevitably followed the same general pattern.[16]

The connection between import prohibitions, licensing sys-

---

[16] See, for example, Heller, *Hungarian Economic Policy*, pp. 100 ff.; Madgearu, *op. cit.*, pp. 15–19; Jussiant, *op. cit.*, pp. 116 ff.; Hoffherr, *op. cit.*, pp. 254 ff.; Lieftinck, *op. cit.*, pp. 41 ff.; *British External Economic Policy*, Part II, pp. 35 ff.

GOVERNMENT THROUGH PRODUCERS 219

tems, and quotas is sufficiently obvious to need little emphasis. Since exchange control systems necessarily involve the issuance of exchange permits, they comprehend a licensing of imports which may be supplementary to, or correlated with, quota systems. It was not an infrequent development for importers to find that licenses to import could not be used for lack of the necessary means of payment. At an early stage of development the pressure to export was often great enough for exporters to take the risk of subsequent payment being arranged with the result that arrears of commercial debt added to the exchange confusion. This has, at times, led even a free-exchange country like Great Britain to acquiesce in, and even encourage, the development of, or reversion to, quota restrictions on its exports.[17]

The earliest forms of global quotas setting a limit to the total quantity or value to be imported, usually within a period as long as a year, and leaving the allocation among importers and ports, as well as among exporters, to the working of competitive forces, quickly led to abuses and administrative difficulties. It was not easy to keep track of imports when a quota was opened, so that a sudden rush of imports was apt to exceed the quota. Gluts of commodities followed by long periods of scarcity caused violent price fluctuations and much irritation to national producers, importers, and exporters. It was inevitable that more elaborate methods of organization should be devised, allocating permitted imports over time and among the parties interested.

There is, however, no inherently equitable basis for such allocations. If they are based on imports at some prior period, they tend to stereotype the economic arrangements then existing.[18] New or progressive importers are apt to be pe-

[17] Cf. Kuyucak, *Exchange Control in Turkey*. The purchasing agreements negotiated by Great Britain for the sale of coal have also resulted in the necessity for import monopolies (as in Norway) or other forms of quantitative restrictions.

[18] The simplest illustration of the way in which the choice of a base period may determine the allocation of quotas is that provided by the experience of the United States in regard to immigration quotas. The shift in the United

nalized and shifts in export advantages are nullified. Despite the attempts of the United States to insist upon the principle of global quotas, unallocated as between exporting countries, the trend has inevitably been in the opposite direction. Indeed, the use of quotas for bilateral bargaining purposes has led to an increasing degree of arbitrary and discriminatory official control almost everywhere. Various devices have been used—reserve quotas, the allocation of unnecessary quotas to certain countries, the transference of unfilled quotas, the negotiation of cartel agreements, purchasing agreements, or voluntary quotas, the withholding of exchange permits, the issuance of supplementary quotas, and even a widespread use of secret clauses in commercial agreements. Detailed illustration of these devices is, however, superfluous, since in fact the general trend has been towards reciprocal bilateral bargaining conducted by official negotiators in large specific transactions. As the machinery for such negotiation has been perfected in most European countries, the allocation of quotas between exporting countries, and indeed the short-term commercial agreements, have become more and more a skeleton framework of legislative authority to conclude particular bargains.

Quite obviously, this has entailed considerable increases of discretionary power in the hands of controlling authorities. Those who negotiate in detail, almost continuously, must have their hands free. Therefore, the mobilization of producers and trading organizations as instruments for the execution of quota policies has, in the end, not increased their influence, but effectively subordinated their power to that of the State. At an early stage the necessity for building up such organizations seemed likely to result in governments of producers,

---

States Emergency Quota Act of 1921 from the 1910 to the 1890 basis was made in order to exclude a greater proportion of certain nationalities, an object that was more successfully achieved in another way by the Act of 1924. Cf. Gayer and Schmidt, *American Economic Foreign Policy,* pp. 245–246. The choice of base periods for import quotas (for example, in the British colonies) prior to the great expansion of Japanese exports after 1931 is another example.

GOVERNMENT THROUGH PRODUCERS 221

by producers for producers; but, in fact, the surrender, voluntary or enforced, of competitive power has ended in trade associations becoming the instruments for executing in technical detail the overriding decisions of government policy.

This development was inevitable, if only because a quota policy cannot for long remain autonomous. As with currency depreciation or any other aspect of international economic relations, national policy cannot hope to count upon other governments passively accepting the disadvantages thrust upon their nationals. Trade in recent years has increasingly taken the form of commercial warfare and, as in any other form of warfare, attack is met by counterattack. Quotas have therefore tended to become reciprocal rather than autonomous, import possibilities being traded for export outlets. Before the dominance of political motives in trade regulation became too obvious to be ignored, there were attempts at direct negotiations between industrial groups, as between French and German trade associations in 1931. Perhaps the best known of these conversations were those begun early in 1939, with government approval on both sides, between the Federation of British Industries and the Reichsgruppe für Industrie. An Anglo-German Coal Agreement, which was essentially designed to divide markets, fix prices, and eliminate competitive undercutting, had been signed in January, 1939. In March, the bases of a wider agreement which would have regulated competition in a wide range of commodities not only in the respective national markets, but in export markets also, was announced. Its execution, however, was frustrated by the German occupation of Prague, which finally alarmed the British government.[19]

One obvious difficulty in carrying through such reciprocal industrial agreements has been the increasing use of export subsidies by most governments, and the correlation of such subsidies with import controls, especially under exchange-control systems. By a curious inversion of protectionism, every country seemed bent on subsidizing the consumers, including

[19] *British External Economic Policy in Recent Years: Supplement*, pp. 1–4.

the tourists, of other countries. Motorists entering Switzerland received warrants which enabled them to purchase gasoline at a price which forewent most of the government tax. Swiss motorists going to France or Italy could, on the other hand, purchase coupons giving them the right to buy gasoline at reduced prices. Each country, endeavoring to secure at least some free exchange, encouraged the tourist traffic of every other. In much the same way, export subsidies provided for consumers (in so far as the import restrictions of their own country permitted) commodities at lower prices and often in better quality than were available to consumers in the exporting country. Australia subsidized butter exports from 1926 onwards. South Africa began the same practice for several agricultural exports in 1931. There were few European countries after that date that did not seek to expand their export outlets by subsidies of one kind or another, directly in payments to producers or exporters, or indirectly by manipulation of the exchange rates. The most ambitious of all such export promotion schemes was that of Germany from 1935 onwards, by which turnover taxes imposed upon national production were used to compensate exporters for the lower prices quoted to obtain orders. Operation of this scheme was secret, in order to minimize reprisals by way of antidumping duties; but it has been estimated that as large a sum as RM. 1,000 m. was paid out annually—approximately one fourth of the total value of German exports.[20] Nearly everywhere, also, governments provided credit facilities for the encouragement of exports, either by various forms of export credit guaranty,[21] by the operation of clearing arrangements, or even by the extension of foreign loans to be expended within the lending country.[22] It was entirely natural that such export promo-

[20] The German budget for 1938–39 included an amount of RM. 1,500 m. "for the promotion of German foreign trade." Cf. the New York *Times*, April 4, 1939.

[21] Cf., e. g., *British External Policy in Recent Years: Supplement*, pp. 7–9.

[22] See von Mickwitz, *Capital Exports to South-Eastern Europe*; Staley, *World Economy in Transition*, pp. 269–279; Hipolit Gliwic, *Les Capitaux étrangers en Pologne*, pp. 11 ff.; Kuyucak, *op. cit.*, pp. 7–8, 48–51; Madgearu, *op. cit.*, pp. 26–27; etc.

tion devices should be closely linked with the negotiation of import facilities.

The administrative evolution of quota systems, therefore, was from the comparatively simple and improvised unilateral methods of global reductions in the total quantities of certain imports, to a highly complex and particularized development of bilateral bargaining extending over a wide range of imports and exports between pairs of countries. These specific bargains were inevitably discriminatory and destructive of multilateral trade based upon price competition. They also led to increasing government direction of trade in detail and, therefore, to an extraordinary degree of administrative protection. But as the discretionary power of public officials over external trade increased, there was a parallel extension of their control over domestic production and prices. Rationing applied to external trade was necessarily the means and the cause of equally extensive rationing of raw materials so that the whole gamut of economic activity became subject to State control. Like a parasitic growth, the emergency assistance and protection extended to private enterprise ended by choking it almost out of existence.

The Incidence of Quotas

Some brief analysis of the economic incidence and effects of quantitative trade restrictions is necessary, not only to demonstrate the erratic and arbitrary distribution of the costs and monopolistic profits created by direct interference with supply, but also because important issues of international policy have arisen in this connection. It is not intended to work out in theoretical detail the differing incidence of quotas limiting a portion of the total supply of a commodity as contrasted with that of a tariff increasing the cost of imported goods. The differences are real and important; but from a practical viewpoint it is well to come directly to the main point, which is that quota restrictions as they developed created situations of State-controlled monopoly. There is little practical utility, therefore, in detailed illustration of the way in which, under hypothetical conditions of free or semimonopolistic competition, quotas differ from tariffs mainly by giving rise to quasi-monopolistic trading profits in the importing countries. It is clear that the possession of a license to import is a valuable property right that may, in certain circumstances, be sold profitably.[23] Most governments have, in fact, appropriated any quasi-monopolistic profits of this kind by the simple means of imposing license fees, which have at times been an important source of revenue, or by regulating the disposal of quota allocations.

The actual incidence of quota restrictions is variable, since it depends upon such factors as the elasticity of demand in the importing country and of production in the exporting country; the proportion of the restricted imports to total consumption in the importing country and to total production in the exporting country; the possibilities of substitution, etc. There appear to have been cases where practically the whole cost of restriction has been thrown upon the consumers in the importing country and others where exporters were crippled by the loss of important markets.

In general, the major effect upon the prices of commodities subject to quota has been a fragmentation of the market. Prices in different national markets began to diverge to an extent far greater than had been possible when international trade was limited only by tariffs. This did not necessarily mean a lowering of prices in the exporting countries. In the case of manufactured goods, for example, where exports to a particular market formed a relatively small fraction of the total production, the prices ruling in the exporting country continued to depend primarily upon conditions of demand and supply, including credit conditions, in the main market. The loss of export outlets probably tended, on the whole, towards increased costs and, therefore, higher prices where such com-

---

[23] In certain conditions the right to export to a quota-controlled market may also become, as did the Danish "pig passports," a valuable transferable property.

modities were produced under conditions of increasing returns. On the other hand, the wholesale restriction of agricultural commodities undoubtedly forced down prices in producing areas and on world markets.

Within the countries of quota restriction the general tendency was towards erratic, and at times large, price increases; but the more powerfully organized governments have endeavored to combat such increases by improved efficiency of distribution and the encouragement and subsidizing of substitutes. Prices have been strictly controlled and rationing systems have been introduced so that shortages, delays, and impaired quality were often substituted for price increases. Since sharp price increases, particularly of food and raw materials, led to increased production costs and therefore to a disadvantageous export situation, every effort has been made to administer the quota and price and production controls in such a way as to limit price rises and confine them as far as possible to commodities of national consumption.

The increasing centralization of control in the hands of governments has given a varying degree of monopoly power to the officials negotiating the specific bargains that came to be the realities behind the negotiation of commercial treaties. In these bargains not only import and export prices (often subsidized), but exchange rates, quota allocations, and flexible tariffs, as well as credit facilities, transport charges, and priorities of payment, can be manipulated. Monopolistic power has at times been increased by the accumulation of clearing arrears that enabled a country whose prior importations had been on a grand scale to demand favorable terms both for the exports necessary to liquidate such arrears and for renewed purchases.

Theoretically it seems clear that a great importing country such as Germany, whose imports from any small country were a relatively small proportion of her total consumption but a relatively large proportion of the small country's production, should have a strong position in bilateral bargaining. Being in a position of partial discriminating monopoly, she might use the bargaining power of her great market, as Great Britain did in bilateral negotiations with the Scandinavian countries, to secure favorable terms of trade. This, all economists will recognize, is a reversal of the classical theory that, on balance, a small country is likely to obtain the greater share of the gains from trade with a larger country. The classical theory, however, was based upon the assumption of a multilateral and competitive world trading system. In a trading system such as the present, consisting largely of canalized bilateral barter transactions in which private enterprise is severely restricted, the traders of the smaller countries have less opportunity to compete on favorable terms in alternative markets. Such possibilities as have remained open for trade with free-exchange countries, however, have been a powerful bargaining instrument in the hands of their governments. Whenever the possibilities of multilateral trade diminished, Germany's monopoly buying position was thereby strengthened.

Nevertheless, it seems doubtful, in the circumstances of the years immediately preceding the present conflict, whether the division of the gains from bilateral trade was to the disadvantage of the smaller European countries. Germany's need for foodstuffs and raw materials was urgent. A great military machine was in process of development. No shortages of essential supplies could be allowed to slow up this major purpose of the German economic organization. Moreover, the German government was intent on building a great continental, if not world, trading system to destroy and replace British commercial supremacy. For this purpose, which is clearly postulated in German economic writings,[24] considerable economic development of the smaller European countries was needed. There was also a political element in the situation, since alliances, or at least benevolent neutrality, were sought. And the possibility of alternative export outlets had always to be reckoned with as the economic struggle between

[24] Cf. von Mickwitz, *op. cit.*

the Great Powers grew in intensity. A Finnish document bears witness, however, to the insatiable German demand for raw materials which was probably the determining factor in the whole situation.[25] As long as this demand remained insatiable, it was altogether natural for German negotiators to refrain from pressing home their bargaining advantages to the ultimate limit.

It is by no means sure that such circumstances will be repeated after the present conflict ends. If it ends in German victory, the fullest use may be made of enhanced monopoly power to squeeze from the smaller countries the utmost advantage in bilateral trade. If, on the contrary, it ends in a British victory, the speedy restoration of a multilateral trading system will not be easy. The political and economic interests of the smaller countries are dependent upon such restoration giving them the opportunity to trade in alternative markets.

The Value of Imports

It is curious to reflect that the systems of quantitative and monetary trade restrictions, which began almost in a panic fear of excessive imports and frantic pressure to increase exports, have in their ultimate development tended towards an enlargement of imports and a conservation of export resources. This paradoxical result is, of course, one aspect of the change from negative to positive policies of trade regulation. It has been most marked in Germany since 1935, when Dr. Schacht launched an extensive trade drive in southeastern Europe by negotiating massive purchases of foodstuffs and raw materials through clearing agreements. In greater or less degree, this initiative has been followed in most of the exchange-control countries in proportion to their means and the efficiency of their trade negotiators.

The Japanese control system which, in Professor Royama's

[25] H. R. Hormi, *The Exchange Clearing and Compensation System as Applied by Finland.*

words, "lays emphasis on the control of exports" has a different origin and follows different methods.[26] Its aim is primarily to "cope with the economic nationalism of other countries . . . to mollify their preventive policies against Japanese goods and at the same time to preserve (Japan's) position in world trade."[27] Because of the spectacular development of Japanese exports after the depreciation of the yen in 1931, there was an almost world-wide campaign of restriction directed against them. Not only were greater quantities of well-established manufactures exported, but a wide range of new Japanese exports made their appearance on world markets. Fundamentally the cause of this uprush of industrial development was not the depreciation of the yen, but a national policy of credit expansion correlated with war expenditures and protected by the fall of the exchange rate. Systematic purchases of raw materials to be later exported at prices based on lower exchange rates gave a transitional advantage to Japanese exports during the years when the yen was depreciating; but it was the combination of modern machine methods and scientific organization with an almost inexhaustible supply of cheap labor that made Japanese competition so formidable. It so happened, however, that this expansion of Japanese trade took place in the years of greatest depression in other countries, so that there was a world-wide demand for the imposition of higher tariffs, import quotas, and exchange-dumping duties against Japanese goods. It was in order to forestall the progressive penalization of exports that threatened to shut off the sources of necessary raw material imports that Japan began to regulate the quantity and prices of export goods, first by voluntary quotas, then by export control legislation, and finally by the compulsory establishment of export guilds. As the system developed, particularly after the "China Incident" took the proportions of a major war, imports of consumer's goods were rigidly controlled, export

[26] Masamichi Royama, *Japan's Foreign Trade and Exchange Policies under War-Time System*, p. 6.
[27] *Ibid.*, p. 6.

credits were advanced, exchange control was tightened, and a trade control system was developed in which imports of essential raw materials were linked with exports of manufactured goods. In order to limit domestic consumption, differential prices were established, national prices being kept at higher levels than those for exports. The attempt to link commodity imports and exports has not been wholly satisfactory. Exports decreased and national consumption increased as prices continued to rise. Various adaptations of the link system have been tried, but, under the strain of war, the whole apparatus of exchange control and trade regulation has tended to become an organization aimed primarily at securing essential raw materials, to the detriment both of the export trades and of the consumers of imported goods.[28]

It is natural in a time of war that consumers should be penalized and exporters handicapped because of the need at all costs to secure imports of strategic raw materials. These results have followed in Germany as well as in Japan since the outbreak of actual hostilities. In some degree also they have followed in Britain and France. But in the period immediately preceding the war, the ironical situation developed that imports were sought on a grand scale by the country which practiced extreme economic nationalism, while those countries which nominally professed adherence to the principles of multilateral trade continued in fact to practice severe import restriction. This development, by which Germany bought large quantities of imports at high prices (in some cases reselling them at a loss) in order to provision her economy and secure future export outlets, was skillfully devised and executed. Not only were the prices paid for imports much higher (at the ruling exchange rates) than those current in free-exchange countries: Germany endeavored to negotiate exchange rates that depreciated other currencies relatively to the mark. The effect of keeping the mark high was to stimulate imports into Germany and retard exports from that country.

In other words, the German negotiators had grasped the

[28] Royama, *op. cit.*, pp. 23–36.

simple fact that economists have found so difficult to popularize—that imports are receipts and exports are payments. That country which by borrowing, bartering, or trading, can secure the greatest inflow of imports, gains most from its international transactions. If it can secure larger imports for a smaller quantum of exports, it has improved its terms of trade. If it can buy, as Germany did, on deferred payment, it can, for a time at least, secure adequate provision for national needs even while devoting an increasing part of its national resources to noneconomic ends, such as military preparations. It is not at all clear that Germany was, in fact, able to improve its terms of trade, but persistent efforts were made in this direction.

The simple truism that an expanding quantum of imports constitutes the only real gain from international trade has been overlaid in most countries in recent years by concern for national employment and the protection of existing vested interests. In fact, the only remedy in the long run for national unemployment is the restoration of a smoothly functioning system of international trade. The German unemployment problem could not have been solved if Germany had not been able to secure large imports of foodstuffs and raw materials. It is probable that if the war should end in a quick German victory, this lesson will not be overlooked. The imports needed for reconstruction based upon German manufacturing development will not only be welcomed but required. In this, as in so many other respects, German economic organization, while using unorthodox methods, has grasped and acted upon the fundamental economic realities rejected by the timorous methods of other countries. It has long been clear that the failure of the freer trading countries to find effective means of practicing the multilateral trading principles to which they professed devotion, played directly into the hands of German negotiators who were ready in the prewar years to purchase imports at almost any price and in any quantity. It would not be surprising if the ultimate result of attempts to evade capital losses and the necessity for painful adaptations of national employment and production were to be, at best, the aggravation of these necessities after a costly war. At worst, they might well result in the domination of economic activity in many countries by a victorious Germany able to bargain on her own terms as the monopolistic center of a new world trading system. Such developments could well be the consequence of attempts to preserve past privileges of occupation and ownership at the cost of wrecking international cooperation.

CHAPTER VII

The Monetary Weapon

The Advent of Monetary Nationalism

SYSTEMS of exchange control, like quotas, were practiced during the war of 1914–18 and the years of its immediate aftermath, were attenuated or abandoned in the years of apparent recovery from 1925–29, and reappeared on an even more extensive scale in the monetary panic of 1931.[1] Their origins are to be found primarily in violent disturbances of invisible items in the national balances of payments. In most cases the proximate causes were withdrawals

[1] The following list of countries where exchange control was in force prior to the outbreak of war is arranged chronologically:
   Before 1931: Bulgaria, Portugal, Turkey
          1931: Brazil, Spain, Germany, Hungary, Chile, Uruguay, Colombia, Greece, Czechoslovakia, Bolivia, Yugoslavia, Latvia, Austria, Argentina, Nicaragua, Denmark, Estonia
          1932: Costa Rica, Rumania, Japan, Paraguay
          1933: Mexico
          1934: Honduras, Italy, Cuba
          1935: Danzig, Lithuania, Hong Kong
          1936: Iran, Poland, Venezuela
          1938: China, Afghanistan, New Zealand
In addition exchange control was imposed temporarily in the following countries: Iran (February, 1930–May, 1933), United Kingdom (September, 1931–March, 1932), Finland (October–December, 1931), New Zealand (January–June, 1932), Ecuador (May, 1932–October, 1935 and July, 1936–July, 1937), United States (March–November, 1934), El Salvador (August–October, 1933), Cuba (June–July, 1934), China (September, 1934–November, 1935), Belgium and Luxembourg (March–April, 1935).

Informal or voluntary exchange restrictions have been used for shorter or longer periods in Australia, Canada, France, Norway, the Netherlands, South Africa, Sweden, and Switzerland.

THE ADVENT OF NATIONALISM 233

of foreign credits, or a cessation of foreign lending, usually aggravated by flights of national capital. As may be readily deduced from the chronological order of the table below, their reintroduction began when a great liquidity crisis was opened in May, 1931 by the revelation of the Austrian Credit-Anstalt's difficulties and extended widely when sterling depreciated in September of that year.[2]

It has already been argued that the practice of monetary nationalism was severely limited as long as adherence to the

[2] For an authoritative and detailed economic analysis of exchange control, see Howard S. Ellis, "Exchange Control in Central Europe," Harvard University Press, 1940. Cf. also for an account of wartime developments in the British Empire London Wall, "The British System of Exchange Control," London, 1940. The importance of these monetary measures warranted separate treatment in preparation for the Bergen discussions. Arrangements were therefore made for national studies to be undertaken in several countries. These studies, together with a summary report by M. André Piatier, who was in charge of the investigation, will be published separately. While they vary in their approach to the problem as well as in length and in quality, they provide in the aggregate a mass of detailed information concerning the actual practice of exchange control.

Cf. André Piatier, *Exchange Control: A General Survey* (Paris, 1940); also the following documents:

A. Valle and Juan M. Ferrer, *The Economic Policy of the Argentine*
A. Tchakaloff, *Exchange Control in Bulgaria*
H. P. Gøtrik, *Danish Economic Policy, 1931–38*
Fritz Meyer, *An Analysis of Exchange Restrictions at Present in Force*
H. R. Hormi, *The Exchange Clearing and Compensation System as Applied by Finland*
J. D. Pintos, *Exchange Control in Greece*
Kalman Buday, *Exchange Control in Hungary*
A. Hirschmann, *Exchange Control in Italy*
M. Royama, *Japan's Foreign Trade and Exchange Policies under Wartime System*
E. Taylor, *The Repercussion of Monetary Difficulties on the External Economic Policy of Poland*
Jerzy Nowak, *Exchange Control in Poland*
V. Madgearu, *Exchange Control in Roumania*
H. A. Kuyucak, *Exchange Control in Turkey*
F. W. Paish, *The Effects of Foreign Exchange Control on British Trade*
Herbert M. Bratter, *Foreign Exchange Control in Latin America*
A. Yovanovitch, *Exchange Control in Yugoslavia*

M. Piatier's survey is supplemented by short studies of exchange control in Austria, Czechoslovakia, and New Zealand.

international gold standard brought into play corrective forces operating on credit issues and therefore on sensitive items in the balance of payments.[3] When the exchange rates were maintained within the gold import and export points, it was not possible for any country to follow an independent monetary policy for any length of time. It was not until the liquidity panic ended in the collapse of international exchange equilibrium that monetary nationalism could develop in full strength. Behind the breakdown of exchange stability, however, both advocates and critics of exchange control agree, were the stiffening rigidities and growing fears engendered by policies of economic as distinct from monetary nationalism.[4] M. Piatier sums up the causes of breakdown as due to "restrictions on the movement of men, merchandise and capital and deviations in those movements which have survived in spite of restrictions."

The reason for such restrictions he finds to be "the intrusion into international economic life of extra-economic considerations, particularly of a political and military order, and because of the preponderant place taken by emotional or sentimental reactions and feelings (such as fear and distrust —which scarcely merit the pompous appellation of 'psychological factors'). Hypertrophic nationalism paralyses the movement of men and closes the frontiers to foreign products. Strategic and military requirements have steadily imposed themselves upon a widening range of economic activity and there has been an evolution from the key industries of List's time total autarky. Rearmament, alliances, and political discriminations have diverted the flow of merchandise from economic channels. Blockade, sanctions, and preferential treatment take precedence over the desire for rational economic organisation, which, with some simplification of the problems involved, was formerly called the international division of labour.

"Fearing insecurity, capital no longer seeks profitable in-

[3] See above, p. 94.
[4] Cf., e. g., Piatier, *op. cit.*, Ch. II, and Fritz Meyer, *op. cit.*

vestment, but a place of safety. . . . Is it surprising that a country which needs to borrow fails to find a lender; that its export trade encounters customs barriers; that capitalists, apprehensive of danger, remove their assets; that the wealthy, for fear of losing their capital, refuse to invest it in hazardous undertakings and prefer to hoard it? Given such conditions, it would be surprising if the balance of payments were equilibrated and if currencies were maintained at stable exchange rates. Spurning the idea of international economic reorganisation, or unable to make any concessions to it, States have multiplied emergency measures to save what they thought could be saved. Exchange control represents an essential part of these measures." [5]

After citing, in more detail, the specific reasons advanced for the introduction of exchange control in the various countries, M. Piatier proceeds to trace the evolution of monetary nationalism. It is obvious that the powerful creditor countries were favorably placed to pursue expansionist credit policies. The mere cessation of foreign lending caused an accumulation of liquid funds in their national banking systems, and in many cases this accumulation was swelled by repatriation of short-term foreign loans and the sale of foreign securities, as well as by flights of foreign capital to whatever monetary center seemed most secure from depreciation at a given moment. Freed by suspension of the legal obligation to convert national currency into gold, Great Britain was able to lower interest rates, carry through a vast conversion operation, and embark upon a reflationary policy as early as 1932. The United States depreciated its currency in April, 1933. The gold bloc countries continued to suffer drains on their balances of payments that inhibited reflationary policies, or if they followed such policies were forced—as was Belgium in March, 1935—to devaluation, or—as was Italy in May, 1934—to the imposition of exchange control. The smaller creditor countries of Europe also depreciated their currencies. Sweden took this decisive step at an early date (September 27, 1931); Switzerland and

[5] Piatier, *op. cit.*, Ch. II.

the Netherlands only in September, 1936. Czechoslovakia, however, surrounded by customers whose currencies were controlled at an early stage of the crisis, was forced to adopt exchange control in October, 1932, and later to carry through a double devaluation in February, 1934 and November, 1936.

It is necessary, at this stage, to draw a clear distinction between policies such as the manipulation of discount rates, open-market operations, or the use of exchange equalization funds, designed to regulate and moderate fluctuations in the exchange market and exchange control by rationing methods. Some writers have claimed that there is no essential difference of principle between regulatory policies and exchange control strictly defined—the former being appropriate to the circumstances of creditor countries and the latter to those of debtor countries. In this view any type of intervention in the exchange market may be classed as exchange control.

It must, of course, be admitted that the exchange market has never been left without regulation. This is to say no more than that monetary policies have always, even under the gold standard, been managed in some degree. But there is a sharp difference of principle between policies that are designed only to moderate fluctuations in the rate of exchange—which means the price of a currency in terms of other currencies—and those which, in an effort to maintain a rate higher than the market warrants, embark upon rationing of the available supplies of foreign exchange, a process that leads to restrictive control of the constituent items of the balance of payments and also to detailed regulation of domestic economic activity. The discussion of political issues that follows is limited to the effects of exchange control in the latter and correct definition of that term.

M. Piatier's analysis traces the evolution of State intervention in the exchange market from simple attempts at pegging the official rate to the very complex methods now used in manipulating differential rates so as to regulate the visible and invisible items in the balance of payments. When such an analysis is made, it becomes very clear that attempts, by using

THE ADVENT OF NATIONALISM

equalization funds or similar market operations, to regulate the price of a currency have very narrow limits of effective action. An equalization fund is, in fact, only an extension and rationalization of classic central banking practice. Essentially it consists in the segregation of a buffer fund of gold or foreign assets designed to take the shock off temporary variations in the exchange rate so that the national credit system is insulated against fluctuations arising from speculative capital movements.

A bear attack can be met by the fund's using its foreign assets to buy all the national currency offered, at whatever rate the exchange is pegged. On the contrary, offerings of short-term hot money can be absorbed by the fund without being allowed to increase the credit base of the national currency, the foreign assets so absorbed being held in reserve against subsequent withdrawals of short-term funds. In particularly favorable circumstances, such as those enjoyed by Great Britain and Sweden for some months in 1932 and 1933, and by France in 1939, the exchange rate may be held at a low level while returning national funds are used to reconstitute or increase the reserve of gold and foreign assets. Such use of an equalization fund, however, is possible only when the balance of payments would in any case be favorable. It is not likely to be possible over long periods. It is improbable, moreover, that any one country could continue for long using an equalization fund in this fashion without provoking retaliation.

In the long run, therefore, equalization funds offer an improved means of smoothing out temporary fluctuations in the exchange rates, but are powerless to remedy long-continued drains of funds (or inward movements of gold and foreign assets) resulting from disequilibria in the balances of payments. These must be remedied by allowing the currency to depreciate (or, on the contrary, by accumulating large excess reserves), or by appropriate action to bring credit issues and therefore the national price-structure into equilibrium with international conditions.

Attempts to peg the rate of exchange at a level above that

warranted by the state of the market have invariably been accompanied by the appearance of a black market in which the pegged currency sells at a discount. Those who fear depreciation will endeavor to get their funds out of the country and, if buyers are not forthcoming at the official rate, they will sell at lower rates. This they can do by selling securities abroad, by exporting the currency to foreign centers, by transferring credits abroad, and in many other ways. The authority which is endeavoring to peg the rate is led, therefore, to attempt at least partial control of the market by placing restrictions and hindrances to the export of gold or foreign assets, by control, official or unofficial, of capital exports, and by restrictions on the payment of external debt service or payments for current imports. Once begun, this process of intervention leads rather quickly to the attempt at complete monopoly of foreign exchange by the institution of exchange control. Partial control tends to become more and more complete, covering not only the major items of the balance of payments, such as export receipts and import payments, but also the invisibles, such as capital movements, tourist traffic, shipping receipts, etc. The only possibility of halting such an evolution is a restoration of equilibrium by action that effectively reduces national purchasing power. M. Piatier gives many examples drawn from various countries of this process of evolution,[6] and quotes in conclusion the statement of M. Auboin (Director-General of the Bank for International Settlements), that "when the authorities undertake to check by administrative measures the draining of foreign currency or gold reserves, they begin by declaring that they have absolutely no intention of hindering commercial transactions, but simply of preventing the 'speculative' exodus of capital by refusing to satisfy 'unjustified applications for foreign currency.'

"It is soon realised, however, that—as if by chance—all calls for foreign currency are needed for commercial purposes. Moreover—also by chance—the influx of currencies slackens and the quantity available falls well below the figure cor-

[6] Piatier, *op. cit.*, Ch. IV.

THE ADVENT OF NATIONALISM

responding to the country's exports. It therefore becomes necessary to carry the measures a stage further and to decide that all foreign currencies derived from exports are to be handed over compulsorily to the monetary authorities and to make a distinction between applications for currencies according as they are 'legitimate' or not.

"Fresh difficulties then arise. The introduction of control automatically involves the appearance of a dual rate of foreign currencies; the official rate at which the authorities continue to supply currencies to fill approved applications, and the depreciated rate at which they negotiate, either beyond the frontiers or within the country, on a clandestine market, which invariably forms despite the severest penalties.

"Naturally currencies at the official rate are unobtainable except from the authorities. Only strictly indispensable sums enter the country, for once they have entered they can no longer be freely exported. The country thus becomes, to use a very apt expression, 'a capital trap.'"

The fact is that exchange control becomes necessary only when the controlling country is unable to meet its commitments abroad—when it is in a state of external insolvency. At a moment of crisis, such as attends the devaluation of a currency or the sudden withdrawal of large short-term funds, the temporary imposition of controls may give time to bring about adjustments of the national balance of payments, either by calling in or mobilizing foreign assets or by restricting national credit. Unless such action is effective in restoring equilibrium in the balance of payments, rationing must be resorted to. Such a drastic step, however, means that the problem is solved by allocating sacrifices among various economic groups. Foreign creditors are usually the first to suffer by the withholding of the foreign exchange necessary to meet their claims. Consumers of imported goods and exporters dependent upon imported raw materials are next in line. As the controllers of the exchange market become more proficient, other ways are found of throwing part of the burden on to foreign exporters. Some aspects of this rearrangement of claims are discussed below. Here it is necessary only to point out that exchange control is essentially similar to a receivership. Its basic cause is external insolvency; its methods of procedure must be the mobilization of assets and the arrangement of priorities of claims to those assets.

In order to carry through such a receivership, control has to be exercised over all incoming and outgoing payments. This means in practice that governments, or their monetary agents, must plan and manage not only the commodity imports and exports, but all external transactions involving payments or receipts. The planning of imports necessarily involves decisions not only as to what may be consumed within the country, but also as to what may be produced, since allocations of available exchange must be made as between finished goods and raw materials for which import permits are demanded. In the effort to obtain foreign exchange, shipping freights, railway tariffs, and even tourist expenses must be controlled. In the summer of 1935, for example, German tourists flocked to Switzerland because a commercial agreement had been signed bartering coal against tourist services. Tourist coupons to a large aggregate amount were promptly issued in Germany, payable at any Swiss post office. The coal did not materialize since the price proved too high and Switzerland was left with a large credit in blocked marks. The following summer saw large contingents of German tourists in Italy, since there were blocked lire balances accumulated as a result of German exports during the Ethiopian campaign. Many similar instances might be cited of the sudden and erratic shifts of trade and other external transactions resulting from the necessity, as exchange control was extended, to fit those transactions into the pattern of payments dictated by government policy rather than by economic considerations.

It is not surprising, therefore, to find that by 1935, when totalitarian governments had begun to discover the latent possibilities of the monetary weapon, exchange control became the principal instrument in the regulation of commerce. It also became the pivot upon which the regulation of national credit and the organization of national production turned. When this stage had been reached, with national and international transactions firmly under control, it became possible to manipulate the monetary weapon in an effort to secure trading advantages abroad. This development from a negative safeguarding of the balance of payments to positive, and even aggressive, use of the bargaining power implicit in State trading monopoly was most marked and effective in the German system; but, according to their means and organizing ability, all the exchange-control countries endeavored to organize their bargaining power along parallel lines.

It is as an instrument of economic warfare that exchange control must be judged. The German contributor to the exchange-control studies made a skillful case for it as the monetary basis of an expanding system of regulated trade. His criticisms of the failure of the free-exchange countries to establish effective conditions for the working of multilateral trade and free exchanges are penetrating and difficult to refute. The conclusion drawn, however, that regulated bilateral trade based on exchange control is not only the inevitable alternative, but a superior system of managed currency and trade, is not borne out by recent experience. As succeeding sections of this chapter will show, exchange control as used in Germany has proved an admirable instrument of rearmament and war preparation, enabling that country to organize a vast military effort of which at least part of the cost was borne by foreign creditors and trade rivals. It is probably true that the countries with which Germany built up a considerable trade on a clearing basis made reasonably good bargains, though the future implications of their political and economic dependence upon a single dominant market need to be considered. It is also true that some of Germany's creditors saved something of their claims by the institution of compulsory clearing, though they were less successful in maintaining their competitive trading position in third countries. The United States has probably been the largest involuntary foreign contributor to the German war effort by the default on its debt claims and direct investments, the blocking of commercial arrears and even banking obligations, and the loss of trade, directly and indirectly.

Exchange control is the chief instrument of monetary nationalism and should be judged as such. It provides a means whereby the national market may be segregated and all external transactions controlled in detail so as to divert trade into the channels desired by government policy. It is incompatible with the principles upon which free international trade is based, since they are essentially co-operative whereas exchange control as now practiced is an instrument of State policy designed for the diversion and regulation of trade in a great effort of economic mobilization.

The Scaling Down of Debt

Pressure of outward capital movements upon available supplies of foreign exchange was the main reason for the imposition of exchange controls in the crisis of 1931–32. The burden of international indebtedness weighed heavily upon many countries. The only possibility of discharging the interest and amortization payments upon such debt might have been the maintenance of a great volume of international trade at high price levels. But the quantum of trade shrunk rapidly and prices fell even faster. The total value of world trade in 1931 was only 58 per cent, and in 1932 only 39 per cent, of its value in 1929. Debt obligations, many of which were expressed in gold, remained at their former level or were increased by short-term borrowings in 1930 and 1931. It was manifestly impossible for most debtor countries to meet their obligations when their only means of payment—their export trade—was struggling under such handicaps. The panic withdrawal of short-term loans and flights of domestic capital that set in as a result of this alarming situation completed the demoralization of the exchange market. As M. Madgearu has pointed out, even the cessation of capital imports was sufficient to have

THE SCALING DOWN OF DEBT 243

caused serious inconvenience to many debtor countries.[7] When capital inflow ceased and was succeeded by massive withdrawals of capital at a time when export outlets were closing and prices were falling rapidly, the debtor States of Europe and Latin America had no option but to suspend the service of their debts. In the year 1931 default, partial or complete, occurred in eight Latin-American countries,[8] while three others followed in the next two years.[9] In Europe important debtor countries declared transfer moratoria—Hungary in December, 1931; Bulgaria and Greece in April, 1932; Austria in June, 1932; Yugoslavia in November, 1932; Rumania in January, 1933; and Germany in June, 1933. These moratoria were not concerned with reparation payments and war debts, which had been suspended at President Hoover's suggestion in June, 1930, the former being effectively abandoned at the Lausanne Conference in July, 1932 and the latter falling into default after the breakdown of the Monetary and Economic Conference in July, 1933. The defaults and moratoria of 1931 and 1932 were in respect of commercial, banking, and public debts other than war obligations. It is not an exaggeration, indeed, to state that all debtor countries except those with preferential access to a great money market, as the British Dominions and colonies had to London, fell into default in these years of crisis.

As the years passed and partial recovery set in, international indebtedness was scaled down. The methods used to reduce the burden of debt were varied. The "gold clause" in loan contracts was repudiated by all debtors, public and private, so that interest and repayments fell due in the paper money. The depreciation of the currencies of creditor countries also lightened the burden on the debtors. The primary reason, indeed, for maintaining the nominal gold value of

---

[7] V. Madgearu, *La Politique économique extérieure de la Roumanie*, pp. 25–26.
[8] Bolivia, Peru, Chile, Brazil, Uruguay, Argentina, Dominica, Colombia.
[9] Costa Rica, Cuba, Paraguay.

debtor currencies was a desire to take advantage of the overvalued exchange rate in so far as debt payments were concerned. There were, in addition, many instances of actual repayment of debt by countries such as India, South Africa, Canada, New Zealand, the Argentine, and Finland, which were able to accumulate foreign assets. Interest reductions were negotiated and conversion operations undertaken notably by Australia. A considerable amount of debt repatriation took place also, by purchasing depreciated securities in foreign markets. Under clearing and payments agreements which were negotiated largely in response to the moratorium declared by Germany in June, 1933, and made more drastic a year later, provision was made for a gradual reduction of debt arrears. The manner in which use was made of such methods of debt collection by the British bilateral treaties has been analyzed in some detail by Dr. Tasca.[10]

Behind the shelter of exchange control, therefore, many debtor countries were able to negotiate with their creditors for reduction of their commitments. There was, in fact, much good will on the side of creditor interests and good faith on the part of debtors. Moreover, as the experience of many small countries bears witness, such good faith and skillful management were capable both of reducing international debt burdens and of devaluing the currencies that had been maintained at overvalued rates behind the shelter of exchange control. The fear of uncontrollable inflation had made it impossible for most of these countries to devalue when sterling was depreciated in September, 1931. It was obvious that not only debt reduction but devaluation was necessary if monetary equilibrium was to be re-established, exchange control relinquished, and multilateral trade restored. Important steps in this direction were taken by Austria between 1932 and 1936. The skillful technique followed by the National Bank of Austria consisted essentially in a gradual extension of the types of transaction permitted to private negotiators at the

[10] Henry J. Tasca, *World Trading Systems*.

free market rate of exchange.[11] It was found that, as the market extended and was officially recognized, the value of the schilling settled at a level below the old parity, but above the rates that had ruled in the illicit transactions of the black market. Austria had certain political advantages in these years, being able to profit both from League sponsorship in the conversion of her external debt and from the rivalries of the great powers in the negotiation of commercial treaties. Her monetary policy, however, was pivoted upon drastic financial controls that inhibited effective measures of attack upon the grave unemployment situation which persisted through the years of financial recovery and monetary stabilization. It may perhaps be questioned whether the social costs and political risks of such a policy were outweighed by the financial results; but at least it is clear that the technical possibilities of devaluation and exchange stabilization were demonstrated. With more concern for social welfare, stabilization might still have been achieved at a somewhat lower level of devaluation.

In other European countries progress was made by other methods towards much the same goal. In Hungary, Yugoslavia, Bulgaria, and Rumania, the system of import surcharges and export premiums, either uniform or variable according to commodities and the countries of their origin, was becoming stabilized and approximated to a devaluation of the currencies. In all these countries, however, as in Greece and Turkey, the German trade drive intervened and checked the progress towards relaxation of exchange control. The technique adopted in Latin-American countries was somewhat different, consisting mainly of the fixation of differential exchange rates for official and private transactions.[12]

The outstanding case of exchange control adopted as a

---

[11] Cf. the summary of these developments by Dr. Lieser-Burger, in Appendix I to Piatier, *op. cit.*

[12] Cf. Herbert M. Bratter, *op. cit.*, and Angel Valle et Juan M. Ferrer, *op. cit.*

mechanism to regulate the balance of payments, however, was that of Germany. In the first stages of its operation, the German exchange-control system, like those mentioned above, was directed mainly to an attempt at restoring monetary equilibrium. The German economy was relieved of reparation payments from June, 1930 onwards; but it was burdened with a considerable volume of public and private external debt, much of it on short-term. Standstill arrangements were entered into in respect of certain banking and municipal debts. Commercial arrears and the service of long-term debt were blocked, but efforts were made to facilitate their discharge by the encouragement of additional exports.

A new phase was entered when, shortly after the advent to power of the National Socialist party, there was centralization of control over transactions affecting blocked accounts and over the repatriation of German securities. At the same time there was begun a vast program of public expenditure for rearmament and the provision of employment. In June, 1933 a transfer moratorium was declared on all external debt except for interest and amortization payments on the Dawes loan, interest on the Young loan, and payments under the standstill arrangements. This moratorium, extended a year later to include the Dawes and Young loans, was met by the imposition of clearing arrangements in all the creditor countries that had passive trade balances with Germany and were therefore able to retain payment by their nationals for imports beyond the value of exports to Germany. These payments were applied to the discharge of debt service. The German decision, modified in some degree by the institution of clearing arrangements, was in fact a refusal to use foreign exchange for debt service. The exchange so withheld was needed for the purchase of imports with which to prosecute the expansionist program, which was, in fact, largely a program of rearmament. The first costs of German rearmament were thrown, therefore, upon the foreign creditors—and particularly upon those in the United States. Americans had not only invested heavily in German securities, but the United States government was unable to institute a clearing system since Germany bought from the United States more than it exported there.

The foreign owners of German securities were not the only involuntary contributors to that country's rearmament program. As the scope of exchange control was extended, all foreigners who had property claims in Germany became unable to transfer abroad either their capital assets or the profits from them. Among those hardest hit were emigrés from Germany who became unable to withdraw any but a fraction of their capital assets. The owners of foreign branch enterprises and direct business investments, and even exporters who were owed arrears of commercial payments, also found their holdings blocked.

The regulations under which the holdings of blocked marks could be used within Germany became steadily more severe, so that, as their use was limited, their value in foreign currencies fell heavily. The lowest valuation naturally was that for emigrant marks, which fell to a pitiful proportion of their nominal value. The blocked marks available for security purchases within Germany sold for approximately one tenth of their nominal value; those (arising mainly from the standstill credits) available for travel purposes fell to less than half their nominal value as the demand for tourist purposes declined.

Little information is available concerning the use made of the credit remaining in the blocked accounts, which from 1933 onwards were concentrated in the Konversionskasse; but it is reasonable to infer that this institution, like every other in Germany, invested its assets in government securities. As the rearmament program expanded, the vast expenditures were met by various types of government bills which were taken up by all banks, financial institutions, business concerns, etc. When every reserve fund, pension account, insurance reserve, and savings bank was a creditor of the Reich, it is reasonable to suppose that the blocked mark accounts of foreign creditors were invested in the same way. The solvency of these claims, therefore, became a function of the German government's credit. The market's estimate of the chances of realizing such foreign claims, even at the end of 1938, before war had been rendered almost inevitable by the German seizure of Prague in March, 1939, varied from about 6 per cent in the case of emigrants' claims, to 10–12 per cent for industrial and commercial investments—or, in betting language, from 16 to 1 to 8 to 1 against. During 1939 and 1940, especially since the outbreak of war, the odds have lengthened considerably and most foreign owners of property in Germany have reconciled themselves to the fact that their assets have, in fact, been hypothecated to build up the German army and air force. The initial step in this process was the moratorium declared in June, 1933 by which foreign exchange that might have been utilized for amortization and interest payments on foreign debt was retained in order to pay for raw material imports.

The Theory of an Autonomous Konjunktur Policy

The tremendous deflationary strain thrown upon the national economies of debtor countries after 1929 does not need emphasis. It has already been argued [13] that one of the major reasons for the breakdown of the international gold standard in 1931 was the desire of every country to escape from deflationary pressure so that national policies of credit expansion might be initiated. In the fantastic situation where the chief creditor country in the world redoubled its import barriers while debtor countries frantically increased their export surpluses in an effort to discharge their international obligations, there was cumulative pressure upon the prices of goods entering international trade. Any country that endeavored by cheaper interest rates to arrest the spiral of deflation ran the risk of unbalancing its commodity trade and causing a flight of capital. Meantime, progressive deflation uncovered successive strata of weakness, each fall in purchasing power causing more unemployment and therefore further declines in pur-

---

[13] See above, pp. 115–116.

chasing power. The canalization of these pressures upon Great Britain's free-trade market finally caused that country to adopt a protective policy, and sharp withdrawals of short-term credit forced a depreciation of sterling. With exchange stability destroyed by this collapse at the center, deflationary pressure was accentuated elsewhere, particularly in the debtor countries. Unemployment rose to catastrophic levels until, at the depth of the depression in 1932, it was conservatively estimated by the Director of the International Labor Office to have affected at least thirty million workers.

Subsequent efforts to cope with this vast disorganization of productive activity necessarily proceeded along national, rather than international, lines. Those countries which allowed their currencies to depreciate, and thereby freed themselves from external drains on their currency reserves, were able to embark upon expansionist credit policies that checked the cycle of deflation. Notable examples of such policies were provided by Australia,[14] and Sweden.[15] It does not detract from the skill with which these countries managed their recovery programs to point out that they were appreciably helped by the fact that the depression touched bottom in Great Britain in the middle of 1932 and sterling prices turned upward from the first quarter of 1933. In the years that followed there was a checkered but definite upswing of the business cycle. Though the pattern of recovery was not uniform in the main trading countries, largely because of the necessity for successive adjustments of exchange parities, there gradually emerged an approximation to exchange equilibrium over the greater part of the trading world. The sterling area was a great region of exchange stability and after the depreciation of the dollar, beginning in April, 1933, and its provisional stabilization in January, 1934, there was a fair measure of stability between sterling and the dollar. The area of *de facto* stabilization appeared to be widening in the years 1935 and 1936. The Latin-American countries found it possi-

[14] Cf. D. B. Copland, *Monetary Policy in Australia*.
[15] Cf. Gunnar Boös, *Survey of Sweden's External Economic Policy*.

ble to loosen their exchange-control regulations.[16] Even the countries practicing exchange control in central and southeastern Europe took steps to regularize their systems of import surcharges and export premiums, and even to mitigate the administration of their exchange-control systems.[17] When the Tripartite Agreement of September, 1936 gave an opportunity to devalue the remaining gold bloc currencies, it seemed as if there was a possibility of a tentative approach once again to the formation of a freer system of multilateral trade based upon stable exchange relationships.

The experience of the totalitarian countries did not fit into the general pattern. The external economic relations of the U. S. S. R. remained subject to complete State monopoly. Its program of national equipment was pursued independently of external trade or monetary considerations, and it continued to illustrate the fact that a completely autonomous national economic policy is possible if two conditions are fulfilled—autarky pursued to the logical extreme and planned economic activity based upon compulsion. An autonomous economic system demands that the State which practices it must be prepared to abandon the advantages of international specialization and force its citizens into compliance with the requirements of a planned economy. If these conditions are fulfilled, it is possible to expand credit, increase (at least for a time) the types of production that are desired, and provide full employment.

These objectives of national policy are characteristic of war economy, or preparation for war. It has long been clear that there was a large strategic element in the U. S. S. R.'s program of industrialization. Japan has been engaged in warfare on the continent of Asia almost continuously since 1931. Her economic policy, as Professor Royama frankly admits, has

[16] See A. T. Bandeira de Mello, *Les Politiques et la paix*, pp. 22 ff.; Herbert M. Bratter, *op. cit.*; L. Ponton, *Le Traits essentiels de la politique économique du Mexique*.

[17] See Madgearu, *La Politique extérieure de la Roumanie*, pp. 12–13; Buday, *op. cit.*, pp. 37–38; Yovanovitch, *op. cit.*, pp. 9 ff.; Tchakaloff and Zagoroff, *op. cit.*, pp. 18 ff.

necessarily been governed by this fact. Behind the shelter of exchange control there has been progressive credit expansion and the stimulation of war industries to the detriment of consumers, and latterly also of the export trades. Spain, torn and impoverished by civil war, has been added to the list of totalitarian States. Whether Italy's adoption of exchange control in May, 1934, as a result of reflationary policies straining the balance of payments, was a preparation for the Ethiopian war may be an open question; but there is little doubt that the economic consequences of that war, of Italian "nonintervention" in Spain, and of subsequent war preparedness have necessitated increasing stringency of exchange control.

The country for whose autonomous credit policies most economic virtue has been claimed is Germany. The exponents of the theory of *Wehrwirtschaft*, however, have never concealed the fact that the primary objective of national economic policy since March, 1933 has been war preparedness. In the light of events since Austria was occupied in March, 1938, it might seem superfluous to stress this point. The whole conduct of German policy fits into a consistent pattern of mobilization. As long as there remained even the slightest hope that actual conflict might be avoided, there was some reluctance outside of Germany to accept this rather obvious, and indeed proclaimed, fact. Foreign economists, especially those who advocated expansionist monetary policies in their own countries, were prone to stress the employment aspect of the German experience. German economists propounded theories rationalizing that experience as a solution of the problem of business fluctuations and as a model upon which other countries might build systems of full employment so that an expanding system of regulated bilateral trade might eventually replace what they described as the anarchy of free multilateral trade.

It must be conceded that the achievements of German economic policy since 1933 are impressive in many respects. Having been finally freed of reparation payments by the Lausanne Conference in July, 1932, and of the greater part of her foreign obligations by her own unilateral moratorium declared in June, 1933, Germany proceeded to finance a vast program of rearmament and public works by means of a great inflation that was not permitted to reveal itself in a rising spiral of prices and wages. The technical devices by which this inflation was carried out were complicated and ingenious. Statistical measurement can only be guesswork since essential information has been progressively withheld. The main body of expenditure has been upon the building up of a great army and its equipment on a scale hitherto unknown, upon accessory services such as fortifications, airports, barracks, storage equipment, roads, canals, strategic railways, and upon the heavy industry needed not only for the production of war materials but for communication services and a great building boom. Having started with an unemployed population of at least six millions, there was a great deal of slack to be taken up in the economic system before labor shortages began to appear and supplies of essential raw materials needed to be conserved. The formulation of a great program of construction, much of which was in the field of civilian construction and even social welfare, though it was practically all accessory to rearmament, was pushed forward vigorously. The necessary costs were met by credit expansion of various types, but mostly by the issuance of short-term bills. Care was taken not to inflate unduly the currency issues that served as instruments of individual purchasing power. As production increased, and with it profits and wages, taxation provided larger revenues. One of the pivots on which the whole financial scheme worked was that the increased production was intercepted for the purposes of the State. Profits were limited, wages and prices were not permitted to rise, and when occasional commodity shortages appeared, rationing and improved distribution were organized. There seems little doubt that in the latter years of the program such shortages, as well as a deterioration of quality and delays in the satisfaction of demands for certain goods, became more marked.

As in any great investment boom, there were apparent

AUTONOMOUS KONJUNKTUR POLICY

signs of increasing prosperity. Greater numbers were employed, savings increased, credit was plentiful and cheap, new construction and invention were apparent on every hand. Despite occasional short periods of difficulty, there was never any real problem in placing the short-term bills. From time to time substantial amounts were funded into long-term loans, but business institutions and even private individuals as well as banks and financial enterprises carried increasing amounts of government paper. There was a slow circulation of this paper and every source of available credit was swept into government use. In addition to foreign holdings of blocked marks, the property of proscribed groups yielded some funds; but all property rights and all labor were closely regulated and, if necessary, conscripted for national service.

Behind all the technical expedients and ingenious devices that were developed to cope with transitional periods of economic friction, there lay the driving force of inexorable and single-minded will power. The economic effort of preparedness displayed all the characteristics of the military campaigns for the support of which it was designed—the same unified purpose and direction, co-ordination of instruments, and determined ingenuity in breaking through or circumventing obstacles. Within Germany itself this ruthless and determined drive to complete mobilization of economic resources successfully enlisted all available labor and materials in the building up of a great military machine. In doing so, heavy demands were made upon the workers as producers, as consumers, and as citizens. Hours of work were lengthened, labor was moved where it was needed, and trade-unions were smashed. Wages were prevented from rising and consumers' goods failed to keep pace with armament production. Individual liberty was subordinated to State necessity.

In this sense the autonomous Konjunktur policy was certainly successful. There was no slackening of production, no decline of employment, and possibly, on the average of social classes, some increase in the standard of living. How long the process of acceleration could have continued without inducing a serious, if slow, decline in living standards is open to some difference of opinion. It has been contended by some observers that there were signs even before the war of such deterioration, as for example in a rising incidence of industrial accidents and deficiency diseases. Whether this intensive limit of effort was being reached or not may be a matter of dispute; but there was clear evidence of an extensive limit of labor power. Not only had unemployment disappeared, but women were called back into industry and immigrant labor was sought. With the strongest will and the finest technical organization, an economic system cannot continue to accelerate indefinitely. Moreover, as will be shown in the next section, there is an external limit also to the ability of any nation to pursue a policy of independent economic development.

The clue to an understanding of Germany's autonomous Konjunktur policy, therefore, is totalitarian preparation for totalitarian war. It is a policy of all or nothing, a throwing of all reserves into one great and sustained effort. If the effort can be sustained until victory is achieved and wider fields of organization are opened up, the costs and sacrifices are counted worth while; but there can be no slackening of effort and sacrifice since the struggle must be renewed on a greater scale. The rewards, like the calculus of advantage, are not individual, but collective. In other words, they do not bring concrete satisfactions to the individual, such as a greater abundance and variety of commodities and more leisure; but instead they consist largely in the consciousness of mystical identification with the growing power of the State. Necessarily the conflict must be renewed after each victory since the whole concept is one of assertion rather than of achievement.

It is impossible that such policies of independent economic nationalism can ever form the basis of international co-operation. They are, in their conception, contradictory and hostile to such co-operation. Instead of a world of interdependent co-operative national communities, they aim at national assertion and aggrandisement. Their ultimate aim is world domination, and their technique is that of conflict.

For the mobilization of national economic activity, exchange control is an essential weapon. Capital cannot be allowed to escape from the national economy, individual citizens cannot be allowed to engage in import or export transactions, or even to pay debt services or to travel, in ways that may weaken the State's control of economic resources. It is natural to find, therefore, that exchange control is an expedient adopted by warring States. Theoretically, it is argued, State expenditure behind exchange control might be directed to the promotion of full employment in production for consumers' satisfactions and not for war. Actually this does not happen when State control of economic activity becomes effective. In any case, there is very good reason to doubt whether any system of full employment reached in this way could provide standards of living as high or as secure as could be provided by a smoothly operating system of international co-operation. There is still more reason to doubt whether it is possible, without a lowering of living standards and the risk of subsequent economic collapse, to maintain a state of full employment that has been reached by national expenditures made possible by an independent monetary policy.

The case put up by German economists for exchange control, as the central feature of a new system of international trade based upon full employment in the various national economies, is essentially dependent upon the belief that a national economy can not only be brought to, but maintained in, full employment by judicious conduct of credit policy unhampered by strains on the national balance of payments. This postulates not only monetary skill, but completely co-ordinated and centralized control of national economic activity in detail. It is theoretically conceivable that such detailed regulation, if conducted with extreme skill, might eliminate unemployment, but only at the cost of sacrificing the advantages of international specialization. Unless centralized control should prove more efficient than individual initiative, it must entail a further lowering of living standards from this cause. It is, moreover, easier to conceive such control being effective when the objectives of organization are dominated by the single aim of military power rather than by the multifarious satisfaction of consumers' demands. As an instrument of war, exchange control is essential. As a safeguard against utter disorganization of a national economy whose balance of payments is out of equilibrium, it is sometimes a necessary evil. As a mechanism for maximizing social welfare, it is sheer humbug.

Exchange Control as an Instrument of Commercial Policy

Exchange control is defended by Dr. Meyer as "the only possible and lasting solution by which the monetary and Konjunktur policies of the various countries can be co-ordinated in such a manner as to permit an autonomous Konjunktur policy side by side with stable exchange rates." He argues that "no currency system can last which, in order to maintain the stability of the exchange rate, i. e., in the interests of equalization of the balance of payments, necessitates a monetary and credit policy contrary to the needs of a Konjunktur policy." [18] Such a currency system, however, did in fact last for many decades while the international gold standard was operating in a peaceful world. The examples which Dr. Meyer gives to prove his thesis are all drawn from the period of economic disorganization after the war of 1914–18. The essence of his argument is that governments must have their hands completely free to pursue whatever monetary and economic policy they wish to follow within their own borders. This emphasis on monetary nationalism is quite clearly incompatible with exchange stability arrived at by national adjustments to international equilibrium. Many economists, impressed by the violence of economic fluctuations and the

[18] Fritz Meyer, *op. cit.*

severity of unemployment in recent years, have sympathized with the view that national monetary policy should not be influenced by pressure on the balance of payments. Dr. Meyer, however, rejects the solution usually proposed by those economists who advocate fluctuating or variable exchange rates, and belittles the practical utility of periodic adjustment of currencies such as took place after the signing of the Tripartite Agreement of September, 1936.

His solution of the problem may be cited in his own words: "By adopting a bilateral equalization policy with the measures set forth in the New Plan, an absolute substitute for the (gold-standard) mechanism was brought nearer. Quotas of raw materials and a preferential allotment of labour to the exporting industries produce the same systematic detachment of goods and services from domestic consumption as is effected by the price mechanism of a free-exchange policy. As, however, the placing of exports presents a price problem which is not solved by simply detaching the goods from domestic consumption, the Supplementary Export Process (Zusatzausfuhrverfahren) reduces the price-level of exports to below the general price-level and to a level necessitated by the competitive situation in foreign markets. This again only creates the situation which would also exist if Germany had depreciated her currency or had lowered the price-level of her export goods within the framework of the gold standard to an extent which would allow the parity selected between the Mark and gold to be upheld. German foreign exchange control can, therefore, with every justification be termed a currency form presenting the most perfect embodiment of the fundamental ideas of the classical gold economy, i. e., a currency which maintains exchange rates by adjusting the domestic price-level. This system is tenable, because by restricting the adjustment of price movements to a partial price-level it can never contradict the requirements of the Konjunktur policy." [19]

This euphemistic and somewhat disingenuous statement, it will be recognized, postulates State control over production by

[19] Fritz Meyer, *op. cit*.

means of the rationing of raw materials, industrial conscription of labor, detailed price regulation, and discriminatory subsidies. By these means, a certain proportion of national labor and material supplies is devoted to the production of commodities for export at prices below those paid by the home consumer. This is no more "the most perfect embodiment of the classical gold economy" than the maintenance of the mark at its par value for debt payments is exchange stability. Both in regard to exchange stability and to the conduct of international trade, Dr. Meyer's statement glosses over the truth. Only in respect of his final phrase, that this system "can never contradict the requirements of the Konjunktur policy," is it possible to accept his argument as an accurate description of German policy in recent years.

M. Piatier has drawn attention to one aspect of the use of exchange control as a mechanism of debt reduction. "It is," as he says, "to the interest of all debtor countries with liabilities expressed in foreign currency to keep a national currency intact. It is the only way in which they can take advantage of foreign devaluations; since currencies are exchanged at the official rate, debtors have to pay a smaller number of units of national currency to obtain the same amount of devisen needed for their payments. Any devaluation in the debtor country would wipe out this advantage.

"Germany is almost alone in increasing the profit realised at the expense of creditor countries by repurchasing, at a low figure, blocked account certificates negotiated on the various financial markets. The profit is equal to the difference between the nominal value of the blocked account certificate and its free repurchase rate." [20]

Differential depreciation of the mark has indeed been characteristic of German trading methods ever since Dr. Schacht launched his great trade drive in southeastern Europe in 1935. In negotiating trade treaties, and in making particular bilateral bargains, the rate of exchange to be fixed between the mark and other currencies is one of the chief points of dis-

[20] Piatier, *op. cit.*, Ch. VI.

cussion. There is differentiation also of blocked marks according to their origin and to the purposes for which their use is permitted. The depreciation of "emigrant marks" is well over 90 per cent. Even in trade with a free-exchange country such as the United States, different commodities have been bought at world market prices or at prices above that of the world market in varying degree according to the German need for them, while exports have been subsidized to meet competition. The net effect of such trading is equivalent to a differential depreciation of the mark. The value of the mark in gold, or in any stable currency, varies from country to country, from time to time, from commodity to commodity, and from transaction to transaction. For statistical purposes the mark values of imports and exports cannot be converted into any other unit of valuation, but are simply question marks.

Nor is this experience confined to Germany. Wherever the new system of bilateral trade balancing by clearing arrangements has spread in exchange-control countries, there has ensued a fragmentation of the external value of the national currency. Only Poland appears to have been exempt from this experience. In Italy, as late as May 15, 1939, an emigrant lira was created. Bulgaria, Rumania, Yugoslavia, Hungary, Greece, and other countries have varied forms of import surcharges and export premiums representing a differential depreciation of their currencies.

It is in the negotiation of clearing agreements, however, that such discriminatory depreciation has been most effectively achieved. On this point something needs to be said of the bilateral balancing of imports and exports which forms the second part of Dr. Meyer's claim for exchange control as a new monetary system. A candid account of this process would start with a description of the massive purchases made by Germany wherever such purchases could be negotiated on a clearing basis. The goods purchased were not necessarily used in Germany, but were on occasion supplied to other clearing countries or sold on free markets to get foreign exchange. The prices at which they were bought were generally well above the market price in free-exchange countries. The prices at which they were sold outside of Germany were negotiated separately and, on occasion, were much below the prices paid, and even below the competitive prices in free-exchange countries. In this way, dumping went far to ruin the export market for the clearing countries in free-exchange areas.

Germany obtained these goods by negotiating with the export institutes or similar official bodies which have been established in most exchange-control countries. Bulk sales at a high price were obviously tempting to such bodies, since they were saved the laborious task of disposing of merchandise in small quantities by hard bargaining in scattered markets. Producers were paid in their own national currency so that the National Banks concerned found their credit and note issues expanded without any corresponding increase of reserve assets except a credit in blocked marks. Since the prices paid were high the exchange value of their currencies was depreciated, in fact if not in law; but they were unable to import freely from free-exchange countries since they lacked the exchange resources necessary to do so.

Ultimately, after a considerable lapse of time, they were able to import from Germany against payment from their blocked accounts. Doubtless the German negotiators attempted wherever possible to drive hard bargains by setting a high value on the mark, by offering unsuitable commodities (including discarded types of armament), and by charging prices as high as the market would bear. It is probable, however, that after the initial devices used in this type of trading became known, the smaller countries were able to make relatively good bargains. The chief strain thrown upon them arose from the fact that they were the involuntary lenders, for long periods, of substantial quantities of foodstuffs and raw materials and have continued to provide the intermediate credit for the trade both ways. German exports at times were pushed not only by subsidized prices but also by long-credit terms, which in fact constituted a risk not for the German exporters but for the creditors of Germany, since nonpayment merely reduced the foreign clearing accounts while the German exporters had been paid in blocked marks. A minor, but characteristic, device was the payment for tourist services, and even for the rent of shooting boxes, in blocked marks.[21] The situation of the National Banks in the exporting countries was impaired for lack of free foreign exchange. They were not able to meet external debt service nor to provide the exchange for imports from free-exchange countries. The main sufferers, therefore, were the exporters in countries such as the United States and Great Britain, and the creditors in those countries. As the bonds of the clearing countries fell on the free markets because of increased default, Germany was able to repeat the device of buying in the securities whose value had been lowered by her own policy. These could then be sold to the debtor country at higher values, to reduce its claims in blocked marks.

Every aspect of this trading system bears the mark of totalitarian methods. Thrusting the financing of trade on to the financially weaker countries, depleting their foreign exchange reserves, depreciating their external credit, pressing down the external value of their currencies, spoiling their export markets by the dumping of surpluses, and raising their domestic price levels, Germany was playing for much more than a mere temporary advantage in current trade. In the totalitarian conduct of trade policies, by using the methods of discriminating State monopoly, the German authorities were doing much more than establish a "bilateral equalization" at the expense of the German consumers. They were, in fact, building a new trading system, the center of which was the German military economy—a bilateral system in which all the traffic should flow to and from the center. This system was not designed to broaden into multilateral interchange in which there would be room for all the great trading countries to co-operate. It was designed to supplant and destroy the world trading system that Great Britain had built up and that

[21] Paul Einzig, *Bloodless Invasion* (London, 1939).

the United States was trying to revive. Its methods are best understood when compared with those by which great monopolistic corporations have attempted, by horizontal and vertical integration, to destroy the trade of their competitors. In such struggles for power full use is made of discriminatory prices, dumping, massive raw material purchases, and even of terrorism. While the struggle is in progress, the smaller traders who supply materials or purchase the finished products may gain substantial advantages; but the achievement of even a partial monopoly advantage by one of the great competitors is apt not only to deprive them of such advantages, but to put them in a position where they must pay tribute.

CHAPTER VIII

Commercial Diplomacy

Treaty Degeneration

THE CONFUSION and deterioration of international relations in recent years is nowhere more evident than in the field of commercial policy. It is significant of the breakdown that diplomacy has been so much concerned with economic affairs, not in the settlement of great principles, but in the administration of detailed and often petty bargaining. There has been a notable commercializing of diplomacy. In the nineteenth century, governments often used political and even military power in support of the private ventures of their nationals; but with the growth of State intervention and planning, trade and diplomacy have been fused. In those countries which still cling to private capitalist enterprise, the traditions of foreign policy have died hard. Consular and commercial services have been extended and economic sections have been added to foreign offices, but control of policy has remained in the hands of men trained in the old school.[1]

There has been no such dichotomy of foreign policy in the totalitarian States. Unified direction and single-minded pursuit of definite objectives have achieved a co-ordination of political and economic policies. It is this fact that has enabled States, which at the beginning of the depression were laboring

---

[1] A notable illustration is provided by the account of his activities in Germany recently written by Sir Nevile Henderson, *The Failure of a Mission* (London, 1940).

under political disadvantages and economic impoverishment, to build up formidable instruments of diplomacy in both spheres as well as in that of propaganda. If war is an extension of diplomacy, diplomacy may serve as a preparation for war; and since totalitarian war is waged on many fronts, of which the economic is not the least important, totalitarian diplomacy has given new meaning to the concept of economic penetration.

It is in the negotiation of commercial treaties that the conflict between the old and the new diplomacy is most clearly revealed. The doctrine of laissez faire dominated nineteenth-century international relations. Commercial treaties were designed to lay a stable foundation on which international trade could be built by the multitudinous and varied activities of private enterprise. Their concern was with legal rights, the protection of property, procedures of arbitration, equitable taxation, and the assurance of equal justice. The guaranteeing of fair conditions for the conduct of international trade rather than the actual conduct of trade was their main objective.[2]

There is a long history behind this attempt to negotiate guaranties of freedom to trade in foreign countries. Mr. Culbertson is able to cite instances of such treaties from ancient

[2] Cf. W. S. Culbertson, *International Economic Policies* (New York, 1925), p. 26. "The following subjects taken from commercial treaties indicate the wide range of subjects covered by provisions in modern commercial treaties: conditions of residence, travel and trade; immigration and emigration; police protection and civil rights; admission of diplomatic and consular officers, their rights and activities; vehicles and instruments of communication and transportation; navigation, quarantine and harbor regulations, and dues relating thereto; conditions for importation, exportation, transit, transfer, and warehousing of merchandise; tariffs and customs laws; protection of patents, trademarks, copyrights, and other industrial property rights; possession and disposal of, or succession to, real and personal property; payment of taxes; rights of commercial, industrial, or financial associations; exemption from military service, forced loans, and extraordinary levies; treatment of commercial travellers and their samples; bounties and drawbacks; internal duties and local loans; treatment of vessels seeking refuge from damage or shipwreck; salvage operations and dues; coasting trade, and port-to-port with foreign cargoes; extraterritorial jurisdiction; freedom of religious worship, and right of burial with suitable decorum and respect."

and medieval history. The earliest recorded commercial treaty made by Great Britain was that with Norway in 1217. Those negotiated with Spain and Sweden towards the end of the seventeenth century are still in force.[3] The wars that marked the struggle for supremacy among the rising European States from the seventeenth century onwards are punctuated by such treaties, a notable example being the Eden Treaty signed by France and England in 1786. It was in the nineteenth century, however, that the multiplication of commercial treaties wove a network of legal obligations among all the great trading countries. These treaties were intended to be permanent. Their scope steadily widened but, once signed, they remained in force for very long periods. Indeed, it is only in very recent years that some treaties negotiated many decades ago have been denounced.

More serious than these isolated denunciations has been the administrative sapping of their guaranties wherever the new controlled systems of trade have gained ground. The two major objectives of commercial treaties are usually described as "national treatment" and "most-favored-nation treatment." The former has been less discussed than the latter because it has, until recently, been taken somewhat for granted, so widespread had been its acceptance in the nineteenth century. It consists essentially of assurance that foreign traders shall receive the same treatment as national citizens. The principle is still maintained, but it is inevitably impaired by the growth of State intervention. Two examples are sufficient to demonstrate this fact. The extension of State enterprise, which normally restricts contracts to nationally produced materials, is a serious blow to international traders. Still more serious is the spread of exchange control and transfer moratoria which effectively prevents the transference of profits made in branch enterprises. Instances could be multiplied, such as policies of nationalization or confiscatory taxation that are general in their terms but in practice affect those industries owned by foreign capital; the fixation of railway

[3] Culbertson, *op. cit.*, p. 24.

rates and even port dues in such a way as to penalize foreign commodities; or the requirement of national participation or management in trading and producing enterprises. It is obvious that a government which exercises detailed control over economic activities within its borders has ample opportunity to regulate prices, raw material supplies, labor conditions, transport facilities, and taxation, by general ordinances designed to favor national producers.

The principle of most-favored-nation treatment is even more seriously undermined by the practice of detailed government regulation of trade and production. This has already been pointed out in connection with tariff policy. It has often been said that a truer description of what has been aimed at in this respect would be "equally-favored-nation treatment," or, as American writers now phrase it, "equality of trading opportunity." The formulation of the most-favored-nation clause recommended by the Economic Committee of the League of Nations stipulates that the imports from either contracting power "shall in no case be subject . . . to any duties, taxes or charges other or higher, or to any rules and formalities other or more burdensome, than those to which the like products having their origin in any third country are or may hereafter be subject." [4] It is entirely natural that every country shall endeavor to secure at least equally favorable treatment for its exports. In a world of reasonably equal competition, such a desire resulted in the past in the equalizing of tariff treatment to all countries. When nations struggle, as they have done in recent years, for preferential and exclusive privileges, it is an obvious symptom of disintegration.

The adoption of discriminatory trading methods, and particularly the vesting of monetary and quantitative trade controls in the hands of administrative bodies with discretionary power, has done far more than impair the working of most-favored-nation treatment. Discrimination is exercised in the

[4] League of Nations, *Recommendations of the Economic Committee Relating to Tariff Policy and the Most-Favoured-Nation Clause* (1933. II. B. 9), p. 21.

allocation of quotas and allotment of exchange priorities, in price bargaining, special freight arrangements, and the fixation of exchange ratios. Indeed, the range of possible discrimination is almost coterminous with the wide scope of trade negotiations. Trade treaties are supplemented by purchase agreements negotiated between industrial interests; tariffs are manipulated for bargaining purposes, and such bargains may be directly between governments, between organized industrial groups, or between the national units of an international cartel. There is hardly any aspect of international economic relations that is not now envisaged as coming within the scope of bilateral bargaining. Like modern wrestling, trade negotiations are not hampered by rules. They are "all in, and no holds barred."

The effect of such a degeneration of trading relations is naturally reflected in the treaty instruments by which they are governed. The elaborate negotiation of comprehensive treaties designed to stabilize and regularize trade over a long period has been replaced by a succession of short-term instruments registering snap bargains. Indeed, there is a strong tendency for these instruments to become merely the means of empowering negotiators to make such bargains. Mr. Obradovic has listed the commercial agreements entered into by Yugoslavia between 1924 and the end of 1938.[5] The list begins with single entries for the years 1924 and 1925, three treaties in 1926 and 1927, four in 1928 and 1929, five in 1930, and three in 1931. After that the tempo increases, fourteen agreements being signed in 1932 and twenty-five in 1936.[6] In the

[5] S. D. Obradovic, *La Politique commerciale de la Yougoslavie* (Belgrade, 1939).

[6] The full statistics are:

1924	1	1931	3
1925	1	1932	14
1926	3	1933	10
1927	3	1934	17
1928	4	1935	11
1929	4	1936	25
1930	5	1937	24
		1938	18

eight years preceding the adoption of exchange control the annual average was three treaties; in the following seven years it was seventeen. The Yugoslav negotiators were obviously kept busy.

Moreover, there is a definite change in the nature of the treaties and agreements. The twenty-four treaties negotiated before 1931 were with no less than eighteen separate countries and most of them were described as "Treaties of Commerce and Navigation." They were, in fact, a reconstitution of the network of trading treaties on the nineteenth-century model. Towards the close of this period, however, degeneration was setting in. Thereafter such descriptions as "Protocole additionel," "Accord additionel," "Arrangement additionel," "Accord provisoire," "Accord complementaire," and "Avenant à l'Arrangement du 7-XI-31" recur more and more frequently. There are special commodity agreements—"Accord sur le betail," "Accord sur le petrole," "Accord sur l'achat du blé." From April, 1932 there is also a new category—"Accord de Clearing." And from March, 1932 an even more significant entry appears in an agreement with Germany entitled "Commission mixte." Moreover, there is clear evidence of the frequent revision of these agreements with particular countries. Indeed, the distribution of these treaties at various times is instructive in regard to the development of Yugoslav diplomacy. A summary table is given in the footnote below, from which the rise and decline of the Little Entente and the Balkan Entente can be clearly seen, together with the French effort at commercial alliances in 1936 and 1937 [7] and the increasing influence of Germany after 1934.[8] It will be seen that Great

[7] France signed five agreements with Yugoslavia on December 8, 1936, and renewed three of them a year later. The two not renewed were for preferential imports of Yugoslav wheat and maize.

[8] *Chronology of Yugoslav Commercial Treaties, 1932–38*

Country	1932	1933	1934	1935	1936	1937	1938	
Albania	–	1	2	–	–	–	–	3
Austria	5	1	–	–	–	1	2	9
Balkan Entente	–	–	–	2	2	1	1	6
Belgium	1	1	–	–	–	1	1	4

(*Continued on next page*)

TREATY DEGENERATION 269

Britain signed only two treaties with Yugoslavia in these years and the United States none. The timing of the treaties is perhaps worth noting. In order to illustrate the frequency with which agreements have been made, and their variety, another footnote records the agreements negotiated by Yugoslavia with Germany within seven years.[9]

The logical outcome of frequent changes in treaty arrangements is the conduct by administrative action of almost con-

Brazil	1	–	–	–	–	–	–	1
Bulgaria	–	–	2	–	–	–	–	2
Costa Rica	–	–	1	–	–	–	–	1
Czechoslovakia	1	–	–	1	1	1	–	4
Denmark	–	–	–	–	–	1	–	1
Estonia	–	–	–	–	–	–	1	1
France	–	2	–	–	5	3	–	10
Germany	1	2	3	1	2	2	4	15
Great Britain	–	–	–	1	1	–	–	2
Greece	1	1	1	1	1	–	1	6
Hungary	–	1	1	1	4	2	–	9
Italy	2	–	1	–	1	2	3	9
Latvia	–	–	–	–	–	1	–	1
Little Entente	–	–	3	3	2	2	1	11
Netherlands	–	–	–	–	1	1	–	2
Poland	–	–	–	–	–	1	1	2
Rumania	–	–	–	1	1	2	–	4
Spain	–	–	–	–	2	–	–	2
Sweden	–	–	–	–	–	1	–	1
Switzerland	1	1	–	–	–	2	2	6
Turkey	1	–	3	–	2	–	1	7

[9]
1932:	September	13	Clearing Agreement
1933:	July	29	Commercial Agreement
	September	14	Protocol
1934:	May	1	Commercial Agreement
	May	4	Clearing Agreement
	July	31	Protocol
1935:	March	1	Mixed Commission
1936:	April	1	Mixed Commission
	October	10	Mixed Commission
1937:	March	24	Commercial Payments Agreement
	September	29	Mixed Commission
1938:	June	4	Mixed Commission
	October	25	Additional Agreement
			Mixed Commission
			Clearing Agreement

tinuous barter bargaining. Yugoslavia does not have the only, or even the most developed, system of administrative control over external trade, but the extent of discretionary power entrusted to officials may be gauged from the passage in which Mr. Obradovic summarizes the law governing exports of cattle and animal products. The law, as he says, merely provides a framework of legislative authority for administrative decisions.[10] The same principle of organization operates in the supervision of bilateral bargaining. The following brief description of Yugoslav commercial arrangements with Germany describes in a nutshell the manner in which the new system of administrative bargaining has come to replace the older form of trade treaties.

"The [German] agricultural protectionism, by limiting Yugoslav exports, brought about the denunciation of the 1927 trade treaty. A new treaty not having proved negotiable in the meantime, trade between the two countries, lacking any contractual basis after March 5, 1933, was subject to the maximum tariff rates. Five months elapsed before a provisional agreement was reached in order to prepare the ground for a new commercial treaty. That treaty, concluded on May 1, 1934, created particularly large bases for Yugoslav-German trade. Yugoslavia agreed to reduce and consolidate a great part of its customs tariff. In exchange, Germany gave large quotas for agricultural, pastoral and forest products. Germany being a totalitarian country, there was established in the agreement the details of a Yugoslav export control and procedures for price-fixing. To this end, a 'permanent economic commission' of the two countries was created. It was given vast powers and must meet twice a year to examine the working of the agreement and take any necessary decisions." [11]

This is the type of trading agreement that is becoming typical—an agreement to put the control of bilateral trade into the hands of officials with discretionary powers. The broad conditions under which the trade is to be conducted are laid

[10] Obradovic, *op. cit.*, p. 21.
[11] Obradovic, *op. cit.*, pp. 23–4.

down in a general agreement, but the interpretation and execution of the agreement is left in the hands of permanent officials who are in practically continuous consultation. There has been a rapid evolution in recent years of government departments specialized in trade regulation.[12] The same specialized civil servants have represented their countries at successive bilateral and multilateral conferences. They have become experts in trade regulation and trade restriction. The treaty arrangements under which they operate are general in terms, contain secret clauses, are capable of flexible interpretation, and are frequently revised. In that revision the expert administrators naturally have most influence.

The segment of trade conducted in this way is still the lesser part of world trade; but the destructive effect of such operations upon the trade of third countries is very considerable. Apart, however, from the strictly economic costs of administrative bilateralism, there is a broader aspect of this problem. International law, never very firmly established in the conduct of national policies, has been increasingly disregarded in every sphere. In the field of commercial policy, the long process by which equality of trading opportunity had been established on a treaty basis has been checked and reversed. Using trade as an instrument of national policy, authoritarian governments have replaced law by administrative discretion. That discretion is used arbitrarily and for discriminatory purposes. Instead of multilateral competition on a basis of equality of trading opportunity guaranteed by treaty, bilateral bargaining is conducted by officials aiming at national advantage. In such circumstances, economic considerations become subordinate to political influences. The nineteenth-century dream of a world of independent Nation-States linked by treaties which gave private enterprise a world-

[12] See, for example, Parkinson, *Bases of Canadian Foreign Policy*, pp. 174–85; Valle and Ferrer, *La Politique économique de L'Argentine*, pp. 60 ff.; *British External Economic Policy*, Part II, pp. 9 ff.; Boös, *Survey of Sweden's External Policy*, pp. 20 ff.; Tuveng, *External Economic Policy of Norway in Recent Years*, pp. 78 ff.; Lieftinck, *External Economic Policy of the Kingdom of the Netherlands*, pp. 41 ff.

wide range is being replaced by the anarchy of State monopolies using trade as an instrument of national power.

Compensation, Clearing and Payments Agreements

The idea of clearing by offsetting credit claims is not new. What is new in recent clearing arrangements is the necessity, since 1931, of devising special machinery for settling international payments on a bilateral instead of a multilateral basis. As soon as credit instruments came into wide use, the advantages and economies of offsetting them by a bookkeeping process were obvious. The London Bankers' Clearing House developed between 1750 and 1770. Other metropolitan banking centers followed this example and special clearing systems for the settlement of accounts developed also in stock and produce exchanges and railway systems.[13] In any clearing system claims and counterclaims are offset and balances settled by drawing on funds maintained at the clearing center by all the participating institutions. In a fully developed banking system local clearings are organized in every important city. Regional clearings and national clearings complete the system.

During the nineteenth century the London Money Market came to function as a clearing center for payments arising out of international trade and investment. It was the most highly developed financial market in the world, and the best supplied with credit. The world markets for staple commodities that grew up in London during the free-trade era supplemented the facilities offered by the money market. In order to cope with the intricate financial transactions on long- and short-term that were the result of world-wide investment and trade, specialized markets grew up dealing with the acceptance, discount, and marketing of bills. The volume of transactions was very considerable, so that almost any type of credit could be had at a price as long as sterling was managed as an

[13] Cf. Palgrave, *Dictionary of Political Economy*, article on "Clearing System."

CLEARING AND PAYMENTS AGREEMENTS 273

international currency and Great Britain remained a free-trade market.

The international clearing that was conducted through London was, in a sense, unorganized. There was no clearing-house, no central institution. On the contrary, there was a dispersed and loosely linked series of specialized markets created by the independent operations of a great number of dealers. These markets were competitive and the clearing of payments between national monetary systems was merely one aspect of a complex process that included the financing of international trade, the determination of commodity prices, the fixing of interest rates, and the flotation of international loans. The foreign exchange market in London was more than a means of settling the value of sterling in foreign currencies. Such exchange markets operated in many other financial centers; but the great volume of transactions that passed through London made it a convenient place for the settlement of international balances.

This settlement was multilateral in the true tradition and meaning of clearing. It was closely integrated with the competitive determination of commodity prices and the flow of international trade in accordance with those prices. It was also free, and reflected the equilibrium arrived at by world-wide competitive bargaining.

The breakdown of this market in 1931, and the subsequent collapse of foreign exchange stability, created immense difficulties in the transference of credit between national economies. The transfer problem so created paralyzed the international capital market and greatly impeded the financing of world trade. It was natural, therefore, that attempts should have been made to institute some method of easing the difficulties of transfer and reviving the flow of international trade. The devices adopted fall into three main groups. There were different kinds of barter transactions, of which the commonest were usually described by the French word "compensation." Such transactions were usually deals by which offsetting transactions were arranged between pairs of importers and exporters in two countries. Occasionally such transactions became somewhat complicated, as when funds were blocked in central European countries and individuals or banking institutions arranged transactions in which commodity exports, security transactions, real estate purchases, and other means of payments were combined. A Hungarian exporter, for example, might find it possible to send a shipment of pigs to Czechoslovakia and arrange with a Hungarian importer of timber to pay him in pengö, the Czech timber merchant being paid by his compatriot who bought the pigs. He might find instead a Czech who wished to realize on a credit in blocked pengö and was willing to take the pigs and sell them for Czech crowns. Or the Czech with blocked pengö might want to have sterling in which case the transaction might be extended to include a Czech owner of British securities. Such transactions in many ingenious forms were used in order to withdraw capital from the countries that had adopted exchange control; but the monetary authorities in those countries soon discovered that such leakages of capital were serious drains on the balances of payment. Increasing restrictions were therefore imposed on private compensation. In general, it was permitted only for so-called "additional exports" over and above those made possible by bilateral trade treaties with the countries concerned.

When it became possible in 1935 and 1936 to relax exchange-control regulations in certain countries, particularly in Austria, the method followed was the progressive extension of the list of commodities in which compensation was permitted. Since, by this time, the organization of such transactions was mainly arranged by banks, this was equivalent to releasing a section of foreign trade to private enterprise financed by the banking methods that had been normal before 1931.[14] The exchange rate at which these transactions

[14] Cf. A. Tchakaloff and S. Zagoroff, *La Controle des changes en Bulgaire*, p. 37: "The exporter sells to the importer, through the agency of a specified bank or the National Bank of Bulgaria, the whole or part of the exchange derived from the exports, at a premium based on the official note. Compensation may be either *total* or *partial*, according to whether the exporter retains the whole amount of the exchange to be compensated or whether he has to deliver part of it to the National Bank of Bulgaria."

took place was well below the official rate, but somewhat above the black market rates, and approximated, therefore, to a depreciation fixed by private trading. A continuation of these developments might have led ultimately to the restoration of multilateral trade and clearing on the basis of depreciated but stabilized exchange rates.

The second type of substitute for multilateral clearing that was devised in the years after 1931 consisted of bilateral clearing arrangements negotiated between pairs of countries. Such clearing treaties were an obvious improvement upon the barter procedures of the early forms of private compensation. As Dr. Schacht once remarked, it was "barbaric to be forced to barter machines for cereals, or radio apparatus for tobacco, like a Negro who exchanges his ivory for glassware or his rubber for cotton goods." [15] On the other hand, as Dr. Schacht admitted in the same interview, the institution of bilateral clearing "substituted the normal play of exchange and credit with a terrible bureaucracy." [16]

The first bilateral clearing agreement was negotiated between Switzerland and Austria in November, 1931. In the same month a conference of the Danubian countries met at Prague and recommended the institution of such arrangements between exchange-control countries in order to revive international trade between them. For lack of available foreign exchange the volume of commodity trade, formerly financed in large part through London, had fallen disastrously. Where there was reciprocal demand, it was obviously wise to institute arrangements whereby imports and exports between pairs of countries could be settled by payments in and out of accounts opened in the national banks of the respective countries.

The movement towards bilateral clearing was further encouraged by the desire of creditor countries to collect pay-

---

[15] Cited by B. Ohlin in Joint Committee Carnegie Endowment, International Chamber of Commerce, *International Economic Reconstruction* (Paris, 1936), p. 94.
[16] *Ibid.*

ment on debts that had been subjected to transfer moratoria, or to liquidate arrears of commercial payments that had been blocked. Many of them took steps to do so by impounding the payments by their nationals for imports from the defaulting countries. France, for example, took steps to block payments for such imports as early as February 15, 1932. Within a few months similar action had been taken by most of the European creditor countries—Belgium, the Netherlands, Sweden, and Switzerland. Czechoslovakia, surrounded by exchange-control countries, was itself forced to the more extreme step of adopting exchange control. Great Britain refrained from such action until the German transfer moratorium was renewed and extended in June, 1934, and she was then able to negotiate a Payments Agreement with Germany.[17]

Faced by this impounding of the payments for their exports, the exchange-control countries, including Germany, hastened to negotiate bilateral clearing agreements and, by the end of 1932, Europe was covered with a network of such treaties. For this type of pressure to be effective, however, it was essential that the creditor country should be in a position to withhold the foreign exchange accruing from the surplus of its imports over and above its exports to the debtor country. Where the creditor country did not have a passive import balance in trade with its debtor, it was impotent. The United States had an active export balance with Germany and most other countries and was, therefore, not in a position to bring pressure on them, even if its policy had not been opposed in principle to bilateral clearing arrangements. Even where a passive import balance existed, the tendency of bilateral clearing was strongly towards its elimination, since every country tried to bring pressure to bear on the other contracting party to increase export outlets. Such pressure was most effective when the first country could point to an excess of imports in

[17] The Argentine (Roca) agreement of May 1, 1933 preceded and was the model for the German agreement of November 1, 1934 negotiated after the Sondermark agreement of August 10, 1934 failed to function satisfactorily.

its trade and threaten to reduce them. In later bilateral clearing agreements an attempt was usually made to establish an agreed ratio between imports and exports. Perhaps the most striking of these instances of proportional trade has been Turkey's effort to establish with each separate country the import-export ratio of 4:5, which is calculated as that ratio needed in her total trade to settle the adverse balance of the invisible items in her aggregate balance of payments.

The scope of bilateral clearing agreements was rather quickly widened to include not only commodity trade but other international payments such as those for debt service, shipping freights, insurance and other financial services, and tourist traffic. It was not long, indeed, before the attempt at bilateral balancing covered all important items in the balance of payments between the two countries concerned. This led to the third type of substitute clearing which came to be known as a Payments Agreement.

The terminology of the new trade regulation has at times been confused and vague. There was a tendency in the early years to speak of private and public compensation, and private and public clearing. It seems best, however, to reserve the term "compensation" for the private barter transactions that soon came to be organized under banking auspices and, therefore, to resemble trade conducted by private enterprise, as in free-exchange countries. Even though there were Compensation Agreements regulating this private trade, it is better to make the distinction between compensation and clearing one of private, as distinct from public, action. Private clearing is compensation and public compensation is clearing.

Payments agreements were an adaptation of the clearing process, as is shown by the existence of many clearing and payments agreements. Such agreements were negotiated between exchange-control countries. In so far as there is any distinction to be drawn between clearing and payments agreements, it arises from the precedent set by the Anglo-Argentine and Anglo-German agreements in May, 1933 and November, 1934. These agreements covered other items in the balance of payments besides commodity trade, and in particular made detailed provision for the liquidation of certain arrears of debt payments. The Anglo-German agreement, for example, stipulated that import permits for British goods could be issued to German importers to a value equal to 55 per cent of the amount realized by German exports to Great Britain during the last month but one. Detailed arrangements were agreed upon whereby freight payments and debt arrears (including arrears under the preceding Sondermark agreement) were to be met from the sterling accruing from German exports to Great Britain; but a substantial amount of exchange was left at the free disposal of the Reichsbank.[18]

It is sometimes stated that the payments agreements differ from clearing agreements in being negotiated between a free-exchange country on the one hand and an exchange-control country on the other, instead of between two exchange-control countries, and in leaving the allocation of payments in the hands of the exchange-control country. But, in fact, the payments for German exports to Great Britain were made into an account held at the Bank of England to the credit of the Reichsbank. It is true that Germany controlled both her imports and exports to Great Britain according to the terms of the agreement. On the other hand, Great Britain has made clearing agreements, as have other free-exchange countries, while clearing and payments agreements have been negotiated between pairs of exchange-control countries. There is, in fact, no clear line of demarcation between clearing agreements and payments agreements and it seems best to regard the latter as an improved version of the former, laying particular and specific emphasis on financial as well as commercial transactions and giving scope for limited transfers of free exchange.[19]

[18] Cf. H. J. Tasca, *World Trading Systems,* Ch. IX for a detailed analysis of British payments agreements.

[19] Definitions of clearing and payments agreements have been worked out by the International Chamber of Commerce in its *Clearing and Payments Agreements* (Basel, 1938), Introduction. The distinction turns on the possibility of liquidating balances by the transfer of free exchange. Under clear-

CLEARING AND PAYMENTS AGREEMENTS 279

The complexity of the new bilateral clearing system may be judged by the fact that at the beginning of 1939 there were 171 agreements in operation between 39 different countries. Of these 79 were clearing, 59 clearing and payments, and 33 payments agreements.[20] The percentage of trade covered is not easy to estimate, but its aggregate direct importance for world trade is easy to exaggerate. In some countries the greater part of the imports and exports are subject to bilateral clearing; but in many the percentage is very small. The proportion of world trade conducted under bilateral clearing arrangements has been estimated at about 12 per cent in 1937.[21]

Throughout this brief and summary description, it may have been noticed, the adjective "bilateral" has been prefixed to clearing agreements. This is to emphasize the fact that the essential difference between the new and the old system is not in the fact of clearing by bookkeeping credits, but in the replacement of multilateral by bilateral clearing. The new system is a makeshift, an inferior substitute, not a new invention replacing what some apologists would represent by implication as a cruder system. The word "clearing" is apt to convey an impression of modern methods, especially when it is contrasted with the gold standard—a suggestion that cumbersome and crude metallic money has been replaced by credit instruments and bookkeeping processes. Actually what has happened is that a world-wide, multilateral clearing has been broken up into a series of bilateral clearings. Such bilateral clearings, as will be argued in the next section, have been destructive of international trade, and particularly of the chains of multilateral transactions that made its extension possible. Their imposition has invariably led also to a conflict of interest between those concerned with current trade and those who own claims to arrears of commercial debt or to interest

---

ing no such transfer is made, balances or arrears of payment being possible only by increased commodity exports from the country in arrears.

[20] On June 1, 1936 the corresponding figures were 51, 69, and 11, a total of 131.

[21] *World Trade,* February, 1939.

on past investments. In many cases current trade has been sacrificed to debt collection. Bilateral clearing agreements, as Professor Haberler points out, are in fact an inevitable accompaniment of exchange control. As he emphasizes, "Bilateral forms of exchange control, represented most strikingly by clearing agreements, which tend to equalize the balance of payments between pairs of countries, have been particularly injurious to 'triangular trade.' The only way of escape from this pernicious system is to give up trying to maintain an artificial rate and to let the exchange depreciate in accordance with purchasing power parity." [22]

The Strategy of Bilateralism

The terms "unilateral," "bilateral," and "multilateral," when used in connection with international trade and commercial policy, have been the source of much confusion. It is essential to distinguish clearly between procedures of negotiation and the type of trading that is the object of such negotiation. As a result of recent experience, it may well be regarded as proven that bilateral negotiations to extend trade are the most likely to achieve results. This is, in fact, not a new discovery. Perhaps the most important step ever taken in the direction of freer trade was the Anglo-French bilateral treaty negotiated by Cobden and Chevalier in 1860. While much nonsense has been talked in high places about the difficulty of negotiating

[22] G. Haberler, *The Theory of International Trade*, pp. 89–90. Professor Haberler adds: "In spite of the complexity in detail of exchange control it is really not difficult to grasp the general situation and to point the way out of this tangle of restrictions, prohibitions and regulations, if one understands the workings of the international monetary mechanism. Most of the 'practical' men who introduced and administered exchange control entirely lacked this knowledge. They had to discover step by step through bitter experience the principles of international trade—a wearisome process very costly to the economic system. . . . The working of exchange control in Germany and in other countries during recent years has been by no means uninteresting. But the results which it has yielded were easily deducible from the theory of international trade and were, indeed, for the most part actually predicted beforehand."

multilateral conventions, it is true that bilateral conversations are easier. In all the great international conferences called by the League of Nations, or outside its auspices, the difficulty in reaching agreement has not lain in the fact that many governments were represented, but in the failure to reach agreement between the three or four leading Powers. Nowhere was this clearer than at the Monetary and Economic Conference held at London in 1933. If an agreement could have been reached between the representatives of France, Germany, Great Britain, and the United States on two or three fundamental issues, and notably on currency stabilization, the remaining fifty-two governments represented at the conference would not have presented an effective obstacle to agreement, even though Italy and Japan were among the fifty-two. Attempts to throw the blame for the conference's failure upon its size are mere camouflage, designed to cover up the irreconcilable disagreements of policy among the Great Powers.

It should be clearly stated that the success of either bilateral or multilateral negotiations, in commercial policy or in any other aspect of international relations, is dependent upon the will of leading Powers to make them succeed. Cobden and Chevalier made a successful bilateral trade treaty because both Britain and France were at the time following unilateral policies of tariff reduction and were anxious by reciprocal concessions to facilitate such reductions. The most successful multilateral conference of the interwar period was that held at Washington in 1921. Its success resulted from the decisive initiative taken by the United States, an initiative that had been prepared in detail and with equal consideration of American and foreign disarmament possibilities. The decisiveness of the American proposals and their prompt acceptance by the British representatives assured acceptance by the other Powers. In the same way, the only proposals that were decisively put forward by United States representatives at London in 1933—those regarding silver and wheat—were the only proposals agreed to by the conference. The fact cannot be stressed too often that the real cause of failure in negotiations to reduce trade barriers has been the absence of any decisive, unilateral will to extend international trade.

A further elementary point must also be emphasized. It is possible to take unilateral, bilateral, or multilateral action in the direction either of restricting or of expanding multilateral trade. The trend to bilateral trade in recent years has, in fact, been primarily due to the unilateral action of certain Great Powers. The bilateral negotiations in which this trend has been brought under formal regulation have merely registered the inevitable consequence of prior unilateral action. No clearer illustration need be asked than the way in which national systems of exchange control and transfer moratoria led to bilateral clearing arrangements. The extension of national economic regulation has led in recent years to bilateral negotiations that have canalized trade between pairs of countries. It is theoretically possible to conceive systems of national regulation designed to facilitate and expand multilateral trade, but in practice such systems have been conservatory of vested national interests to the detriment of multilateral trade.

The criticism of bilateralism which follows is directed therefore against the trend towards bilateral trade, and not against bilateral procedures of trade negotiations. Not only Cobden and Chevalier, but Mr. Hull, have shown that bilateral negotiations can be conducted in a multilateral spirit and can be made to yield results. Given decisive leadership and determination by the Great Powers to maintain and extend the multilateral trading system, it is simply a matter of administrative convenience whether negotiations to this end are conducted bilaterally or multilaterally. Either type of negotiation can be made effective.

There is abundant evidence of a strong trend towards bilateral balancing of commodity trade. This trend has been measured for five countries by Dr. A. Hirschmann.[23] Of the five countries studied—Belgium, Great Britain, Germany, the

[23] Albert Hirschmann, *Etude statistique sur la tendance du commerce extérieur vers l'equilibre et le bilateralisme.*

Netherlands, and Sweden—only Germany has practiced exchange control. Using the formula of standard deviation to measure the extent to which imports and exports from and to particular countries are consistent with the relation between total imports and exports, Mr. Hirschmann has calculated indices of bilateralism. In his index a figure of 100 would represent a complete absence of bilateral tendencies, while a figure of zero would represent perfect bilateral balancing of imports and exports with each particular country. Mr. Hirschmann's calculations are summarized in the following table.

Indices of Bilateralism

Year	Great Britain	Germany	Netherlands	Belgium	Sweden
1929	25.8	25.2	23.7	22.3	25.6
1930	25.0	26.1	27.3	22.3	26.9
1931	24.9	29.0	31.0	25.3	31.6
1932	24.3	28.5	28.3	24.8	29.1
1933	24.3	28.9	24.9	23.2	26.7
1934	22.8	28.8	24.1	20.8	22.6
1935	21.2	22.8	22.6	22.5	18.0
1936	19.2	17.8	23.0	22.8	19.2
1937	17.5	21.5	21.2	20.8	18.2

The trend revealed by these figures is striking in every country. It suffers somewhat, as all such calculations do, from using annual figures. The upturn of the German figure in 1937, for example, was due rather to an unbalancing of trade relations by fresh buying in new markets while blocked balances were being liquidated by exports to other countries. In the case of Great Britain, the steady trend to bilateralism is clear and especially marked after the agreements negotiated with the British Dominions and other countries came into effect.

Dr. Hirschmann's results, confirming previous studies made with different methods by the Economic Intelligence Service of the League of Nations, offer striking evidence of the extent to which bilateral is replacing multilateral trade. There are three main reasons why this trend to bilateralism has been economically disadvantageous in recent years. It destroys the effective international specialization that is based upon price comparisons in a world market, directs trade into politically rather than economically advantageous channels, and renders this trade more erratic since the bilateral bargains on which it depends may be abruptly terminated for political reasons. The *World Economic Survey, 1935–36*, prepared by the present author for the League of Nations in the summer of 1936, contained the following comments on the League's studies of bilateralism first made available in that year. The comments are even more applicable to later developments.

"It is possible that the conduct of balanced bilateral trade along these lines may, in certain circumstances, result in an increased volume of trade being conducted. Some aspects of the canalizing of trade into bilateral channels need, however, to be stressed. It is abundantly clear that bilateral trade, directed as it has recently been by currency, and sometimes political, considerations, is not usually as economical as that directed by private interest. Trade conducted by bilateral national bargaining will hardly be able to follow the channels laid down by private interest in seeking out the best bargains. The deterioration of Germany's barter terms of trade in 1935 is clear evidence of the cost of the new methods.

"Moreover, the balancing of imports and exports as between each pair of countries eliminates the triangular trade that was necessary to carry payments for past indebtedness. The control of commodity trade and its direction into new channels whereby imports can be paid for by commodity exports renders acute that division of group interests within each national community which has been analyzed in another publication of the Economic Intelligence Service.[24] In the past, international lending has gone hand in hand with the development of

---

[24] *Balances of Payments, 1934* (Geneva, 1935), p. 17: "It has become increasingly clear, therefore, that, in the present situation, the financial interests of many countries conflict to a certain extent with their industrial and agricultural interests and, accordingly, that measures affecting their international transactions frequently involve a selection between the interests the country may wish to protect."

international specialization and the growth of foreign trade. The connection of trade and investment was, however, very loose. The payments due on account of debt were effected by roundabout and multiangular trading transactions. It is very unlikely that bilateral trade will provide an effective substitute for such transactions in promoting future investment. In the meantime, it has rendered the payment of existing obligations much more difficult.

"Bilateral balancing of trade strikes at many important economic advantages arising from international specialization and co-operation. For the flexible and effective organization of world-wide trade by private enterprise, it substitutes a much more rigid and narrower series of bilateral national bargains. Efficiency is lowered as the scope for specialization is limited.

"Finally, and more than is commonly recognized, the economic welfare and stability of the modern world has, until recently, been dependent upon the trading mechanism by which the whole body of international economic and financial relations was linked in one continuous chain of trading transactions. Not only were commodities exchanged, but national price levels were adjusted, and production and investment regulated, by a world-wide trading system with manifold ramifications and interconnections. The breaking of essential links in the chains of transactions has been a major cause of the unprecedented fluctuations of prices, the disorganization of production, default on financial obligations and piling up of stocks that have been characteristic of the recent years of depression. Attempts to form new trading connections and to dispose of stocks or surplus production in new areas have led, and are still leading, to fresh disturbances of international economic relations. The whole world was organized as a series of closely connected and interdependent markets, the smoothness of whose adjustment led perhaps to an underestimate of their value. The substitution of more rigidly planned and directed systems of independent and closely regulated, if not closed, markets has not eliminated but exaggerated the fluctuations of prices and production, and at the same time has destroyed a large part of the specialized international cooperation by which the rapid advance of living standards has in the past been made possible." [25]

Certain political implications of these economic disadvantages of bilateralism need to be stressed in a study of economic policy in relation to world peace. In the first place, the elimination of triangular balances—making the payment of debt service, financial commissions, and shipping freights more difficult—struck a heavy blow at the specialized functions of Great Britain as a center of multilateral trade. It was inevitable that this should lead to the mobilization of British financial power as an instrument of diplomacy. So was launched another phase of the great struggle for hegemony over the southeastern European and Near Eastern States. Great Britain endeavored to counter massive German purchases of foodstuffs and raw materials by trade treaties that included provisions for financing British exports by the medium of export credit guaranties, and, at first hesitantly and then more boldly, added political to export credits. There was a steady progression from the first rather small and narrowly calculated use of financial resources to the negotiation, on September 2, 1936, of the Anglo-Turkish agreement by which, in addition to export credits, a loan was given for Turkish rearmament.[26] With the approach of war, the full financial power of Britain and France was called into use in an effort to buy up raw materials, gain control of productive enterprises and transport facilities, and facilitate the rearmament of neutral States.

As Mr. Folke Hilgerdt has pointed out also, the bilateral canalizing of trade has greatly accentuated the difficulties of access to raw materials and sharpened the struggle to gain free exchange with which they may be purchased. Writing as early as August, 1935, Mr. Hilgerdt pointed out that "as bilateralism particularly renders the supply of raw materials to certain countries difficult, it threatens to lead to an intensified

[25] League of Nations, *World Economic Survey, 1935–36*, pp. 183–184.
[26] Cf. Kuyucak, *Exchange Control in Turkey*.

fight for influence upon (or domination of) the undeveloped countries, and thereby to political controversies, which may adversely effect all forms of peaceful collaboration between nations." [27]

This prediction was amply fulfilled in the years that followed, and it is now so obvious as hardly to need statement that bilateral trade took on aggressive and destructive aspects as international rivalries were sharpened in the era of what is now known as pre-belligerency. Not only was bilateral trade made to depend upon political relations with particular countries; it was also used to harass and replace the trade of those nations which clung to multilateralism. The manner in which trade could be switched on and off is well illustrated by the relations between Germany and the U. S. S. R. It is also clear that massive German purchases of raw materials from the Baltic and Scandinavian countries in 1938 and early 1939 were not only a means of securing these materials (as far as possible without using free exchange) and building up future export outlets, but a means of economic penetration into what were destined to become important theaters of war.

Economic penetration of this type, moreover, served a double purpose. It gave footholds in strategic regions, but it also weakened the multilateral trading system from which the free-exchange countries drew their strength. Bilateralism cannot be judged merely as an economic development; it has become a revolutionary instrument designed to weaken and eventually destroy the so-called plutocratic control of world trade which carried with it the control of strategic raw materials by the opponents of the totalitarian Powers. It is a mistake to regard exchange control and clearing agreements as a mere instrument of economic self-protection, or even as a substitute for free multilateral trade. They have not been used in this way by the totalitarian States, though the smaller debtor countries of Europe had no option but so to use them. The totalitarian Powers, on the contrary, have used them as a

[27] Folke Hilgerdt, "The Approach to Bilateralism—a Change in the Structure of World Trade," *Index* (August, 1935).

means of destroying and ultimately supplanting multilateral trade and investment. There is no reasonable doubt that these Powers, given political domination of smaller States and colonial areas, might well launch a considerable program of economic development in those areas, building up the production of those materials and finished products that fitted into their own requirements, and particularly into their armament programs.

The real purpose of organized bilateralism, therefore, has been commonly underestimated. It has been used to complete the destruction of nineteenth-century trade and investment, and with it the organization of world production by private enterprise to meet the needs of consumers by competitive multilateral marketing based on equality of trading opportunity. Such organization was being replaced by State regulated trade of a monopolistic and discriminatory character designed to build up the military strength of the dominant totalitarian Power. To be successful it was necessary that all trade channels should lead to and from the center, and that bilateral bargaining should be conducted separately with each of the smaller States. In bargaining of this type the great and controlled market of the totalitarian Power might well be used as an effective bargaining instrument. During the period of building, concessions were necessary, but once alternative outlets were limited or closed that bargaining power would be irresistible. Bilateralism was not an economic system and should not be judged as such. It was a play in a great game for high stakes.

The Tactics of Bilateral Bargaining

In order to illustrate the manner in which bilateral bargaining has proceeded through clearing agreements and exchange control it is necessary to examine the working of these agreements in detail. Dr. Tasca had done this for the British and American bilateral treaties negotiated in recent years.[28] Detailed reference has already been made to his work.[29] His con-

[28] H. J. Tasca, *World Trading Systems*.
[29] See above, Ch. IV.

clusion is that Great Britain made considerable use of the bargaining power of her great market. The pressure was exerted primarily to increase outlets for British exports and one consequence was that the smaller countries were forced to retain, or even to introduce, measures of import or exchange control, in some cases to the extent of impairing their ability to continue most-favored-nation treatment.

Not only the northern European countries, but the central and southeastern European countries also faced the pressures on their economic organization from the policies of great Powers. It should be pointed out, however, that the German policies of controlled trade take a different form and are directed more to securing adequate and suitable supplies of imported raw materials than to assuring export outlets.

It may well be argued that Germany's dependence upon the smaller countries was at least as great as their dependence upon Germany, so that the bargains they had been able to make were on the whole favorable. There seems no reason to doubt this argument; but against it must be set a statement from a small southeastern European country which is worth quoting.

"The increase of regulation has been a conscious and deliberate policy only in the case of certain great Powers, and above all the countries which have chosen the system of autarky in order to prepare for war. All the other countries have been forced to introduce and increase regulatory measures in order to defend themselves against the consequences of disorganisation of economic activity caused by the depression—consequences which persisted even during the period of relative prosperity which was only partial and not general in every country.

"The little countries had no freedom of choice. They were compelled to introduce methods of regulation. All the extensions of regimentation have been produced by these pressures; but to be completely objective, it must be added that there arose also a desire in certain countries to organise their economic activity more completely. Certain tendencies towards partial autarky have had an important influence in that direction.

"But it remains true that if we have come to this, the fundamental cause is the collapse of the international economic system directed from its centre at London. The collapse of the gold standard followed by the collapse of London as a commercial clearing-house, is the fundamental cause of this situation. It has been asked whether another centre could not replace London, now that Great Britain has fallen into a nationalist policy. The United States which might do so is also entrenched in a nationalist policy.

"I would like to complete these observations by a statement that is too often overlooked today, which is that Germany has the desire to become the centre, a new centre of a new international economic organisation. This manifest desire—today limited—can be seen in the tendency shown by Germany to reorganise the economy of the whole of southeastern Europe. In German political thought today, both official and unofficial, we find this categorical assertion—Germany wishes to have a free hand in central and south-eastern Europe. And when Germany asserts that exchange control is a system capable of restoring international economic relations, she does so after a happy experience for herself.

"To illustrate my thought, I shall refer to certain circumstances in my own country which is in a critical situation. On one side it is a debtor to the western countries, on the other it finds in Germany a great complementary market. To escape from the prospect of ending in a quasi-monopolistic situation as far as economic relations with Germany are concerned and to meet financial obligations to the western countries, it has sacrificed its currency and accepted the necessity of limiting the scope of exchange control by leaving some of the free exchange accruing from exports to free-exchange countries, to be sold on the free market. The aim of this measure was to gather enough free exchange to trade with free exchange countries, to import raw materials, and in an important proportion, to meet financial obligations towards those countries. The result of the experiment has been negative. In the present year (1939) the total of free exchange has diminished in an extraordinary manner and external trade is distorted in favour of trade with Germany which is much more than half the total. How have we come to this? By the rigorous application of the monetary and commercial methods practised by Germany, by the systematic extension of the German system. One must recognise that there is, today, a revival, in other forms of the struggle of imperialisms. These imperialisms found themselves in conflict in the last war. They have ended in this war after having exhausted all warlike tactics in the framework of international relations before war began. New methods are employed nowadays. The official declaration of Germany that it has no intention of returning to the gold standard should be taken most seriously. Germany has found its system: it is exchange control. By means of exchange control it intends to reorganise the economic world on another basis."

This serious appraisal of German aims could be proved by many illustrations of the tactics by which German negotiators approached the task of reorganizing the economic activity of southeastern European countries so as to increase the production of commodities suitable for the German market. The first step in this direction was taken in the negotiations with Hungary which resulted in the commercial agreement on February 21, 1934. A clause in the agreement stipulated that Hungary should take steps to increase the production of the commodities needed by Germany. In subsequent years this tentative beginning was greatly elaborated. Massive purchases of imports were later followed by exports of manufactured goods and of capital equipment. In the bargaining process the equipment necessary to produce the materials needed by Germany was sold on favorable terms.

The trade treaty signed with Germany by Rumania in March, 1939 begins with a declaration that "the Kingdom of Roumania and the German Reich, having the intention, in the interests of the two countries to draw closer their economic ties which are in continuous development, and to collaborate on a large scale in accordance with a program in the economic field with the object of realizing their pacific aims, have agreed to conclude a treaty." The first article of the treaty provides for the establishment of an "economic plan, to cover several years. The economic plan will take into account, on the one hand, German import necessities, and on the other hand, the possibilities of developing Roumanian production, Roumanian domestic needs, and Roumanian need of economic exchange with other countries."

The fields of Rumanian production to be included in the plan are then specified, beginning with "the development of Roumanian agricultural production, the cultivation of new agricultural products, as well as the intensification of those already cultivated, especially forage, oleaginous and textile plants; the development of existing agricultural industries and the creation of new agricultural industries and of processing installations." The list goes on with the development of Rumanian forestry and forest industries; "deliveries of machines and installations for mining exploitations in Roumania; the foundation of mixed Roumanian-German companies for the opening up and valorization of deposits of calcium pyrites of Dobrogea and chrome minerals of the Banat, and of manganese minerals in the Vatra-Dornei-Brosteni region. Similarly valorization of the bauxite deposits and eventually the creation of an aluminum industry will be examined."

Provision is next made for "the foundation of a mixed Roumanian-German company which will concern itself with petroleum exploitation and the execution of a program of drilling and refining of crude oil."

Further provisions of the treaty cover collaboration in the industrial field, the creation of free zones, the delivery of armaments, the development of means of communication and transportation, the construction of public-utility installations, and collaboration between German and Rumanian banks.

The execution of the treaty is to be entrusted to governmental mixed commissions and provision is made for the two governments to give the necessary aid to the organizations

TACTICS OF BILATERAL BARGAINING

and firms involved in preparing and executing the projects mentioned above. The whole organization of the plan is to be effected by utilizing the Rumanian-German clearing agreement.

In accordance with the provisions of this treaty, a considerable number of German experts were immediately dispatched to Rumania in order to consult with Rumanian experts in the elaboration and execution of the new agricultural, forestry, mining, petroleum, and industrial development. In so far as the work of these experts bore fruit, it was quite clearly in the integration of Rumanian production with the needs of the German economy.

It is apparent, therefore, that a new system of international trade was rapidly forming before the present war broke out —a bilateral system centered upon Germany, conducted behind the shelter of exchange control and through the medium of highly elaborated clearing and trade agreements. This system was intended to cripple and finally destroy the multilateral trade that had been centered upon Great Britain. It diverged from that system in almost every respect. The trade conducted through bilateral clearing agreements proceeds at a level of prices considerably higher than those ruling in trade between exchange-control and free-exchange countries. In other words, Germany has endeavored to maintain a high value for the mark and a low value for the currencies of her partners in clearing agreements, being thus enabled to pay prices which are well above the prices ruling in world markets when these are converted at the rates of exchange ruling with free-exchange countries. This tactic, which has not always been successful, is calculated to achieve several objects. It reduces the possibilities of exports to the free-exchange countries, thereby reducing the exchange available for debt service as well as increasing the German hold over the market concerned. High prices in local currency also stimulate the production of the goods Germany needs and create popular pressure, particularly among the peasants, in favor of economic (and political) co-operation with that country. Since such commodities can be sold at high prices only to Germany through clearing agreements, the German negotiators are able to insist upon the acceptance (and payment) of German technical advisers whose task is to reorganize economic activity in the directions complementary to the German economy. There is a solid geographic and economic basis for such developments. Germany is a great industrial country needing the foodstuffs and raw materials that her neighbors can supply and well fitted to equip them in return with capital goods and manufactured consumption goods. In any circumstances there would be a considerable volume of mutually beneficial trade. Nor is there any reason to doubt that the clearing trade has been mutually beneficial. What Germany loses in the high prices paid for imports is regained to some extent by the high prices received for her exports. The main losers by the new system have, in fact, been creditors and trade competitors in third countries.

The ultimate explanation of the new trading devices, however, is political rather than economic, and the most serious criticisms of it from the point of view of the small countries derive from its political implications. Apart altogether from the use made by the German government of its enhanced power vis-à-vis the smaller countries or vis-à-vis other great Powers, it is evident that anything approaching monopolistic German domination of the markets of southeastern Europe may well reduce the bargaining advantages they have enjoyed in the past. It had, even before the war, impaired their economic sovereignty by forcing them to accept a measure of German advice and control in the organization of their economic activity and by necessitating their acceptance of economic regulation modeled upon and fitted into the German system. It would not require much extension of such dominance to impair their political independence and place them in the position of economic satellites dependent upon, and serving the purposes of, the German market upon Germany's own terms.

CHAPTER IX

The Limits of Regionalism

The Teachings of Experience

THERE has in recent years been increasing discussion of the possibilities of regional agreements to extend the advantages of specialization beyond narrow national boundaries, or at least to preserve some measure of international trade. It is not surprising that the collapse of the international trading system that was restored on the nineteenth-century model should have stimulated such discussion.[1] The years between 1931 and 1938 were fruitful in regional initiatives, particularly in war-haunted and tariff-

---
[1] Cf. Erik Colban, La Convention d'Oslo
Franz Grosse, Regional Trade Agreements between Groups of Nations
Elemer Hantos, Le Régionalisme économique en Europe
Klaus Heinrich, The Formation of Past Customs Unions
Mirko Lamer, Regional Economic Agreements concerning Yugoslavia
von Mickwitz, The Economic Structure of Capital Exports to Southeastern Europe
C. A. S. Hawker, Australia's Foreign Trade Treaties
J. F. Parkinson, The Bases of Canadian Commercial Policy, pp. 89–97, 134–143, and 222–226
T. Voionmaa, Finnish Commercial Policy, pp. 22–23 and 33–34
René Hoffherr, La Politique commerciale de la France, pp. 55–68, 72–74, and 245
P. Lieftinck, The External Economic Policy of the Kingdom of the Netherlands, pp. 7 and 39–40
Morten Tuveng, External Economic Policy of Norway in Recent Years, pp. 34–36
Erling Petersen, The Repercussions of Modern Commercial Policies on Economic Conditions in Norway, pp. 9–10
H. P. Gøtrik, Danish Economic Policy, 1931–38, pp. 61–66
Gunnar Boös, Survey of Sweden's External Economic Policy, pp. 74–83
British Coordinating Committees, British External Policy in Recent Years, pp. 15–18

ridden Europe. For the most part these anxious and somewhat unrealistic discussions of economic measures to promote the common trade of neighboring countries were a desperate reaction to the debacle of multilateral negotiations in the Monetary and Economic Conference held at London in 1933 —the last and most ambitious, but least successful, attempt to restore a multilateral trading system. As will be shown later, these regional economic discussions were, in turn, all wrecked upon political rocks. Yet there is vitality in the regional idea, which keeps recurring in proposals for European reconstruction after the war now in progress.

In order to gain perspective, it is necessary to recall the fact that the nineteenth century was prolific of customs unions that proved enduring. It was an era of rapidly extending world trade; but political change was incessant. Old empires fell to pieces and new States were carved out of them. The Latin-American republics arose from the wreck of the Spanish and Portuguese empires, as the United States of America had broken away from the British Empire just before the century opened. Belgium was separated from the Netherlands and the Balkan nations strengthened themselves at the expense of the Ottoman Empire. In what remained of the British Empire the most advanced colonies of settlements claimed, and were granted, economic independence.

But there were, on the other hand, strong tendencies towards federation and the formation of larger areas of free trade to counteract, in some measure, the centrifugal forces of nationalism. The United States was developing into a great free-trade area. In 1833 the German Zollverein was formed, to be consolidated in 1870 into the German Reich. Switzerland abandoned its intercantonal trade restrictions in 1848. Mexico went through two stages of federation in 1857 and 1873, the Argentine federated in 1861, and Canada in 1867. Italy became a united nation in 1870. Brazil federated in 1891, Australia in 1901, and South Africa in 1903.[2] At a later stage, China carried through the long and difficult task of

[2] Cf. Klaus Heinrich, *op. cit*, p. 6.

abolishing the "likin" charges that hampered trade within her borders.

It is important to notice, however, that all of these economic developments, widening the area within which trade might be conducted freely, were accompanied by organic political union. The customs unions were integral parts of a political process and were enforced by the police power of centralized government. A German writer has presented this development in dialectic form. Free trade is the thesis, opposed by the antithesis of nationalism, but transcended in the synthesis of federation based on customs union.[3]

The importance of common political aims, and generally of geographical propinquity, in these customs unions of the past is clear; but two factors must be stressed before they can be regarded as affording valid guidance for the solution of modern problems. In the first place, most of the cases cited are those of new countries—colonies of European settlement which joined together as they grew. The three cases of union within Europe—Germany, Switzerland, and Italy—had behind them a large measure of cultural unity, the essential basis of true national feeling. Their experience, therefore, does not afford conclusive evidence that economic union is a means to political rapprochement. On the contrary, it may plausibly be argued from the policies pursued by all these federations after achievement of their customs unity that one of the main reasons for their drawing together was to mobilize and augment their economic resources. Switzerland is an exception to the general rule that most federations have followed a policy of external trade restriction; but it might perhaps be argued that Switzerland lacked the area or resources to do so.

Dr. Heinrich, following Schmoller, argues that the prime motive of all such customs unions in the past has been the desire, by free trade within an enlarged but politically homogeneous territory, to develop productive forces that would en-

---

[3] J. Pentmann, *Die Zollunionsidee und ihre Wandlungen im Rahmen der Wirtschaftspolitischen Ideen und der Wirtschaftspolitik des 19 Jahrhunderts bis zur Gegenwart* (Jena, 1917), quoted by Klaus Heinrich, *op. cit.*, p. 15.

able the young nations to compete on terms of greater equality with older and more developed countries.[4] They have not consisted of homogeneous economic territories, but have rather endeavored to combine heterogeneous resources into a more balanced economic whole. This argument, it will be noticed, is consistent with the traditional autarkic thesis that a certain degree of economic self-sufficiency is an essential characteristic of statehood.

The war of 1914-18 gave renewed impetus to the forces of nationalism within Europe. Long subordinated linguistic groups—the Finns, Estonians, Letts, Lithuanians, Poles, Czechs and Slovaks—were given independent nationhood. There was, it is true, a considerable rearrangement of territory, particularly in central and southeastern Europe, involving the creation of new minority groups; but, on the whole, the settlement of Versailles was based on the principle of nationality. This fact renders more important the second point that needs to be stressed in connection with past customs unions. Throughout the nineteenth century there was a great and continuous expansion of international trade, and, on balance, a steady movement towards freer trading relations, the main instrument of that enlargement of freer trade being the most-favored-nation clause in commercial treaties. The new Nation-States of the twentieth century, on the contrary, were born into a world of restrictive economic nationalism. The creation of a series of small independent Nation-States at such a time was a highly dangerous experiment.

It is not surprising to find, therefore, that, in a period when the free-trade thesis was weakened and its national antithesis greatly strengthened, all attempts to find a synthesis in regional agreements have been greatly hampered. As was foreshadowed early in the twentieth century, such attempts at regional economic agreement have taken the form of reciprocal negotiations aimed at preferential arrangements rather than the more developed form of customs unions.[5] The

[4] Heinrich, *op. cit.*, p. 23.
[5] Heinrich, *op. cit.*, p. 35.

controversies which they aroused, therefore, centered about the conflict between proposed preferential concessions within a regional group and the principle of equality of trading opportunity as guaranteed by the most-favored-nation clause in commercial treaties. Heinrich lists no fewer than fourteen regional derogations from most-favored-nation treatment.[6] Few of these derogations, however, have been accepted as valid by the great trading nations. Regional agreements indeed have been effective only when the contracting parties have been powerful enough to secure recognition of exceptions to most-favored-nation treatment. The most conspicuous cases of such success have been the acknowledgment by the United States of the British imperial preferential arrangements and the acceptance of the Cuban clause by other trading nations. It is a significant fact that none of the groupings of small powers discussed in the next section has been able to secure acceptance by the great trading powers of the preferences it was desired to establish in their regional agreements. Most of the clauses listed by Dr. Heinrich are aspirations rather than established policies.

Nevertheless, the fact that the struggle to achieve regional trade agreements has taken the form of attempts to modify the most-favored-nation principle reveals the essential nature of the problem. That principle was the essence of the nineteenth-century trading system. It remains the keystone of American policy and is accepted also by Great Britain, with the qualification of imperial preference. Indeed, as Professor Rist has argued, it is inevitably claimed by all nations in regard of their exports.[7] At the instance of those who despaired of restoring a world-wide system of international trade, but were unwilling to accept the triumph of autarky,

[6] The British imperial, Scandinavian, Baltic, Russian, Balkan, Bulgarian, Iberian, South American, Central American, Cuban, Japanese, Netherlands, Asiatic, Egyptian, and southeast European clauses.
[7] Cf. Charles Rist and J. H. Herberts, "The Past and the Future of the Most-Favoured-Nation Clause in its Limited and Unlimited Forms," in Carnegie Endowment–International Chamber of Commerce, *The Improvement of Commercial Relations between Nations* (Paris, 1936), pp. 111–123.

the Economic Committee of the League of 1936 considered the possibility of circumstances arising in which the unconditional application of most-favored-nation treatment might be modified in an effort to form regional areas of freer trade.[8] The result of the Committee's deliberations, however, afforded little satisfaction to those who wished to obtain from the great trading powers freedom to negotiate reciprocal concessions within regional groups without their being extended generally by the operation of most-favored-nation treatment.

In any case, apart altogether from the arguments in favor of maintaining the principle, and from the uncompromising attitude of the great trading powers in this respect, political events in Europe quickly relegated discussions of regionalism to the status of academic exercises. As the threat of war grew more ominous, it became evident that whatever grouping of the nations was effected would be for strategic rather than economic reasons. This fact became so clear after the absorption of Austria into the German Reich that there was little further discussion of attempts of free trade among regional blocs.

Regional Initiatives in Europe

The progressive disintegration of trading relations between the European States may be traced in the growing feverishness of the regional conferences that succeeded each other ever more rapidly until the assertion of German hegemony over Austria in March, 1938 made it obvious that other solutions of the problem were in the making. The complicated story of these conferences might be reported by attempting to treat each region separately. In this fashion, separate treatment might be given to the almost continuous discussions of the northern countries,[9] from the time of the con-

[8] League of Nations: Economic Committee, *Equality of Treatment in the Present State of International Relations—The Most-Favoured-Nation Clause,* C. 379. M. 250 (1936. II. B. 9).

[9] Denmark, Norway, Sweden, Holland, and Belgium, joined by Finland in 1932.

vention signed at Oslo on December 22, 1930 until the virtual abandonment of their hopes by the declaration signed at Stockholm on May 11, 1938. Following the same regional pattern, the Danubian, Balkan, and Baltic conferences might be treated, with the frequent meetings of the central European agricultural-exporting countries running across this pattern like a connecting thread.

The reality behind these conferences, however, is to be found in a relentless political struggle between the great Powers for control over the smaller nations of Europe. In that struggle economic relations were steadily worsened and all attempts at regional understanding were thwarted.

The story begins with the Anglo-French domination of Europe after the war of 1914–18. Provision was made in the Treaties of St. Germain (article 222) and the Trianon (article 205) whereby Austria, Hungary, and Czechoslovakia were relieved of most-favored-nation obligations in respect of preferential concessions they might make in mutual trading arrangements.[10] It was realized that the replacement of the old Austro-Hungarian monarchy by the independent succession States brought grave danger of economic dislocation in what had been a well-balanced economic union. The years immediately after the treaty settlement, however, were not propitious for international co-operation in the Danubian region. All the central and southeastern European States were overtaken by financial and monetary disorders. Self-preservation was their first thought and anything more than emergency measures was out of the question. The stronger States were able to survive, in part with financial assistance extended to them by the Allies, and particularly by France. Austria and Hungary fell into disastrous inflation which was ended only when international assistance and control was organized under the aegis of the Economic and Financial Organization of the League of Nations. The League also intervened with assistance to Greece and Bulgaria in the settlement of refugees. It was very clear to the experts who worked in these schemes

[10] Franz Grosse, *op. cit.*, pp. 37–55; Mirko Lamer, *op. cit.*, p. 7.

of international reconstruction that their emergency assistance depended for its ultimate success upon active efforts to restore international trade in this whole region. Reporting to the Financial Committee of the League in September, 1925, Sir Walter Layton and M. Charles Rist pointed out that "the protectionism of Central Europe is run to extreme lengths compared with that of the larger commercial countries of Europe. The result has been a very great shrinkage of the trade of Austria with the succession States and though the foreign trade figures show that some compensation has been obtained in markets further afield, it is impossible that the latter should prove an adequate substitute for the lost markets of contiguous countries." [11]

Trade between the Danubian countries continued to decline.[12] When the flow of loans to Europe ceased abruptly, and agricultural prices fell heavily, in the first stages of the depression, there ensued a succession of conferences among the agricultural countries. The scene of these meetings shifted rapidly. In June, 1930, representatives of Hungary, Rumania, and Yugoslavia met in Bucharest and a further meeting was held in Sinaia between the two latter countries at the end of July. A more important meeting attended by representatives from Bulgaria, Czechoslovakia, Estonia, Latvia, and Poland, as well as the three countries mentioned above, was held at Warsaw at the end of August. In all of these meetings, as in the demands formulated at the League Assembly in September, an effort was made to secure preferential treatment for grain and other agricultural exports from central and eastern Europe. The demand was maintained in numerous conferences in succeeding years, but was never successful.[13] The

[11] League of Nations: Document C. 440. M. 162. 1925. II.
[12] Cf. Kalman Buday, *Exchange Control in Hungary;* Madgearu, *La Politique économique extérieure de la Roumanie;* Yovanovitch, *Le Contrôle des changes en Yougoslavia.*
[13] Cf. Marko Lamer, *op. cit.,* p. 10. "In the following years of economic distress, Yugoslavia took part in numerous conferences, i. e.
23–28. II. 931 Comité d'études pour l'union europeenne, Paris
26. III–2. IV. 1931 Conférence internationale du Blé, Rome
18–23. V. 1931 Conference in London

REGIONAL INITIATIVES IN EUROPE 303

economic need of these small countries was desperate, but economic motives were not strong enough either to move the great trading countries or to secure unanimity of action among the eastern European countries themselves. The former were preoccupied with their own economic difficulties and unwilling to penalize the great agricultural-exporting countries outside Europe. The latter were divided by political differences and under heavy pressure from the even more bitter struggle among the Great Powers for political hegemony.

Throughout the years after 1918, France had endeavored to build up the economic and military strength of the Little Entente—Czechoslovakia, Rumania, and Yugoslavia—all of whom had received territory in the Versailles settlement. After the failure in 1932 of the Stresa conference and the misfiring of its "Convention for the Valorization of Cereals" and other proposals prepared in anticipation of the great Monetary and Economic Conference at London, impetus was given to closer collaboration between the Little Entente Powers. A plan of economic co-operation was worked out in some detail in January, 1934. This plan, involving transport arrangements, credit facilities, and co-operation of commercial policy, was based largely on increased Czech purchases of agricultural exports from its partners.[14] There was, at the same time, a vigorous revival of French diplomacy in this region, brought to a sudden end by the assassination at Marseilles of the Yugoslav king and the French foreign minister by a Croat terrorist. The international background of this incident threw a lurid light on the political struggle for control of the Danubian area.

The elements of the struggle had revealed themselves in the successive emergence of the proposed Austro-German

---

5–20. IX. 1932 The famous Conference in Stresa
10–13. XII. 1932 Conference of agricultural countries in Sofia
5–20. IX. 1933 Wheat Conference in London
4–6. VI. 1933 Eastern European Agricultural Conference in Bucharest, etc. The results of none of these conferences were sufficient to justify their cost." Cf. also Franz Grosse, *op. cit.*, pp. 37–55, and Elemer Hantos, *op. cit.*

[14] Lamer, *op. cit.*, pp. 13–14; Hantos, *op. cit.*, pp. 26–33.

Customs Union in 1931; the Tardieu plan announced in January, 1932; the drawing together of the Little Entente in 1933–34; and the Rome protocol of March 17, 1934, followed by the Three Power Pact of May 15, 1934 between Italy, Austria, and Hungary. The latter pact, based essentially upon transport, marketing, and credit arrangements that evaded conflict with the most-favored-nation principle, resulted in increased exports from Austria and Hungary to Italy. Though the statistical measurements are complicated by the fact that Italian trade was diverted from other countries during the Ethiopian campaign, it is broadly evident that Italy was prepared to pay an economic price for increased political influence in the Danubian area. The tangled story of political and economic collaboration in this region during the years from 1935 onwards was further complicated by the vigorous economic activity of Germany and by the growing rapprochement between Yugoslavia and Italy which sensibly weakened the Little Entente.[15]

The division between the political interests of the southeastern European countries was further evidenced by the evolution of discussions at the so-called Balkan conferences. Beginning at Athens in 1930, and continued in successive years at Istanbul, Bucharest, and Salonika, these discussions followed the normal course of proposals for reciprocal treaties based upon preferential concessions safeguarded by a Balkan clause from generalization by most-favored-nation treatment. The final result of these discussions, however, was not an economic agreement, but the Balkan Pact signed in February, 1935, by the four antirevisionist powers in the Balkans —Greece, Rumania, Turkey, and Yugoslavia.

This interplay of German, French, and Italian policy in southeastern Europe was increasingly affected by the economic influence built up by extensive German import purchases as the new controlled system of German trade developed. When Austria was joined to the Reich in March, 1938 it was evident that the balance of political power in

[15] Cf. Lamer, *op. cit.*; Grosse, *op. cit.*, pp. 37–55; Hantos, *op. cit.*, pp. 15–54.

the Danubian area was altered. The acquisition of the Sudeten region of Czechoslovakia in September, 1938 and the protectorate extended over the remainder of that country in March, 1939 emphasized the achievement of German hegemony over this region.

It remains only to consider the attempts at regional agreement in the northern European countries. The Baltic conferences may be dismissed rather briefly. Conversations began as early as 1924, but became more effective at the Baltic Economic Conference in April, 1928. Successive meetings between Estonian, Latvian, and Lithuanian representatives continued in December, 1929, June, 1930, September, 1933, and September, 1934, the main object being to secure acceptance of the Baltic clause as a recognized exception to most-favored-nation treatment.[16] Something was achieved by mutual interchange of information and by joint agreement upon the administration of exchange and quota allocations; but the Baltic Powers were always in a weak bargaining position, as became obvious in their bilateral negotiations with Great Britain and Germany The dependence of economic policy upon political power was dramatically demonstrated after the outbreak of hostilities in Europe by the rapidity with which the U.S.S.R. secured a privileged position in the Baltic countries.

Negotiations between the Oslo group of northern and western European Powers represented the most promising and determined effort between the years 1930 and 1938 to form a "low-tariff club" of like-minded small Powers. Its origins are to be found in the proposals for a tariff truce that sprang out of the World Economic Conference convened by the League of Nations at Geneva in 1927. Delegates to this conference did not have plenipotentiary power so that the debates and reports, though containing a mass of valuable information and interesting suggestions, did not have practical results in government commitments. The whole conference, in fact, illustrated the reliance at that time

[16] Cf. Hantos, *op. cit.*, pp. 52–54.

placed upon the power of educated public opinion. Following the conference, a strong drive was made under the leadership of Great Britain to secure acceptance of a draft convention that embodied what was popularly described as a tariff truce. This convention, adopted on March 24, 1930, never secured effective ratifications; but, at the 1930 Assembly of the League, Denmark, the Netherlands, Norway, and Sweden endeavored to revive it.[17] These Powers were joined by Belgium at a meeting at the Hague in October, and further meetings were held in November at Geneva and in December at Oslo. Finally the Oslo Convention, providing broadly that the contracting parties would not add new duties or increase existing duties without consultations among themselves, was signed on December 22, 1930.

New impetus was given to this initiative of the small Powers by negotiations between November, 1931 and July, 1932, which issued in the Ouchy agreement between Belgium and the Netherlands, providing for reciprocal and progressive tariff reductions.[18] At this time the Lausanne Conference was meeting and a final settlement of Germany's reparation obligations was being arranged,[19] together with plans for calling the Monetary and Economic Conference which met at London in June, 1933. The Belgian-Dutch proposals were launched as a practical step towards the freeing of trade restrictions. It was the last chance of restoring a multilateral trading system. Recovery from the depth of the economic depression had begun in the summer of 1932 and the prospects of international agreement seemed propitious; but the prime support upon which the whole Oslo-Ouchy initiative had depended was now lacking. Great Britain, which had fought for the tariff truce, had introduced a protectionist tariff and was unwilling to commit itself to a

[17] Finland joined the group in 1932.
[18] Cf. Colban, *op. cit.*, for a detailed analysis of this whole movement, including the texts of the Oslo, Ouchy, and Hague declarations; also Grosse, *op. cit.*, pp. 28–37; and Hantos, *op. cit.*, pp. 48–52.
[19] One result of this settlement was default on the Allied War Debts to the United States after the failure of the London Conference.

stabilization of sterling. In July, 1932 the Ottawa agreements reinforced British protectionist policy and extended the imperial preferential system to the greater part of the non-self-governing colonial empire. At the same time the Imperial Conference at Ottawa insisted upon most-favored-nation treatment in regard to any reciprocal tariff concessions that might be granted within the Oslo group, while maintaining imperial preference as a recognized exception to such treatment. The Ouchy initiative, confronted with this decision, was stillborn.[20]

The Oslo group, meantime, continued to meet and to exchange information, even to collaborate on common problems. Shorn of British support, it encountered insuperable difficulties in its attempt to expand a freer-trading initiative. The northern countries, as M. Colban points out, are not an economic unit. Their trading connections with the Great Powers were more important than trade within their own region, a fact which was emphasized by the British bilateral treaties negotiated in supplement of the Ottawa agreements. The "new protectionism," involving the increasing use of quantitative and monetary restrictions, lessened the importance of the tariff agreements upon which the Oslo Convention was based. The group was split also in the formation of the monetary blocs discussed later in this chapter, Belgium and the Netherlands forming part of the gold bloc and the others depreciating their currencies to remain within the sterling bloc.

A last attempt was made on Dutch initiative by the signing of the Hague agreement on May 28, 1937. This agreement, in specific detail, endeavored to enlarge trade among the contracting countries by relaxing the quantitative restrictions on enumerated articles; but before the first year of the agreement was ended, economic depression supervened once more, and the agreement was ended by the declaration of May 11, 1938 at Stockholm. The Oslo Convention

[20] It was formally abandoned at the London Conference. Cf. Colban, *op. cit.*, p. 47.

remained in force, and consultation between the contracting powers was frequent until first Finland, and later Denmark and Norway, became involved in hostilities.

The long and persistent attempt of the Oslo Powers to form a nucleus of freer trade illustrates the dependence of economic policies upon the play of power politics. As a reinforcement of British free-trade policy, it might have proved a powerful lever in the reduction of tariff barriers. If British insistence on most-favored-nation treatment and hard bargaining in bilateral treaty negotiations had not weakened the bargaining position of these small Powers, at a later date they might have reinforced the freer-trading initiative launched by the United States reciprocal trade treaty program. There is little reason to doubt the desire of the smaller Powers in Europe to expand their trade by regional agreements; but, as M. Hantos has pointed out, "the restoration of a world economy is one of those crucial human problems that, like war and peace, in the last analysis are decided by the political intentions of peoples." [21] Political conflicts among the smaller Powers have been a cause of disunion; but the political conflict that has wrecked all the regional initiatives launched in recent years has been the bitter struggle of the great Powers for hegemony on the continent of Europe.

Imperial Consolidation

By the end of the nineteenth century, virtually all the economically undeveloped areas of the world had passed under the control of one or other of the great trading Powers. Africa was partitioned. Spheres of influence were established in China and elsewhere in Asia. Even the scattered Pacific islands were taken over. The scramble for territory was caused mainly by the desire to secure control of raw materials and was accelerated by the growing importance of oil. Openings for investment and markets for manufactured exports were sought also, and in some cases

[21] Hantos, *op. cit.*, p. 14.

the necessity of establishing coaling stations or of safeguarding strategic trade routes played an important role. In the scramble, the weaker peoples generally lost political as well as economic independence, a process that has continued in the twentieth century not only in Africa and Asia, but even in Europe.

Though the economic profit to be derived from colonial territories has sometimes been exaggerated, the tenacity with which territorial expansion has been sought on the one hand, and resisted on the other, is sufficient proof that there must be political and economic advantages worth struggling for. These problems will not be canvased here.[22] It is essential, however, to stress the fact that the spread of economic nationalism has both aggravated the difficulties of the Powers without colonies and encouraged the colonial Powers to strengthen regional organization within their empires. Territorial ownership, though not without importance, was less vital when trade was freer. As long as the Open Door and the mandate principle, in which the welfare of native peoples was regarded as "a sacred trust of civilization," were recognized as practicable ideals, if not actual realities, it was possible to look forward to an era of "Peaceful Change." There is a sharp conflict of principle between imperial consolidation and the Open Door, between the formation of great autarkic empires and the transformation of mandates and protectorates into independent membership of the League, between the political mobilizing of imperial economic resources and free multilateral trade and investment among independent States, great and small, developed and undeveloped.

The ideal of interwar Liberalism envisaged evolution of the British colonies of settlement into independent Nation-States, joined in the free association of a Commonwealth; the progress of other colonies towards Dominion status; the acceptance of trusteeship as a guiding principle in the administration of less advanced colonial territories; the main-

[22] Cf. International Studies Conference, *Peaceful Change* (Paris, 1938).

tenance of equality of trading and investment opportunity in these territories; and the approaching prospect of transferring colonial responsibilities from a Commonwealth to an international trust as the power of the League of Nations was consolidated. These constituted a dream of independent but co-operative Nation-States accepting joint responsibility for the welfare and political education, as well as the economic development, of dependent and industrially backward peoples. Even though the political realities did not correspond with this dream, it was a noble vision and its influence on practical policies was not negligible.

In recent years, however, the dream has faded. It was always an Anglo-American aspiration, a theory of political scientists, rather than an expression of government policy. The public opinion to which it owed its practical importance had its triumphs—in the launching of the mandate experiment, in the renunciation by the United States of interference with the domestic affairs of other American countries, in the promised restoration of Philippine independence, in the grant of provincial self-government to India, and in the restoration of sovereignty to Egypt and Iraq. Until 1932 also, British colonial policy may be put to its credit. The free-trade policy pursued in the Belgian and Netherlands colonial empires and the Congo Treaty assuring the Open Door in central West Africa are other examples of its working.

Monopolistic policies, however, have always been followed by most colonial Powers. Japanese and American territories are regarded as coming within the shelter of national tariff and shipping legislation. There is never any question raised of this extension of protective policy. France has steadily pursued a policy of assimilation. Algeria is an integral part of its metropolitan area and the remaining colonies are administered within a great system of imperial protection. Impetus was given to this system by a series of Colonial Conferences after the war of 1914–18,[23] and it is

[23] Cf. Michel Carsow, *Quelques aspects du commerce impérial de la France* (Paris, 1935).

IMPERIAL CONSOLIDATION 311

clear that policies of imperial integration were gaining ground in France before the present war.[24]

The greatest change in colonial policy, however, has come in recent years from the reversion by the British Commonwealth to imperialist integration and consolidation. The first British colonies of settlement were lost in consequence of an attempt to maintain the monopoly of colonial trade that called forth the thunders of Adam Smith's invective, and Edmund Burke's even more picturesque, rhetoric. In the century that followed the American Revolution there was growing disillusion with "the baleful spirit of Commerce that would govern a great Empire by the Maxims of the Counter." Adam Smith's dictum [25] that "the monopoly of the colony trade, like all the other mean and malignant expedients of the mercantile system, depresses the industry of all other countries, but chiefly that of the colonies, without in the least increasing, but on the contrary diminishing, that of the country in whose favor it is established" was accepted as incontrovertible.

It is no longer so accepted. While no attempt was made until war broke out in September, 1939 to re-establish a State-controlled monopoly of colonial trade, long steps were taken at Ottawa in 1932 towards the creation of exclusive privileges in that trade. This reversal of British policy, while perhaps not intrinsically as important a factor in the restriction of world trade as the tariffs of high protectionist countries, or even the moderate tariff adopted by Britain itself in 1931–32 (and still less important than the conduct of monetary policies in a spirit of nationalism), was of the greatest political and psychological significance. It marked the passing of the Open Door policy and the exacerbation not only of trading, but of colonial rivalries.[26]

Three aspects of recent British policy need to be clearly

[24] Hoffherr, *op. cit*
[25] Cf. *Wealth of Nations*, Book IV, Ch. VII, Part III.
[26] Grosse, *op. cit.*, pp. 8–28; British Coordinating Committee, *op. cit.*, pp. 15–20.

distinguished in this connection. The adoption of tariff protection, supplemented by quota restrictions on certain agricultural imports, is the first and intrinsically the most important of these, especially since it was combined with the depreciation of sterling and its subsequent management as a national rather than an international currency. The second is the extension and consolidation of regional preferences within the self-governing units of the British Commonwealth, including India. This extension of the preferential system is maintained and recognized by other Powers, including the United States of America, as an exception to the most-favored-nation principle. The Ottawa Conference at which the British reciprocal trade treaties were negotiated in July, 1932 not only adopted a resolution maintaining that imperial preferences were not inconsistent with most-favored-nation treatment, but also affirming the objection of the British Commonwealth to the recognition of similar preferences granted mutually by other regional groups. This resolution dealt the deathblow to the Oslo and Ouchy initiatives. It is difficult, however, to discover any essential differences between the nations of the British Commonwealth and those of the Oslo group, except that the former owe allegiance to the same monarch whereas the latter obey separate kings. If the Statute of Westminster and independent membership of the League are to be taken as tests, the British Dominions, apart from the common link of the Imperial Crown, are sovereign States.

The third important aspect of British imperial consolidation is the inclusion of the dependent colonies within the scope of the preferential agreements negotiated at Ottawa by Great Britain with the Dominions. Certain of the West African colonies in respect of which Great Britain is bound by the Congo Treaty were exempted, and, of course, the mandated areas also; but even the colonies with representative institutions were committed by the British government to the new preferences. This was a distinct break with the traditional Open Door policy, and its significance was made

IMPERIAL CONSOLIDATION 313

clearer when, in the case of Ceylon, the reserved powers of the Governor were invoked to implement the Ottawa agreements against the expressed wish of the Colonial Assembly.

The British Commonwealth and Empire, therefore, conducting about 30 per cent of the world's trade, has provided the most conspicuously successful example of regional integration in recent years. It is impossible to be dogmatic concerning the economic consequences of this development. For a time there was an evident strengthening of interimperial trade, though how far this was due to the new trade agreements, to co-ordinated monetary policies,[27] or to other factors such as world recovery in the period 1932–37, is impossible to estimate. There is evidently more doubt concerning the beneficial results of the agreements in those Dominions, notably Canada and to some extent Australia, which must seek markets outside the Empire for a considerable proportion of their exports than in New Zealand to which the British market is of overwhelming importance.[28] The wider effects of the agreements upon world trade as a whole, as distinct from interimperial trade, are less obscure. Great Britain was able to extend preferences to the Dominions only because it had adopted a protectionist tariff, and the increased Dominion preferences were granted in large part by raising the tariff against foreign imports. No conclusive evidence can be gained from comparing statistics of imports in the years before and after 1932, since there were wide fluctuations in economic prosperity; but, even if the effect of increased tariffs on foreign markets cannot be measured precisely, it is sufficient, for the problems here studied, to note the political effects of the Ottawa agreements. There can be no doubt that they were received with apprehension by neutral powers such as the Scandinavian

[27] One of the most important resolutions at Ottawa was that approving common principles of monetary policy. Monetary expansion based on exchange stability within the Empire, and pegged on sterling as a managed currency, was a potent instrument of economic recovery during the period before the Tripartite Agreement of September, 1936.

[28] Cf. Parkinson, *op. cit.*

and Low Countries, with regret by the United States, and with resentment by Japan and the other countries which had embarked on policies of political expansion. They have contributed much ammunition to the advocates of imperialism in these countries, and in this way must be regarded as having contributed to political tension.

Indeed, the drawing together of the scattered areas of the British Empire into closer economic regionalism must be counted as an ominous symptom of increasing political conflict and disintegration of the world trading system. It is significant that before Great Britain could negotiate a reciprocal trade treaty with the United States, it was necessary to modify certain of the Ottawa agreements. The British Empire was essentially a product, almost a by-product, of the nineteenth-century multilateral trading system. It was lightly held, in both an economic and a strategic sense. To turn it into a closely integrated regional economic group in a world of economic nationalism involves sacrifices as great in their way as the effort to defend it in a period of renewed imperialism. Wide as are its boundaries and varied as are its resources, it is still far from self-sufficient. The past investments of Great Britain in areas outside the Empire and Britain's dependence for raw materials, foodstuffs, and markets upon foreign countries are very considerable. The division of the trading world into autarkic blocs, to which so much impetus was given by the Ottawa negotiations, threatens the loss of a considerable proportion of British investments, trade, and markets outside the Empire. This, together with a further push towards the economic mobilization that led ultimately to war, has proved a heavy offset to the concessions within the Empire secured at Ottawa. It may be argued that these risks and losses were not the result of Ottawa, but, on the contrary, that the negotiations there saved the most valuable British investments, trade, and markets from further deterioration. No one can prove or disprove such a statement. Imperial regionalism may be the only practical policy in present circumstances; but no economist would admit that it has enhanced the prosperity and promoted the peaceful development of the Empire as did the expansion of multilateral trade.

The mobilization of economic resources for the prosecution of hostilities has increased the probability that the consolidation of this great regional bloc will be maintained. Every effort must be made to economize the free exchange needed for armament and raw material imports. Supplies will be purchased as far as possible within the Empire. Production will be increased and investments will be made that cannot hope to survive renewed competition from extra-imperial sources of supply when the war ends, so that there must be pressure to maintain and extend the system of imperial preferences. Moreover, the elaborate machinery of controls and commandeers, supplemented by price regulation and rationing, is being incorporated into the machinery of government. The adoption of exchange control as the mechanism through which those controls work is itself an indication of increasing discrimination.

No one can foresee what territorial changes the war may bring. As these lines are written, the German occupation of Denmark and Norway has resulted in the Allies taking over the Faroe and Lofoten Islands, while Iceland has proclaimed its independence and the status of Greenland is the subject of concern in the United States. The prospect of hostilities spreading to the Netherlands has already brought rumors of Anglo-American conversations concerning the Netherlands East Indies, rumors that promptly brought from Japan a semiofficial statement that, in case of war, the future of these islands was of great concern to Japan.[29] The Belgian colonies, particularly the rich copper areas of the Belgian Congo, may become a tempting prize of war. Italian aspirations for imperial expansion in North Africa are still maintained. While the battle has as yet hardly been joined and its possible extension into new areas of conflict, to say nothing of its probable result, cannot be foreseen, it seems

[29] The New York *Times,* April 18, 1940, and ff.

clear that a great impetus must be given to the transformation of colonial empires into more closely organized economic regions. The empires of the nineteenth century, in which trade was free to all nations, cannot survive in the modern world.[30]

The Formation of Monetary Blocs

The extension of economic nationalism into the closer organization of existing empires gives the clue to the sort of regionalism that has proved to be practical politics since the breakdown of multilateral trade in 1931. The effort of colonial Powers to bind their territories into closer economic union, moreover, has found a parallel in the territorial expansion of the Powers which at present pursue aggressive policies. Since 1931, the Japanese Empire has set up puppet regimes in Mukden, Peiping, and Nanking, and has occupied islands off the southern coast of China. Italy has added Ethiopia to its empire and taken control of Albania. The U. S. S. R. has absorbed Lithuania, Estonia, and Latvia, destroyed Finland's possibilities of effective defense, and absorbed a large part of Poland as well as Bessarabia. Germany has reoccupied the Saar, Danzig, and Memel, and conquered Austria, Czechoslovakia, Poland, Norway, Denmark, Belgium, Holland, and France. These are tremendous territorial changes; but greatly as they change the political map of the world, they are not sufficient to solve the economic problems of these dominant countries.

Side by side with political expansion a process of economic penetration of neighboring territories has been going on. The beginnings of German economic expansion and the foreshadowing of its technique were early apparent. In the commercial treaty signed with Hungary on February 21, 1934, less than a year after the National Socialist party had come into power, there was inserted a clause to the effect that "special attention was to be given to the question of

[30] Subsequent events, particularly the defeat of France and the entry of Italy into the war, have added significance to these developments.

adjusting portions of Hungarian agricultural production to German import needs." [31] Such a provision foreshadowed the supplementing and, if need be, the supplanting, of price competition by special measures of planning to render Hungary a more effective feeder of the German market. The technique necessary for this development was brought to a high pitch of perfection in the treaty signed between Germany and Rumania on March 18, 1939. The measures of co-ordination there agreed upon amounted virtually to direction by German technical experts of a great part of Rumanian productive activity.[32]

In order to understand the formation of such regional trading groups, it is necessary to consider the way in which the breakdown of monetary equilibrium resulted in the creation of so-called monetary blocs. The conduct of monetary policy is now so important in the organization of economic activity that the alignment of national price systems by pegging the national currencies to one or other of the great trading currencies has proved to be a potent means of reorganizing trade connections. It is probable that this result was not foreseen. The first reactions from the breakdown of monetary equilibrium were largely defensive. When sterling depreciated in September, 1931, the smaller countries were faced with a problem of immense difficulty. Those to which the British market was of overwhelming importance quickly followed the British lead. Within the British Commonwealth and Empire there were powerful monetary and commercial forces that prompted parallel depreciation and continued pegging on sterling. The currencies of the dependent colonies followed this procedure automatically. Their whole monetary and credit system depends upon variants of the gold exchange standard. Their economic development has been promoted by British investments and their major market is in London, even when the ultimate destination of their exports may be elsewhere. India stands, in these as in

[31] Grosse, *op. cit.*, p. 68.
[32] See above, Ch. VIII.

other respects, halfway between the position of the dependent colonies and that of the Dominions. Her currency is a classic example of the gold exchange standard, and any other course than continued association with sterling would have involved the disturbances of economic activity reported in countries like Denmark, Greece, and Turkey, whose currencies also were pegged on sterling.[33] Australia and New Zealand operate a credit exchange standard which is even more closely linked with sterling than a gold exchange standard currency would be. For them the British market is of overwhelming importance. South Africa hesitated for many months to follow the British lead, partly for political reasons, but mainly because the commodity gold is of such basic importance in the South African economy that any step that might tend to discredit its use in monetary systems was distrusted. By December 28, 1932, however, South Africa had depreciated to the level of sterling. Canada had an even more difficult problem to solve since it was torn between the financial and commercial influences emanating from London and New York.[34] The Canadian dollar for some months pursued an independent course midway between the levels of sterling and the United States dollar. The depreciation of the latter in April, 1933, and its temporary stabilization in January, 1934 at approximately the same relation with sterling as before September, 1931, relieved the strain on Canadian policy; but whenever the British and American currencies diverged the strain was renewed. At the outbreak of war in September, 1939, however, the dominance of political over economic forces was manifested. Canada became an integral part of the Anglo-French economic group, the Canadian dollar depreciating and being held at the level of sterling.

There is a solid nucleus, therefore, of the sterling bloc,

[33] Cf. Gøtrik, *op. cit.;* Pintos, *Le Contrôle des changes en Grèce;* Hazim Kuyucak, *Exchange Control in Turkey.*
[34] Cf. Parkinson, *op. cit.,* pp. 203–204.

consisting of the member-states of the British Commonwealth and the dependent colonial empire.[35] The divergent commercial interests of Canada have at times caused the counter-attraction of its great neighbor to be reflected in commercial and monetary policy; but the effect of war has been, as always, to close the ranks. There is, however, a large group of independent countries to which trade with Great Britain has, in the past, been of great importance. It was significant that, immediately after the successful conclusion at Ottawa of reciprocal trade treaties within the Commonwealth, Great Britain made a drive to conclude a series of bilateral treaties with countries that lay definitely within the influence of its trade. The most important of these countries had quickly aligned their currencies with sterling in 1931 so that they could be regarded loosely as members of a sterling bloc. British policy was directed towards expanding trade, reviving international capital movements, and maintaining exchange stability within this bloc.

It is apparent, however, that even before war was renewed in 1939 there was no clear-cut regional grouping. The Scandinavian countries—Denmark, Finland, Norway, and Sweden—managed their currencies in parallel with sterling, but the latter in particular maintained the independence of its currency policy. The Baltic countries endeavored also to maintain and extend their connection with the British market. The trade treaties which Britain negotiated in this area were hard bargains, postulated on the necessity for these countries to retain access to a great market in which they could obtain free exchange. In return they

[35] London Wall, "The British System of Exchange Control," confines the definition of the sterling area to "the United Kingdom, any part of H. M. Dominions outside the United Kingdom (except Canada, Newfoundland and Hong-Kong), any territory in respect of which a mandate on behalf of the League of Nations has been accepted by His Majesty and is being exercised by His Majesty's Government in the United Kingdom or in any Dominion, any British protectorate or protected State, Egypt, the Anglo-Egyptian Sudan and Iraq."

granted concessions to British exports, particularly of coal and textiles.[36] Elsewhere in Europe the influence of the British market was mainly seen in the depreciation of the Greek and Turkish currencies, and in trading agreements with those countries which gave export credits and even a loan to Turkey in an effort to expand reciprocal trade.[37] British influence was evidently stronger in the Near East than in central and southeastern Europe, both because of close relations with Egypt, Iraq, Iran, and the Arabic States and because of British political and economic connections with Greece and Turkey.

In the Far East, the Japanese expansion in Asia tended to create a yen bloc covering the Japanese Empire, Manchukuo, and part of northern China, while a bitter currency warfare was waged in the coastal ports of China in the course of the undeclared war that broke out on July 7, 1937. The Chinese currency had abandoned its silver bullion basis on November 9, 1934, and was pegged on sterling and the dollar, though increasingly on the latter rather than on the former. The obscure conflict between the American system of free exchange and multilateral trade, the British system of managed sterling, and the Japanese controlled trade within a closed yen bloc, was still unresolved when hostilities broke out in Europe.[38]

In Latin America the sterling bloc registered its greatest success in the negotiation of trade agreements and exchange understandings with the Argentine. The reluctance of the United States to accept the characteristic Argentine exports, or even to remove the veterinary restrictions on meat imports from that country, gave Great Britain, which had large investments there and provided a great market with only

[36] Cf. British Coordinating Committee, *op. cit.*
[37] *Ibid.* See also Kuyucak, *op. cit.*
[38] Masamichi Royama, *Japan's Foreign Trade and Exchange Problems in War Economy.* See also George Taylor, *The Japanese Sponsored Regime in North China* (Institute of Pacific Relations, 1940), and Chi Chao-Ting, *War Time Economic Development in China* (Institute of Pacific Relations, 1940).

mild quantitative restrictions and moderate import duties, a great bargaining advantage.[39]

To sum up, it is evident that, after the depreciation of sterling in 1931 and the consolidation of imperial trade in 1932, Great Britain endeavored by a series of bilateral trade treaties to consolidate its trading position in the countries whose currency alignment with sterling was evidence of complementary economic interests. At the same time, efforts were made in various clearing and payments agreements, notably that signed with Germany on November 1, 1934, to retain trade, collect arrears of commercial debt and at least part of the interest due on long-term debt from countries practicing exchange control. As Dr. Tasca's study bears witness, this aspect of British policy consisted of a series of particular arrangements involving considerable compromises with the regulated system of trade operating through exchange control.

In order to complete the picture of the involved currency situation out of which great trading blocs seemed slowly to be emerging, it is necessary to recall briefly the pertinacity with which a group of European countries defended the gold parity of their currencies in the years after 1931. The gold bloc, which was never, despite early conferences, closely organized, included at first not only France, Switzerland, and the Netherlands—all of whom persisted in their opposition both to devaluation and to exchange control until September, 1936—but Belgium, Italy, Poland, and, in certain respects, Czechoslovakia. The group had in common only its resistance to monetary adaptation, and one by one its members were forced either to exchange control or to devaluation. Czechoslovakia, surrounded by exchange-control countries, was forced early into similar policies and into devaluation in February, 1934. Belgium found the effects of depreciation in its great Western markets and exchange control in its

---

[39] See Angel Valle and Juan Ferrer, *La Politique économique de l'Argentine;* also Tasca, *World Trading Systems.*

Eastern markets involved too great a deflationary effort and devalued on March 30, 1935.[40] Italy, even before the invasion of Ethiopia, had embarked in March, 1934 on a policy of reflation which led quickly to exchange control.[41] Poland for many years maintained the gold parity of the zloty without exchange control, but at the cost of severe deflation and with quantitative import controls that achieved much the same purpose as exchange control, to which it was finally forced on April 26, 1936.[42]

The negotiation, in September, 1936, of the Tripartite Agreement between France, Great Britain, and the United States was avowedly aimed at forming a great area of exchange stability that could offer an opportunity for the gold bloc countries to devalue without the risk of provoking inflation.[43] France devalued and was quickly followed by Switzerland and the Netherlands, which, with Belgium, adhered to the agreement in October. There were some other currency devaluations, notably in Italy and Czechoslovakia; but the major purpose of the agreement, the promotion of freer trade in a great region of assured exchange stability, met with disappointing results. There is a sense in which the Tripartite Agreement was an attempt to form a bridge between the dollar and sterling blocs and to afford an opportunity for the gold bloc countries to join with Great Britain and the United States in the gradual re-establishment of monetary equilibrium upon the basis of which freer trade might be promoted over a widening area. Though this purpose was not achieved, the method of the agreement offers an instructive illustration of the way in which a bridge might be built between great regional trading blocs organized around leading currencies.

No mention has been made up till now of the great trading campaign pursued by Germany, particularly in central

[40] Jussiant, *L'Evolution du commerce extérieur de la Belgique.*
[41] Hirschmann, *Le Contrôle des changes en Italie.*
[42] Jerzy Nowak, *Le Contrôle des changes en Pologne.*
[43] See Bank for International Settlements, *The Tripartite Agreement* (Basle, 1937).

and southeastern Europe. Out of the difficulties and weaknesses of the smaller Powers, Germany endeavored to build a great trading empire. Some of the technicalities of that system have already been discussed. Such a system consists essentially of barter transactions negotiated bilaterally with each of the smaller Powers. Like the communications map of a highly centralized community, all the lines of negotiation lead to and from the metropolis, with little cross-traffic. The transactions are negotiated on a large scale by government officials so that the odd trades which depend upon individual enterprise and ingenuity tend to be crushed out. There is elaborate bargaining on quantities, prices, exchange rates, and transport charges; but this bargaining resembles the barter methods of primitive tribes rather than the processes by which equilibrium is established in a competitive market.

For the most part, the cost of financing is thrown on the smaller countries. Germany buys their exports on a great scale and the purchase price is distributed to individual producers by the central bank of the exporting country. In return the central bank receives a credit in blocked marks which, at a later date, must be liquidated by the import of German products determined by a comparable process of barter bargaining. Many tales are told of German efforts to get rid of products not suited to its creditors' requirements; but there seems good reason to believe that, on the whole, the small countries have made satisfactory deals. They clearly finance the trade since it is normal for them to have a large credit balance in blocked marks. Even if their imports from Germany are in the form of capital goods, and on occasion payment for these capital goods is financed over a term of years, there has been a net export of capital from the smaller agricultural countries to Germany. Such capital development as is taking place in these regions therefore is, in the last analysis, financed by the smaller countries themselves.

There has grown up a cleavage between the trade which they conduct with Germany on the one hand, and the free exchange countries on the other. The former is conducted on a clearing basis. Prices both of exports and imports range higher than those ruling in free markets. This is an indication that, for trade within the clearing system, currencies are substantially depreciated. The comparative degree of depreciation of the mark and of the other currencies is a matter of negotiation in practically every major transaction, or at least for periodic readjustment. Such trade conducted by clearing arrangements within an area of exchange control offers obvious facilities as contrasted with the more complicated processes of competitive bargaining in a free market.[44] An essential condition of its development, however, is that each of the smaller countries trades bilaterally with Germany and organizes its production so as to meet the needs of the German economy. It is obvious that, in any circumstances, the industrial development of Germany offers a great market for the raw materials and food supplies of the agricultural countries. This natural economic attraction, however, is offset by both economic and political disadvantages. The centralized German trading system operates on the principle of discriminating monopoly. As long as its suppliers have access to alternative markets, they may perhaps be able to strike advantageous bargains; but if they are deprived, by lack of free exchange, of access to other markets and are dealt with separately, their bargaining power may be very weak. If, and when, they get into such a position, they may be forced not only to produce what Germany wants, but to sell it on Germany's terms. Moreover, there are always ominous political implications involved in a situation of economic dependence.

It is already clear that the formation of great regional blocs dominated by the monetary policy of a great trading country has been carried a long step forward by the economic pressures of war. There is a world of difference, however, between a regional system in which trade proceeds

[44] See Meyer, *Analysis of Exchange Restrictions at Present in Force;* and von Mickwitz, *op. cit.*

FORMATION OF MONETARY BLOCS

on a basis of exchange stability by price competition within a free market and a system in which trade proceeds by monopolistic State barter transactions on a bilateral clearing basis. The sterling bloc is of the first type; the German trade area is of the second type. How the smaller countries of Europe are divided between these two groups, and the extent to which the sterling bloc will be forced to adopt stricter methods of quantitative import restriction and exchange control, will depend upon the outcome of hostilities and cannot now be foreseen. Nor can it be foreseen whether Japan will succeed in organizing a closed system of trade within a great Asiatic region. On the other hand, the most exclusive and centralized of all State trading monopolies, that of the U. S. S. R., has already extended the area of its effective control and, in a disillusioned, impoverished, and war-weary world, may extend it yet further.

There has been, in the strict sense of the word, no dollar bloc, since the United States has made no attempt to conduct its monetary and trading policies so as to build up a regional group.[45] This was very clear from the trade negotiations which were conducted with Brazil, the only important country with which the United States has a passive import balance that might be used as a bargaining weapon.[46] The policy of the United States has been directed, on the contrary, towards the rebuilding of a multilateral system of world trade based upon equality of trading opportunity. The great economic power of the United States, as symbolized by its enormous gold reserve, might conceivably be used to further a policy of freer trade after the present war; but it is already evident that the point of effective pressure must be the relations of the United States with the regional groups now formed or forming. Since the structure of these groups depends essentially upon the monetary relationship between

---

[45] For later developments in regard to Western Hemisphere negotiations, see below, Ch. XI.

[46] See Tasca, *op. cit.;* see also Bandeira de Mello and Alfonso Toledo, *Les Politiques économiques et la paix.*

their constituent units, it is obvious that some such form of monetary understanding as that attempted in the Tripartite Agreement of September, 1936 might well prove an effective means of linking those regional groups which are ready to co-operate with the countries of freer trade now grouped around the United States. Such monetary policies might lead to an expanded area of exchange stability in the maintenance of which the United States gold reserves might be used effectively. Upon the basis of such exchange arrangements, whether achieved by direct consultation or through the medium of an international monetary authority, it might be possible to negotiate reciprocal trade agreements with individual countries that would first curtail and finally discard the monetary and quantitative trade controls that have proved discriminatory in practice, if not in intent. There would appear to be no insuperable technical difficulties in this procedure. A plan has recently been projected for the creation of an International Monetary Authority with power to discipline States that pursued tariff, quota, and monetary policies inconsistent with the expansion of freer trade.[47] It is highly desirable that such plans should be invented and their possibilities explored. Political and economic progress in the past has not come from waiting on events, but from precisely such political inventions, even though in their first projection they may appear idealistic and unrealizable.[48] But the invention of machinery is perhaps the least difficult problem to be faced. The same general result might well be obtained by the unilateral initiative of a powerful trading country such as the United States, provided always that there was a genuine will to co-operate in the other contracting powers. One point, at least, is clear. The designer of the plan for an International Monetary Authority makes it clear that such an Authority, to function effectively, must be endowed with power to enforce its decisions. Among the specific powers needed is the power to veto autonomous exchange

[47] J. E. Meade, *The Economic Bases of an Enduring Peace* (London, 1940).
[48] Cf. Graham Wallas, *Men and Ideas* (London, 1940), Ch. I.

policies![49] Power there must be, but it might well be the economic power of a great nation or group of nations, exercised as was the financial power of the London Money Market during the latter half of the nineteenth century. No economic pressure, however, can enforce collaboration in a world trading system upon a State in which economic activity is regimented and mobilized for strategic purposes. The only force to which such a State will yield is military defeat. As long as State authority is used to promote individual welfare, ways and means can be found to bridge the trading needs of regulated and unregulated systems; but no compromise is possible in the long run between States that are organized to serve the purposes of individual citizens and those in which the individual is subordinated to the service of the State.

[49] J. E. Meade, *op. cit.*

CHAPTER X

New Aspects of International Organization

The Growth of International Business

THE INCREASING efficiency of communications in the modern world has tended greatly to reduce national differences of costume, food, amusement, and ways of working as well as of living. One modern metropolis tends to be like any other. The countryside moves more slowly into conformity with prevailing fashions. National, and even local, characteristics persist in country regions, but even there the influence of the automobile, radio, and moving-picture theater is increasingly powerful. Knowledge of modern inventions spreads almost as rapidly as any other form of news. Machine equipment therefore becomes as desirable, if not as necessary, for village life as for life in a cosmopolitan big city. Cash registers in stores, typewriters in offices, mechanical implements on the farm, radios, electric light, and mechanical cooking appliances in the home are no longer confined to a few advanced industrial communities. It is this generalizing of conveniences and labor-saving inventions that has given new significance to the spread of business enterprises across national frontiers. The world is not yet organized on a uniform pattern. There are still large populations too poor to afford mechanical aids to production and mechanical means of consumption. There are many other peoples whose purchasing power is so limited that they must go without much equipment that they would wish to have. But the pattern of production and consumption becomes steadily more uniform at least in the Western world, and in much of the Eastern. No longer must peculiar local needs be met almost entirely by local effort.

There have been foreign traders and trading settlements lodged more or less precariously on alien soil for many centuries. At the beginning of the modern age commercial outposts were multiplied by the great companies of Merchant Adventurers. The rapid development of British manufacturing and trading enterprise in the nineteenth century led to further extension of British business establishments in foreign countries. In many a port and trading center, on the continent of Europe and elsewhere, British merchants built thriving businesses handling the import of coal, textiles, and machinery, or purchasing raw materials. They were followed by merchants from other countries as industrialization progressed; but until very recent years this spread of business enterprise beyond national frontiers was essentially connected with shipping and merchandising, rather than with manufacture.

The rather rapid change by which, in recent years, branch manufacturing establishments have become more important than trading concerns has not yet been adequately studied. Behind it lies a growing demand for fabricated commodities that are costly to transport or difficult to install. Most of these manufactures embody devices that are protected by patents or trade-marks taken out simultaneously in every important market. The great trade in locomotives and other heavy machines in the latter part of the nineteenth century, a trade that continues to newly developing countries, indicates that transport costs are not the only factor in the problem. As manufacturing industry develops greater capacity in one country after another, the price-differentials between local and imported products tend to fall below the cost of transport for exceptionally bulky or heavy articles. Protective tariffs further narrow the price-differential in many cases; but as long as essential patents are effectively protected it is necessary to take account of the property rights embodied in such patents. This can be done by buying the rights for a particular area, by paying royalties for the use of the processes or devices, by encouraging the foreign owners to erect factories abroad or to participate with national capital in the erection of such factories. In particular cases, machines embodying patent processes will not be sold, but must be leased.

The spread of such international enterprises was rapid and cumulative in the latter part of the nineteenth and the early twentieth centuries. The first important examples occur naturally enough in the field of transportation. British capital built railways and established coastal and even river as well as transoceanic shipping services in many parts of the world. As the need for raw materials grew more extensive, mining companies and plantations were organized until there was a great international network of productive enterprises feeding the needs of the industrial countries. Tin mines in Bolivia and Malaya, tea plantations in India and Ceylon, rubber plantations in the Dutch East Indies, land development and mortgage companies in the River Plate, refrigerating plants in Australia and New Zealand, are examples of this phase of extension. One of the most striking illustrations of this whole development is provided by the world-wide search for oil as the internal combustion engine was perfected. Venezuela, Borneo, Iraq, Iran, Rumania are only a few of the cases where the new fuel was produced after exploration and heavy investment by great international companies. In many instances the first processes of manufacture—the smelting of tin, refining of oil, preparation of rubber—were located for economy near the source of supply.

At a somewhat later stage there was transplantation to the consuming countries of branch factories for the production of finished manufactures. Cotton factories in India, cigarette factories in China, automobile assembly plants in practically every important market, are examples of a general trend. With these industries also went essential services. The motorist traveling across Europe is apt to take for granted the gas pumps dispensing well-known brands of gasoline at a uniform price within the same wide region; but such conveniences are very new and owe their existence to the initiative, and often to the capital investment, of great international businesses.[1]

The capital investment side of this problem is considered later in this chapter. Here it is necessary only to repeat that there have been powerful economic forces at work promoting the spread of international business enterprise. These forces operate both from the side of demand and from that of supply. The cumulatively increasing demand for raw materials, and particularly mineral ores, forces industrial concerns in the manufacturing countries to extend their extractive operations over a world-wide area. The modern manufacturing enterprise tends to spread its roots like a great tree. Thus, Henry Ford has dredged the River Rouge to make a port at Dearborn connected with the Great Lakes so that his own ships may bring ore from his mines on the Canadian shores of Lake Superior to the very door of his furnaces, while rail transport brings coal, timber, and other materials from his own sources of supply in other areas. Great American manufacturers of rubber tires have established rubber plantations in Liberia and Brazil. Standard Oil, already established in many widely separated areas, has recently bought a large concession of oil-bearing strata in Saudi Arabia. A diagrammatic representation of the interests of Unilever Ltd. is like a maze, with its branch factories and plantations in many tropical countries. This process has gone so far that South African interests working from London operate gold mines in West Africa, and Australian base-metal interests work through London in Burma, Siam, and Malaya. Still on the side of demand are the forces which have led the International Business Machines Corporation to establish

[1] Frank A. Southard, Jr., *American Industry in Europe* (New York, 1931). Cf. also Bureau of Foreign and Domestic Commerce, "American Direct Investments in Foreign Countries," *Trade Information Bulletin* No. 731 (Washington, 1931).

first offices and then branch factories in European centers. The Ford Motor Company has set up assembly plants near London, Antwerp, Copenhagen, and in many other areas. It has also entered into arrangements whereby the U. S. S. R. uses its patents in great factories built on the American model. Instances could be multiplied of this powerful trend towards international business connections.

On the side of supply are all the expansive forces that derive from the economies of large-scale production and drive manufacturing establishments organized for mass production to seek wider markets. In this search they build subsidiary or finishing plants and furnish supplementary services. The old Pacific Island story of the wise administrator who presented the ruling chief with a carriage and pair and so secured the building of a much-desired road finds many parallels in the practices of industrial firms who wish to extend their markets abroad.

Even in a period of rabid economic nationalism, these forces of industrial and commercial internationalism have remained vigorous. Direct business investments were the only form of international lending to withstand, in substantial measure, the financial panic that swept the world from 1931 onwards. It is true that the operation of international businesses was hampered greatly by widespread economic depression and still more by the stiffening of tariffs and the imposition of quotas and exchange control in many countries. The stimulus to protectionism which resulted from quantitative and monetary trade restrictions acted, however, as a reinforcement in some cases of the already marked tendency towards the establishment of branch enterprises. Exchange control, in particular, blocked payments which accumulated to the point where many trading concerns were tempted to use them for investment in national production.

These scattered and illustrative notes are not intended as an exhaustive treatment of the problems raised by the extension of business relationships across national boundaries. There is a wide field of research awaiting political economists in this connection. It is apparent that the comparatively simple problems of international trade must give place increasingly to a wider consideration of international economic relations. Theories and policies based upon the early nineteenth-century experience of trade conducted between national enterprises are no longer adequate in a world where so many powerful international enterprises have vested interests in more than one country. Between Canada and the United States, for example, there is a considerable degree of economic integration in many industries.[2] The automobile manufacturers of Michigan have erected Canadian factories on the northern shores of the Great Lakes and the lumber industry of the Pacific Coast, together with the related manufacture of pulp and paper, is an economic entity in which the political boundary between British Columbia and the Puget Sound region has important but somewhat obscure influences on trading negotiations not only between Canada and the United States, but also between Canada and Great Britain and between Great Britain and the United States. In the same way, the activities of productive enterprises functioning within exchange-control countries with capital and patents belonging to American manufacturing concerns, and even competing in third markets with products of the parent companies, raise trading and political problems that are novel.

Finally, it is clear that the fusion of politics and economics which is so marked a development of recent years is as characteristic of international economic relations as it is of national economic regulation. In the new world after the war any discussion of international trade policy must reckon with linked economic enterprises subject to varying degrees of government control and regulation. It is perhaps significant that, at various stages of diplomatic discussion, both before and after hostilities broke out in Europe, business leaders have appeared as go-betweens or agents of negotiation.

It is, indeed, inevitable that increasing ease of communica-

[2] Cf. J. F. Parkinson, *The Bases of Canadian Commercial Policy.*

tion shall continue to render national frontiers anachronistic. The rapid development of aviation offers the clearest case of an industry that must operate by international agreements in which business and governments are vitally concerned.[3] Even more than ocean shipping and ocean cables in an earlier stage of communications, aviation, and radiotelegraphy with its related development of broadcasting, must ultimately be managed as international businesses, by agreement, if not by fusion; but no government, even a world government, could allow such vitally important enterprises to escape from control. There is a gradation from such obviously international enterprises through many forms of manufacture to purely local services; but the center of gravity shifts steadily from local to international forms of business organization. No peace plans can afford to ignore this trend and, if ever it becomes possible again to consider the refashioning of peaceful international relations and the redefinition of national sovereignty, serious thought must be given to the tendency of business organization, as well as capital investment and trading relations, to become international in scope.

International Commodity Controls

There is perhaps no field of economic research in which the difficulty of access to reliable quantitative material is greater than in the shadowland that lies between business and government. Yet this field has gained in importance during recent years and its significance for international relations has considerably increased. There are connections that are obvious enough between the spread of international business enterprise discussed briefly in the preceding section and international economic agreements, whether the latter are of a private business character, are business understandings supplementary to and reinforced by trade treaties, or are agreements between States enforceable upon private busi-

[3] Cf. League of Nations, *Economics of Air Transport in Europe* (Geneva, 1935) (C. 97. M. 44. 1935. VIII).

ness enterprise. International commodity controls, indeed, must be considered as a bridge between the expansion of business enterprises across national frontiers and the problems of national economic planning in an international world. There is, however, little accurate knowledge of the extent of such controls or of their precise relations with government regulation of international trade. This lack of information is due both to the secrecy with which international business agreements have always been enshrouded and to the difficulty of assessing the influence exerted by their negotiators upon government policy.

A French study of international cartels published in 1937 listed 140 such agreements, great and small, operating over restricted or wide areas, loosely or with an approach to complete monopoly control of the markets.[4] Between the years 1933 and 1938, a German investigator was able to trace the formation of no fewer than 46 new agreements as against seven agreements dissolved. It is evident, therefore, that the development of such undertakings has taken on greater importance in the years since international monetary equilibrium was destroyed and the world-wide trading system broke up into a series of disparate national economies. The new cartels have in many cases taken a different shape from the older type.[5] Instead of being organized to regulate total production by the allocation of production quotas to national territories, they have attempted to regulate export quotas while leaving national production uncontrolled. This important change in tactics is symptomatic of the disappearance of international economic equilibrium. Control could be maintained over national production only as long as economic activity in the various countries concerned moved roughly in parallel. Since the development of autonomous credit policies this parallelism has disappeared. The mechanisms of quantitative

[4] Mme. Laurence Ballande, *Les Ententes économiques internationales* (Paris, 1937).

[5] Cf. Albert Prinzing, *The Bearing of International Cartel and Control Schemes upon International Trade Organization.*

trade restriction and exchange control by which expanding national economies have been protected from import competition have effectively destroyed the methods of fine and indemnity by which the older cartels regulated production quotas. On the other hand, in these systems of regulated trade the negotiation of export quotas has been a means of safeguarding national markets and controlling access to export markets. Necessarily, such export quota systems have been closely integrated with national economic policy as expressed in bilateral trade and clearing agreements.

The conclusion to which Dr. Prinzing comes is worth quoting since it throws into clear relief the concept of an expanding system of regulated trade based upon independent national economic policies.

"If we take a long view," he writes, "international trade appears from the point of view of maximal commodity provision, to have developed in a threefold rhythm. The period of international free trade originally tended to reach this aim by way of international division of labour in a state of completely free movement of production factors. After the limitation of this free movement, International Cartels were organized as instruments for the same purpose, so that, in the second period there was a change in the form of economic organisation, not in the content of its aims. Today we witness the beginning of a third solution, viz. that of rationalising of national economies which will, through the full use of their productive capacities, develop not only a stable but also a large demand for the commodities of the world market. Thus the paradoxical result is that world-wide striving for relative autarky will at the same time lead to stabilisation and expansion of international trade and probably to the elimination of unnecessary restrictions. From the thesis of international free trade and the antithesis of autarky will probably result the synthesis of our third solution: through national economic planning to a peaceful international exchange." [6]

While this conclusion does not necessarily follow, it is indis-

[6] Prinzing, *op. cit.*, p. 32.

putable that there has, in recent years, been a strong tendency to link cartels and business agreements with the new methods of trade regulation. After 1929 the attack on trusts and cartels was vigorously prosecuted in many European countries as a measure of deflation.[7] Fixed and cartelized prices were an element of rigidity in the price structure. After the breakdown of exchange stability, however, the attempt to restore international equilibrium by deflating prices in countries with overvalued currencies became more and more hopeless. As the new trading restrictions spread, they involved the necessity of organizing domestic production and trade more systematically, so that government pressure on cartels and trade associations was soon replaced by co-operative consultation with, and then by direct encouragement of and support for, such bodies. It was not long before they were delegated some of the powers and responsibilities of regulation, a process that led logically to their incorporation in the machinery of government. It has already been argued that this was by no means an unmixed blessing to the industrialists and traders concerned since, in accepting the minor administrative functions allotted to them, they became instruments for the execution of government policy. The apparent extension of their power led, in fact, to the loss of their independence.

The international implications of this development may be seen in a growing tendency for international cartel and trading agreements to be correlated with commercial treaties. Governments have on numerous occasions supported their nationals in cartel negotiations by manipulating tariff duties and other trade barriers so as to provide bargaining counters in the negotiations.[8] In the same way, governments have encouraged their nationals to engage in parallel negotiations with their competitors or customers while commercial treaties were under discussion with the country concerned.

---

[7] Cf., e. g., Roman Piotrowski, *Le Problème des cartels en Pologne.*

[8] The extent to which trading associations have been linked with trade agreements may be illustrated by reference to the *Memorandum on British External Economic Policy in Recent Years,* pp. 32–34 and 43–51.

The results of such business negotiations have usually issued as private agreements which in effect form part of the trade treaty and, indeed, have often been used as a convenient method of evading most-favored-nation obligations to third Powers.

Together with the rapid development of international cartel agreements linked with commercial treaties between governments, there must be reckoned the semiofficial and official international commodity control schemes which endeavor to regulate the export of raw materials. While both have been affected by the outbreak of war, it is probable that the increased regimentation of national economies for war purposes will lead to their greater importance in any plans for the restoration of international trading connections after the war. There is a baffling complication of control arrangements in which it is difficult to distinguish types. Both production and prices are controlled. National merges into international control. Raw materials, semifinished products, and manufactures are covered, and there are varying combinations of technique in these different fields. For the most part, however, the new cartel arrangements are based upon independent development of production for national markets combined with regulation of exports. The commodity control schemes, while in most cases involving restriction of production by the allocation of export quotas to producing areas, are intended primarily to maintain prices at levels that will preserve the financial structure of the raw material producing enterprises. Both cartel and commodity control agreements, therefore, are designed to regulate trade—in the former case, trade in manufactures, and in the latter, trade in raw materials. It is inevitable that any attempt to restore international trade at some uncertain period in the future will need, at least for a transitional period, to incorporate and connect these elements of international industrial agreements. It is probable, therefore, that there will be a greater degree of "planning" in any such restoration of international trade.

Access to raw materials was not a problem for any country, even for inland continental countries like Poland and Switzerland, as long as trade remained reasonably free so that materials could be bought in the open market. The advent of control schemes, however, created a situation in which, for some important commodities of which tin is a good example, a few countries within whose territories the most extensive and accessible supplies were located were able to regulate supplies to the market. Such regulation was undertaken in the interests of producers, or, more strictly, in the interests of the owners of shares in the producing enterprises. There was little or no representation in the various control schemes of the consumer interest. This raises a general problem of the regulation of economic activity; but within that general problem there is a particular international problem of great political significance. For countries which lack important raw materials in their own territories, but are large consumers of those raw materials, some of which are of great strategic importance, international control schemes appear as monopolistic controls in the hands of countries more fortunately placed than themselves. The price of essential commodities is regulated in the interests of those who own the territories in which they are produced. In that regulation the "have-not" countries have no voice. No great consuming country is likely to accept such a situation quietly. The United States, for example, protested vigorously against the Stevenson scheme for regulating the output and raising the price of crude rubber.

While, in most instances, a good case may be made out for temporary regulation of output in periods of depression, when unrestricted competition may endanger the solvency of large capital sums invested in raw material enterprises, the tendency for regulation to persist after the worst of the depression has passed raises large issues of international politics. If production and trade in vital commodities such as rubber, tin, and copper are to be controlled by international agreement between a comparatively few countries, every country which feels its national security imperiled by the possibility of being cut off from supplies in an emergency will endeavor to secure permanent access to such supplies, if necessary by the historic method of military conquest. Even in times of peace, a control which squeezes consumers in the interests of organized producers is likely to lead to protests and to the search for substitute materials.

It is apparent, therefore, that the abandonment of a free trading world economy and the substitution therefor of regulated production and trade in important raw materials, must either proceed to the logical end of international regulation or run the risk of embittering international relations. Most international commodity control schemes are, in fact, international only in the sense of giving representation to the producing countries, and it cannot be expected that this situation will be accepted gracefully by other countries. There is, in fact, no very satisfactory halfway house between a free trading system based on laissez faire and a system in which national production is co-ordinated in a system of international planning. It is unlikely that either alternative will be easily attainable, but it is certain that the linking of cartel agreements and commodity control schemes in regulated trade requires very careful consideration. The key to the situation may perhaps be found in more effective consumer representation, if possible including consumer interests in countries outside the controlling group. A means of securing such representation might possibly be found by a linking-up of cartel agreements between the manufacturing countries with the commodity controls over raw materials. But in the long run the most important practical consideration is likely to be the spirit in which such controls are administered. If they are motivated primarily by the desire to preserve a level of prices which will enable older-established and more costly sources of supply to maintain some output, and therefore the financial value of their investment, they will be driven to monopolistic attitudes. In this, as in so many other aspects of international economic organization, control which works towards a freer market and acceptance of competitive forces is not only economically beneficial, but politically wise.

The Financing of International Enterprise

International lending has naturally changed its character as the form of international business enterprise has changed. The international capital market that was the pride of nineteenth-century economists was only loosely related to international trade and the expansion of particular manufacturing enterprises in foreign countries. The speculative fund and the cosmopolitan loan fund, which Bagehot describes as running "everywhere as it is wanted, and as the rate of interest tempts it," were essentially banking funds—liquid credit resources directed into investment channels by the operations of financial specialists. Bagehot, indeed, speaks of "the whole of the loan fund of the country lying in the hands of bankers and bill-brokers, which moves in an instant towards a trade that is unusually profitable, if only that trade can produce securities that come within banking rules." [9]

This description of the method by which business was financed, nationally and internationally, calls up a vivid picture of financial specialization in a competitive era. It was the period when trade, both domestic and international, was financed by the drawing of bills, the handling of which gave employment to many specialized markets. Bill brokers, acceptance houses, and discount houses were merchants dealing in short-term credit applied to the financing of commodity trade. In the same way the Stock Exchange, with its division between brokers and jobbers, and its specialized markets handling different types of securities, was not as concerned with the speculative reappraisal of old investments as it was with forecasting the profits of new enterprise, "when enterprises were mainly owned by those who undertook them or by their friends, and associates." [10] The growth of absolute

[9] W. Bagehot, *Economic Studies* (London, 1880), p. 45.
[10] J. M. Keynes, *The General Theory of Employment, Interest and Money*, p. 150.

ownership, however, has constantly tended to enhance the purely speculative side of Stock Exchange operations. In Mr. Keynes's phrase, "Speculators may do no harm as bubbles on a steady stream of enterprise. But the position is serious when enterprise becomes the bubble on a whirlpool of speculation. When the capital development of a country becomes the by-product of the activities of a casino, the job is likely to be ill-done." [11]

There is abundant evidence that the floating of new securities representing shares in foreign enterprises has in recent years been steadily replaced by methods of self-financing, or the "placing" of shares. Liquid credit for new capital investment has less often been gathered up by public subscription and flotation. The extension of great business enterprises has been increasingly financed by the use of reserve funds withheld from distribution as dividends, or by direct banking loans. Their profits have not been distributed to shareholders, but retained, so that decision in regard to new investment has passed in greater measure to the managers as distinct from the individual owners of large businesses. Investment across national frontiers has been markedly influenced by this trend. There is still a great market for international securities, and this market is often replenished by the capitalization of direct investments and their issuance to the general public after the original promoters have successfully launched the venture; but direct international lending was tending to dry up [12] even before the breakdown of exchange stability brought the collapse of the international capital market after 1931.

Direct investment took many forms such as, for example, the purchase of shares in a foreign enterprise by a great corporation wishing to enter the foreign market, the establishment of branch factories or the flotation of new enterprises in which the parent corporation retained a minority or ma-

[11] *Ibid.*, p. 759.
[12] Except for the great flow of American loans to Europe in the reconstruction period 1925–29.

jority interest. Nearly always the right to use patented processes or devices was part of the arrangement.

Very intricate and difficult problems of valuation and accounting arise in connection with such businesses and these are rendered of more than statistical importance by the practice of double taxation in many countries.[13] It is all but impossible to determine a sound basis for valuing royalties to be paid by branch factories for patent rights, or for the invoicing of parts and replacements supplied to such factories by the parent company. Allocation of profits between the main concern and its branches is clearly a matter of accounting policy, depending upon such prior decisions of valuation.

In the period of growing nationalism after the war of 1914–18, the increasing use of direct investments appeared likely to offer a solution of the conflict between national control and international economic expansion. This solution was endangered when the spread of exchange-control systems blocked the transfer of earnings from branch factories as effectively as the payment of interest on public securities. Many devices—usually in the form of additional exports—were used to secure some transfer of these blocked earnings; and there was for a time, before war broke out, some disposition on the part of many great corporations to reinvest them either in an extension of the businesses or in other channels of investment in the defaulting country. Such an arrangement, however, could only postpone the problem without solving it, since it was equivalent to funding the transfer obligation. In the long run, direct investments would appear as likely to suffer default as other forms of international lending.

Meantime, however, it is important to notice that, on the model of private direct investment, a new form of capital construction in backward industrial countries has developed within systems of regulated trade conducted by clearing ar-

---

[13] Cf. Ralph C. Jones, "Allocation Accounting for the Taxable Income of Industrial Enterprises," *Taxation of Foreign and National Enterprises,* Vol. V (League of Nations, Geneva, 1933).

rangements. This development has been justified as typical of the way in which international capital movements should, in the future, be integrated with commodity trade.[14] Rejecting the nineteenth-century system of multilateral trade and foreign investment as anarchic and unworkable, Dr. von Mickwitz argues that Germany's clearing agreements with non-creditor countries had made possible a considerable capital export from Germany to the agricultural countries of south-eastern Europe. This capital export was closely linked with bilateral trade treaties which provided for the liquidation of the debt incurred in the only sound economic manner—by the export of goods. The essential point in his argument, however, is clearly expressed in his own words: "A favourable clearing balance represents a means for financing foreign trade, in which, paradoxically enough, interest payments precede capital supplies, since the financing of the export transaction has perforce to be taken over by the agricultural clearing partner. The intermediary stage of providing cash is eliminated in a clearing capital export of this type, and thus the economic monopoly held by those nations who are able to make cash transfers of foreign loans is broken. It is not the country which can offer substantial loans that can conclude an agreement for supplies of capital to south-eastern Europe, but the country which is prepared to take south-eastern European goods in payment.

"By this means, trade policy takes the place formerly occupied by financial policy, so that the country which, by devising a really supplementary exchange of goods can offer more to the raw material country, which is short of foreign exchange, ultimately becomes the bearer of the new foreign investments, in contrast to the pre-war era, when the creditor position of a country actually depended on a too liberal offer on the money and capital markets."

A distinction must be drawn, however, between the export of capital and the export of capital goods. Germany's

[14] von Mickwitz, *Memorandum on the Economic Structure of Capital Exports to South-eastern Europe.*

trade policy has for many years been based upon large imports of foodstuffs and raw materials, payment for which swelled the clearing balances of the agricultural countries. Those balances were gradually liquidated by the export of manufactured goods from Germany, of which a substantial part was durable capital equipment. In this way industrial development had been promoted, but the capital had been provided by the agricultural countries, not by Germany. Indeed, any capital export was in the opposite direction since the agricultural countries were, in fact, creditors of Germany, financing the clearing trade by having large balances in the clearing accounts—balances which did not pay interest.

Whether such a method of industrialization was in the best interests of the countries concerned, or more economical than the flotation of loans which under a multilateral trading system might have been spent in the purchase of German capital goods, is a question that could be answered only by detailed scrutiny of the terms by which the clearing trade has been conducted.[15] In such a calculation the reluctance of creditor countries, such as the United States and Great Britain, to modify their protectionist policies must be taken into account.

Whatever judgment might be arrived at on purely economic grounds, the political factors in any comparison between the old and the new system cannot be ignored. Quoting with approval an article from the London *Times* arguing

[15] Cf. von Mickwitz, *op. cit.*, p. 19: "If Germany buys South-Eastern European products at a higher price than the world market price, it must be remembered that Germany pays a price unaffected by trade cycles and will not be affected in the prices she offers by the jump in prices of boom years. But as Germany is exchanging goods, the higher price which she is prepared to pay corresponds to the higher price which the German machine exporter can obtain from the South-Eastern European clearing country, one part of which, it is true, represents the credit interest on the machines delivered. Payment of interest is at any rate no necessary part of this new system of exporting capital—this must be considered in judging the price which the raw material country has to pay for capital supply in kind (machinery, etc.) for in pre-war days the purchase of such production goods was made more expensive for the national economy of a country as a whole by the interest which had to be paid to the intermediary provider of the cash. £1,000,000 at 5 per cent for 20 years represents a repayment obligation of £2,000,000."

that not only should exports be connected with loans, but interest payments with imports, Dr. von Mickwitz argues that this is achieved in the new clearing system.

"Germany also adopted that method of securing interest payments on her capital exports in kind which was adjudged the only correct method in the *Times* article mentioned above. She was careful to see that the south-eastern European countries could guarantee 'to produce such goods or services as would form a basis for additional reciprocal trade.' She built up an 'exchange of primary products and her own complicated finished products' and she erected an economic system that would 'complement' Germany's."

Two observations must be made in concluding this very brief and summary raising of some of the problems of direct investment. The first is that the new system of clearing arrangements designed to take care of capital movements as well as trade is primarily a governmental system. Direct investments have been associated in the past with private business enterprise. In form the German investments may still be transactions of business firms, but in fact they are part of national policy. The investment is not determined by profit possibilities nor by the demands of consumers in the country concerned, nor indeed by the wishes of the real owners of the capital. By a complex and subtle series of negotiations, exchange rates and prices are manipulated so that it appears to be profitable for business enterprises to use the capital of another country in ways that serve the needs of trade so directed and controlled as to carry out the policy of the dominant industrial debtor. It is the purposes of German industry which are promoted, and German industry is the creature of the German State.

The second point is equally clear. The new regionalism promoted by such investment behind the shelter of exchange control is not a means of extending international trade on a multilateral basis, but a method of binding satellite countries to the economic power of a dominant metropolitan industrial area.

The Dilemma of Planning

"Planning" is a word that carries with it a background of emotional approval. It suggests wise forethought and rational control of complicated problems by "minds that sway the future like a tide." Such words are dangerous since their use is apt to prejudge the issues of debate. Wherever there is a subconscious connotation of approval or disapproval in the expressions used as tools or instruments in discussing social questions, the scientific investigator ought to be particularly on his guard. Everyone is tempted to accept or advocate policies that claim to substitute order for chaos, foresight for muddle, and intelligence for stupidity. It is, therefore, wise to scrutinize with special care whatever is labeled by such an attractive word as "planning," suggestive as it is of "capability and god-like reason."

It is obvious that the increasing complexity and range of international economic contacts brings the need for careful reconsideration of the institutions and procedures by which such contacts are regulated. Some evidence of the changing character of international economic organization has been presented in the preceding sections of this chapter. The spread of industrial enterprise across national frontiers and the growth of direct business investments have in recent years encountered an increasing tendency for governments to regulate and control international trade. The result has been a marked stimulus to cartels and trade organizations which tend to be linked with, and form part of, government policy. Such developments naturally encourage the advocates of planned economies since they offer a prospect of highly organized and elaborated institutional procedures in the conduct of international relations.

There is always a subordination of private to public interests in time of war, or more correctly a subordination of private interests to the purposes of the State, which are public interests only as long as the State is the servant and not the master of its citizens. It becomes increasingly difficult, however, to separate the conduct of modern war from its prior preparation. The acceptance of State regulation even in times of peace is greatly facilitated by this fact. It is essential, however, to realize that the superficial efficiency of the new type of centralized organization is primarily due to the fact that the purposes of such organization are simpler and easier to achieve than the conflicting purposes of an economy aimed at maximizing the economic welfare of a great community. Economic welfare is a vague generalization that sums up a great diversity of conflicting and complementary individual consumers' satisfactions. Moving-picture films and steel trusses for bridge building, millinery and motorcars, art and alcohol, all enter into such satisfactions. It is true that a modern army needs almost as great a variety of production for its maintenance. It would be surprising if it did not, since warfare now demands the support of the whole embattled population. But there is one single test of utility in such production—its contribution to fighting efficiency. Decision is therefore concentrated in the hands of those who control the fighting machine. In the last resort, therefore, the reason for centralized State control in wartime is the necessity to concentrate economic power in the hands of those who are responsible for war strategy. This is usually described as a system of "power economics" as contrasted with "welfare economics"; but there is a secondary meaning of the phrase "power economics" that is worth noting. In general, the phrase connotes an attempt to increase the military power of the Nation-State, but in so doing it is inevitable that the power of those who control the institutions of the State shall be increased also. Perhaps because of the old habit of referring to States as Powers, great or small, the expression "power economics" calls up a vision of a vast military machine; but, in fact, the most insidious aspect of "power economics" is the power it gives to a small group of important officials to direct and mobilize the activities of their fellow citizens. This, rather than the power to hurl the activities so mobilized into conflict with those of another people, is the most dangerous risk to be run in a system of State-regulated economic activity. And it is this concentration of power and decision in a relatively few hands that gives the appearance of efficiency and order to such a system. It is theoretically possible that such despotism may prove to be benevolent and use its centralized efficiency to promote the infinitely various satisfactions demanded by the citizens of a great community; but the teaching of history is that it has seldom proved safe to allow such concentrations of power to develop.

Against this risk of arbitrary concentration of power must be set the admitted fact that the increasing complexity of modern life calls for a higher degree of organization than was compatible with the more localized and less complex personal relations of a premechanical age. To allow the new forces of industrial invention and speedier communications to operate unchecked by social controls is to run a risk that competition will result in power passing into the hands of ruthless groups of "economic royalists." The social history of the nineteenth century is largely a history of political inventions designed to protect the weak in bargaining power and to control the strong. It is inevitable that this process of political invention shall continue; but there is a clear distinction to be drawn between legislation governing economic activity and attempts actually to concentrate the effective operation of such activity in the hands of government agents.

There is good reason to believe that the former type of regulation is not incompatible with the preservation of international equilibrium. It is, after all, a setting of the market rather than its replacement by State monopoly. The regulation of wages and hours in factory employment, progressive taxation, the provision of social services, and similar types of social legislation alter the rules within which economic bargaining is conducted and make such bargaining more equal; but they do not destroy the bargaining process. In this respect, they are similar to the regulatory controls imposed upon international trade by such measures as tariffs and exchange equilization accounts. If such regulations are pushed to extreme lengths, they may seriously hamper market processes; but in principle they are consistent with multilateral bargaining within and between national economies. Essentially they represent the type of social control which leaves a great deal of initiative to individuals in the pursuit of their own satisfactions. Whether stress is laid upon consumers' choice, freedom of contract, or individual enterprise, the basic concept in such a system is that government and economic organization exist to promote individual welfare. It follows naturally that the individual is, within rather wide limits, the best judge of his own welfare. Freedom to exercise judgment is, indeed, a value in itself.

Such emphasis on individual rights is not inconsistent with government action designed to limit privilege and ensure equality of bargaining power. The establishment of decent minima of subsistence and the relief of distress and misfortune have long been accepted as valid objects of legislation. Community action to provide equality of economic opportunity, particularly by the expenditure of funds derived from progressive taxation to furnish educational, health, and recreational facilities for the community as a whole, is broadly accepted now in most countries. There is, in addition, a range of public services—differing in various countries, particularly those into which enters an element of natural monopoly—which are recognized as being best operated by some form of government enterprise. None of these broad categories of government intervention in economic activity has proved incompatible with the mechanism of the market. The idea of town planning, in the sense of public control exercised over the zoning of economic activities, does not now meet open opposition although it may conflict sharply with particular vested interests. There seems no reason why its extension cannot be envisaged over wider areas, the beginnings of which may perhaps be discerned in national conservation movements in many countries.

Planning has moved into new and more debatable ground, however, with attempts to rationalize and organize national economic activity by administrative control exercised at the center of national power. In recent years the most effective weapon utilized in such centralized control has been the power exercised by governments over public credit and monetary policy. The monetary weapon is a powerful one since all economic activity proceeds in a medium of credit. Moreover, control of the credit mechanism is comparatively easy to acquire. Coinage is a prerogative of governments and, in an age when credit is more important than circulating media of exchange, it is obvious that its control must pass from the hands of private interests to those of governments. Central banking is perhaps the most important of all the public services which are necessarily monopolistic and therefore destined for public control.

A debatable problem arises, however, as soon as the principle of control is conceded and the manner of its exercise is examined. There is an increasing tendency in many quarters, responsible and irresponsible, in almost every country, to advocate the manipulation of monetary policy as an effective means of economic reorganization and social reform. A parallel might perhaps be drawn between the use of a municipal water scheme, not to provide water and perhaps power supplies open to consumers on equal terms, but to effect a reorganization of consumption and production. In fact, since credit operates in such multifarious ways in every aspect of economic activity, generalized measures such as lowering the rate of short-term interest and increasing the supply of available money have not up till the present proved an effective means of social reorganization, except when supplemented by more direct and positive action such as control of investment and government spending of various kinds. Even then, their success has been most marked in countries like Germany where the ends of expenditure are known and simple, and where monetary policy has been merely one aspect of totalitarian economic policy.

The difference between providing credit conditions that facilitate dispersed efforts by private initiative to reorganize economic activity, and the attempt to stimulate such reorganization in detail by government action, raises again the distinction between regulation of the market and actual government operation of economic activity. The baffling complexity of economic relations in a modern State is such that monetary policy must embark upon discriminatory rationing if centralized operation is to be effective as a means of planning. This distinction between setting the conditions within which private enterprise must function and the supplanting of such enterprise by government action in detail is peculiarly important in regard to the international repercussions of independent monetary policies followed by sovereign States. There seems no insuperable obstacle to the international co-ordination of national policies if they are confined to the regulating function; but there is little possibility of co-ordinating detailed plans of rationing and credit control. Specifically, it seems technically possible to envisage national policies of credit expansion (or theoretically of credit contraction) if such policies are confined to action upon the price of credit without discrimination or rationing. Consultation and concerted action between central banks might even result in parallel action. Strains on national balances of payments might be met by the use of equalization accounts (which are, indeed, simply an expansion of well-tried central banking practice) or by clearing accounts through an international monetary institution. Some economists are willing even to contemplate periodic adjustments of exchange ratios of national currencies with each other or with some international unit of account,[16] though this raises difficulties for any resumption of long-term international lending.

On the contrary, there is no practical likelihood that independent or autonomous monetary policies based on exchange control can be fitted into a system of international economic co-operation and equilibrium. Regulation of credit by control of its price, the rate of interest, might be worked by international consultation or by clearing through an in-

[16] Cf. J. E. Meade, *The Economic Bases of a Durable Peace*.

ternational authority; but centralized rationing cannot be so adjusted. It is significant that the most precise plan yet projected for an International Monetary Authority gives power to that Authority to forbid exchange control and to supervise and gradually eliminate quantitative controls of international trade.[17] Such rationing is impossible of international co-ordination and is, in fact, inextricably bound up with that concentration of economic power in the hands of State officials which is an essential attribute and hallmark of militarist policies. Not all exchange control and quota systems by any means have been devised for militarist reasons; but their existence facilitates the purposes of militarism and no militarist regime can survive without them.

Like the preceding sections of this chapter, the foregoing discussion does not pretend to analyze, but merely to raise, certain new aspects of international economic organization. It is clear that any future attempt to restore international economic co-operation must reckon with greatly extended schemes of economic "planning," in which public control of the monetary mechanism is an essential instrument. If such "planning" takes the form of detailed management from the center, its integration into schemes of international co-operation will be so difficult as to be impossible in practice. If, on the other hand, it takes the form of regulation rather than operation, such integration is not inconceivable, but will demand the invention of new types of international political and economic institutions. This distinction is all the more important if, as now seems probable, the tendency towards the formation of great economic blocs dominated by important trading currencies should emerge as the pattern of international organization. The following chapter deals with some aspects of this problem. Meantime, it is clear that to the spread of economic enterprise across national frontiers, the transference of investment from specialized banking to business enterprises, and the increasing domination of both business and investment by government policy, must be added the

[17] *Ibid.*, pp. 84 ff.

emergence of credit regulation as the most powerful instrument that governments can use in such domination. The way in which that instrument is used will largely determine the possibilities of international economic co-operation in the immediate future.

CHAPTER XI

The Conditions of Economic Co-operation

The Approach to Peace

IN THE midst of a great war, the outcome of which is still obscure, it requires some hardihood of idealism even to contemplate the restoration of peaceful economic co-operation. Few now entertain the illusion that years of bitter conflict and impoverishment can do other than make more difficult the solution of already difficult international problems. The unloosing of virulent hatreds, mobilization of economic resources, and harsh individual sacrifices inherent in modern warfare are not good foundations on which to build co-operative relations. It is true that a great social upheaval, such as war or revolution, loosens the grip of traditional concepts and types of organization. In such calamitous circumstances men may be readier to accept new ideas; but this fact offers constructive possibilities for the future only if those who grasp the need for social and international reconstruction are prepared to seize such possibilities. The necessities and disillusions that inevitably follow a great war may be powerful factors of constructive co-operation; but only if they are used in that direction.

No one can yet foresee the course that hostilities may take, the new battlefields that may be opened up, the grouping and regrouping of nations that may result, or the duration of the conflict. Still less is it possible to envisage the ending of the conflict, or whether it will end. The first months of actual hostilities have taken a course which was not foreseen, in the actual form of the struggle, in the use made of new weapons and in the theaters of war.

It is equally impossible to foresee how or when the conflict will end, which countries will be victorious in the military sense, or even which will be the final protagonists in the struggle. More, perhaps, than in any preceding major war, the relations of neutrals to the contending parties, and even the definition of neutrality, are so ambiguous that there remain possibilities of realignment. There remains a possibility also that victory will not be decisive, but that hostilities will end in stalemate while the economic war continues and embattled nations go underground to renew the struggle whenever and wherever opportunity seems to offer. Or an uneasy peace may come to provide an interlude of armed neutrality. Whether such a pause comes to the interlocked death struggle or outright victory results in a reorganized Europe over the prostrate body of Germany, or, on the contrary, in German hegemony over Europe, the destruction of British sea supremacy, and the redistribution of colonial territories the world over, including perhaps the colonies of neutrals as well as belligerents—whatever the outcome may be, there will remain an extremely complex and difficult task of economic reconstruction and rebuilding of international communications.

If the war results in a rapid and complete German victory and German political organization remains unshaken by the war and its immediate aftermath, the task of reconstruction will fall to German initiative and will clearly be attempted by methods that are radically different [1] from the traditional procedures of international co-operation. A Germany, united and supreme, even if impoverished by the struggle, might proceed to organize a vast trading empire, the nucleus of which was an extended, but consolidated Reich. The pattern of such an empire is already traced in theory with economic satellites grouped around, and integrated with, the metropolitan

[1] Cf. "Implications to the United States of a German Victory," The National Policy Committee, Washington, D. C., 1940.

area. Such hegemony by a single dominant Power over the European continent, with access to the sea and possession of mineral and other raw material resources in colonial areas, might be supplemented by bilateral barter agreements with Latin-American and other agricultural-exporting countries. Provided only that political unity was not impaired and morale undermined by the privations and psychological exhaustion of a long conflict, economic poverty and deterioration of equipment might be repaired rather quickly. Indeed, the problems of demobilization and civilian reorganization might be facilitated by the immense task of empire-building financed in the first instance by extensive imports under clearing agreements of foodstuffs and raw materials from countries outside Europe.

It is obvious that a reorganization of Europe along totalitarian lines could not be confined to territorial changes or within continental boundaries. It must comprehend economic as well as political activity, and be world-wide in its scope. The unification of Europe might well be achieved not in a federation, but in the creation of a cluster of satellite, puppet States around the industrial heart of a great German Reich. In that event, only five great economic systems would remain in the world and two of them would be subordinate to the Reich. The extended Italian and Japanese empires would exist by the grace of a dominant Germany, and the U. S. S. R. and the United States would remain outside this great alliance. Even if the British Empire should manage to preserve some independence, its lifeblood would be drained by the collapse of the free international trade and finance upon which its prosperity and power have been built.

Moreover, great colonial areas and rich raw material resources are dependent upon the European market. The map of Africa would need to be redrawn, with the mineral resources of the Belgian Congo and tropical products, such as vegetable oils, becoming available to the newly created European system. The Dutch possessions in the Far East and the French Empire in Asia, as well as the mineral oils of the

Near East, would become available also. On the American continent there are French, Dutch, and British colonies, while many island possessions in the Atlantic and Pacific Oceans might gain new importance as air bases.

More important perhaps than territorial redistribution must be the reorganization of international trade, in which the Latin-American countries would be pivotal. Unless alternative outlets for their exports are found, a clearing system might well draw them within the German orbit. Debt payments and imports from free-exchange countries, such as the United States, would necessarily diminish and, if European precedents are followed, corps of German technicians would be established, by treaty agreement, to reorganize production in the exporting countries. It is, indeed, evident that a complete German victory must result in the replacement of London by Berlin as the center of a new type of world trading system. Nor may it be expected that semi-totalitarian methods, such as the organization of a Pan-American export cartel, could effectively combat German trade controls. As long as Europe provides the only real market for Latin-American exports, the State-controlled trading monopolies under German domination will be able to barter for these exports on favorable terms. Only if the United States is prepared to absorb such imports at the cost of disturbing her own agricultural and extractive industries can she become the center of an alternative trading system.

It is, perhaps, difficult to imagine that any continental country or continental group could in one relatively short campaign achieve such a complete and far-reaching victory over enemies that began the struggle with not only access to, but command over the sea, and have been able, therefore, to draw upon the material resources of the world outside Europe. Such a decisive and rapid outcome of the war is, however, the only hypothesis upon which it might possibly be argued that European economic reconstruction might not necessitate a considerable measure of outside assistance, particularly from the United States. Unless one Power emerges strong enough to dominate and direct the reorganization of both belligerents and neutrals into one great European union, there must be financial, technical, and economic pooling of effort. Even if the winning country is united in victory and not utterly drained of resources, the exhaustion and demoralization of the vanquished must present tremendous problems of reorganization and reconstruction. In fact, the strain of modern war is such that the greater probability is that both victors and vanquished will be impoverished and torn by political dissension. The longer the war lasts, the wider its range, and the more intense its conduct, the greater become not only the financial but the real economic, and behind them the physical and psychological, strains. High taxation and impaired productivity level incomes and destroy property rights. The conduct of monetary policies that concentrate purchasing power in the hands of governments leads to grave inflationary risks unless rigid wartime price and production controls can be strengthened after the inducement of war conditions to their acceptance has ceased. There are very definite real economic costs—reserves are used up, stocks of finished goods and raw materials disappear, basic equipment falls into obsolescence and disrepair, productive plant and energy is adapted to wartime needs and proves difficult to readapt, capital is diverted to unproductive uses. Malnutrition, long hours, and intense effort, prolonged over months and years, take their toll of physical fitness. The psychological costs, accentuated by physical weakness and tense emotional strain, are no less real and are likely to become apparent when defeat or disillusion follows the buoyant optimism of national effort and may be aggravated by the collapse of authority and accepted social institutions.

There would seem to be three stages of postwar reconstruction in which economic policy may require concerted international action. The first is a humanitarian phase which has already arrived in some stricken countries—a phase of relief, calling primarily for the activities of the International Red Cross. If the experience after previous wars is any guide it will include the provision of elementary relief—the distribution of food and clothing—as well as medical aid, drugs and hospital equipment, and preventive public health measures to arrest the spread of epidemic diseases. The more complete organization of totalitarian warfare promises to prolong the present conflict to the point where even greater exhaustion of human and material reserves will call for swifter and more extensive measures of relief than proved necessary in 1919.

Beyond the immediate problem of relief, however, there looms an emergency problem that was not tackled after the last war until many countries had experienced extreme inflation, economic collapse, and even revolution, and was attempted then only on a limited scale in the international assistance extended to Austria and Hungary. It is a problem of maintaining or restoring essential services, of keeping the railways running, of maintaining the supply of electric current, coal output, petroleum, and even food supplies, of retaining control of the public finances, and of maintaining public confidence in monetary systems. While, up till the present,[2] the devastating aerial bombardment of civilian areas has been confined to a few unfortunate towns, the destruction of public utilities and means of communication wrought in those areas is sufficient evidence of the damage that may be done if aerial warfare takes the amplitude and intensity that was generally anticipated at the outbreak of the war. Even apart from such direct destruction, however, there are likely to be engineering and economic problems of great magnitude and urgency beyond the capacities of the stricken countries.

The formulation of programs of action for needs that cannot yet be foreseen in detail is obviously speculative. Perhaps the most that can be done is to have developments in each country watched carefully by expert national groups. The essential information must remain secret for military reasons; but it might be assembled and kept up-to-date within each country. It is unfortunate that one of the casualties of the war must be an impairment, temporarily at least, of the eco-

[2] May, 1940.

nomic information collected and analyzed by international institutions. Governments at war must refuse information that could be serviceable to the enemy, but it might be possible for those governments to keep accurate record not only of data bearing on the war effort, but also of data that will be needed for reconstruction after the war.

The organization of at least a skeleton crew whose activities could form the nucleus of more extended salvage operations is another obvious preparatory measure. The steps recently taken to reconstitute the technical services of the League of Nations into an autonomous organization [3] appeared to offer possibilities in this direction; but an international body, however efficient, from which Germany, Italy, the U. S. S. R., and Japan are absent, while the co-operation of the United States is unofficial, labors under difficulties that do not need to be stressed. Moreover, there are other international organizations, official and unofficial—the International Labor Organization, the Bank for International Settlements, the International Institute of Agriculture, the International Institute of Intellectual Co-operation, the International Red Cross, and the International Chamber of Commerce (some of which, even in wartime, are able to maintain contacts with the belligerents on either side)—that have contributions to make by providing information, expert contacts, ideas, and public support. Unless there is some prior preparation, it may be difficult in the immediate postwar period, with national and international problems crowding on all concerned, to improvise an emergency service. In particular, the preoccupation of statesmen, experts, and public opinion with the peace settlement may divert attention from the immediate task of restoring normal economic activity until it is too late to avert frustration and despair leading in the most stricken countries to blind social revolution.

The principles of a peace settlement are beyond the scope

[3] League of Nations, *The Development of International Cooperation in Economic and Social Affairs; Report of the Special Committee* (Geneva, August, 1939) (General. 1939. 3).

of this volume. Discussion of the redrawing of national frontiers or of similar political issues could, in any case, be merely speculative. It is probable that, as in the past, the settlement of such issues will be determined in large part by the outcome of the conflict. More important in the long run, however, are the principles of economic co-operation that may be adopted in the working out of international relations in the new world.

It is, indeed, necessary to insist with all possible emphasis upon the fact that peace is not to be obtained by a formula, however elaborate it may be. Reliance upon a peace settlement laid down in a treaty is sheer word magic. Our conceptions of peace, even more than of war, need revision. Peace is a dynamic process, the other name for which is co-operation. It can be achieved only by a laborious and sustained effort based on a realistic acceptance of basic economic and political factors by belligerents and neutrals alike. To that effort every people must contribute, since all are bound up in the same world economy. Some of the more fundamental economic factors to be borne in mind are briefly outlined in the remainder of this chapter.

Autarky and Sovereignty

Wherever new boundary lines may eventually be drawn in Europe, the riveting of totalitarian controls on production and trade must involve fundamental reconsideration of the concept of national sovereignty. Economic mobilization has gone further and taken a different shape in the present conflict. After the war of 1914–18 emergency controls of various aspects of economic organization were rapidly, and in most cases completely, abandoned. Industry, finance, banking, and international trade reverted to prewar methods of private enterprise regulated by a moderate degree of government intervention. In the present conflict, and even before it began, government intervention has penetrated much more deeply into economic activity. It is no longer a question of State regulation of private actions. The organization of production, and still more of finance and trade, has become part of the machinery of government in practically all the belligerent countries. The totalitarian State has actually been realized. Where this process has reached its logical fulfillment there can be no question of relinquishing wartime controls unless, indeed, the whole system tumbles in ruins. If it does, then both government and business must be rebuilt from the foundations up. Even where some measure of private enterprise has survived while great strides have been taken towards totalitarian organization, the relinquishment of speedy modification of State controls is unlikely.

It follows that the type of economic reconstruction attempted after the war of 1914–18 is impractical. That reconstruction was based primarily upon the principle of self-determination, with the implicit assumption that a world of independent sovereign States, great and small, would find means of economic co-operation reconciling the principle of nationality with the necessity of world-wide economic specialization and interchange. That assumption was falsified in the twenty years that followed and has even less justification now that economic activity is not merely dominated by, but a part of, government organization. The Nation-States that were created in 1919 were not self-sufficient economic units, but all of them, even the smallest, proceeded to erect barriers to international trade and increasingly to practice autarkic policies. Little-known languages were revived and made official, new customs frontiers were organized, new central banks administered independent monetary policies, and new systems of national legislation and administration broke up what had formerly been stabilized, if not balanced, economic units into unstable and unbalanced national economies dominated by political rather than economic forces.

It is unlikely, whatever the outcome of the war, that self-determination of this type will be the operative principle of reorganization. It is certainly desirable that a large degree of cultural autonomy and domestic self-government shall be restored to homogeneous national groups. There are cultural and artistic values worth preserving—national forms of literary, musical, artistic, and craft expression, the loss of which would leave the world poorer. There is real importance to be attached also to long traditions of self-government enshrining safeguards of individual and group liberties—intellectual freedom, freedom of worship, of political expression, and of economic choice. In the past, such countries as Switzerland, the Netherlands, and Scandinavia have proved that self-government in citadels of freedom need not be inconsistent with international co-operation. But the nineteenth-century freedom of international trade, in which State sovereignty was reconciled with a world economy, is now so greatly impaired that another solution must be sought, at least temporarily.

Such a solution might follow one of two lines—the expansion of national territories by conquest or fusion, or the voluntary relinquishment of certain aspects of sovereignty in some form of regional federation. The varieties of these alternatives are, of course, legion and discussion concerning them is perhaps the most urgent task confronting political theorists at the present time. The case against independent State sovereignty in a system approximating international anarchy is overwhelming and has been made with sufficient force to carry widespread conviction.[4] It may well be argued that not sovereignty in itself, but the way in which it has been exercised, is the cause of our difficulties. This is very true, but it is necessary to consider what safeguards can be erected against the improper use of national sovereignty, especially in a period of social unsettlement and embittered feeling after a great war.

There are already some signs that the practical solution of this problem, combining political practicality with economic efficiency, may prove to be a combination of territorial expansion with some steps towards federation. Even if the smaller nations that have recently been overrun regain some measure of autonomy, it is likely to be limited autonomy

[4] Cf. Clarence K. Streit, *Union Now* (London, 1939), Annexes: Chs. 2 and 3.

within a greater unit, the shape and constitution of which it is not yet possible to foresee clearly. Much discussion of this problem has run in terms of formal treaty decisions and constitution making. To suggest that history does not, in general, proceed in this fashion is not to deprecate such discussion. It is, indeed, urgently necessary to project paper schemes of reorganization so that every possible alternative and variety of federation proposal may be examined. Political inventors should be encouraged and taken seriously, and it should never be forgotten that some of the most far-reaching inventions, in politics as in other fields, have been the work of men who for long were derided as cranks.[5] The more actively the scope and territorial composition of projected federations and the manner of their possible creation is canvased, the more likely it is that unrealistic practical experiments will be avoided and that any steps taken after the war will be solidly based on workable hypotheses.

Nevertheless, political change has in the past grown out of economic and military pressures rather than speculative idealism; and it is likely to do so in the future. The longest single steps taken in recent years towards the leveling of national frontiers as far as economic relations are concerned have been the brief experience of Anglo-French fusion on the one hand, and, on the other hand, the extension, either by conquest or by economic domination, of Soviet hegemony over neighboring territories to the east as well as to the west; of German hegemony over central, southeastern, and northern Europe; and Japanese hegemony over the north and northeastern provinces of China. Whether the territories won by conquest can be retained or whether they will be added to in vaster empires, with Italy carving out wider dominions in southeastern Europe and North Africa, will be determined by the arbitrament of war and not by rational discussion. It seems altogether

[5] Cf. Graham Wallas, *Men and Ideas*, Ch. I. The greatest advances in modern scientific discovery were made in face of the skepticism of leading authorities, even when the new theories were advanced not by cranks, but be recognized scientific leaders of the younger generation. Cf., e. g., A. S. Eve, *Rutherford* (London, 1939), Chs. V–VI.

probable, however, that, unlike its predecessor, this war will end in the creation of larger units of governments rather than in the Balkanization of Europe. If this happens, the creation of great economic regions with enlarged metropolitan territories surrounded by satellite areas enjoying varying degrees of political autonomy, but essentially dependent upon the financial, monetary, and economic strength of the dominant Power, may prove to be the units between which international relations must be organized.

Such a prospect does not, by any means, exclude the possibility that on the continent of Europe regional federations of what are now independent States, based not on vague reciprocity but on actual customs unions and perhaps political fusion, may prove to be the effective units of governments. Defeat for Germany would turn this possibility into a probability. Whether the recent advance of the U. S. S. R. in Finland, along the Baltic, and through Poland can be consolidated, and whether, in the frustration and disillusion of defeat, other great areas in central Europe will turn to Soviet forms of government and link themselves with the U. S. S. R., need not be discussed here. It is at least clear that unless the Soviet system should collapse entirely—which would seem unlikely except in the sense that in such unpredictable times nothing is impossible—there will be a great autarkic region stretching halfway across Europe and perhaps halfway into China, and even pushing southward towards the Persian Gulf, if not the Indian Ocean. In the same way, unless actual defeat or collapse, rather than stalemate, overtakes the Japanese adventure on the mainland of Asia, another great autarkic region will be formed in the Fast East.

The political reorganization of continental Europe must inevitably be influenced by these facts and, in any case, the experience of twenty years of extreme nationalism seems altogether likely to result in some form of closer economic union, whether voluntarily accepted or imposed by some dominant Power.

In the long run, however, the short-lived fusion of Anglo-

French diplomacy, strategy, economic mobilization, and finance—comprehending as it did not only the metropolitan countries themselves, but their great dependent Empires, and in some measure the autonomous British Dominions—may prove to have been the boldest and most significant experiment of all in the formation of larger regional units of governments. Moreover, it raises the most significant possibilities of building a bridge between the old and the new order of international relations. The anomalous and undetermined position of the Dominions, and especially of Canada, would have raised great problems of policy if the fusion of war effort could have been developed, as some of its advocates were already urging, into permanent union after the war. Still more, the relation to the new federation of smaller States which for decades have moved within the economic orbit of the British trading and currency system would have accentuated those problems. A federation, or even a consultative conference, of the British and French empires would in itself have been a greater aggregation of political and economic power than the world has yet seen. If to it had been added close, and perhaps reciprocal, trading arrangements with the Scandinavian and Low Countries, Switzerland, the countries of the Near East, and some of the leading Latin-American countries, it would have comprehended by far the larger part of the world's trade and controlled a very large proportion indeed of the most important raw material resources of the world. If such a grouping of countries, whether closely united or merely dependent upon the trading power of a federated nucleus, had followed autarkic policies within this great region, the restoration of economic co-operation on a world-wide scale would have been impossible.

No mention has been made of a possible dollar bloc centered around the United States of America, because the policy consistently followed by the United States has not envisaged such a development. There is much discussion of the "good neighbor policy," particularly in relation with the Latin-American countries, and of co-operative measures of mutual economic assistance; but the foreign policy of the United States remains firmly fixed on the restoration of a multilateral trading system with equality of trading opportunity. In the words of the Secretary of State, this policy "requires not only that nations refuse to grant preferences in their own markets, but also that they refrain from seeking a preferred position in the markets of other countries." [6] In negotiations with the other countries of the Pan-American Union, this principle has been affirmed and reaffirmed. "With respect to international economic relations, the Lima Conference reaffirmed the policy enunciated at the Buenos Aires meeting. The Hull trade principles were endorsed. Reciprocal tariffs based on the most-favored-nation system were declared to be the fixed policy of the Americas; barter and discrimination were condemned even by the countries then engaged in such practices.[7]

At this point it is convenient to stress the fact that the foregoing brief discussion is not intended to outline or suggest the precise forms of regional grouping that should, or will, emerge from the many proposals for federation now being canvassed. In particular, no attention has been given to the many proposals for European federation, or federation of the democracies within and outside Europe. These range from Mr. Clarence K. Streit's specific projection of a united federation of fifteen democratic nations,[8] and Sir William Beveridge's plan for a federated western Europe including Germany, France, and Great Britain,[9] to various other proposals for partial federations in Europe. The object of this discussion is not to canvas these proposals either in principle or in detail, but merely to suggest that the world after the war will prob-

[6] Cited by Tasca, *World Trading Systems*, p. 153.
[7] Arthur D. Gayer and Carl T. Schmidt, *American Economic Foreign Policy*.
[8] Cf. Streit, *op. cit*. The countries concerned are the United States, the United Kingdom, Canada, Australia, New Zealand, South Africa, Irish Free State, France, Belgium, the Netherlands, Switzerland, Denmark, Norway, Sweden, and Finland.
[9] Sir William Beveridge, *Peace by Federation* (London, 1940).

ably consist of larger units and that small States, whatever political autonomy they preserve, must seek shelter in some larger grouping or under the wing of a dominant Power, and, in so doing, surrender much of their economic sovereignty. In particular, they must peg their currencies to that of some great trading country and refrain from monetary and economic policies likely to strain that relationship. Within the larger trading areas thus constructed there will probably be freer trade and certainly greater exchange stability. This, in itself, is sufficient to make the emergence of such trading regions a powerful factor of integration. Any federation, or political arrangement, that may be envisaged after the war is likely to prove unrealistic if it does not achieve such an economic integration.

The crucial question of postwar economic policy, therefore, is likely to be not the specific constitution of European federal arrangements, important as decisions on this point will be, but the degree to which the emergent units of a new world economy will endeavor to follow policies of self-sufficiency with regard to other groups and to the United States. In the event of a British victory, the policies of the British Commonwealth will be decisive in determining whether world-wide economic co-operation can be restored, or whether the world will enter an era of closed economic empires. The choice for British statesmen may be put broadly as one between entering a European confederation or joining with the United States in an effort to re-establish a world trading system. The choice may not be clear-cut and may not lie entirely with them, since the United States itself must be prepared to use its great economic, financial, and political power more effectively, and above all more consistently and continuously, than it has done hitherto. An opportunity for it to do so may be presented by the exhaustion of the belligerents at the close of the war; but if this opportunity is not seized decisively and followed through to its logical conclusion in the creation of an international system in which the United States takes a large share of permanent responsibility for the maintenance of political as well as economic world order, the British choice may well need to be an unhappy compromise. It cannot be doubted that the British Dominions, and probably the smaller European countries, would greatly prefer that the British system should not become embedded in Europe, but should seek by all means to link itself with the New World. Their choice would be determined not only by their political and cultural affinity with the United States, but also by the dependence of their prosperity upon a restoration of world trade.

Moreover, the distribution of raw material resources in the world is such that any movement in the direction of great autarkic empires must accentuate economic and political rivalry and lay the foundations for even more devastating wars between larger combatant groups in the not-too-distant future. No great industrial country can now afford to remain dependent upon the good will of its rivals for access to essential supplies of minerals and oils. These supplies are so scattered over the earth's surface that there are no other alternatives open than a continuous struggle for their possession or, on the contrary, assurance of equal access to them in a multilateral trading system buttressed by collective security. Which alternative will govern the future of international relations will be determined very largely, on the one hand, by the willingness of the United States to make good its professed policy of peaceful trading development, and, on the other, by the readiness of the British Commonwealth to give up immediate strategic and economic advantages for the larger security and economic opportunity of participation in a world trading system.

If the choice should lie not with Britain, but with a victorious Germany, it will not be a choice between clinging to exclusive privileges and participation in a collective system, but one between mobilization for bigger and better wars and the abandonment of "power economics" in favor of "welfare economics."

The Economics of Insulation

The most distressing economic fact of recent years has been the persistence of economic insecurity for large masses of the population in most countries. Fluctuations of economic activity have been violent and unpredictable, speculation of a destructive type has threatened one currency after another, capital has been afraid to venture upon long-term undertakings but has sought safety in liquidity and, at times, in rapid flight from one financial center to another. Underinvestment has been paralleled by underemployment, and not the least tragic aspect of this whole problem is that only in dictatorial mobilization of human and material resources has there appeared to be any solution of the employment problem.

Not only has international equilibrium given place to a series of desperate attempts to organize security and stability within national boundaries; the theoretical reasoning by which international economic co-operation was formerly justified is now challenged. The challenge is directed primarily to that cosmopolitan financial enterprise which has been described above as the mainspring of economic expansion in the nineteenth century.[10] In the economic convulsions that followed the breakdown of exchange equilibrium in 1931, the risk of surrendering the control of national economic activity to "the operation of blind forces" emanating from international disequilibria has seemed too great, and the task of restoring international equilibrium too impracticable, to warrant either the stabilizing of currencies or effective measures to reduce trade barriers. Every country has desired to keep its hands free to follow whatever economic policy might seem necessary in an emergency. In particular, monetary policy has been determined by national rather than by international considerations.

This has entailed considerable interference with the flow of trade and has paralyzed international investment almost completely. Yet there is, even among those who are most emphatic

[10] Cf. Ch. III.

in their criticism of the international techniques that have been discarded, a lively recognition of the desirability, and even the necessity, of restoring international equilibrium. Such a restoration is sought, however, by new methods that can be reconciled with national stability of employment. As one example may be cited the conclusion which Mr. J. M. Keynes appended to his statement of the case for revising the orthodox economic theory of international economic relations. In his own words: "If nations can learn to provide themselves with full employment by their domestic policy (and, we must add, if they can also attain equilibrium in the trend of their population), there need be no important economic forces calculated to set the interest of one country against that of its neighbours. There would still be room for the international division of labour and for international lending in appropriate conditions. But there would no longer be a pressing motive why one country need force its wares on another or repulse the offerings of its neighbours, not because this was necessary to enable it to pay for what it wished to purchase, but with the express object of upsetting the equilibrium of payments so as to develop a balance of trade in its own favour. International trade would cease to be what it is, namely, a desperate expedient to maintain employment at home by forcing sales on foreign markets and restricting purchases, which, if successful, will merely shift the problem of unemployment to the neighbour which is worsted in the struggle, but a willing and unimpeded exchange of goods and services in conditions of mutual advantage."[11]

It may be noted in passing that Mr. Keynes's description of competitive trade seems to fit the restrictive national policies followed since the onset of depression in 1929, and the breakdown of international equilibrium in 1931, rather than the normal working of international trade.[12] This point, however,

[11] J. M. Keynes, *The General Theory of Employment, Interest and Money*, pp. 382–83.
[12] Cf. J. E. Meade, *The Economic Bases of a Durable Peace*, pp. 16–17. "The great depression had, moreover, a rather more direct influence upon

THE ECONOMICS OF INSULATION 373

is mainly of academic interest at the present time since the chances of restoring a freer-trading system based on exchange stability maintained by gold standard methods are rather slim. The conflict of opinion that is likely to be important in the months and years that lie immediately ahead is between those who advocate a positive policy of monetary and direct government action intended to stimulate domestic markets, and those who rely upon negative and restrictive competitive policies to maintain exchange stability.[13] It is, perhaps, probable that

---

international relations. When a slump occurs within any country there are, broadly speaking, two types of policy which may be adopted to overcome the general decline in the demand for goods and services. In the first place, by means of protective tariffs and import quotas, by export subsidies of a disguised or open character, by cutting wage-costs in the industries producing for export, and by an unjustifiable depreciation of the national currency designed to reduce prices in foreign markets, measures may be taken to expand a particular nation's markets at the expense of other nations. Such measures were adopted on a large scale to meet the post-1929 depression. Not only were they largely ineffective—for in most cases they led to counterbalancing retaliatory measures on the part of the nations whose markets were threatened—but they naturally led to a rapid deterioration in international political relations."

[13] Cf. Meade, *op. cit.*, pp. 17–18. "The second main method of meeting a general slump is for each nation to rely primarily upon the re-expansion of its internal demand for goods and services by a monetary and economic policy designed to restore money incomes. Various measures may be taken for this purpose. The banks, by increasing the supplies of money and by reducing interest rates, may induce producers to borrow fresh funds for expenditure on new capital developments. The state and other public authorities may support this 'easy money' policy by borrowing fresh funds to spend on various schemes of public construction. These new streams of money expenditure upon capital construction will raise employment, wages and profits in the construction industries. This in turn will lead to the expenditure of some part of the increased incomes upon various goods required for current consumption. Employment, wages and profits will rise in the industries producing consumption goods. This in turn will lead to further increases in expenditure on consumption goods; and the consequent restoration of profits will re-stimulate private capital construction. Such a policy has the advantage that it will help to increase the demand in the nation which practises it not only for home-produced goods but also for foreign-produced imports; and thus it positively eases for other nations that search for markets which is the most common feature of a widespread depression. It is true that this may lead to an unbalanced excess of imports into any particular nation which is alone adopting such a policy of internal 'reflation,' and that this danger may have to be met by special protective measures; but if the generality of nations

as long as the war continues the "full employment of all available resources at the best possible terms of trade for the provision of imports" will lead to increasing use on the British side of such measures as clearing agreements and differential export prices based on subsidies.[14] On the German side, the continuance of such trading methods may be taken for granted. These are war necessities. When hostilities cease, however, urgent problems of demobilization and the reduction of public expenditure to more normal levels will again raise the issue between monetary policies designed to support national purchasing power and those which are conceived in more orthodox terms of balancing budgets and restraining inflationary tendencies.

This conflict, it may be presumed, will arise both within and between the great trading groups, the emergence of which has been foreshadowed as probable. For the smaller trading countries, moving within the orbit of a great metropolitan country, the problem will be primarily one of maintaining employment while at the same time keeping intact the exchange relationship of their currencies with the great trading currencies. For Australia and New Zealand, to take a simple case, it will be a matter of watching the sterling reserves needed to keep their currencies pegged at the same level on sterling. Their ability to do so without reducing purchasing power at home, and without restricting imports, will depend largely upon the volume of their exports that can be absorbed by the British market and the prices at which those exports are absorbed. In great part, therefore, the prospects of maintaining exchange stability and the free flow of international trade within the sterling area will depend upon the monetary policy followed in Great Britain.

---

simultaneously adopt policies of internal expansion each individual nation will discover that its external markets are expanding as quickly as its own demand for imports. The moral may, therefore, safely be drawn that the adoption of proper principles of policy to meet trade depressions is one of the chief economic bases of a durable peace."

[14] Cf. T. Balogh, "Foreign Exchange and Export Trade Policy," *Economic Journal* (March, 1940), p. 22.

The continuance of expansionist monetary policies at such a time, however, leads to the risk of strain on the external balance of payments, a strain that concentrates upon London the burden of payment for imports not only into Great Britain but into the whole sterling area. In Mr. Meade's words, "this may lead to an unbalanced excess of imports into any nation which is alone in adopting such a policy of internal 'reflation,' and this danger may have to be met by special protective measures; but if the generality of nations simultaneously adopt policies of internal expansion each individual nation will discover that its external markets are expanding as quickly as its own demand for imports." [15]

Even if it be granted that, at the end of a long and exhausting war, monetary policies of an expansionist character can be continued to tide over the extraordinary costs of demobilization and resettlement into civilian life, without running the risk of uncontrollable inflation, there arises the problem of maintaining some degree of exchange stability while pursuing such monetary expansion. There are two tests of currency inflation, internal and external. It cannot, unfortunately, be taken for granted that the risk of internal inflation is negligible. Indeed, it is probable that the only practical way of avoiding the kind of monetary collapse that overtook many European countries after the last war is by international cooperation pivoted on the maintenance of external exchange stability. On the other hand, it seems obvious that the only way to avoid social disorder when war discipline is relaxed will be by prompt and expensive government programs of reemployment. It becomes necessary, therefore, to examine whether there is any alternative to continued policies of monetary expansion conducted within trading areas whose leading currencies must be protected from exchange depreciation by the progressive tightening of exchange and import controls. Such tightening, it is evident, will be necessary unless parallel expansionist policies are financed in other areas and some mechanism is devised to keep the exchange rates stable while

[15] Meade, *op. cit.*, p. 18.

trade flows freely. If the rates are held steady by a tightening of exchange control, trade cannot flow freely. If trade flows freely, exchange rates will be disturbed unless prices move at least in the same direction in other trading countries. If the exchange rates are disturbed, controls must then be strengthened to avoid undue depreciation. Unless means can be found whereby monetary policies are co-ordinated, there is every possibility that a restoration of multilateral trade will be impossible. At best, the great trading regions that are forming will become closed blocs, and there will even be difficulty in maintaining exchange stability between their constituent units.

The mere fact that exchange stability has been aimed at and, for the most part, successfully achieved within the great trading blocs is in itself evidence of its importance as a factor in facilitating the smooth working of international economic co-operation. It is, of course, unnecessary if trade is conducted by bilateral barter transactions as in the German system; but if there is to be multilateral international trade conducted by the mechanism of the market, and supported by capital movements, stability of the units of valuation is important. It is significant that even the advocates of variable exchange rates are clearly aware of the disadvantages and risks to be run if their proposal is adopted. Mr. Meade, for example, argues that "in order to avoid the continual raising of trade barriers for the purpose of adjusting the balances of international payments, it would be preferable to rely upon the mechanism of variable foreign exchange rates for this purpose." [16] But he lists four serious disadvantages of such a mechanism: the sacrifice of convenience in having a stable unit of account, increased uncertainty of trading calculations, the encouragement of speculative capital movements, and the risk of competitive exchange depreciation. He does not mention, moreover, what is perhaps the most serious disadvantage of fluctuating exchange rates—the impediment to international lending that results from uncertainty as to the future

[16] Meade, *op. cit.*, p. 58.

valuation of the investment. In order to safeguard against improper national action in regard to exchange rates, Mr. Meade would give the power of adjusting such rates into the hands of an International Authority.[17]

Before proceeding further on this point, two suggestions may perhaps be made to simplify the argument. In the first place, it is probable that much difficulty might be avoided in the postwar period if exchange stabilization was attempted by multilateral agreement between the leading countries instead of by unilateral national decisions, as was the case after the last war. The determination of workable exchange ratios, after due interchange of the best available information regarding the international economic situation of the countries in question, would be likely not only to result in a closer approximation to exchange equilibrium, but in decisions that would carry with them the political conviction necessary to defend by concerted action the rates chosen.

The second suggestion is that the case for variable exchange rates is not, in fact, what the term might suggest—a case for indeterminate and uncontrolled fluctuation—but is rather a case for periodical revision and adjustment by mutual consent.

A first, though only partially successful, effort to put these principles into execution was the Tripartite Agreement signed by France, the United States, and the United Kingdom on September 25, 1936. This agreement, subsequently reinforced by the adherence in October and November, 1936, of Belgium, the Netherlands, and Switzerland, was essentially a mutual undertaking to maintain exchange stability between the dollar, franc, and sterling.[18] It was hoped that stability could be maintained within the trading area dominated by each of those currencies, which in turn would maintain stable ratios among themselves so that, in fact, a large proportion of the world's currencies would be stabilized. Upon this basis, a movement towards freer trade might have been initiated.

If, as seems probable, economic negotiations after the pres-

[17] *Ibid.*, p. 64.
[18] Bank for International Settlements, *The Tripartite Agreement*.

ent war follow this precedent of attempting to secure agreement for provisional stabilization between the leading currencies, upon the assumption that other currencies will either join the agreement or be pegged to one or other of the leaders, certain conditions will be necessary for success. The first, and most obvious, is that there shall be broad general agreement between the monetary authorities concerned, both as to the rates that should be established and as to the currency and economic policies to be followed in maintaining them. It is probably inevitable that the former belligerent countries must continue to follow policies of monetary expansion; but if they do so while maintaining exchange rates that are high in relation to the dollar, and if the United States follows a less expansionist policy, the only result can be an accentuation of the present accumulation of gold reserves in the United States. Even if the United States should extend credit on a large scale in order to finance the reconstruction of Europe, and in doing so to promote its own export trade, the relief given to Europe could only be temporary. The only way in which multilateral trade can be restored is by the establishment of such price relationships as will enable trade to flow freely without disturbing the balances of external payments. Imports from the United States will be needed in large amounts and, for a time, they must probably be financed by the extension of credit. But in the long run, and not too long a run, the United States must accept a large passive balance of imports. This can be brought about by a reduction of the American tariff, by prices rising in the United States faster than elsewhere, by other currencies depreciating against the dollar, or by some combination of all three of these developments. There can be no restoration of multilateral trade unless the United States is prepared to accept the position, proper to a great creditor nation, of receiving a volume of imports much in excess of its exports. This need not diminish the absolute volume of its exports. Indeed, an expanding two-way trade is necessary; but the United States must be prepared to accept and welcome heavy imports as the benefit to be drawn from its strong economic position in the world, even if the competition of those imports is destructive, as it must be, of some sheltered American industries.

An exchange agreement of the type described would need, however, to be buttressed by provisional arrangements for the replenishment of currency reserves that have been depleted over many years. It is unlikely that any set of exchange rates that may be fixed will prove tenable without reserves adequate to offset panic or speculative flights of capital. The protection of the agreed rates might be achieved in a variety of ways. Mr. Meade has made the bold suggestion that an International Bank might be given a sufficient fund to use as an international equalization fund, the national use of such funds being prohibited.[19] Such a bank, without being given sole authority, might have a considerable gold fund at its disposal to use as a *masse de manoeuvre* in support of national action in defense of a threatened currency; but in this case there would need to be provision for adequate consultation in regard to national monetary policies. A simpler, and probably more practical, solution would be agreement among the leading countries to maintain the agreed exchange rates by concerted action taken independently. Whichever of these devices was adopted, its success or failure would depend mainly upon the United States which already possesses over 80 per cent of the world's stock of monetary gold and (if gold is not used) has very considerable financial influence. The vigorous use of an American equalization fund to prevent appreciation or depreciation of the dollar relatively to other currencies would almost certainly be sufficient to maintain exchange stability against speculative attacks.

No equalization fund, however, national or international, could maintain exchange stability if the economic and monetary policies followed in particular countries were out of alignment with those elsewhere. If, for example, Switzerland obstinately followed a deflationary policy while expansionist policies were followed in other countries, no fund could for

[19] Meade, *op. cit.,* p .71.

long prevent the appreciation of the Swiss franc. If, on the other hand, Germany, beset by grave social and unemployment problems, followed a policy of rapid monetary expansion, no fund could prevent the mark from depreciating. In such circumstances, the assistance of an international fund (or of a fund operated in another country) might well be made conditional upon a revision of the national policy in question. It might well be that the circumstances would also call for a revision of the exchange value of that particular currency.[20]

Two final observations may be made before leaving this problem. Whether gold is used in future as the most convenient method of settling international balances, or whether some device of international clearing is worked out, the only satisfactory way in the long run by which monetary reserves can be replenished is by so adjusting the terms of trade that impoverished nations can earn the reserves they borrow temporarily. It may well be argued that the possession of a large gold fund and unimpaired credit facilities puts the United States in a position to influence the nations which now practice exchange control and quantitative import restrictions to abandon these obstacles to multilateral trade. The gold might be put at the disposal of an international bank in which the United States retained predominant control, and might be used in support of policies which promoted multilateral trade. The same effect might be produced by lending the gold to, or opening credits for, such countries as needed assistance in mitigating, and finally abandoning, their monetary and quantitative trade restrictions. But, unless the debt is ultimately to be transformed into a free gift, the United States must make it possible for the countries concerned to repay the loan. The only way they can do so is by selling to the United States more than they buy.

The second observation is that the choice of mechanism is a

[20] Mr. Meade would give to the International Authority power to require appreciation or depreciation of a national currency out of alignment with international equilibrium, *op. cit.*, p. 64.

THE ECONOMICS OF INSULATION 381

matter of secondary importance, depending upon administrative and political expediency. The same essential results, from an economic point of view, could be achieved by the institution of an international authority, by agreement among a very few great trading countries, or, in less effective degree, by the unilateral action of a dominant financial Power. As will be argued in the next section, the most important aspects of international economic relations are the national economic policies of the great Powers, not the international consultations through which they are cleared. An international bank would work effectively if the leading Powers were determined to make it work. They could equally well make their policies effective by agreement among themselves. Whether formal agreement is necessary, or a permanent institution desirable, is merely a matter of convenience in administration and perhaps of political prejudice. There can be no effective international economic co-operation unless there is a will to co-operate and to make the adjustments of national policy necessary in a co-operative system. Mr. Keynes has written that "one can almost hope that in Great Britain the technique of bank rate will never be used again to protect the foreign balance in conditions in which it is likely to cause unemployment at home." It ought to be possible, with the technical devices now at the disposal of the controllers of managed credit policies, to utilize buffers such as secondary reserves or equalization funds to stave off sudden speculative attacks on a currency. On the other hand, it ought to be possible, given a reasonably co-operative attitude on the part of a comparatively few men in control of great monetary systems, to concert parallel policies of controlled credit in the leading countries so that the necessity for abrupt disciplinary action to preserve international equilibrium need not arise to create vast unemployment. In this sense everyone will share Mr. Keynes's hope; but if his phrase is to be interpreted as advocacy of national monetary policies pursued independently and in despite of their international repercussions, it can lead only to the abandonment of any possibility of constructive international co-operation in the monetary sphere. In another passage Mr. Keynes has drawn attention to the limitations of an immoderate policy of economic nationalism in the sphere of commercial policy, describing it as "a treacherous instrument even for the attainment of its ostensible object, since private interest, administrative incompetence and the intrinsic difficulty of the task may divert it into producing results directly opposite to those intended." [21] These words are surely applicable with even greater force to a policy of extreme monetary nationalism. Insulation is desirable as a means of achieving security of full employment; but it is practicable only when combined with measures to preserve and extend international collaboration.

The Clearing of International Co-operation

Throughout this volume an effort has been made to focus attention upon the conduct of national economic policies. Little attention has been paid to proposals for the creation of international institutions. It has been argued that not only are the great Powers in a position to make or mar the prospects of co-operation, but that modern economic and monetary as well as military developments have placed the smaller Powers under the necessity of grouping themselves as satellites around one or another of the great Powers. A series of trading blocs is in process of formation so that the relations between their nuclei gain added importance. As long as independent national sovereignty was capable of being defended and international trade was conducted by multilateral chains of transactions with a minimum of government regulation, it was possible to think of international relations, political and economic, as being conducted by competitive bargaining in a loosely organized co-operative process. There will be a place again for independent small countries practicing national economic sovereignty only if multilateral trade is restored and some system of collective security can be established.

[21] J. M. Keynes, *op. cit.*, p. 339.

With the formation of great trading blocs and the increasing tendency to link government, business enterprise, and investment more closely, there is more need than ever for international institutions to act as clearinghouses. It is probable, however, that the type of international institution based upon national equality and independence in a collective system will not prove adequate to the new situation. The League of Nations that was constituted after the last war was primarily Anglo-Saxon in its origins. It has been described as a blend of diplomatic and parliamentary institutions. Its inspiration was clearly political rather than economic and its methods were derived from democratic parliamentary procedure. That procedure, however, was worked out in an age when parliaments did not attempt to regulate, and even to direct, the detail of economic activity.

Incorporated in the League machinery were technical organizations designed in recognition of the fact that the modern world has brought all governments into close neighborhood and made necessary the negotiation of practical working understandings in matters of common concern. It is significant that the first, and in many ways the most smoothly operated, institutions of international co-operation were established in the field of communications before the League was brought into existence. The most effective of them all, the Universal Postal Union, never became a part of the League machinery. Anyone at all familiar with the actual working of the League, however, must have soon become aware that among its many functions was the humble, but essential, task of facilitating co-operation in technical problems of concern to more than one government. These covered a wide range of activities, from technical problems of public health such as the standardization of sera and vaccine, transport facilities such as the uniform marking of level crossings, control of the traffic in opium and narcotics, and economic matters such as the simplification of customs nomenclature, to great issues which, though technical in character, had far-reaching political implications. Apart altogether from the political tasks of the League, arising from its functions as an institution designed to preserve peace, such matters of international concern as minority problems, the supervision of mandated colonies, and economic discussions particularly in the field of international trade, monetary policy, double taxation, and nutrition, raised issues of far-reaching political importance.

It is impossible, however, to avoid the fact that in the economic sphere the most important aspects of international relations escaped the competence of League organs. Cartels, the new types of trade agreements, exchange control, direct investments, and similar phenomena were studied from time to time; but the operative committees of the League never had any control, or even influence, over their development. How far this was due to the origins of the institution, to the subordination of technical to political functions, or to political factors outside the machinery of the League, is a question that need not be discussed here. All that need be stated is that the urgent practical problems demanding international action in the immediate future arise from the interaction of economic and political factors in policies that have not hitherto been effectively controlled or influenced by League action. There has been remarkable work in many fields, but this major problem of the fusion of political and economic power in the external policies of great nations has developed outside the League's sphere of influence.

It may be remarked in passing that this is even truer of other official international institutions. The International Labor Organization, which was an autonomous organ of the League, has endeavored to build up a code of labor legislation that might be accepted internationally; but it has not been able to exercise any more than indirect influence on national labor and employment policies. The Bank for International Settlements, though discharging valuable liaison and other functions, has not been the instrument of major financial and monetary policies. The International Institute of Agriculture has been confined almost entirely to the collection, analysis, and dissemination of current information.

CLEARING OF CO-OPERATION 385

It is no criticism of these institutions to point out the limits that were imposed upon their operation. Within these limits their work was effective, and there is no doubt that much more could have been done if they had not been weakened by important defections of membership and even if their mechanism had been fully used by the remaining member-states. The fact must be recognized, however, that States-Members of the League retained full sovereignty in all important matters and utilized the international machinery merely for registration of national decisions (often arrived at by consultation among leading Powers) or for plenipotentiary discussion of issues of minor political importance. There was no power at the center, even in such minor matters as the right to call for statistical information or to inspect mandated areas. In all such matters the international secretariats were dependent upon the good will of national governments. That they achieved so much by persuasion is a high tribute to the quality of their work.

Just before the war an important step in the direction of rationalization was taken by the grouping of the League's technical services into an autonomous organization.[22] This partial separation from the more directly political activities of the League might conceivably facilitate co-operation in a worldwide institution whose functions were primarily those of a clearinghouse of national plans and an instrument for co-ordinating national policies. It might also facilitate solution of the overriding problem of peace by making possible the negotiation of regional pacts of collective security. It is at least a recognition of the fact that the organization of peaceful international relations is an extremely complex problem not to be solved by a simple formula embodied in a single institution, but requiring specific action by varying methods in many different fields, sometimes on a world scale, sometimes in smaller regional units. The process of rationalization, however,

---

[22] League of Nations, *The Development of International Cooperation in Economic and Social Affairs; Report of the Special Committee* (Geneva, August, 1939) (General. 1939. 3).

was only begun. It is inconceivable that international economic problems can be effectively handled unless their various aspects—migration, labor, production, trade, finance, investment, and money—are considered in relation to one another. This does not, indeed, mean that a single institution can deal effectively with such a wide range of problems on the international, any more than on a national, plane; but it does imply the necessity of close liaison between such institutions as may be handling various aspects of a related problem.

Paper plans for the re-creation of international institutions must be regarded as Utopian at the present time. Whether they will ever reach the stage of practical politics must depend upon the outcome of the war and upon the attitudes taken after the war by the statesmen of the victorious Powers. The suggestion may be made, however, that rather radical changes are needed in the administrative organization of the international bodies that functioned in the interwar period. If Germany is victorious, the problem will not arise. If, on the contrary, Germany is defeated, it may become a vital issue.

In the first place, there should be a broadening of the League Assembly into a supreme legislative authority by giving it ultimate control not only over the technical and political organs of a reconstituted League, but also over the other technical organs of international co-operation—an International Bank, the International Labor Office, the International Institute of Intellectual Co-operation, the International Institute of Agriculture, the International Cinematographic Institute, the Permanent Court of International Justice, and even the Universal Postal Union. These institutions might well retain a considerable measure of autonomy and be located in different centers; but they should at least submit regular reports of their activities for debate by the international assembly. If that assembly is to function effectively, it must be constituted by some method of indirect election rather than by the nomination of States representatives. The International Labor Conferences have established the precedent of giving places to representatives of organized labor and employers' associations as well as governments. In the League Assembly some governments have regularly sent members of their parliamentary oppositions. Direct electoral representation would probably be cumbrous and unworkable; but unless some form of indirect election is established, the international assembly cannot exercise independent criticism, still less legislative control, over the action of States.

In the second place, there must be a vitalizing and differentiation of the executive functions that in the past have gone through the political bottleneck of the Council. The executive liaison between a representative international assembly and the various technical and political organs might be assured by a series of executive commissions, constituted of experts in the various fields, rather than by a single political organ. This would mean, in practice, giving a considerable measure of executive power (subject to the legislative authority of the Assembly) to the governing boards (or commissions) that at present control many of the institutions concerned, and to others that might be created. As long as their annual budgets were subject to a vote of the assembly, these governing commissions might well be given increased power.

At the same time there should be a clearer division between technical and political activities, with direct access to the assembly on both sides by way of the appropriate governing commissions. The regrouping of the technical activities of the League is a step in this direction that might well be supplemented by the addition of other technical services. Political functions might then be organized in a series of regional conferences or federations. It is probable that such conferences would have to be organized in different forms according to political conditions in various areas. Some might be actual federations and others merely loose consultative groups. They would, in any case, have to be overlapping so that Powers with dispersed interests might be represented in more than one conference. They could come into existence only as the result of regional pacts of collective security entrusted to the administration of executive commissions. Their regional functions would undoubtedly cut across the universal application of the technical commissions, thus creating the necessity for demarcation of functions such as occurs between State and federal jurisdictions.

The chief administrative weakness of international organization up till the present time, however, has been the lack of power and positive responsibility at the center. Admirable administrative instruments were built up, but they were forced to adopt the negative attitude of waiting to be used. Wherever successes were registered, they were in the discharge of positive functions entrusted to the institution concerned. The excellent research work of all these bodies is a clear illustration of this point; but wherever they were given responsibility —in the financial reconstruction of Austria and Hungary, in the erection of a *cordon sanitaire* to check the spread of typhus after the last war, in the settlement of Greek and Bulgarian refugees, in technical assistance to the Chinese government— their efficient discharge of such responsibilities has received widespread recognition. Where, on the contrary, action depended upon persuading States to follow lines of policy recommended by international experts, success was meager. Only when the experts were themselves responsible officials prepared to execute the decisions agreed upon in consultation —usually in politically minor, but not unimportant, matters— have effective results followed.

This fact of past experience has important bearings on proposals to reorganize and reconstitute international institutions after the present conflict. To be effective, they must have responsibility and power. This means, in practice, the transfer to such institutions of some attributes of national sovereignty. One way in which this could be done would be by the allocation to them of definite constructive tasks. If the responsibility for refugee settlement were given to the Migration Section of the International Labor Office, or the powers of an International Tariff Commission entrusted to the Economic Section of the League, or those of an international equalization fund to the Bank for International Settlements, those institutions would have positive functions to discharge. To do so, however, they would need both the financial means of discharging such duties and the power to make their decisions effective. Such agreed delegations of sovereignty might constitute the beginnings of effective world government. It is essential to realize, however, that this process, once begun, is far-reaching in its implications, involving as it does the ultimate creation of a world-state.

This fact may be illustrated by examining briefly the proposals recently made (in his private capacity), by a temporary League official, for establishing the economic bases of a durable peace on the assumption "that after the peace settlement some International Organisation is in existence—whether this organisation takes the form of the present or a revised League of Nations, or, for example, of a Federated Union of previously independent states; and that the Member-States, which join together to form this International Organisation, hand over certain economic questions for decision and administration by a duly constituted International Organisation." [23]

The powers which, after examination of the nature of economic policy in "planned" and "liberal" systems, Mr. Meade deems it essential to transfer to the International Authority constitute a truly formidable array. They are, even so, less extensive than the powers which Mr. Streit would transfer to the federal government of his proposed union of democracies.[24] Mr. Meade would give to an International Central Bank power to regulate the issue of international currency so as to combat the onset of economic depression and "the ultimate power of controlling the total supply of money within the Member-States" (p. 50); as well as the sole power to vary exchange rates (p. 64); engage in open-market operations (p. 69); and forbid the use of national exchange equalization

[23] J. E. Meade, *op. cit.*, p. 10.
[24] C. K. Streit, *op. cit.*, pp. 325, seq. The Union is given powers of legislation and taxation, the right to grant citizenship, make treaties, maintain power, raise armies, regulate commerce, issue money, operate postal and interstate communication services, etc.

funds (p. 71). In addition, the International Authority would be empowered "to appoint representatives to the national boards of control over the foreign trade of the Member-States with planned economies; and these representatives would need to possess the final power of decision over the actions of such national bodies" (p. 96). Other powers to be handed over to the International Authority include supervision of the operations of "the various bodies which already control prices, production, sales or exports of various primary commodities such as tin, rubber and tea" (p. 100); "powers to prevent any Member-State from putting an embargo upon the issue of foreign loans or upon the purchase of foreign securities or of other forms of property in foreign countries" (p. 110), together with other powers in respect of international capital movements (p. 112); power to forbid the type of trading system which uses exchange control and clearing agreements (p. 137); supervision of exchange controls directed against speculative transfers of capital and also of import and export controls (p. 139); power to enforce the principle of the Open Door (p. 162), which "might be assured by handing over the colonial territories to the International Authority itself for actual administration by a competent international body" (p. 163); supervision of international cartels (p. 166); and power "to insist gradually and without undue distress upon the relaxation of restriction schemes as a permanent method of maintaining the incomes of the producers of raw materials" (p. 169).

Freedom of migration is another condition of international co-operation which would be a responsibility of the International Authority, which might also have an army, and police, as well as taxation, powers. Moreover, Mr. Meade relegates to a footnote (p. 92) the vital assumption that must underlie any scheme for an International Authority—the assumption of some effective means of ensuring collective security.

These are heroic suggestions which, if adopted even in part, would result in the creation of an International Authority vastly different from that of the League of Nations which throughout its twenty years of existence had to rely upon persuasion and the force of public opinion. It will be noted, moreover, that the various organs of international economic regulation, including a World Central Bank, are brought into organic relationship with the projected International Authority. Bold as such proposals may seem, they, or some equivalent, are necessary if such an Authority is to function successfully at the present time. Mr. Meade's proposals, based largely on the necessity of combining "liberal and planned" economies, suggest not only a world-state, but what looks very like a totalitarian world-state. In a more reasonable world less authority might be needed at the center, but the world after the war is likely to be less, rather than more, reasonable. Even if the creation of a supreme International Authority of this type should prove impracticable on a world-wide scale, there is every reason to believe that centralized powers of the type outlined by Mr. Meade must be established within great trading regions. They must, for example, form the basis for any reorganization of a federated Europe. It is possible that centralized controls may be realized by different political methods in different regions. A formal constitution based upon treaty arrangements may be necessary to achieve in Europe the co-ordination that might well be realized by less formal understandings within a British trading region. The relations between a closed Soviet region, a federated Europe, a Japanese-dominated area, a loosely but effectively organized British group and the United States and Latin America would still need careful organization by some such technique as that of the Tripartite Agreement. A still more delicate and complicated problem would be the relations of individual States-Members of a regional group with States outside that group and with any supreme international authority that may be established. Fortunately, precedents exist for the solution of these problems mainly in the experience of the British Commonwealth. It is not unduly difficult to conceive trade treaty relationships crossing the boundaries of a trading region and independent membership of an International Authority by member-states of a regional group, provided only that the monetary relationships between the groups as a whole are stabilized effectively.

It may perhaps be argued that the world is not yet ready for such radical measures as the transfer of extensive powers and responsibilities to an international institution. There is a great body of sentiment in favor of international co-operation, but little real appreciation of its practical necessities. Good will and uplift, however, are not effective substitutes for hard political thinking. If international co-operation is to be effectively organized, long steps must be taken in the direction of a world-state. This means the transfer to some international authority of many aspects of economic sovereignty. Such transfers would affect employment, prices, and property values everywhere. They would also place national legislation in some measure under the control of other peoples. The mere constitutional problems involved in the setting up and practical working of international institutions call for a greater effort of political imagination and invention than most people are as yet willing to contemplate.

Whatever solutions may be found in practice for these problems of international organization, one fact will remain of supreme importance. The national policies of the great Powers will determine what kind of organization, if any, can be brought into being, what powers will be entrusted to it, and whether those powers can be effectively discharged. After the war, which will certainly exhaust and impoverish the European Powers, the greatest responsibility must inevitably devolve upon the United States. The responsibility may be unsought and unwelcome; but it is inescapable. Not what Americans think, but what the United States does, will largely determine the pattern of international relations for the immediate future. Even inaction is a policy, negative but nonetheless decisive. The United States may refuse the responsibility and retreat into isolation. That is a logical policy to follow, provided its costs are weighed against its advantages.

Among those costs are the probability that great autarkic

trading regions will form and extend their control over the relatively undeveloped sources of food supplies and raw materials. Their economic penetration is likely to carve out spheres of economic influence in Asia, Africa, and Latin America. Multilateral international trade will be still further restricted and access to natural raw materials such as rubber, tin, copper, manganese, nickel, antimony, mercury, tungsten, and bauxite, will be determined by bilateral barter arrangements. The struggle between great economic empires for control of such materials will certainly lead to an intensification of regulated production and trade. In such circumstances, the United States might well lose a large part of its export markets as well as its overseas investments, and have to pay dearly for essential imports. It would, at the same time, be faced with the necessity for greatly increased rearmament expenditures, involving much higher rates of taxation and a considerable measure of economic regimentation. Standards of living must fall and a considerable reorganization of industry, including agriculture, be undertaken. Retreat into isolation would in fact bring, in an exaggerated form, the structural economic dislocation and financial crisis that were at the root of the social unrest after the breakdown of international equilibrium in 1931. No tariff or huge gold stock could forestall a great and continuing depression.

If, on the contrary, the United States should take bold constructive steps to initiate the creation of international institutions, that also would be a logical policy; but its costs should be squarely faced also. Some of them have already been suggested. On the economic side, it would be necessary to acquiesce in a practically world-wide depreciation against the dollar, in a substantially greater rise of prices in the United States than elsewhere, and in an effective lowering of the American tariff. This would mean heavy transitional losses in protected industries, particularly in agriculture, and a further displacement of labor in mineral and agricultural employment as well as in some of the older manufacturing industries. These losses would be more than compensated by the gain in other industries, but the transitional costs would be heavy and would bear harshly on particular interests.

Moreover, no system of economic or financial co-operation can be effective for long unless it is firmly based on political security, which means collective security. In assuring collective security, the United States must assume a large share of responsibility and make far-reaching political and military commitments. It is simply unrealistic to blink this fact. If an international system is to be restored, it must be an American-dominated system, based on a Pax Americana.

The worst of all policies in the long run, though the most tempting, would be the extension of international loans or proposals for international action that were not followed up by consistent leadership in the working out of continuing means of international co-operation. No doubt the extension of liberal credit might give temporary relief to a stricken Europe and even create a substantial reconstruction boom. It did so from 1925 to 1929. No doubt also the countries of the New World, including those of Latin America and the British Dominions as well as the United States, may well and rightly insist that Europe should settle its own feuds by some pact of regional security or outright federation. But economic co-operation and peaceful security cannot be divided into regional segments. Nor can they be established once and for all by a magnanimous gesture. If co-operation is begun it must be seen through, or, as after the last war, the world will in the long run be worse off than if it had never been attempted. Peace and prosperity, it must be repeated over and over, cannot be achieved by a formula. More than word magic and idealistic wishful thinking is needed. If peace and prosperity are ever to be restored to an unhappy world, they must, like freedom, "be re-created year by year."

Appendix

THE factual material for this volume has been drawn mainly, but not entirely, from the studies listed below. These studies were undertaken as research preparation for the Bergen meeting of the International Studies Conference. The subject—Economic Policies in Relation to World Peace—had grown naturally out of previous discussions on "The State and Economic Life" (Milan, 1931 and London, 1933), "Collective Security" (Copenhagen, 1935), and "Peaceful Change" (Paris, 1937). In the course of these discussions it had become evident that the conflict of economic and political forces in the modern world demanded thorough investigation. Such an investigation was begun in November, 1937 by calling for detailed national studies of economic policy in all the countries where co-operating committees of scholars were in existence. The minimum asked from each group was an answer to five questions:

a) A brief outline statement of the main features of external economic policy in recent years;

b) A statement of the legal and administrative machinery by which external economic policy is decided and administered (including a statement on indirect methods of protection);

c) An exposition of the principal social and economic factors which have influenced the recent evolution of external economic policy;

d) A similar exposition of the principal political factors that have influenced external economic policy;

e) A statement of the international pressures responsible for such policy.

APPENDIX

The attempt to secure such national studies had for its primary purpose an experiment in the method of comparative analysis that is, perhaps, the best substitute in the social sciences for the experimentation that has proved so fruitful in the natural sciences. The national studies, uneven in quality and different in treatment as they proved to be, demonstrated the utility of this method. They present a surprising degree of unanimity on many important issues, enabling the student to trace in the varying circumstances of different countries similar effects from similar causes.

A parallel series of studies on the narrower problem of exchange control was undertaken in a smaller number of countries with equally useful results. In addition to a definite convergence of results, it produced a clear statement of opposing theses in regard to exchange control as an instrument of national policy.

The co-operating national groups were not confined to the minimum program thus outlined, but were free to present additional studies relevant to the main subject of discussion. Many of them did so, and it is notable that several studies of regionalism were independently produced, showing that there is a widespread search for practical means of escaping from the narrow limits of nationalism. The Program Committee also invited individual experts to submit studies dealing with general problems common to more than one country, and in particular arranged for a series of studies to raise controversial issues.[1]

The great bulk of this material was circulated in published or mimeographed form to members of the conference in time for them to study it before coming to Bergen. An analytical program also was drawn up and circulated in order to pose a long list of questions that appeared to emerge from the documentation and to relate those questions to the relevant documentary material. This program, however, was not mandatory and provision was made for the meeting to organize its own discussions by means of a committee of round-table chairmen.

Preparation, therefore, consisted essentially of three main stages. In the first, emphasis was placed upon the collection of relevant information by a co-operative process of investigation using the

[1] The following studies were invited in this way: W. F. Fitzburgh, *The Economic Effects of Diminished Emigration from Europe*; Karin Kock, *Capital Movements and Economic Policy*; L. Baudin, *Free Trade and Peace*; M. A. Heilperin, *International Monetary Organisation*; M. J. Bonn, *Wealth, Welfare, or War*; H. J. Tasca, *World Trading Systems*.

APPENDIX   397

broad outlines of an agreed plan of study. In the second stage, the material was analyzed and the possible shape of a conference program was suggested. The third stage should have been the actual organization of round-table discussions by the committee set up for that purpose. Circumstances prevented the organization of the round-table discussions; but the studies listed below remain a useful source of detailed information.

List of Memoranda on Economic Policies in Relation to World Peace, Submitted to the Twelfth Session of the International Studies Conference

ARGENTINE MEMORANDUM:
  1: Angel Valle and Juan M. Ferrer, *La Politique économique de l'Argentine* (1927–1938).

AUSTRALIAN MEMORANDA:
  1: H. L. Harris, *Australia's Economic Policy.*
  2: W. S. Kelly, *The Australian Tariff.*
  3: C. A. S. Hawker, *Australia's Foreign Trade Treaties.*
  4: D. B. Copland, *Monetary Policy in Australia.*
  5: Australian Institute of International Affairs, *The Department of Commerce (Commonwealth of Australia).*

BELGIAN MEMORANDUM:
  1: Jean Jussiant, *L'Evolution du commerce extérieur de la Belgique.*

BRAZILIAN MEMORANDUM:
  1: Alfonso Toledo Bandeira de Mello, *Les Politiques économiques et la paix.*

BULGARIAN MEMORANDA:
  1: C. Bobtcheff, *La Politique commerciale extérieure de la Bulgarie après la guerre.** [2]
  2: A. Tchakaloff and S. Zagaroff, *Le Contrôle des changes en Bulgarie.*†

CANADIAN MEMORANDUM:
  1: J. F. Parkinson, *The Bases of Canadian Commercial Policy.*

[2] Documents marked with an asterisk (*) have been published. All others were submitted in mimeograph. Documents marked with a dagger sign (†) were submitted in a special exchange control series.

APPENDIX

CARNEGIE ENDOWMENT MEMORANDUM:
1: Erik Colban, *La Convention d'Oslo*.

DANISH MEMORANDUM:
1: H. P. Gøtrik, *Danish Economic Policy (1931–1938)*.*

FINNISH MEMORANDA:
1: T. Voionmaa, *Finnish Commercial Policy*.
2: H. R. Hormi, *The Clearing and Compensation Policy of Finland*.

FRENCH MEMORANDUM:
1: René Hoffherr and other authors, *La Politique commerciale de la France*.*

GERMAN MEMORANDA:
1: Kurt Kroyman, *Problems of German Foreign Trade Policy*.
1a: M. von Mickwitz, *The Economic Structure of Capital Exports to South-eastern Europe*.
2: Fritz Meyer, *An Analysis of Exchange Restrictions at Present in Force*.†
3: Albert Prinzig, *The Bearing of International Cartel and Control Schemes upon International Trade Organisation*.
4: Klaus Heinrich, *The Formation of Past Customs Unions*.
5: Franz Grosse, *Regional Trade Agreements between Groups of Nations*.

GERMAN MEMORANDUM:
1: J. D. Pintos, *Le Contrôle des changes en Grèce*.†

HUNGARIAN MEMORANDA:
1: Elemer Hantos, *Le Régionalisme économique en Europe*.*
2: W. Heller, *Hungarian External Economic Policy*.
3: K. Buday, *Exchange Control in Hungary*.†

INDIAN MEMORANDUM:
1: Sir B. L. Mitter, *India's Economic Policy* (Speech delivered at the International Studies Conference).

ITALIAN MEMORANDUM:
1: O. A. Hirschmann, *Le Contrôle des changes en Italie*.†

JAPANESE MEMORANDA:
1: M. Royama, *Japan's Foreign Trade and Exchange Policies in War Economy*.† *

APPENDIX 399

2: T. Ueda, *The Population Movement in Japan.**
3: Tesuji Kada, *Social and Political Factors Determining Japan's External Economic Policy.**
4: S. Kawashima, *The Trend of Japan's Foreign Trade Policy and Her Indirect Protective Measures.**
5: K. Takahashi, *Economic Conditions in Japan and Their Bearing on International Affairs.**
6: S. Kojima, *Natural Resources of Japan.**
7: Zenichi Itani, *Social and Economic Factors in Japan's Foreign Trade.*
8: K. Kimpara, *Changes in Japan's Exchange Policy and Foreign Exchange Fund Account.** †

MEXICAN MEMORANDA:

1. L. Ponton, *Les Traits essentiels de la politique économique du Mexique.*
2. M. Quintana, *Les Problèmes économiques et la paix.*
3: G. Loyo, *Les Bases minima d'une politique demographique.*
4: R. Ricalde, *Les Mesures sanitaires appliqués au commerce d'importation et d'exportation dans les parts mexicains.*
5: Ing. Manuel Meza A., *Le Crédit agricole du Mexique.*

NETHERLANDS MEMORANDUM:

1: P. Lieftinck (Netherlands Economic Institute), *The External Economic Policy of the Netherlands.*

NORWEGIAN MEMORANDA:

1: Morten Tuveng, *External Economic Policy of Norway in Recent Years.*
2: Erling Petersen, *The Repercussions of Modern Commercial Policies on Economic Conditions in Norway.*

POLISH MEMORANDA:

1: K. Bretoni, *Les Traits essentiels de la politique économique de le Pologne.*
2: S. L. Zaleski: *Le Surpeuplement et l'émigration en rapport avec la politique économique de la Pologne.*
3: Witold Stanewicz, *La Politique agraire de la Pologne.*
4: Edward Lipinski, *L'Industrialisation de la Pologne.*
5: Roman Piotrowski, *Le Problème des cartels en Pologne.*
6: Hipolit Gliwic, *Les Capitaux étrangers de la Pologne.**
7: Edward Taylor, *La Répercussion des difficultes monétaires*

sur la politique économique extérieure de la Pologne.*
8: Czeslaw Strzeszewski, La Politique du commerce extérieure de la Pologne.
9: Pawel Czechowicz, L'Organisation du commerce extérieur de la Pologne.
10: J. Nowak, Le Contrôle des changes en Pologne.† *
11: Adam de Heydel and Wojciech Zaleski, Le Protectionnisme indirect dans les divers pays et ses répercussions sur les exportations de la Pologne.
12: Adam de Heydel and Bronislow Oyrzanowski, Le Protectionisme en Pologne.
13: Cezary Berezowski, Du Rôle de l'état et de l'individu dans les relations économiques de la Pologne avec l'étranger.
14: Antoni Deryng, La Politique économique de la Pologne et le problème de la paix.
15: Karol Bertoni, Les Besoins économiques et demographiques de la Pologne et la question des colonies.
16: Bohdan Nagorski, Les Ports de Dantzig et de Gdynia et leur rôle dans la vie économique de la Pologne.

RUMANIAN MEMORANDA:

1: Virgile Madgearu, La Politique économique extérieure de la Roumanie (1927–1938).*
2: V. Madgearu, Le Contrôle des changes en Roumanie.†

SWEDISH MEMORANDA:

1: Gunnar Boos, Survey of Sweden's External Economic Policy.
2: Berthold Josephy, Exchange Depreciation in Scandinavia and Its Bearing on the International Economic Relations of the Scandinavian Countries.
3: Karin Kock, International Capital Movements and Economic Policy.

SWISS MEMORANDUM:

1: J. Wackernagel, J. de la Harpe and C. Burky, La Suisse et l'autarcie.*

TURKISH MEMORANDUM:

1: Hazim Atif Kuyucak, Exchange Control in Turkey.†

UNITED KINGDOM MEMORANDA:

1: Study Group of the British Coordinating Committee of In-

APPENDIX 401

ternational Studies, *British External Economic Policy in Recent Years*, and *Addendum*.
2: F. W. Paish, *The Effects of Foreign Exchange Control on British Trade*.*

UNITED STATES OF AMERICA MEMORANDA:
 1: Eugene Staley, *World Economy in Transition*.*
 2: Percy W. Bidwell, *The Invisible Tariff*.*
 3: Benjamin H. Williams, *Foreign Loan Policy of the United States Since 1933*.*
 4: H. M. Bratter, *Foreign Exchange Control in Latin America*.* †
 5: Raymond Leslie Buell, *The Hull Trade Program and the American System*.*
 6: A. D. Gayer and C. T. Schmidt, *American Economic Foreign Policy*.*

YUGOSLAVIAN MEMORANDA:
 1: S. D. Obradovitch, *La Politique commerciale de la Yougoslavie*.*
 2: Goyko Grdjic, *Un Aperçu des traits les plus marquants de la politique économique extérieure de la Yougoslavie*.
 3: Miya Mirkovitch, *Les Principaux facteurs sociaux et économiques qui ont exercés une influence sur la recente évolution de la politique économique extérieure*.
 4: Alexandre Bilimovitch, *La Nouvelle politique économique extérieure de la Yougoslavie*.
 5: Mirko Lamer, *Regional Economic Agreements Concerning Yougoslavia*.
 6: Georges Andrassy, *L'Arbitrage international comme moyen de réglement des conflits économiques*.
 7: A. Yovanovitch, *Le Contrôle des changes en Yougoslavie*.†

INTERNATIONAL MEMORANDA:
 1: Louis Baudin, *Free Trade and Peace*.*
 2: Michael A. Heilperin, *International Monetary Organisation*.*
 3: M. J. Bonn, *Wealth, Welfare or War*.*
 4: Henry J. Tasca, *World Trading Systems*.*
 5: William W. Fitzhugh, Jr., *The Economic Effects Caused by Diminished Emigration from Europe*.

ADDITIONAL MEMORANDA PREPARED FOR THE CONFERENCE:

1: O. A. Hirschmann, *Etude statistique sur la tendance du commerce extérieure vers l'équilibre et le bilateralisme.*
2: A. Piatier, *Exchange Control: A General Survey* (Paris, 1940).*

PUBLICATIONS PLACED AT THE DISPOSAL OF THE MEMBERS OF THE CONFERENCE:

1: F. L. McDougall, "Food and Welfare," Geneva Studies, Vol. IX, No. 5.
2: Leopold Wellisz, *Foreign Capital in Poland* (London, George Allen & Unwin, Ltd., 1938).
3: John Foster Dulles, *War, Peace and Change* (New York and London. Harpers, 1939).

Officers of the Conference

PRESIDENT OF THE CONFERENCE: Frede Castberg, *Professor of International Law in the University of Oslo, President of the Norwegian Co-ordinating Committee for International Studies.*

CHAIRMAN OF THE STUDY MEETINGS: Malcolm W. Davis, *Associate Director of the European Centre of the Carnegie Endowment for International Peace.*

GENERAL-RAPPORTEUR: J. B. Condliffe, *Professor of Commerce in the University of London, now Professor of Economics in the University of California.*

SECRETARY-RAPPORTEURS: H. O. Christophersen *and* A. Piatier.

SECRETARIAT OF THE CONFERENCE: Henri Bonnet, *Director of the International Institute of Intellectual Co-operation;* Leo Gross, Oliver Jackson *and* Jiri F. Vranek, *Secretaries at the International Institute of Intellectual Co-operation.*

List of Participants in the Study Meetings [3]

BERTONI, Karol—*President of the Central Committee of Polish Institutions of Political Science; Former Minister Plenipoten-*

[3] It will be recalled that participants in the Study Meetings attend in their personal capacity (as individual scholars or experts). A participant in the Study Meetings is in no sense a representative of the institution by which he may have been nominated. See *The International Studies Conference. Origins-Functions-Organisation* (I. I. I. C., Paris, 1937), p. 23.

APPENDIX 403

tiary; *Professor in the Diplomatic Section, University of Lwow.*
—Central Committee of Polish Institutions of Political Science.

BIDWELL, Percy W.—*Director of Studies, Council of Foreign Relations.*—American Co-ordinating Committee for International Studies.

BILIMOVITCH, Alexandre—*Professor.*—Yugoslav Scientific Committee.

BOBTCHEFF, Constantin N.—*Professor of Economic Policy at the Free University, Sofia.*—Bulgarian ad hoc Committee.

BURTON, John W.—*Member of Australian Public Service.*—Australian Institute of International Affairs.

CASTBERG, Frede—*Professor, University of Oslo.*—Norwegian Co-ordinating Committee for International Studies.

DAVIS, Malcolm W.—*Associate-Director, European Centre of the Carnegie Endowment for International Peace.*—Carnegie Endowment for International Peace.

DEAN, Vera M.—*Research Director and Editor, Foreign Policy Association.*—American Co-ordinating Committee for International Studies.

FORSYTH, William D.—*Research Fellow, Melbourne University.*—Australian Institute of International Affairs.

GØTRIK, Hans P.—Institute of Economics and History, Copenhagen.

HAMBRO, Edvard—*Christian Michelsen Institute for Science and Intellectual Freedom, Bergen.*—Norwegian Co-ordinating Committee for International Studies.

HEBBARD, Lawrence—*Assistant to Mr. C. F. Remer.*—European Centre of the Carnegie Endowment.

HEILPERIN, Michael A.—*Formerly Assistant Professor in the Graduate Institute of International Studies, Geneva.*—Expert invited by the Conference.

HELLER, Wolfgang—*Professor, University of Technical and Economic Sciences, Budapest; Chairman, Hungarian Co-ordinating Committee.*—Hungarian Co-ordinating Committee for International Studies.

HEYDEL, Adam de—*Professor Jagellons University, Cracow.*—Central Committee of Polish Institutions of Political Science.

HOFFHERR, René—*Maître des Requêtes at the Conseil d'Etat; Professor at the Ecole Libre des Sciences Politiques, Paris.*—French Co-ordinating Committee for International Studies.

APPENDIX

HOOVER, Calvin B.—*Dean of the Graduate School, Duke University, United States of America.*—American Co-ordinating Committee for International Studies.

HUBBARD, Ursula P.—*Division Assistant, Division of Intercourse and Education, Carnegie Endowment for International Peace.*—European Centre of the Carnegie Endowment for International Peace.

KITTREDGE, Tracy B.—*Assistant Director. The Social Sciences, Rockefeller Foundation.*—Observer invited by the Conference.

KOCK, Karin—*Professor at the University of Stockholm.*—Swedish Co-ordinating Committee for International Studies.

KUYUCAK, Hazim A.—*Professor, School of Political Science, Ankara.*—Expert invited by the Conference.

LEAL, Herbert Allan—*Holder of the G. T. Alexander Travelling Scholarship from McMaster University, Hamilton.*—Canadian Institute of International Affairs.

LEDERMAN, Lazlo—*Privat docent, Geneva University.*—Swiss Co-ordinating Committee for International Studies.

LUNDSTRÖM, Ragnvald—*Secretary of the Swedish Co-ordinating Committee and of the Committee of International Information.*—Swedish Co-ordinating Committee for International Studies.

MADGEARU, Virgile—*Professor of Economic Politics at the Academy of Commercial and Industrial Studies, Bucharest, former Minister.*—Centre of International Studies (Rumanian Institute of Social Research).

MILLER, Francis P.—*Secretary, American Co-ordinating Committee; Organisation Director for Foreign Relations Committees, Council on Foreign Relations.*—American Co-ordinating Committee for International Studies.

MITTER, Sir Brojendra Lal—*Advocate-General of India.*—Indian Institute of International Affairs.

PEDERSEN, H. Winding—*Head, Economics Section, Institute of Economics and History, Copenhagen.*—Institute of Economics and History, Copenhagen.

POTTER, P. B.—*Professor, Graduate School of International Studies, Geneva.*—Graduate School of International Studies.

REMER, C. F.—*Director, Geneva Research Centre.*—European Centre of the Carnegie Endowment.

ROBLES, A. G.—Mexican Committee for the Scientific Study of International Relations.

SKYLSTAD, R. B.—*Director for questions of Intellectual Co-operation, League of Nations.*—Observer invited by the Conference.
TASCA, H. J.—*Assistant to Professor J. B. Condliffe.*—Expert invited by the Conference.
TCHAKALOFF, Assan C.—*Head of the Credit and Research Department of the National Bank of Bulgaria, Sofia.*—Bulgarian ad hoc Committee.
TUVENG, Morten—*Secretary at the Central Bureau of Statistics, Oslo.*—Norwegian Co-ordinating Committee for International Studies.
VIDELA, Ricardo—*Consul General of the Argentine Republic, Geneva.*—Argentine Co-ordinating Committee for International Studies.
VINER, Jacob—*Professor of Economics, University of Chicago; President of the American Economic Association.*—American Co-ordinating Committee for International Studies.
VOGT, Johan Herman—*Lecturer in Political Economics, University of Oslo.*—Norwegian Co-ordinating Committee for International Studies.
VULCAN, Constantin—*Secretary-General of the Centre of International Studies.*—Centre of International Studies (Rumanian Institute of Social Research).
WALKER, Sydnor H.—*Associate-Director, The Social Sciences, Rockefeller Foundation, New York.*—Observer invited by the Conference.
WEDERWANG, Ingewar—*Professor, Commercial High School, Bergen.*—Norwegian Co-ordinating Committee for International Studies.
WRISTON, Henry M.—*President of Brown University.*—American Co-ordinating Committee for International Studies.
YOVANOVITCH, Alexandre—*Head of the School of Higher Economic and Commercial Studies, Belgrade.*—Yugoslav Scientific Committee.
ZAGOROFF, Slavtcho—*Director General of the Bulgarian Central Board of Statistics; Dean of the Faculty of Law, Sofia.*—Bulgarian ad hoc Committee.

SUGGESTIONS FOR FURTHER READING

CHAPTER I

Toynbee, A. J. *A Study of History*. Oxford University Press, 1934. Vol. I, pp. 1–50.
Royal Institute of International Affairs. *Nationalism*. Oxford University Press, 1939.
Wallas, Graham. *Human Nature in Politics*. Constable, 1908.
Staley, Eugene. *World Economy in Transition*. Council on Foreign Relations, 1939.
Gayer, Arthur D., and Schmidt, Carl T. *American Economic Foreign Policy*. Council on Foreign Relations, 1939.
Condliffe, J. B. *The Changing Structure of the Economic World*. International Chamber of Commerce, 1939.
Robbins, Lionel. *Economic Planning and International Order*. Macmillan, 1937.
Baudin, L. *Free Trade and Peace*. Columbia University Press, 1939.
Staley, Eugene. *Raw Materials in Peace and War*. Council on Foreign Relations, 1937.
Emeny, Brooks. *The Strategy of Raw Materials*. Macmillan, 1937.
Shepardson, W. H., and Scroggs, W. O. *The United States in World Affairs*. Council on Foreign Relations, yearly.

CHAPTER II

Hansen, Alvin H. *Full Recovery or Stagnation*. W. W. Norton & Co., Inc., 1938.
Moulton, Harold G. & Others. *Capital Expansion and Economic Stability*. Brookings Institution, 1940.
Temporary National Economic Committee. *Investigation of Concentration of Economic Power*, Hearings, Part 1. Economic

408 SUGGESTIONS FOR FURTHER READING

Prologue; Part 9, *Savings and Investments,* pp. 3495–3559. U. S. Government Printing Office, 1939–40.
Robertson, D. H. "The Future of International Trade," *Economic Journal,* March, 1938.
McDougall, F. L. *Food and Welfare.* Geneva Research Center, 1938.
Wright, Fergus Chalmers. *Population and Peace.* Columbia University Press, 1940.
League of Nations. *World Economic Survey* (annually since 1931–32).
Bagehot, Walter. *Lombard Street.* C. Scribner's Sons, 1897.
Royal Institute of International Affairs. *The Problem of International Investment.* Oxford University Press, 1937.
Harris, C. R. S. *Germany's Foreign Indebtedness.* Royal Institute of International Affairs, 1935.

CHAPTER III

von Hayek, F. A. *Monetary Nationalism and International Stability.* Longmans Green & Co., 1937.
de Vegh, Imre. *The Pound Sterling.* Scudder, Stevens and Clark, 1939.
Hodson, H. V. *Slump and Recovery 1929–1937.* Oxford University Press, 1938.
Carr. E. H. *The Twenty Years Crisis, 1919–1939.* Macmillan, 1940.
Toynbee, A. J. *A Study of History.* Oxford University Press, 1939, Vol. IV.
von Haberler, G. *The Theory of International Trade.* Macmillan, 1937.
Drucker, Peter F. *The End of Economic Man.* Heinemann, 1939.
Mannheim, Karl. *Ideology and Utopia.* Harcourt Brace & Co., 1936.

CHAPTER IV

League of Nations. *World Economic Survey 1938–39.*
Tasca, Henry J. *World Trading Systems.* Columbia University Press. 1939.
Ellis, Howard S. *Exchange Control.* Harvard University Press, 1940.

SUGGESTIONS FOR FURTHER READING 409

Gordon, Margaret S. *Barriers to World Trade* (to be published), 1940.
International Chamber of Commerce and Carnegie Endowment. *The Improvement of Commercial Relations Between Nations.* 1936.
International Chamber of Commerce and Carnegie Endowment. *International Economic Reconstruction.* 1936.
Wright, Carl Major. *Economic Adaptation to a Changing World Market.* Copenhagen: Einar Munksgaard, 1939.
Dietrich, Ethel B. *World Trade.* Henry Holt & Co., 1939.
McIver, R. M. *Leviathan and the People.* Louisiana State University Press, 1939.

CHAPTER V

Hecksher, Eli F. *Mercantilism.* Allen & Unwin, 1935.
Keynes, J. M. *The General Theory of Employment, Interest and Money.* Macmillan, 1936. Ch. 23.
Tasca, Henry J. *The Reciprocal Trade Policy of the United States.* University of Pennsylvania, 1938.
Bidwell, Percy W. *Tariff Policy of the United States.* Council on Foreign Relations, 1933.
Bidwell, Percy W. *The Invisible Tariff.* Council on Foreign Relations, 1939.
Liepmann, H. *Tariff Levels and the Economic Unity of Europe.* Allen & Unwin, 1938.
Rappard, W. E. *Post-War Efforts for Freer Trade.* Geneva Research Center, 1938.
Beveridge, Sir W. H. & Others. *Tariffs: The Case Examined.* London & New York: Longmans Green & Co., 1931.
Buell, R. L. *The Hull Trade Program.* Foreign Policy Association, 1939.
Political and Economic Planning. *Report on International Trade.* London: P. E. P., 1937.

CHAPTER VI

Royal Institute of International Affairs. *World Agriculture.* London: Oxford University Press, 1932.
League of Nations Economic Committee. *The Agricultural Crisis* (1931.II.B.12′ and 12″).

410 SUGGESTIONS FOR FURTHER READING

Ellsworth, P. T. *International Economics*. Macmillan, 1938.
Rowe, J. W. F. *Markets and Men*. Macmillan, 1936.

CHAPTER VII

Ellis, Howard S. *Exchange Control*. Harvard University Press, 1940.
Waight, Leonard. *The History and Mechanism of the Exchange Equalisation Account*. Cambridge, 1939.
Hall, N. F. *The Exchange Equalisation Account*. London: Macmillan & Co., Ltd., 1935.
Poole, Kenyon E. *German Financial Policies, 1932–1939*. Harvard University Press, 1939.
Gayer, A. D. (ed.). *The Lessons of Monetary Experience*. Farrar & Rinehart, Inc., 1937.
Explorations in Economics. *Notes and Essays Contributed in Honor of F. W. Taussig*. McGraw-Hill Book Co., Inc., 1936.
Balogh, Thomas. "The National Economy of Germany," *Economic Journal*, September, 1938.
―――― "Foreign Exchange and Export Trade Policy," *Economic Journal*, March, 1940.
Angell, James W. *The Financial Foreign Policy of the United States*. Council on Foreign Relations, 1933.
Williams, Benjamin H. *Foreign Loan Policy of the United States Since 1933*. Council on Foreign Relations, 1939.
Whittlesey, Charles R. *International Monetary Issues*. McGraw-Hill Book Co., Inc., 1937.
League of Nations. *Monetary Review* (*Money and Banking*, Vol. I) (annually since 1931–32).

CHAPTER VIII

Culbertson, William S. *International Economic Policy*. D. Appleton & Co., 1925.
League of Nations. *Recommendations of the Economic Committee Relating to Tariff Policy and the Most-Favoured-Nation Clause* (1933.II.B.9).
League of Nations. *Enquiry into Clearing Agreements* (1935. II.B.6).

International Chamber of Commerce and Carnegie Endowment. *International Economic Reconstruction.* 1936.
Dietrich, Ethel B. *World Trade.* Henry Holt & Co., 1939.

CHAPTER IX

Wolfers, Arnold. *Britain and France Between Two Wars.* Harcourt Brace & Co., 1940.
International Studies Conference. *The State and Economic Life.* International Institute of Intellectual Cooperation, 1934. Pp. 46–77.
Benham, F. C. *South-eastern Europe: A Political and Economic Survey.* Oxford University Press, 1939.
Hancock, W. K. *Survey of British Commonwealth Affairs.* Oxford University Press, 1940. Vol. II.

CHAPTER X

Southard, Frank A., Jr. *American Industry in Europe.* Houghton Mifflin Co., 1931.
Marshall, Herbert, Southard, Frank & Others. *Canadian-American Industry.* Yale University Press, 1936.
U. S. Bureau of Foreign and Domestic Commerce. *American Direct Investments in Foreign Countries.* Trade Information Bulletin, 1931. No. 731.
Royal Institute of International Affairs. *The Problem of International Investment.* Oxford University Press, 1937.
Phelps, Dudley Maynard. *Migration of Industry to South America.* McGraw-Hill Book Co., Inc., 1936.
Remer, C. F. *Foreign Investments in China.* Macmillan, 1933.
Holland, W. L. (ed.). *Commodity Control in the Pacific Area.* Stanford University Press, 1935.
Elliott, W. Y. & Others. *International Control in the Non-Ferrous Metals.* Macmillan, 1937.
Rowe, J. W. F. *Markets and Men.* Macmillan, 1936.
League of Nations. *Report of Committee for the Study of the Problem of Raw Materials* (II Economic and Financial, 1937. II.B.7).
Royal Institute of International Affairs. *Raw Materials and Colonies.* R. I. I. A., 1936.

412 SUGGESTIONS FOR FURTHER READING

Jones, Ralph C. "Allocation Accounting for the Taxable Income of Industrial Enterprises." *Taxation of Foreign and National Enterprises*, League of Nations, 1933. Vol. V.

Fisher, Allan G. B. *The Clash of Progress and Security*. Macmillan, 1935.

Russell, Bertrand. *Power, a New Social Analysis*. W. W. Norton & Co., Inc., 1938.

CHAPTER XI

Meade, J. E. *The Economic Bases of a Durable Peace*. Allen & Unwin, 1940.

Hawtrey, R. G. *The Economic Aspects of Sovereignty*. Longmans Green & Co., 1930.

Buell, Raymond L. *Isolated America*. Alfred A. Knopf, 1940.

Streit, Clarence K. *Union Now*. Harper & Bros., 1939.

——— *International Economic Relations*. University of Minnesota Press, 1934.

McIver, R. M. & Others. *Economic Reconstruction*. Columbia University Press, 1934.

Royal Institute of International Affairs. *World Order Papers*. Oxford University Press, 1940.

Mannheim, Karl. *Man and Society in an Age of Reconstruction*. Kegan Paul, 1939.

Index

Administration, 31-34, 269-271
Administrative protectionism, 196-203
Agricultural prices—fall in, 76-78, 210-211, 302
Agricultural protectionism, 78, 105, 210-213, 214-216; *see also* individual countries
Albania, Italian occupation of, 49, 316
Angell, Sir Norman, 55
Anglo-American Trade Agreement, 174, 189, 207
Anglo-French economic bloc, 160, 176-177, 318, 365, 366-367
Anglo-Turkish Agreement, 286
Antidumping legislation, 202-203
Argentina
— and the fall in agricultural prices, 48
— and the sterling bloc, 320-321
Commercial relations with the United Kingdom, 174, 175, 276, 277, 320-321
Commercial relations with the United States, 207
Default on debt service, 243
Federation of, 296
Repayment of debt by, 244
Asiatic clause, 299
Auboin, R., 238
Australia
— and the fall in agricultural prices, 48
Business cycle policy of, 249

Commercial relations with New Zealand, 185
Conversions in, 244
Difficulties with balance of payments, 91
Export subsidies in, 222
Federation of, 296
Interest reductions in, 244
Postwar monetary policy of, 374
Trade agreement with Canada, 185
Australian Institute of International Affairs, 198n.
Austria
Absorption of, 49, 300, 304, 316
Bankruptcy of, 48
Clearing agreement with Switzerland, 275
Inflation in, 301
Proposed customs union with Germany, 303-304
Regional derogation from most-favored-nation clause, 301
Relaxation of exchange restrictions by, 244-245, 274
Transfer moratorium declared, 243
Austrian Credit-Anstalt, 48, 75, 90, 94, 233
Autarky, 161-167
— and sovereignty, 362-370
— and the postwar settlement, 392-393
— and the uneven distribution of raw material, 370, 393
Ayres, L. P., 74

Bagehot, Walter, 80-81, 341
Balance of payments
  Effect of monetary policy on, 41-42
  Effects of trade barriers on, 105-106
  German regulation of, 245-246
  Strain on, 22, 96-97, 140, 232-233; see also individual countries
Balkan clause, 299
Balkan conferences, 301, 304
Ballande, Mme. Laurence, 335
Balogh, T., 180n., 374n.
Baltic clause, 299, 305
Baltic conferences, 301, 305
Baltic countries
  Commercial relations with the United Kingdom, 175, 319; see also individual countries
Bandeira de Mello, A. T., 250, 325n.
Bank for International Settlements, 322n, 361, 377n., 384, 388
Bastable, C. F., 116
Baudin, L., 51n., 52, 53, 54, 55
Belgium
  Agricultural protectionism in, 212
  Bilateralism in, 282-283
  Colonial policy of, 310
  Devaluation in, 235, 321-322
  German occupation of, 160, 316
  International debt collection, 276
  Milling regulations in, 215
  "New Deal" policy in, 41
  Quotas in, 212
  Tariff policy in, 181, 186; see also Oslo conferences, Ouchy initiative, Tripartite Agreement
Beveridge, Sir William, 368
Bidwell, Percy, 33n., 35n., 159n., 170n., 198n., 199n., 202n., 213n.
Bilateral treaties, 270-272, 275-280
  Working of, 288-294
Bilateralism, 139
  Economic disadvantages of, 283-286
  Measurement of, 282-283
  Strategy of, 280-288
Bingham, A. M., 195n.
Black market, 237-238
Blocked accounts in Germany, 246-248, 258-259, 260-261, 323, 343
Bobtcheff, C., 179n., 181n., 183n.
Bolivia
  Default on debt service, 243
Bonn, M. J., 34, 50
Boös, G., 181n., 249n., 271n., 295n.,
Branch manufacturing establishments, 329-332
Brassey, Thomas, 81, 98
Bratter, H. M., 233n., 245n., 250n.
Brazil
  Default on debt service, 243
  Federation of, 296
  Rubber plantations in, 330
  Trade treaty with the United States, 325
Bridges, Robert, 27n.
British Commonwealth
  — and postwar international economic co-operation, 369-370
  Imperial marketing agreements, 34
  Monetary policy in, 317-319; see also United Kingdom, Imperial Conference of the British Commonwealth, and Ottawa Agreements
British Co-ordinating Committee, 24n., 187n., 191n., 193n., 213n., 218n., 221n., 222n., 271, 295n., 311n., 320n., 337n.
Brussels Conference (1920), 47
Buday, Kalman, 233n., 250n., 302n.
Buell, R. L., 195n., 205n.
Buenos Aires Conference, 368
Bulgaria
  Export duties in, 179
  Import surcharges and export premia in, 245, 259
  Transfer moratorium declared, 243
Bulgarian clause, 299
Burke, Edmund, 127, 311
Burky, de la Harpe, and Wackernagel, 16n., 161n., 162n., 163n., 164n., 165n., 166n., 167n., 181n.
Business cycle policy, 45-46, 248-256
  — and international cartels, 335-337
  — and international equilibrium,

INDEX

39-42, 110-114, 371-375; see also individual countries

Canada
— and the Ottawa Agreements, 186
Commercial agreement with Australia and New Zealand, 185
Commercial relations with the United States, 184-185
Federation of, 296
Investment relations with the United States, 333
Monetary policy of, 318-319
Capital market; see International capital market
Carr, E. H., 116, 117, 118, 119, 121, 122, 123n.
Carsow, Michel, 310n.
Central American clause, 299
Chalmers, H., 178n.
Chevalier, 281, 282
Chi, Chao-ting, 320n.
Chile
Commercial relations with United States, 207
Default on debt service, 243
China
Abolition of "likin" charges, 296-297
Monetary policy in, 320; see also Sino-Japanese conflict
Clapham, J. H., 107n.
Clearing
International, 272-273
Clearing agreements, 259, 275-277
— and direct investment, 343-346
— as a method of debt collection, 244, 246, 275-276
Working of, 288-294; see also individual countries
Cobden, Richard, 18, 55, 204n., 281, 282
Colban, Erik, 295n., 306n., 307
Colombia
Default on debt service, 243
Colonial policies, 308-316; see also individual countries
Commercial policy, 263-294

Effect of monetary and other policies on, 29-30
Exchange control as an instrument of, 240, 256-262
Types of modern, 155-160; see also individual countries
Commercial treaties
Degeneration of, 263-272
Discrimination in, 266-267
Political aspects of, 136
— under laissez faire, 264-265
Communications, 18-19, 328, 333-334
Compensation agreements, 273-275, 277
Congo Treaty, 312
"Convention for the Valorization of Cereals," 303
Copland, D. B., 23n., 249n.
Corporative State, 217-218
Costa Rica
Default on debt service, 243
Credit exchange standard, 318
Cuba
Default on debt service, 243
Cuban clause, 191, 299
Culbertson, W. S., 264, 265n.
Currency depreciation
— and agricultural protectionism, 210-213
Consequences of, 93, 133
Differential, 258-260; see also individual countries
Customs unions
— and the peace settlement, 366
— of the nineteenth century, 296-297; see also Germany
Czechoslovakia
Absorption by Germany, 49, 160, 221, 248, 305, 316
Adoption of exchange control by, 173, 232, 236, 321
Devaluation by, 236, 321, 322
Milling regulations in, 215
Regional derogation from most-favored-nation clause, 301

Danubian conferences, 301

416 INDEX

Danzig
  German reoccupation of, 316
Dawes loan, 246
Default on debt service; see individual countries
Deflation after 1929, 248-249
Denmark
  Commercial relations with the United Kingdom, 175
  Devaluation by, 133
  Exchange control in, 22, 157
  German occupation of, 160, 315, 316
  Monetary policy of, 318, 319
  Tariff policy of, 181; see also Oslo conferences
Devaluation
  — and fear of inflation, 244
  — and international indebtedness, 258; see also individual countries
Diplomacy
  Commercializing of, 263-264
Direct investment, 342-346
  — and the financial panic of 1931, 332
Disarmament Conference, 1932, 49
Discrimination
  — and war preparations, 160, 166-167
  — in commercial treaties, 266-267
  — in currency depreciation, 258-262
  — in quota policies, 223; see also Bilateralism, Bilateral treaties, Trade regulation, etc.
Dollar bloc
  — and U. S. commercial policy, 367-368
Dominica
  Default on debt service, 243
Donham, W. B., 27n.
Drucker, P. F., 128n.
Dumping, 202

Economic blocs
  Development of, 155-156, 357-358, 382-383
  Possibilities of co-operation between, 176, 391-392; see also Monetary blocs, Regionalism
Economic nationalism
  — and direct investment, 332, 343-346
  — and imports, 229-231
  — and international co-operation, 254-256
  Causes of, 39-40, 115-116
  Costs of, 56-58; see also Nationalism
Economic penetration, 92, 287-288, 290-294, 316-317
Economic planning
  — and international equilibrium, 349-350, 352-353
  — and monetary policy, 351-354
  — and war preparation, 347-349
  Dilemma of, 347-354
  — in international trade, 335-336
  National and international, 113-114
Economic policy
  — and peace, 47-58
  Autonomous, 248-256
  National and international, 41-42; see also individual countries
Economic reasoning
  Rejection of, 123-131
Eden Treaty, 265
Egyptian clause, 299
Einzig, Paul, 261n.
Ellis, H. S., 233n.
Equality of trading opportunity, 158-159, 172, 266; see also Most-favored-nation clause and United States commercial policy
Estonia
  Absorption by U.S.S.R., 316; see also Baltic conferences
Ethiopia
  Italian occupation of, 49, 188, 316, 322
Eve, A. S., 365n.
Exchange control, 232-262
  — and business cycle policy, 248-256
  — and establishment of branch enterprises, 332

INDEX

- and external insolvency, 239-240
- as an instrument of commercial policy, 240-241, 256-262
- Causes of, 22, 76-77, 133
- Countries employing, 232
- Origins of, 232-240
- "Exchange dumping," 202-203
- Exchange equalization fund, 32, 236-237, 352, 379-380
- Exchange notes
- Variable, 376-377
- Exchange stability
  - and future monetary policy, 373-382; *see also* International equilibrium
- Exchange stabilization, 375-382
- Exchange stabilization fund, 32, 236-237, 352, 379-380
- Export controls
  - after the World War (1914-1918), 179-180
- Export premia, 245; *see also* individual countries
- Export promotion, 221-223
- Export subsidies, 133, 138, 221-222; *see also* individual countries

Fanno, Marco, 93n.
Federation
  - and monetary and economic policy, 368-369
  - and the peace settlement, 364-365, 366-367
Proposals for European, 368; *see also* individual countries
Ferenczi, Imre, 64n., 104n.
Financial rigidities, 106-108
Finland
  - and the U. S. S. R., 316
Monetary policy of, 319
Repayment of debt by, 244
Tariff policy of, 181
Fitzhugh, W. W., 62n., 70n.
France
Administrative protectionism in, 201
Agricultural protectionism in, 135, 137, 211-212

Colonial policy of, 24, 310-311
Commercial treaties with the United Kingdom, 265, 280, 281
Devaluation by, 49, 322
Export subsidies in, 222
Foreign investment of, 53
German occupation of, 316
Monetary policy of, 184, 237, 321
"New Deal" policy in, 41
Quotas in, 213, 216
Stabilization of franc, 91; *see also* Anglo-French economic bloc, Tripartite Agreement
Free trade
  - and peace, 52-53, 54
Economic argument for, 119-120
Frontiers
Closing of, 59-71, 117-118

Gayer, A. D., and Schmidt, C. T., 25, 194n., 220n., 368
Germany
Adoption of gold standard by, 102
Agricultural protectionism in, 212, 270
  - and the reconstruction of international trade, 356-357
Bilateralism in, 282-283
Blocked accounts in, 246-248, 258-259, 260-261, 323
Clearing and payments agreements, 293-294, 322-324, 343-346; *see also* "Commercial policy," etc.
Coal Agreement with Great Britain, 221
Commercial policy of, 137-138, 158, 159-160, 171, 204, 225-227, 229-231, 256-262, 289-294, 316-317, 322-324, 344-346
Commercial relations with Rumania, 289-293, 317
Commercial relations with the United States, 159, 169-171, 203, 276
Commercial relations with the U. S. S. R., 287

418　INDEX

Germany (*continued*)
Commercial treaties with Yugoslavia, 1932–38, 267-270
Commercial treaty with Hungary, 291, 316-317
Default on debts, 243, 246
Economic policy in, 40, 251-256
Exchange control in, 240-241, 245-248, 255, 256-262, 323-324
Expansion of, 49, 160, 221, 248, 300, 304-305, 315, 316, 356-357
Export promotion in, 222; see also "Commercial policy"
Foreign investment of, 53
"New Plan," 257
Payments agreement with the United Kingdom, 276, 277-278, 321
Possibilities of trade with Latin America, 358
Proposed customs union with Austria, 303-304
Results of victory in the present war, 208, 356-358
Sondermark agreement, 276, 278
Tourist agreement with Switzerland, 240
Transfer moratorium in, 241-242, 243, 276
Unification of, 296, 297
Withdrawal from the League of Nations, 49
Zollverein, 296; see also National Socialist party
Gliwic, H., 222n.
Gold
The future of, 379-380
Gold bloc, 49, 235, 250, 307, 321-322
"Gold clause"
Repudiation of, 243
Gold Delegation of the League of Nations, 31
Gold exchange standard, 317-318
Gold standard
Abandonment of; see individual countries
Adjustment under, 30-31, 42-43
Criticism of, 23-24, 101-103
Possibilities of return to, 373
Gordon, M. S., 213n.
Gøtrik, H. P., 22n., 181n., 233n., 295n., 318n.
Government regulation
– and cartelization, 138, 336-338
– and international equilibrium, 35, 103-104, 121-122, 131-132, 139-141, 349-350
– and protectionism, 110, 136-137
– and war, 347-349, 362-363
– in agriculture, 67, 114
– in the exchange market, 236
Influence of organized producers in, 34, 217-223
Internal and external, 148-149
Mechanism of, 149-150; see also Nationalism, Regulation, Trade regulation
"Great Powers"
– and the outcome of the war, 357, 382
Importance of, 28, 281-282, 381, 392
Greece
Depreciation of currency, 320
German trade drive in, 245
Import surcharges and export premia in, 259
Milling regulations in, 215
Monetary policy of, 318, 320
Trade regulation in, 22
Transfer moratorium declared, 243
Grosse, Franz, 295n., 301n., 304n., 306n., 311n., 317n.

Haberler, G. von, 52n., 120n., 280
Hague agreement, 307
Hall, N. F., 36n., 159n.
Hantos, Elemer, 295n., 304n., 305n., 306n., 308
Harris, H. L., 23n., 182n.
Hawke, C. A. S., 295n.
Hayek, F. A. von, 100
Hecksher, E. F., 189n.
Heilperin, M. A., 37, 38
Heinrich, Klaus, 295n., 296n., 297, 298n., 299

INDEX 419

Heller, W. (ed.), 23n., 180n., 181n., 183n., 218n.
Henderson, Sir Nevile, 263
Herberts, J. H., 299n.
Heydel, Adam, 200n.
Hilgerdt, Folke, 96n., 286, 287n.
Hirschmann, Albert, 176n., 233n., 282, 283, 322n.
Hoffherr, René, 24, 77, 186n., 211n., 218n., 295n., 311n.
Hogben, L., 62n.
Hormi, H. R., 23n., 227n., 233n.
"Hot" money, 78, 92-93
Hull, Cordell, 170, 171, 189, 205, 282, 368
Hungary
 Béla Kun regime in, 109
 Commercial treaty with Germany, 291, 316-317
 Import surcharges and export premia in, 245, 259
 Inflation in, 301
 Regional derogation from most-favored-nation clause, 301
 Transfer moratorium declared, 243

Iberian clause, 299
Imperial Conference of the British Commonwealth (Ottawa Conference), 195, 207, 307, 311, 312-313; see also Imperial preference and Ottawa Agreements
Imperial preference, 174, 185-186, 299, 307, 311-312; see also Imperial Conference of the British Commonwealth and Ottawa Agreements
Imperialism, 308-316
 — and autarky, 165
 British, 88-89
Import licensing systems, 78, 179, 216-217
Import monopolies, 215
Import surcharges, 138, 140, 245; see also individual countries
India
 Administrative protectionism in, 201

Gold exchange standard in, 317-318
Repayment of debt, 244
Indirect protectionism, 196-203
Industrialism, 16
 — and nationalism, 15-26
Industrialization, 105, 329-330
 — in southeastern Europe, 344-346; see also Industrialism
International Authority
 Mr. Meade's proposals, 389-391
International Bank, 379-380, 386, 389-390
International business enterprise
 — and economic nationalism, 332
 — and international commodity controls, 334-335
 Financing of, 341-346
 Growth of, 328-334
International capital market, 79-90
 Effects of war on, 91-92
 Marxian criticism of, 88-90; see also Liquidity panic
International cartels, 334-338
 — and government, 337-338
International Chamber of Commerce, 361
International Cinematographic Institute, 386
International commodity controls, 34, 334-341
International economic co-operation
 — and a British victory, 369-370
 — and a German victory, 356-358
 — and economic nationalism, 254-255, 371-382
 — and economic planning, 352-354
 — and exchange stability, 376-380
 — and national sovereignty, 122, 364
 — and war preparedness, 114-115
 Breakdown of, 116-122
 Clearing of, 382-394
 Conditions of, 355-394
 League of Nations and, 383-386
 Possibilities of, 167-177
 The challenge to, 371-372
 The United States and, 392-394

INDEX

International economic (*continued*)
    The war and, 142-143
International equilibrium, 41-43, 99-101
    — and economic planning, 352-353
    — and government regulation, 110-113, 140-141
    — and international cartels, 335-336
    Breakdown of, 70, 71-79, 97-98, 114, 121-122, 371
    Business cycle policy and, 110-113, 371-374
    Effects of price inflexibilities on, 106-109
    Effects of war on, 69-70, 71-73
    Methods of restoration of, 374-382
    Monetary policy and, 110-113, 234, 351-353, 374-382
    Results of breakdown of, 95-97; *see also* Monetary equilibrium
International indebtedness, 242-244, 258
International Institute of Agriculture, 361, 384, 386
International Institute of Intellectual Co-operation, 361, 386
International investment
    — and nationalism, 79-80, 89-90, 343-346
    Change in character of, 342-346
    Distrust of, 89, 93-94
    Effect of currency depreciation on, 93, 97
    Effect of war on, 91-92
    — in Poland, 86-87
    — in the nineteenth century, 80-81, 341
International Labor Organization, 361, 384, 386, 388
International lending
    Interwar, 73, 91-92
International Monetary Authority, 326-327, 353, 377
International Organization
    Proposals of Mr. Meade, 389-391
International organizations

    Reorganization of, 385-392
International Red Cross, 359, 361
International Tariff Commission, 388
International trade
    — and economic planning, 336-338
    — and national equilibrium, 372
    — and population expansion, 63-65
    — and the international capital market, 82-87
    — between industrial countries, 67-68
    Change in character of, 56-58, 135
    Importance of, 59-62
    — in agricultural products, 60, 63-65, 66-67
    Quantum of, 134-135
    Restoration of, 146-148
    Totalitarian organization of, 356-358
International trading system
    Breakdown of, 101-103, 146-148, 188
    Criticism of, 113
    Defects of mechanism of, 99-116
    — of Germany, 256-262
    Politics and the breakdown of, 116-123
Iran
    Commercial policy of, 159
    Import monopolies in, 215
    Milling regulations in, 215
Italy
    Agricultural protectionism in, 212
    Colonial policy of, 316, 365-366
    Commercial policy of, 159
    Devaluation by, 235, 321
    Economic policy of, 251
    Exchange control in, 240, 251, 259, 321
    Export subsidies in, 222
    Milling regulations in, 215
    "New Deal" policy in, 41
    Occupation of Albania, 316
    Unification of, 296
Iversen, Carl, 80, 82n., 86n.

Jacks, G. V., and Whyte, R. O., 66n.

INDEX

Japan
  Colonial policy of, 310, 316, 365, 366
  Commercial policy of, 159, 227-229
  Commercial relations with the United States, 159
  Depreciation of yen, 133
  Economic policy of, 250-251
  Formation of yen bloc, 320, 325
Japanese clause, 299
Jones, R. C., 343n.
Jussiant, J., 19n., 57n., 181n., 198n., 216n., 218n., 322n.

Kada, Tetsuji, 182n.
Kawashima, S., 199n.
Kelly, W. S., 195n.
Keynes, J. M., 96, 108, 189n., 341n., 342, 372, 381, 382
Kock, Karin, 76, 84n., 87n., 90n., 91n., 92n., 95n., 97n.
Kreider, Karl, 206
Kriegswirtschaft, 142; see also War economy
Kroymann, Kurt, 37n.
Kuyucak, H. A., 181n., 219n., 222n., 233n., 286n., 318n., 320n.

Laissez faire
  Commercial treaties under, 264-265
  Decline of, 116-123, 148
Lamer, Mirko, 295n., 301n., 302n., 304n.
Larkin, J. D., 206n.
Latin America
  – and the German trading system, 358
  "Good neighbor" policy of the United States, 367-368
  Monetary policy in, 245; see also individual countries
Latvia
  Absorption by the U. S. S. R., 316
  Milling regulations in, 215; see also Baltic conferences

Lausanne Conference, 115, 243, 251, 306
Layton, Sir Walter, 302
League of Nations, 57n., 134n., 181n., 184n., 197n., 198n., 212n., 266n., 284n., 300, 302n., 334n., 361n., 383, 385n., 386
  – and postwar reconstruction, 361
  Future construction of, 386-389
Le Bon, Gustave, 55
Liberalism
  Interwar, 309-310
Lieftinck, P., 19n., 181n., 212n., 218n., 271n., 295n.
Liepmann, H., 103n., 181n.
Lieser, Burger, 245n.
"Likin" charges
  Abolition of, 296-297
Lima Conference, 368
Linked-purchasing
  – in New Zealand, 215
Liquidity panic, 90-98
Lithuania
  Absorption by the U. S. S. R., 316; see also Baltic conferences
Little Entente, 303-304
Locarno treaties, 115
London Bankers' Clearing House, 272
London Money Market
  Changes in, 91-92
  Functions of, 69, 83-84, 272-273
  Strain on, 71-72
Luxembourg
  Milling regulations in, 215

McDougall, F. L., 66n., 204n.
Madgearu, V., 22n., 140n., 214, 216n., 218n., 222n., 233n., 242, 243n., 250n., 302n.
Meade, J. E., 155, 326n., 327n., 352n., 372, 373n., 375, 376, 377, 379, 380n., 389, 390, 391
Memel
  German reoccupation of, 316
Mercantilism, 189-190
Merchant Adventurers, 329

INDEX

Mexico
Federation of, 296
Meyer, Fritz (comp.), 23, 24n., 40, 42, 51, 69n., 134n., 233n., 256, 257, 258, 259, 324n.
Mickwitz, von, 37n., 222n., 226n., 295n., 324n., 344, 345n., 346
Migration, 62-64
Substitute for, 104-105
Milling regulations, 78, 201, 215
Mises, L. von., 53
Mitter, Sir B. L., 23n., 182n.
Mobilization of economic resources, 160, 167, 314-315, 362-363
 — in Germany, 251-254
Monetary and Economic Conference, London, 1933, 47, 188, 243, 281, 296, 303, 306
Monetary blocs
Formation of, 316-327
Monetary equilibrium
Breakdown of, 71-79, 234-236, 371-372; see also International equilibrium
Monetary policy
 — and economic planning, 351-354
 — and nationalism, 371-372, 381-382; see also Nationalism
 — and international equilibrium, 110-113, 233-234, 352-353
 — and postwar reconstruction, 372-382
1931–36, 232-236, 316-327
Monopolies
Import, 215
Monopolistic power
 — used by governments, 225-226
Most-favored-nation treatment, 266
Denunciation of by Switzerland, 173
Evasions of, 153-155, 266-267, 337-338
 — in British policy, 174-175
Regional derogations from, 298-299, 301; see also Equality of trading opportunity, and United States commercial policy
Moulton, Edwards, McGee & Lewis, 76n.

Mun, Thomas, 189n.

National Policy Committee, 356n.
National Socialist party
Accession to power of, 188, 246, 316
National sovereignty
 — and autarky, 362-370
 — and the peace settlement, 363-364
National treatment, 54, 99, 265-266
Nationalism, 16
 — and industrialism, 15-26
 — and the breakdown of international economic equilibrium, 74-76, 128-129, 234, 371-372
 — and war, 167, 298
Monetary, 110-113, 232-241, 256-257, 381-382; see also Monetary policy
Nationality; see Self-determination
Netherlands
Agricultural protectionism in, 77, 212
 — and international economic cooperation, 364
Bilateralism in, 283
Colonial policy of, 310
Devaluation by, 49, 236, 322
German occupation of, 160, 316
International debt collection, 276
Milling regulations in, 212, 215
Monetary policy of, 321-322; see also Oslo conferences, Ouchy initiative and Tripartite Agreement
Netherlands clause, 299
New York Times, 177n., 199n., 222n., 315n.
New Zealand
Commercial policy of, 157
Commercial relations with Canada, 185, 186
Credit exchange standard in, 318
Depreciation of currency, 133
Linked-purchasing in, 215
"New Deal" policy in, 41
Postwar monetary policy of, 374
Repayment of debt by, 244

Norway
  Commercial treaty with England, 265
  German occupation of, 160, 315, 316
  Introduction of milling regulations in, 215
  Monetary policy in, 319-320
  Tariff policy of, 181; see also Oslo conferences
Nowak, J., 233n., 322n.

Obradovic, S. D., 180n., 181n., 267, 270
Ohlin, B., 275n.
"Open Door," the, 53, 309, 310, 311, 312-313
Oslo conferences, 174, 184, 300-301, 305-308, 312
Ottawa Agreements, 133, 174, 185-186, 207, 306, 311, 313-314, 319; see also Imperial Conference of the British Commonwealth *and* Imperial preference
Ouchy initiative, 173-174, 306-307, 312
Oyrzanowski, Bronislaw, 200n.

Paish, F. W., 233n.
Pan-American export cartel, 358
Pan-American Union, 368
Paraguay
  Default on debt service, 243
Parkinson, J. T., 182n., 184n., 185, 195n., 199n., 271n., 295n., 313n., 318n., 333n.
Payments agreement, 277-278
  Anglo-Argentine, 276-277
  Anglo-German, 276, 277-278
Peace
  — and economic policy, 47-58
  The approach to, 355-362
Peace settlement
  — and national sovereignty, 362-364
  — and the present war, 359-362
Pentmann, J., 297n.
P. E. P., 195n.

Permanent Court of International Justice, 386
Peru
  Default on debt service, 243
Petersen, Erling, 23n., 295n.
Piatier, A., 233n., 234, 235, 236, 238n., 245n., 258
Pintos, S. D., 22n., 233n., 318n.
Piotrowski, Roman, 337n.
Planning; see Economic planning
Poland
  Administrative protectionism and, 200-201
  German occupation of, 316
  Monetary policy of, 322
  Quotas in, 214
  Reconstruction of (after 1918), 86
Policy
  The making of, 26-37
Politics
  — and the breakdown of the nineteenth-century trading system, 116-123
Political changes
  — and economic military pressure, 365-366
Ponton, L., 250n.
Postwar reconstruction, 355-394
  — and a British victory, 369-370
  — and a German victory, 356-358
  — and the war of 1914–18, 363
  Phases of, 359-362
  Problems of, 359
  The United States and, 358, 369-370, 392-394
"Power" economics, 348-349
Price competition, 61-62
  — in the nineteenth century, 68
  Regulation of by business, 107
Price inflexibilities, 106-107
Prinzing, Albert, 335n., 336
Protectionism
  — and government regulation, 110
  — and international business, 332
  — in Central Europe, 302
  The new, 135-137, 190; see also Administrative protectionism *and* Agricultural protectionism

INDEX

Quintana, Miguel, 88, 89
Quotas, 210, 231
   Administrative problems of, 218
   Bilateral bargaining in, 220-223
   Discrimination through, 153-155, 220, 223
   Effects upon prices, 224-225
   Export, 210
   Global, 219-220
   Incidence of, 223-227
   Origins of, 210-217
   Tariff, 210; see also individual countries

Rappard, W., 183n., 203, 204n.
Raw materials
   — and autarky, 370
   — and trade barriers, 56-58
   Colonial areas rich in, 357-358
   — in international trade, 19-20, 57-58, 135
   International control of, 34, 338-341
Regionalism, 44-45, 295-327
Regulation
   — and war, 142
   Criteria of, 151-160
   Maintenance of, 131-143
   National and international, 37-47
   Scope of, 146-147
   Spread of, 132-134, 144-151; see also Nationalism, Government regulation and Trade regulation
Reparations, 92
   Default on, 95-96
   Suspension of, 242-243
Ricalde, Ruben, 198n.
Rist, Charles, 176, 299, 302
Robertson, D. H., 68n.
Rogers, J. H., 61n.
Rome protocol, 304
Royama, Masamichi, 227, 228n., 229n., 233n., 250, 320n.
Rumania
   Commercial relations with Germany, 289-293, 317
   Import surcharges and export premia in, 245, 259
   Quotas in, 214, 216

Transfer moratorium declared, 243
Russian clause, 299

Saar
   German reoccupation of, 316
St. Germain, Treaty of, 301
Salter, Sir Arthur, 71, 75
Scandinavian clause, 299
Schacht, H., 227, 258, 275
Schmoller, G. F. von, 297
Self-determination, 17, 363
Shakespeare, William, 130, 165
Sino-Japanese conflict, 49, 228-229, 250
Smith, Adam, 111, 112n., 116, 121, 190, 311
Snyder, Carl, 124
Social legislation, 107-110
Socialism
   — and peace, 89
South Africa
   Currency depreciation of, 318
   Export subsidies in, 222
   Federation of, 296
   Repayment of debt by, 244
South American clause, 299
Southard, F. A., Jr., 331n.
Southeast European clause, 299
Spain
   Commercial treaty with Great Britain, 265
Staley, Eugene, 16n., 18, 19, 20, 21, 125n., 195n., 222n.
"Standstill" arrangements, 246
Sterling bloc, 307, 317-320
   Exchange stability in the, 249
Stevenson rubber restriction scheme, 339
Stock exchange
   Operations of, 341-342
Streit, C. K., 364n., 368, 389
Stresa Conference, 303
Strzeszewski, C., 214
Substitute products, 137
Sumptuary laws, 78
Sweden
   Bilateralism in, 283
   Business cycle policy in, 249

INDEX

Sweden (*continued*)
   Commercial treaty with Great Britain, 265
   Co-operatives in, 137
   Devaluation in, 235
   International debt collection, 276
   Milling regulations in, 215
   Monetary policy in, 237, 319
   Tariff policy of, 181; *see also* Oslo conferences

Switzerland
   Abandons intercantonal trade restrictions, 296
   Administrative protectionism in, 200-201
   Adoption of protectionist measures by, 186
   Agricultural protectionism in, 212
   — and international economic co-operation, 364
   Clearing agreement with Austria, 275
   Commercial policy of, 161-163
   Commercial treaty with the United States, 162
   Denunciation of most-favored-nation clause, 162, 173
   Devaluation by, 49, 162, 235-236, 322
   Export subsidies in, 222
   Introduction of quotas in, 214
   Monetary policy of, 321
   Tariff policy of, 181
   Tourist agreement with Germany, 240; *see also* Tripartite Agreement

Tardieu plan, 304
Tariffs, 178-196
   — and the new protectionism, 149-150
   "Conventionalized," 192-193, 213
   Effects of, 103-104, 149-150
   Elaboration of, 192
   Flexible, 189
   Height of, 103-104
   Importance of, 178-189
   Multiple, 190-191

Postwar, 179-182
Recent developments in, 189-196
Retaliatory, 185-186
Single, 191
Tasca, H. J., 24n., 25, 29, 169n., 171, 172, 174, 175n., 176, 191n., 204, 205, 244n., 278n., 284, 321, 325n., 368n.
Taylor, E., 180n., 233n.
Taylor, George, 320n.
Tchakaloff, A. (and Zagoroff), 233n., 250n., 274n.
Territorial Redistribution
   — and the outcome of the war, 356-358, 364-366
Three Power Pact, 304
Times (London), 345, 346
Tinbergen, J., 108
Toynbee, A. J., 16n., 17, 118n.
Trade barriers
   Attack on, 203-209
   Effects on balances of payment, 103-104
Trade regulation
   — and international commodity controls, 334-341
   — and international co-operation, 134
   — as an instrument of national policy, 137-138, 141-142, 159-160
   Discriminatory, 152, 158-160
   Effects of, 56-58
   Exchange control as a weapon of, 240-242
   Maintenance of, 139-143
   Postwar, 179-183
   Results of, 134-136
   Scope of, 146-147
   Spread of, 144-151; *see also* individual countries
Trade restrictions
   Effects of, 22-23, 132-136
   Multiplication of, 186-188; *see also* various instruments of trade restriction
Transfer moratoria
   Countries declaring, 243; *see also* individual countries
"Transfer problem," 92, 95-96, 273

INDEX

Triangular trade
  Elimination of, 279-280, 284-286
Trianon, Treaty of, 301
Tripartite Agreement, 162, 250, 257, 313, 322, 377, 391
Tunis
  Milling regulations in, 215
Turkey
  Agreement with the United Kingdom, 286, 320
  Bilateral agreements of, 277
  Commercial policy of, 159
  Depreciation of currency, 320
  German trade drive in, 245
  Monetary policy in, 318
Tuveng, M., 180n., 181n., 271n., 295n.

Unemployment
  — and international equilibrium, 371-372
United Kingdom
  Abandons gold standard, 29, 48, 71, 95, 145, 187, 235, 249, 317
  Administrative organs for regulation of external policy, 187
  Adoption of protectionist tariff by, 77, 133, 185-188, 249, 306-307
  Agreement with Turkey, 286, 320
  Bilateralism in, 282-283; see also "Commercial policy"
  Coal Agreement with Germany, 221
  Colonial policy of, 310-314
  Commercial policy of, 24, 29, 43, 133, 157, 160, 174-176, 185-188, 191-192, 204-205, 288-289, 319-320
  Commercial relations with Baltic countries, 174, 175, 319-320
  Commercial relations with Denmark, 174, 175
  Commercial relations with regulated countries, 174
  Commerical relations with the Argentine, 174, 175, 207, 276, 277, 320
  Commercial relations with the United States, 174, 185, 189, 206-207

Commercial treaties with France, 265, 280, 281
Commercial treaty with Norway, 265
Commercial treaty with Spain, 265
Commercial treaty with Sweden, 265
Congo Treaty, 312
Effects of bilateralism on, 286
Exchange control in, 176
Foreign investment of, 53
Import Duties Advisory Board, 148, 186, 193-194
Import licensing in, 216-217
Livestock Marketing Act, 218
Monetary policy of, 237, 313, 317-320
Payments Agreement with Germany, 276, 277-278
Quotas in, 213, 219
Statute of Westminster, 312
Strain on balance of payments in, 96-97; see also British Commonwealth, Imperial preference, Ottawa Agreements, Tripartite Agreement, etc.
United States
  Active export balance of, 276
  Administrative protectionism in, 197, 199-200, 202
  — and Latin-American trade, 358
  — and postwar reconstruction, 358, 369, 392-394
  — and the German debt default, 246-247
  Commercial policy, 24-25, 73-74, 75, 156, 158-159, 168-171, 174, 191, 205-209, 325, 367-368
  Commercial relations with Canada, 333
  Commercial relations with Germany, 158-159, 170-171
  Commercial relations with Japan, 159, 169
  Commercial relations with the United Kingdom, 174-175, 189, 206-207
  Commercial relations with the U. S. S. R., 172-173

INDEX 427

United States (*continued*)
  Commercial treaty with Brazil, 325
  Commercial treaty with Switzerland, 162
  Consequences of isolation, 392-393
  Devaluation by, 48, 235, 249, 318
  Export subsidies in, 169
  Flow of credit to Europe, 73, 94
  Fordney-McCumber Tariff, 25, 182
  Foreign investment of, 53
  Future monetary policy for, 325-326, 378-380
  Immigration Restriction Act, 182
  Investment relations with Canada, 333
  National Industrial Recovery Act, 148, 206
  Postwar commercial policy for, 358, 378, 392-394
  Quotas in, 159, 169, 213, 220
  Reciprocal Trade Treaty Program, 168, 191, 192, 194, 205-208; see also "Commercial policy"
  Smoot-Hawley Tariff, 25, 133, 162, 168, 184, 185, 191, 205, 206
  Tariff Commission, 194
  Veterinary and quarantine restrictions, 199-200, 320; see also Tripartite Agreement
United States Bureau of Foreign and Domestic Commerce, 331n.
Universal Postal Union, 383, 386
Uruguay
  Default on debt service, 243
U. S. S. R.
  Commercial policy of, 159, 250, 325
  Commercial relations with Germany, 287
  Commercial relations with the United States, 172-173
  Economic policy of, 250
  Expansion by, 316, 365, 366
  Import monopoly in, 215

Valle, Angel, and Ferrer, Juan M., 23n., 181n., 233n., 245n., 271n., 321n.
Veblen, Thorstein, 18

Versailles treaty, 44, 298, 303
Veterinary and quarantine restrictions, 78, 199-200, 320
Viner, J., 202 n.
Voionmaa, T., 181n., 295n.

Wage rigidities, 107-110
Wallas, Graham, 128n., 130, 326, 365n.
War
  – and government regulation, 142-143
  – and social revolution, 360
  – and the distribution of raw material, 370
  Effects of, 355-356, 358-359
  Origins of, 55
  Possible outcome of the present, 356-359
  Results of, 74-75
War debts, 92
  Default on, 95-96, 242-243
War economy, 165-167
  – and economic planning, 347-349; see also *Kriegswirtschaft*
Wehrwirtschaft, 142, 253-254
Welfare economics, 348
Wellisz, Leopold, 86
Wheat
  Government regulation and, 215
Whitehead, A. N., 27
World Economic Conference, Geneva (1927), 47, 184, 305
Wright, C. M., 216n.
Wright, F. C., 70n.
Wright, Quincy, 70n.

Young loan, 246
Yovanovitch, A., 233n., 250n., 302n.
Yugoslavia
  Commercial treaties negotiated, 1924–38, 267-270
  Conferences taken part in by, 304
  Import surcharges and export premia in, 245, 259
  Tariff policy of, 180-181
  Transfer moratorium declared by, 243

Zaleski, Wojcieck, 200n., 201n.
Zeeland, Paul van, 47, 62

Books That Live

The Norton imprint on a book means that in the publisher's estimation it is a book not for a single season but for the years.

W · W · NORTON & CO · INC.
70 FIFTH AVENUE
NEW YORK